Advertising

Made Simple

The Made Simple series
has been created
especially for self-education
but can equally well
be used as
an aid to group study.
However complex the subject,
the reader is taken
step by step,
clearly and methodically,
through the course. Each volume
has been prepared by experts,
taking account of
modern educational requirements,
to ensure the most
effective way of
acquiring knowledge.

In the same series

Accounting
Acting and Stagecraft
Additional Mathematics
Administration in Business
Advertising
Anthropology
Applied Economics
Applied Mathematics
Applied Mechanics
Art Appreciation
Art of Speaking
Art of Writing
Biology
Book-keeping
Britain and the European Community
British Constitution
Business and Administrative Organisation
Business Calculations
Business Economics
Business Law
Business Statistics and Accounting
Calculus
Chemistry
Childcare
Child Development
Commerce
Company Law
Company Practice
Computer Programming
Computers and Microprocessors
Cookery
Cost and Management Accounting
Data Processing
Economic History
Economic and Social Geography
Economics
Effective Communication
Electricity
Electronic Computers
Electronics
English
English Literature
Financial Management
French
Geology
German

Housing, Tenancy and Planning Law
Human Anatomy
Human Biology
Italian
Journalism
Latin
Law
Management
Marketing
Mathematics
Metalwork
Modelling and Beauty Care
Modern Biology
Modern Electronics
Modern European History
Modern Mathematics
Modern World Affairs
Money and Banking
Music
New Mathematics
Office Administration
Office Practice
Organic Chemistry
Personnel Management
Philosophy
Photography
Physical Geography
Physics
Practical Typewriting
Psychiatry
Psychology
Public Relations
Public Sector Economics
Rapid Reading
Religious Studies
Russian
Salesmanship
Secretarial Practice
Social Services
Sociology
Spanish
Statistics
Technology
Teeline Shorthand
Twentieth-Century British History
Typing
Woodwork

Advertising

Made Simple

Frank Jefkins, BSc(Econ), BA(Hons), FIPR,
MCAM, ABC, MInstM

Made Simple Books
HEINEMANN : London

Printed and bound in Great Britain
by Richard Clay (The Chaucer Press), Ltd., Bungay, Suffolk
for the publishers William Heinemann Ltd.,
10 Upper Grosvenor Street, London W1X 9PA

First Edition, March 1973
Second Edition, October 1977
Reprinted, March 1980
Third Edition, April 1982
Fourth Edition, January 1985

British Library Cataloguing in Publication Data

Jefkins, Frank
    Advertising made simple.—4th ed.—
    (Made simple books)
    1. Advertising—Great Britain
    I. Title
    659.1′0941   HF5813.G7
ISBN 0 434 98554 6

Preface to First Edition

Advertising Made Simple has been written to meet the needs of a wide readership.

First, its comprehensive coverage of the subject matter, including a number of case studies, should make the book a valuable source of help and reference to many different kinds of student: to those working for examinations of the Communication, Advertising and Marketing Education Foundation (CAM), the Institute of Marketing, the Royal Society of Arts and the London Chamber of Commerce and Industry, and BTEC Higher and Communication studies students; to fifth and sixth formers studying Economics and Commerce at GCE levels and to those many young people in secondary schools who may be looking at career opportunities or contemplating the business world in general. In this latter connection, careers masters may also find the book useful in dispelling some of the illusions about advertising.

At a higher level of education the book may well be valuable to both undergraduates who are thinking of seeking jobs as trainee account executives, copywriters or market researchers and those who recognise that an understanding of advertising is important in most business careers. Presenting, as it does, a broad picture of a very complex subject, the book's links with social science courses are obvious.

Second, I hope that the book will prove useful for a large number of businessmen, including, in particular, those for whom advertising is but one of several activities or responsibilities and who have to 'do their own advertising'. Among these might be small industrialists, sole traders such as shopkeepers, caterers, hoteliers, entertainment proprietors, transport operators or suppliers of services and local branch managers of larger businesses.

Last, but not least, there are very many people engaged in various types of business activity who may simply be interested to know how advertising 'ticks'. For many such readers, advertising is something of a mystery, and an intelligent understanding of its ramifications might be both useful and a revelation.

Preface to Third Edition

The advertising scene changes so rapidly that it is difficult to keep a definitive book absolutely up to date. In this Third Edition the British Airways, Brooke Bond, Guinness and Woolworth case studies have been retained and updated. BARB has replaced JICTAR. New television contractors have appeared. Chapter 5 has been rewritten to omit organisations which have closed down, and to include new and additional ones and to update references to those which remain. Chapter 22 has been rewritten to reflect the revolution in cinema advertising as a young people's medium. The revisions also reflect the growth of direct response advertising and direct marketing, and the growth of electronic media and of alternative television media. There is also a revised bibliography.

However, the general format of the book has not been changed as the book has proved so popular: the second edition had to be reprinted to meet the demand from overseas, especially from Nigeria.

Advertising Made Simple has become a standard book with CAM, BTEC and LCCI students, particularly with the international growth of entries for the LCCI Marketing Diploma. The success of this book has led to the publication of the author's companion volume, *Public Relations Made Simple*.

FRANK JEFKINS
January, 1982

Preface to Fourth Edition

In this edition, the British Airways Shuttle Service and Brooke Bond PG Tips case studies have been retained and brought up to date, but others have been dropped because different advertising agencies handle the accounts or trading circumstances have changed.

In the short time since the third edition appeared there have been more changes in the advertising world, although some were forecast as far as was possible. Even now, it is too early to know what effect cable and satellite television will have.

But we are able to discuss major changes and developments in the spheres of traditional television, advertising agency operation, direct response marketing, sales promotion, public relations and sponsorship.

Advertising is a continually changing business which reflects the changes in the society in which it is conducted.

Note is taken in this edition of possible changes in the future structure and management of CAM examinations which are expected to take place after the report-back of the CAM Planning Committee in the summer of 1985. Any references made to CAM in this book should therefore be read in conjunction with any new developments which are announced and introduced in 1985/6.

This new edition contains a completely revised index which should be especially valuable to students and lecturers.

FRANK JEFKINS
January, 1982

Acknowledgments

To cover such a complex subject as advertising it is essential to have the willing co-operation of many people. Where possible, this assistance is implied in the text.

Special thanks are due to the secretaries of the numerous organisations described in this book, and to those who allowed me to quote from their works. The media chapters include statistics and lists of advertisers, which were compiled for me by officers and executives of the organisations and firms mentioned. The case studies resulted from correspondence, telephone calls and personal interviews with company and agency personnel who were most co-operative.

Finally, I should like to thank all the hundreds of students whose work and questions have revealed areas of knowledge that a book such as this should cover.

F.J.

This book is dedicated to students of advertising, marketing and public relations everywhere, particularly those I have taught during the past twenty-five years in London, Croydon and elsewhere in the UK, and including those who have attended my short courses in Abeokuta, Accra, Amsterdam, Athens, Blantyre, Brussels, Cairo, Cape Town, Dublin, Enugu, Gaborone, Harare, Hong Kong, Jakarta, Johannesburg, Jos, Kabwe, Kano, Kuala Lumpur, Kuwait, Lagos, Lusaka, Nairobi, Nicosia, Port of Spain, Singapore and Stockholm.

Other Books by Frank Jefkins

Part 1: The Advertising Scene

1
Why Advertise?

1.1 A Simple Answer

The simple answer to the question 'why do we advertise?' is that either we have something we want to sell, or someone else has something we want to buy. Alternatively, we may want to give something away, seek an exchange or invite donors or gifts. We advertise, or make known, our offer or need. We bring together people who would not otherwise know of the existence of those able to supply and those with a demand, very often complete strangers.

Most people use advertising at some time, either privately or in business. And most people respond to advertisements and so enjoy the choices available to them in every sphere of life.

This elementary answer applies whether we want to sell a private house, dispose of kittens, raise funds for a charity, sell the production of a million pound business, buy a second-hand tape recorder, attract shoppers to our store, launch a new product, engage staff or simply find a pen friend. The technique is the same: there is merely a difference of magnitude and sophistication between an inexpensive classified ad to sell one budgerigar and a national campaign on ITV to sell bird seed to hundreds of thousands of budgerigar owners. In short, **advertising is the means by which we make known what we have to sell or what we want to buy.**

1.2 Specific Reasons for Advertising

However, there are many special and specific reasons why we may use advertising, in one of its many forms, as the tool for the job and the following 22 examples offer a broader idea of the versatility and value of advertising:

(*a*) **To announce a new product or service.** Here, prospective buyers are presented with details of a new product, and this usually means a costly and dramatic launch. Announcements for new brands of cigarettes, involving the use of full pages in full colour in the national press, plus giant posters, are typical examples. So, too, are the much more comprehensive announcements of new forms of insurance and unit trust. These launches generally use large advertisements which are frequently repeated, and this 'weight' of advertising makes the campaign hard to miss or overlook.

Is it necessary to spend so lavishly on the launch of a new product? To break into the market with a new product is not easy: the world simply does not beat its way to the better mouse-trap. Novelty is not enough. Nor is quality or obvious desirability. The buying public is conservative, apt to be sceptical, hard to shift from established habits. For decades people thought all doors should be painted brown because they were made of wood, that ice cream was to be eaten only in the summer, and that buses must have conductors. To promote something new the advertising has to be bold, dramatic, persuasive and convincing, whether it be for a complete innovation like a convenience food or an entirely new kind of car. A solitary big splash will not work: a sustained campaign is required. If a fire-engine sounds its siren only on leaving the station this warning will not clear the road all the way to the fire. The siren has to be sounded persistently and insistently all the way, and so with advertising.

(*b*) **To expand the market to new buyers.** Good examples of this are when a paint or a fertiliser has been used successfully for industrial or commercial purposes, and is then packaged and promoted to the consumer market. The do-it-yourself and weekend gardener markets are full of such products, put there by advertising. Alternatively the product may be directed at an extra market, as when sewing machines are sold to girls' schools, cars to commercial fleets and domestic equipment to hotels. The advertising in such cases is likely to have greater impact because the goods have already been proved in professional, commercial or some other accepted use.

(*c*) **To announce a modification.** An existing product may be given a 'face lift' with an additive, a refinement, a new finish or casing, or perhaps even a new pack or container. The attempt may be made to revive the sale of a product whose life-cycle is waning too quickly or because of competition. Detergents, toiletries, foodstuffs, confectionery, petrols and medicines come under this heading, as do such items as foundation garments, domestic appliances and garden tools. Sales Promotion schemes may replace traditional advertising to promote product changes.

(*d*) **To announce a price change.** This was a more common form of advertising before resale price maintenance was made illegal and 'recommended prices' came about. But there are still occasions when this appeal can be used, as when fares are reduced, or when a store announces cut-prices or a sale. It may be necessary, also, to announce a price increase, as happens with public transport.

(*e*) **To announce a new pack.** Pack identification at the point-of-sale is always important, and is a reason why packages are shown in advertisements. Colour advertisements work well here. This becomes even more important if there is a change of pack—carton, container or label—and new sales may be attracted by this ability to awaken new product interest or because the change benefits the customer. It may be lighter in weight, unbreakable, capable of preserving the product longer, or be in keeping with modern trends. Perhaps a very old-established and probably old-fashioned container or label has been updated and it is necessary to promote the new look while assuring customers that the product is the same or better in quality. Consumers are apt to suspect that a new pack means a

different or inferior product, and the advertising—and the public relations—has to dispel such dangerous misgivings which could easily inhibit
sales. Public relations is dealt with in Chapter 13.

(*f*) **To make a special offer.** For various reasons—competition, slack
season, policy to expand sales—advertising may be used to make a special
offer. It could be a banded pack (two bars of chocolate with two pence
off), a premium offer of a coffee table at a bargain price if so many packet
tops are sent with the cash, a limited time price reduction or free gifts or
samples. New products may be launched with 'introductory' special offers.
Dry cleaners, driving schools and tailors may make special offers when
trade is quiet. Hotels may offer special low rates to old-age pensioners
during out-of-season weeks of the year.

(*g*) **To invite enquiries.** Businessmen as diverse as hoteliers, mail order
traders, seedsmen and travel agents rely on a flow of enquiries for their
services. In response to these enquiries they despatch tariffs, price lists and
brochures and business is conducted by post. But the potential customers
are scattered and unknown—especially with a business which has to find
new customers rather than repeat business—and prospects can be discovered through advertising. Most of these advertisements contain a
coupon.

(*h*) **To sell direct.** Department stores, book clubs and firms specialising
in direct response marketing—sell direct to customers. They may buy 'off
the page' from press advertisements, or from catalogues and direct mail
shots, or (as with gramophone records) from TV commercials. Orders may
be posted or telephoned. Payment may be by postal order, cheque or charge
card. Retailing without stores has become big business.

(*i*) **To test a medium.** Some large advertisers prefer to test a new or
untried medium rather than accept or reject the claims made by the space
salesman. Testing is usually achieved by advertising a free gift—a food
manufacturer may offer a recipe leaflet or a sample—and counting the
requests received. This response is then related to the cost of the space to
arrive at a cost per reply figure which will indicate the pulling power of the
medium.

(*j*) **To announce the location of stockists.** To support dealers, to encourage 'selling-out' of the stocks which the company sales representative
(or wholesaler) has 'sold-in' and to urge action on the part of readers,
space may be taken to list the names and addresses of stockists. Addresses
may appear in a display advertisement which promotes the product, or the
space may be occupied primarily by the addresses in the form of a directory.
The concessionaires for foreign cars tend to adopt the first method, while
paint firms often adopt the second at Easter when the do-it-yourself season
opens.

(*k*) **To obtain stockists.** This is a subtle use of advertising whereby consumers are entreated to ask retailers for the product by name. Their demands encourage retailers to place orders with wholesalers or the advertiser's salesmen. When a manufacturer is trying to get distribution for a
new product this is a useful method, but there is the risk that the consumer
will accept a substitute. Obviously, the method is most likely to be successful when the product is novel or the first of its kind. It is unwise to
expect such advertising to act as a substitute for an inadequate sales force,

and it can be fatal to advertise something if its unavailability can only provoke frustration and ill will. That is wasteful advertising, and bad PR.

(*l*) **To educate consumers.** Rather unfairly it is sometimes said by critics of advertising that there are two kinds, **informative** and **persuasive,** and that the former is more socially acceptable or ethical than the latter. The educational advertisement is necessary when a commodity, service or an offer needs careful explanation. This technique can also be used to show new uses for a well-established product. The market can often be extended if extra uses can be suggested. Public transport is promoted by suggesting places to visit, while insurance companies and building societies seek to educate people about family responsibilities and the virtues of thrift. Or it may be that prejudice and ignorance are inhibiting sales of a product whose performance is doubted. Packaged holidays abroad took many years to popularise, and it has taken fish and chips and bingo to overcome fears about funny foreign food and other doubtful pleasures. It is still necessary to educate some potential passengers about the merits of air travel.

(*m*) **To maintain sales.** Yes! One of the secrets of successful advertising is that it is continuous, in one form or another, however seasonal the main emphasis may be. To prove the point one has only to look at one of those old pictures of horse buses jammed together in a crowded London street and to read the names of the advertisers whose placards were fixed to every available space on the buses. Many of them will be familiar as the biggest names in trade today.

Not all advertising is aimed at promoting new and exciting products. There are everyday products such as beer, custard powder, salt, matches, toothpaste, aspirins and soap which have been on the market for generations. Guinness, Cadbury's, Aspro, HP Sauce, Shell are good examples of products whose sales have to be maintained, although increased sales are no doubt welcomed. Just how original one can be in advertising an identical product year in and year out can be seen by studying the advertisements of Guinness whose best-remembered slogan 'Guinness is good for you' is nearly fifty years old! Guinness advertising also demonstrates that sales do have to be maintained: however famous and popular the product it will not sell itself and not to advertise would be to invite extinction. In this truth can be seen the folly of a tax on advertising: our topic is an economic necessity, not a luxury of capitalism, as is discovered when a communist economy expands and is able to offer the people a choice of goods to buy.

(*n*) **To challenge competition.** This motive will be apparent in most of the other sections, and of course no advertisement is necessarily restricted to only one of the 22 possible uses listed here. But the specific purpose of a campaign may be to take up the challenge, as when a new substitute material comes on the market, to mention only man-made fibres to which wool has had to give battle through the International Wool Secretariat, or rail versus air travel and then the reverse as high speed trains rivalled domestic air services. Challenges are frequently seen at the point-of-sale where money-off, premium offers, free gifts and other devices are used to capture or re-capture predominant market shares.

(*o*) **To remind.** Perhaps this is similar to 'maintaining sales', but not quite. There are products which are bought repeatedly—usually small-unit items like razor-blades, tea, margarine, milk, chocolate or cigarettes—and reminder advertising aims to remind customers to ask for the same brand again. Thus, while very similar products, and ones less frequently bought, need advertising to maintain continuity of sales, it is also necessary with repeat-purchase goods to encourage re-purchase of that brand. Reiteration of brand names, and use of catchy slogans and jingles, are used. 'Don't Be Vague, Ask For Haig' is an oldie from the 30s which was revived in the 70s! Some, like 'Player's Please', have never been bettered. 'Persil Washes Whiter' has the measure of the 'whiter than white' detergents. Another oldie which has returned, with innovations, is the 'Ah, Bisto!' advertising which was popular fifty years ago.

Another kind of reminder ad keeps the product or service in mind against some future need. When we go to buy a lawnmower, or a typewriter, a tea-set or a pair of sheets, we are familiar with the makes and often already pre-sold on a particular one. For months we have said to ourselves: 'Next time I buy a so-and-so I'll buy a such-and-such.' Reminder advertising encourages us to stick to that decision.

Much of this kind of advertising concerns **brand names** and it is worth noting that a **brand** is a valuable property which has to be constantly publicised. Moreover, a manufacturer stakes his **reputation** on his brand, and that involves goodwill. And goodwill is a trading asset which must be cherished by repetitive advertising and also public relations. The value of brand names is demonstrated by the following quotation. It is taken from a letter in *The Guardian* (January 19, 1972) in which K. B. Hopkins, Director of Public Relations, British Leyland, refuted the suggestion that the name *Rover* might be dropped. In the 80s these names still exist.

'In Triumph, Rover and Jaguar we have three of the greatest car names in the world and we have no intention whatsoever of jeopardising our own future by dropping either the names or the technological expertise which have made them great.'

There is a lot to be said for *paying for the name* because this is a guarantee of quality, and reminder advertising is part of the process of ensuring customer satisfaction.

Most outdoor advertising, including the night lights of Piccadilly, Leicester Square and other city centres, and the large bulletin boards or supersites placed on strategic solus roadside sites, fall into this category—but more about media in their respective chapters.

(*p*) **To retrieve lost sales.** Again, this is not unlike one or two previously discussed purposes except that here there is a much more urgent need to use advertising. It has to reverse a negative sales trend and not just compete. Sales may have been lost by default—maybe a foolish cut-back in advertising expenditure, as happened with a cigarette manufacturer who stopped advertising and then spent three years climbing back to popularity—or because the product has suffered from a fashion craze or has been temporarily unobtainable owing to strikes or restricted imports. The advertising will probably be linked with a special sales promotion exercise involving, say, a premium offer, a cut-price offer, or an in-store promotion and the use of commando salesmen and special trade terms. In this campaign we must not forget advertising to the trade through the media of trade press or direct mail.

Another example of the use of advertising to regain sales is after a war. During the Second World War there were no branded margarines, only 'Standard' margarine which was rationed. Nevertheless, Van den Berghs advertised Stork right through the war, believing that they had an investment to protect. When rationing ceased, the product returned with a memorable advertisement showing a stork in prison clothes behind bars, the copy stating that Stork margarine had now been 'released'!

(*q*) **To please stockists.** The trade press and direct mail advertising mentioned above is aimed at **selling in**, and consumer advertising and sales promotion seeks to **sell out** (not in the sense of a shop being 'sold-out' but in helping the retailer to move goods off the shelves). Nowadays, with so many rival brands—and the 'house' brands of stores of the Sainsbury and Tesco type—shopkeepers cannot afford to tie up capital in goods which sit on the shelves. The mark-up of most small-unit mass-market goods is so small that profitability for the retailer means rapidity of turnover which in turn means repeat purchasing as well as impulse buying. Thus, a successful retail trader in the grocery, confectionery or druggist fields depends on quick turnover so that the same capital is reused as many times as possible. In contrast, the jeweller or the motor-trader, selling high-priced goods less often, relies on a high profit margin and accepts a much slower turnover.

Nevertheless, whether one is selling cornflakes or motor-cars, the original manufacturer or supplier can maintain the optimum and profitable turnover of production or imports only by helping to promote sales at the retail end. He may do so by running big prize contests or giving away plastic toys, or—in the case of the motor-car manufacturer—by entering car rallies or by participating in the Motor Show.

Dealer support is critical with supermarkets and chain stores which have evolved techniques which permit only a certain area of shelf space to a limited number of accepted brands. Woolworth go so far as to test sales of a new product in a single branch where sales are observed, before ordering stocks for their chain. It is therefore extremely difficult to break into a market which already has a large number of competitive brands. Consequently, it takes more than a persuasive salesman to sell goods 'in', and much of his success will depend on whether the retailer can be convinced that there will be adequate advertising support to sell the goods 'out'. The modern retailer, before agreeing to order stocks, is liable to ask: 'Will there be TV advertising?'

This does not mean that advertising appears on TV solely to please retailers, but it is the one medium seen by most retailers—as members of the great viewing public—and they may be more impressed by this support (which they can see with their very own eyes) than by advertisements in women's magazines which they may not see. Consequently, it may pay to invite retailers to see TV commercials at their regional independent television station; to send them mailing shots telling them when commercials will be screened; or to make video-cassette presentations of commercials to buyers at their premises.

Broadsheets may be mailed which also refer to other advertising aids to mention only display material, free blocks or artwork which the retailer can use in his own advertising in the local press, and offers to meet part of the cost of the retailer's own advertising. The last two examples are called 'co-operative' advertising.

(*r*) **To please the sales force.** Some companies with large field sales forces believe that a bold advertisement in a national publication seen by their sales staff will act as a morale booster. Salesmen will tend to boast about their company's whole page ad in *TV Times*, the *Financial Times* or the *Architect's Journal* as the case may be. If these advertisements are also relevant to the main advertising campaign, so much the better.

Salesmen, constantly aware of the competitive advertising in the local press from local manufacturers, may appeal to their head office for advertising support in their locality, not realising that they already have the support of much more influential national (or TV regional) advertising which the local firms cannot enjoy. Misunderstanding on this point can cause friction between field salesmen and national sales managers or marketing managers, and it is a subject which needs to be fully explained through sales bulletins, house magazines, sales training courses and sales conferences.

(*s*) **To recruit staff.** Recruitment advertising has become much more sophisticated than the 'situations vacant' classifieds which used to be the normal way of seeking staff. Large employers are conscious of the PR effect of their 'job ads' and use **displayed classifieds** which are not just nicely laid out with the company symbol but tell prospective applicants something about the employer and the conditions of employment. They sell the job. Although displayed, recruitment advertising space is bought from the classified advertisement department of the publisher, hence the expression 'displayed classified'.

Displayed recruitment advertising became common in the 50s and 60s when skilled labour was scarce, and it represented the competition between employers. Whereas previously such advertisements might have been used solely to engage a managing director it now began to be used to attract factory floor and office staff, and much of it was used for executive and technological positions. In recent years there has been some criticism of expenditure by local and public authorities on these larger and more expensive advertisements despite a legal commitment to publicise public appointments.

Among these recruitment advertisements will be found those by management consultancies and employment agencies. The boom in recruitment advertising led to advertising agencies setting up special departments or subsidiaries to place it in the media. But recession in the late 70s and early 80s cut the volume of this kind of advertising. Some agencies went out of business. However, leading specialists like Austin Knight Advertising and Whites Bull Holmes have survived, while the *Guardian* has competed energetically for recruitment advertising.

(*t*) **To attract investors.** Although financial advertising is discussed again in the next chapter as a class of advertising, the need to raise funds—whether by a building society, a public company or a local authority—calls for publicised information about the nature of the investment and its likely return. Interest rates and security, ease of withdrawal of savings, the chance to spread a modest investment over a portfolio of major shares, the opportunity to invest in a new or well-known enterprise, or the provident investment in equity-linked bonds or units, endowment life assurance and hospital benefit schemes—all these are forms of financial advertising just as much as the two-page prospectuses that appear in *The Times* and the *Financial Times*. They are forms of financial advertising which are of ever-growing variety. How else could you tap the market of unknown investors and give the offer the substance which will create confidence? To this may be added the PR support of comments by City editors.

(*u*) **To export.** Here we touch on a very specialised field where expert advice can be obtained from advertising agencies with overseas departments, branches or associates. Media abroad are usually quite different. A national press like the British is rare—mostly it is regional or local—while radio is generally much more important than it is ever likely to be in Britain. Radio is especially strong in developing countries because people can listen even if they cannot read. Export advertising also requires knowledge of national idiom, traditions and religions, and translations are best made by a national living in his own country and familiar with the subject.

British advertisers receive excellent assistance from the **Central Office of Information** which organises British stands at overseas trade fairs, distributes British documentary (*not* advertising) films, and operates a world-wide news service (press, radio, TV) about British achievements, while further facilities can be enjoyed through the overseas services of the BBC.

A British manufacturer wishing to promote export business can make good use of advertising, provided he studies his markets and advertises wisely, but each market is different. To advertise in Europe, West Africa and Japan calls for the use of completely different techniques. The European market has some similarities to the British, whereas only the westernised part of the West African population may be likely buyers. Meanwhile, the Japanese may have a huge potential market which must first be educated into accepting a strange product. The latter happened in the case of New Zealand mutton, the Japanese not being a meat-eating nation until the introduction of mutton, and eventually lamb, from New Zealand in the 50s.

Moreover, export advertising without adequate market and media research, can be a costly failure. A great mistake is for a company, famous in its own country, to imagine that it is equally well known in other countries. The great Nissan-Datsun Motor Company of Japan was practically unknown in Britain until the 70's. Until fairly recently, British people were unaware of names such as Daihatsu, Nordmende, and Cathay Pacific. Reverse this mental process, and the marketing problem of the British exporter becomes alarmingly apparent. This is the great problem of the Common Market where European companies have been operating on a continental basis for a very long time and American supra-national organisations have straddled the continent since the 30's. Those British firms which have taken advantage of containerisation and ferry services to tackle the European market will have already dealt with some of the advertising problems across the Channel and North Sea, but many firms now confronted by a complex market five times larger than the British market have got to look very seriously at their European advertising.

(*v*) **To announce trading results.** This is another form of financial advertising, and whether a full chairman's report is published or a digest of essentials for the lay reader's benefit, it is a necessary procedure to announce trading results. In a good year, it is an opportunity to boast, and there have been some original attempts to interest the lay reader by presenting an edited version of the chairman's report, illustrated with simple charts, sketches or photographs.

In setting out these 22 reasons for advertising it has also been possible to give a glimpse of the varied world of advertising, and its application to many undertakings. Inevitably, it has been necessary to use the jargon of the business—and there is plenty of that!—but as the reader proceeds through this book these terms will become easier to understand as they take their natural place as the vocabulary of the topics to which they refer.

We have, for instance, mentioned 'medium' (singular) and 'media' (plural) so that we do not make the mistake of referring to the *Daily Mirror* or commercial radio as 'a good media'. Sales promotion has, in the 80s, replaced what used to be known as merchandising, and the Institute of Sales Promotion has, for instance, established standard rules for competitions. Sales promotion has itself changed. Because of competitive retail trading some of the household items once used for self-liquidating premium offers are not the bargains they were, and customers are less induced to send in tokens and cash for them. Instead, other promotional methods have been introduced such as High Street redemption schemes (with discounts off goods in certain shops), cross-couponing offers and charity schemes, while money-off offers have remained constantly popular.

Deliberately, we have dropped in a few mentions of PR where they are relevant. A quick explanation at this stage can differentiate between the two by saying that advertising persuades and sells while PR informs and educates. There is a world of difference between the two although they may often operate side by side. It is also very true that advertising may fail if PR has not been applied to educate the market. There was the expensive disaster when NSM (New Smoking Mixture) was introduced; the smoking public refused to buy and the product had to be abandoned. Had there been a two- or three-year build-up of public relations work, smokers might have welcomed a safe alternative to tobacco.

We have also spoken of **displayed advertising**, and this is an interesting expression of historical significance since the original press advertising of some two hundred years ago consisted of line upon line of repetitive statements all set in the same size type. When advertisers were able to use a variety of type sizes and styles, and especially when drawings could be reproduced, these more imaginative advertisements became known as **displayed** in contrast to the **classifieds** (or 'smalls') which were—and still are—run on in small type, and classified under different headings. Most publishers have separate departments to handle the sale and insertion of these two types of advertisement.

We also made a brief distinction between a documentary and an advertising film. The first is a PR film—variously called documentary, sponsored or industrial—and is mainly intended for invited audiences and other PR occasions, whereas the advertising film (or commercial) is shown on the public cinema screen or, in a very short form, on commercial TV. Documentaries may be used as straight programme material on either BBC or ITV, and their purpose is to inform, educate and create understanding and goodwill. Very occasionally, the PR film will be slotted into commercial advertising time as with the ICI, British Gas, TI, Esso and other corporate commercials, but this is exceptional.

2
The Ten Classes of Advertising

We shall now look at ten distinct and particular classes of advertising, each of which calls for a distinct treatment and sometimes different media. From these studies we shall begin to appreciate the diversity of advertising even better. The classifications are as follows:

(a) PERSUASIVE	(f) RETAIL
(b) INFORMATIVE	(g) CO-OPERATIVE
(c) INSTITUTIONAL	(h) INDUSTRIAL
(d) FINANCIAL	(i) GOVERNMENT
(e) CLASSIFIED	(j) TRADE

These 10 classes do not include what is sometimes incorrectly termed 'mail order' advertising because this is a contradiction in terms. Mail order is a form of distribution, but direct mail is an advertising medium. Some clarification occurs with new names such as **direct response** and **tele-marketing**. Significantly, in 1982 the mail order exhibition was renamed *Direct Marketing Fair*. Goods supplied direct, instead of through shops, are advertised in the press, by direct mail, on television, and by Viewdata, aided by credit cards. Retail advertising is included as a separate class because this is distinct from that of the manufacturer, one promoting a store and the other a product.

(a) **Persuasive.** Also known as 'hard-sell' advertising, this is the most obvious kind which surrounds us in our daily lives, urging us to buy all manner of products and services. Without such sales-promoting advertising it is hard to imagine how modern society—with its mass production and mass consumption—could survive. Scathing comments are made about the 'admass', but its critics happen to enjoy the plentiful supply of goods which satisfy their economic needs, food, clothes and shelter. Countless pleasures and former luxuries are also enjoyed simply because economies of scale can be exploited, thanks to advertising and other aids to distribution to national and international markets. The argument for advertising is very much the same as the argument for the Common Market.

The alternative to advertising is to revert to a medieval style of life with self-sufficient production and modestly adequate incomes for most craftsmen, little commercial intercourse with other towns, exports of certain primary commodities of which wool predominated, no banking, no credit and religious antipathy towards money-lending and making profits. It is interesting that economic historians have noted the link between capitalism and Protestantism with the leap into capitalism in Tudor times and into banking in Stuart, while much of the industrial revolution concerns Noncomformist entrepreneurs. Or the comparison may be made with the primitive conditions, low standard of living and unsophistication of an undeveloped country where there is little or no use for advertising. In developing countries advertising is taking its place alongside industrialisation and urbanisation, and advertising (and PR) has been used in the national family planning campaign in several countries.

Persuasive advertising is the inevitable companion of industrialisation. There is no point in having machines if markets cannot be found for their output: *persuasive advertising* finds the markets and keeps the wheels of industry turning by maintaining demand. But not only machines need advertising. A holiday resort cannot fill its hotel bedrooms, nor can a theatre attract a nightly audience, without advertising. Moreover, this kind of advertising persuades people to consider the variety of choices available to them, which is rather different from the criticism that advertising persuades people to buy things they do not want!

The persuasive, hard-selling advertisement must perform five functions if it is to succeed, these being to:

  (i) attract attention.
 (ii) command interest.
(iii) create desire.
 (iv) inspire conviction.
  (v) provoke action.

This process means that attention has to be attracted from elsewhere, and interest held by the message which makes the reader, viewer or listener want to own and enjoy the product or service. The message convinces the customer of performance or value for money and some form of inducement—maybe a coupon or special offer—urges action. All this may require an elaborately planned, created and presented advertisement, or it may be achieved with something as direct and simple as FREE GLASS WITH EACH EXTRA PINTA THIS WEEK.

Here, then, is the powerful sales-promoting advertisement which employs all the ingenious techniques of copywriting, design and media planning to achieve its objectives. And in this we can begin to see why advertising calls for such a medley of skills, and why the advertising agency has become the means of providing the advertiser with the brains and talents necessary to plan and create sales-promoting campaigns.

(*b*) **Informative.** Not everything is bought right away. It may have to be thought about very carefully, and there may be quite a bit of window-shopping and budgeting before the final purchase is made. Or it may be one of those once in a lifetime buys, or a present for some lucky person some day in the future. More leisurely and often more expensive purchases can result from a study of helpful and explanatory advertisements over a period of time. Central heating, double glazing, a new car, kitchen cabinets, a refrigerator or a sewing machine are typical products of this sort. Mostly, they are ones we call **consumer durables**, things that last a long time, and are bought infrequently.

So here we have a very different kind of advertising, less dramatic and compelling but none the less attractive, interesting and convincing. The pace of the appeal is quieter, there is more copy to read, perhaps more pictures to look at, and the object of the ad may be to invite the reader to obtain more detailed information by applying for a brochure or arranging for a demonstration.

Of course, a lot of advertisements fall mid-way between the persuasive and the informative. There are exceptions such as proprietary medicine and treatment advertisements which sell by means of facts, evidence, testimonials and other lengthy copy, but, generally speaking, persuasive advertisements tend to appear on TV and in the popular press, while informative ones are more likely to appear in magazines or weekend newspapers which are read more thoroughly or in less hurried circumstances.

There is also the informative ad which hardly seems to sell at all, telling us interesting things that are somewhat removed from the product itself, or creating a mood which makes us feel favourably disposed towards the product. Here we have the 'soft-sell' as opposed to the 'hard-sell' appeal. The tobacco firms are adept at using this technique, promoting leisure and pleasure activities to associate pleasure with their products.

Yet another version is the reader advertisement which simulates editorial style and is very informative. Because reader ads are easily mistaken for real editorial—and, after all, that was presumably the original intention!—editors object to them, and the *British Code of Advertising Practice* now stipulates that reader-style advertisements must be clearly distinguished by the words 'Advertiser's Announcement'. This has nullified the attempt to resemble editorial, and not surprisingly the method has become less common with this loss of effectiveness. This statement needs to be read with care: while it would be wrong to attempt to trick readers into reading an advertisement because it looked like an editorial, there is nothing unethical about presenting a sales message in an agreeable reading form free of typical hard-selling blandishments. But to put the words 'Advertiser's Announcement' above the reader ad is surely to suggest that it is merely an advertisement and therefore not really worth reading. It implies that the editorial is superior to the advertising, and that is sometimes debatable! There is no reason why advertisements and editorial are not equally important. But this is not to agree with the cynical advertisement manager who regards the editorial as the stuff that fills the space between the advertisements. From these remarks the reader may gather that in some publishing houses, especially the larger ones, a gulf can exist between the editorial and advertisement departments. A lot depends on whether the major source of revenue is sales of copies or sales of advertisement space.

However, some journals, such as *Reader's Digest* and *TV Times*, promote their own reader ads. These are not to be confused with the genuine product news stories supplied by PROs, and **product publicity** is a legitimate form of news which will be discussed more fully in the chapter on public relations.

(c) **Institutional.** Also known as **prestige** or **corporate** advertising, this is the type of advertisement used to present the company image, as when an oil or pharmaceutical company takes space to describe its research skills, its contribution to society, or its efforts to combat pollution. In this case advertising techniques and media are being used to perform a PR task. At one time there was a tendency to direct corporate image PR campaigns through advertisements in *The Times*, *Sunday Times*, *The Observer* and business magazines, but as PR techniques were more fully developed it became less necessary to resort to press advertising. The advantage of using institutional press advertising is that the message can be issued in a precise and controlled fashion on specific dates. Thus urgency may occur in the throes of a takeover bid, or if an industry is threatened with nationalisation. Most PR work is rather less urgent, and the effort to establish a corporate image—that is, what the organisation is, does and stands for—is usually spread over a continuous and accumulative effort. Corporate commercials now appear on television.

(*d*) **Financial.** Financial advertising does not have to be sober. Some banks have used humorous TV commercials, others have used colourful electric signs in London's West End. In recent years there has been a re-volution in financial advertising as the banking world has shed some, but not all, of its inhibitions and traditions of bowler-hatted conformity. Banks, unit trusts, building societies and insurance companies have sought users of their services and investors from wider and sometimes younger sections of the public.

There are, of course, many traditional forms of financial advertisements such as those required by the Stock Exchange in the event of a new share issue, and very formal pages of small print, setting out a company's history and prospects, appear in business newspapers. Companies also issue very formal announcements about their trading results, but some go further and offer readers attractively presented information based on the fuller annual report and accounts.

Perhaps the chief characteristic of financial advertising is its detail. Readers usually want to know a lot about the offer being made, whether it be a unit trust, a life insurance policy, a building society investment, a new share issue or a local authority's efforts to raise a loan. The reader wants to know 'what's in it for him', what are the risks and the rewards and what are the safeguards. This calls for meticulously detailed copy, even more so than in the case of the informative or educational advertisement already discussed. The copy has to answer all likely questions, and be convincing about it.

(*e*) **Classified.** While a great many classifieds (or 'smalls') are inserted by private individuals, others are placed by commercial firms as will be seen, for instance, in the vacancy columns of both national newspapers and magazines. The Personal Column of *The Times* and other newspapers is used by both private and commercial advertisers, even if publishers do separate one kind from the other in the same column. Nevertheless, build-ing societies and correspondence schools vie with promises that 'all is for-given' if Vera will come back to Victor.

There is a special art in writing an almost telegram-like ad in a few lines, using an intriguing opening to catch the reader's eye, squeezing as much abbreviated but intelligible copy into as few lines as possible. The impact of a classified is lost if the copy is too long.

In the previous chapter we have already defined the *displayed classified* under Recruitment Advertising.

By classified we mean not only that the advertisements are small and run-on but that they are grouped together under identifying headings such as HOUSES FOR SALE, OFFICES TO LET, SITUATIONS VACANT or EDUCATIONAL. There are also special headings to distinguish the makes of car in a section on second-hand cars or the breeds of livestock in a farming feature.

This class of advertising is a very important source of revenue to publishers. Provincial newspapers are frequently called the *Advertiser* (e.g. *Croydon Advertiser*, *Chesterfield Advertiser*, *Peterborough Advertiser*, *Turriff and District Advertiser*, *Wishaw Press and Advertiser*) because readers often buy these newspapers as much for the ads as for the news. *Advertiser* is therefore a very appropriate part of the title. People *do* buy papers to read the ads! Other examples are *Exchange and Mart*, *Homefinder* and *London Weekly Advertiser* which are bought solely for their advertising content, while *The Times Educational Supplement* carries an enormous volume of classified announcements for teaching posts.

Roy Brooks, the Chelsea estate agent, advertises like this:

> Just under Mile 'down the road' from TOWER BRIDGE. Last Remaining, Grd Flr Flat in refurbished block, GAS CENT HEAT. 15 ft Drawrm. 2 Bedrms. Fit. Kit. New Bath. Lse 99 yrs. GR £25 p.a. Just £25,500! Call Sun. 2–3 p.m. Anne Boleyn Hse, Pearl Street, Presum Street, Wapping, London E.1.

Regrettably, these small ads are sometimes a source of worry to publishers and the advertising business. It is so easy to walk into a publisher's office, or telephone the appropriate department, and insert an announcement for which it is difficult to check the credentials of the advertiser. Consequently, a number of rackets have been perpetrated through the classified columns, notably homework schemes whose operators collect 'registration fees' but pay out nothing for work done.

(*f*) **Retail.** With the exception of productive retailers—bakers, florists, hairdressers—most retailers are selling other people's goods. Their advertising has four objectives:

   (i) To sell the *stock*.
  (ii) To establish the identity or *character* of the store—a kind of 'image' advertising.
 (iii) To identify the *location*.
 (iv) To attract personal, telephone or mail order *shoppers*.

Obviously, retail advertising has to work very hard, even harder than a persuasive advertisement for a manufacturer. The rewards, or lack of them, will be equally obvious. Such advertising is critical to the success and survival of a shopkeeper. Not only does he have to buy skilfully, and provide good service to his customers, but he has to understand how to make advertising achieve the four objectives set out above. This task becomes all the more difficult when one considers what little understanding the smaller trader is likely to have of advertising techniques and that his total expenditure probably does not justify the services of an agency. He can, however, take advantage of the service departments of local media. Further advice may be offered him from time to time in his trade magazine, while some of his suppliers may invite him to join in co-operative schemes.

In announcing stock an economic division may have to be made between types of products, or between departments in a big store. Conversely, the policy may be to offer a bargain, or a 'loss leader' (a sprat to catch a mackerel in the form of a price cut on one item).

But the second objective, establishing character, demonstrates the use and value of advertising in this field. Whether the advertisements are splashed with the bargain offers of a supermarket or hyperstore, or whether they are set out in the sophisticated style of Harrods or Heals, the character emerges to the extent that both Harrods and Heals are each clearly differentiated in their own particular way.

One of the pioneers of store advertising was Gordon Selfridge who took the front page of the *Daily Mail* and created the idea of having a 'day out' to enjoy shopping at his Oxford Street store. Boots put everything on the counters before the customer's very eyes, and Marks & Spencer strive for quality at reasonable prices. While Marks and Spencer seldom use media advertising, Woolworth have made great use of commercial TV, as have Sainsbury and other food chains. Marks and Spencer have expanded many existing sites, and these huge stores have become permanent advertisements. Similarly, Boots is a household name and a familiar landmark in numerous High Streets. But Fenwick, Lillywhites and other stores advertise in the press and do mail-order business in addition to counter sales. Each of the stores mentioned has a distinct character. This store personality is not unlike the brand image of a product, but it is more than that, even when the original founder is no longer connected with the business. In retail advertising this personality has to be preserved and projected. To make a violent change in the advertising style would be like putting on a disguise.

From the above remarks it will be seen that retail advertising is more complicated than advertising by manufacturers. The retailer has two things to sell, his store and the merchandise he stocks. The merchandise may be much the same as that offered by rival stores, and the advertising has to promote the special benefits offered by the store.

(*g*) **Co-operative (four kinds).** The four types of co-operative advertising are:

(i) *Co-operative society* (Co-op) and agricultural and similar co-operative trading organisations. This is really only a form of retail advertising, and is introduced here merely for the sake of clarifying the succeeding forms.

(ii) *Joint advertising* placed by a trade association, a national export organisation or a publicity committee set up on behalf of an industry. Those benefiting from such joint efforts are levied to pay for the campaign. Examples of these three versions are the advertisements of the Brewers' Society, the Joint Venture overseas trade fair facilities of the Department of Trade and Industry, and the campaigns of the National Milk Publicity Council.

(iii) *Mutual advertising schemes* where two or more firms combine their advertising, as in the cases of fashion houses and department stores, bread and butter, packaged holidays and swim suits.

(iv) *Dealer support schemes* which are also known as co-operative schemes. The manufacturer may either subsidise the stockist's advertising, usually on a 50–50 basis, or supply free advertising material, such as stock-blocks of products or complete stereos or artwork of advertisements with a space left for the insertion of the dealer's name and address. Much of the new car advertising in the local press makes use of these stereos. Stock-blocks of products and trade marks can also be inserted in the dealer's own press advertisements or used to illustrate his catalogues and direct mail literature.

In these ways, the manufacturer can encourage the dealer to promote the goods while the dealer can obtain assistance from the manufacturer both financially and creatively. Hence the expression 'co-operative'. A typical example of co-operative advertising occurs when a manufacturer introduces a new model of, say, a sewing machine, and the product is sold by several hundred appointed stockists throughout the country. To back up national advertising in the women's press the manufacturer will invite each stockist not only to stock the new model but to identify the local source of supply by advertising in the local press. Each stockist is invited to claim stock-blocks and/or a contribution to the cost of the space, and since there will be a budget for this campaign the stockists may be asked to present these claims by a certain date. A co-operative scheme like this is clearly more effective than if the manufacturer put his own advertisements in local newspapers. However, as the example implies, co-operative dealer schemes are more applicable to consumer durables which are sold through appointed dealers than to mass-consumer products which are sold through every available outlet. (N.B. Letterpress-printed newspapers require blocks; litho-printed, artwork.)

(*h*) **Industrial.** Most industrial advertising offers raw materials, components and services to manufacturers and users who convert these technical things into finished products which, in turn, are advertised to the end user or final consumer. A house or a motor-car, a television receiver or a central heating system is an assembly of items made by others. It is sometimes said that a fault of the British motor industry is that it comes to a halt if the maker of steel, glass, wheels or engine components goes on strike. Industrial advertising aims to sell, say, plastic rainwater pipes, pretreated timber, infill panels, wood block flooring, windows, bricks, roofing tiles, insulation materials and so on to housebuilders. The media, in this case of the building industry, will consist of the trade press, exhibitions, direct mail and demonstrations in building centres.

The advertisers are sometimes referred to as **secondary suppliers.** Their promotional activities—often making good use of PR techniques such as press relations, documentary films and technical seminars—are called **back selling.** The advertiser has the problem that his product may be seldom or never known to the final customer, and so sales can rarely be achieved by appealing to the final customer for support. The new car has a certain make of battery, tyres, instruments and so on, and the buyer has no say in what shall be under the bonnet, on the wheels or on the dashboard. It is only at the replacement stage that the car owner can exercise a choice, and then he may decide to fit his own choice of tyres.

A principal medium for this kind of advertising is the trade and technical press (which also run most of the trade exhibitions), and Britain is favoured with one of the world's most extensive ranges of specialised journals, such as *Heating and Ventilating News*, *Caterer and Hotelkeeper* and *Electronics Weekly*, which bring industrial advertisers and their markets close together. In this we see just how valuable is the advertising side of the trade and technical press.

The controlled circulation (cc) journal is an innovation which enables advertisers to gain great penetration of the market since a free list is inevitably larger than that of subscribers to a journal with a cover price. However, controlled circulation journals are not distributed indiscriminately and in order to attain an Audit Bureau of Circulations figure the mailing list has to be substantially based on requests from readers. Another innovation has been the journal made up entirely of postage-paid tear-out enquiry cards.

(*i*) **Government advertising.** Many of the forms of advertising already described are embraced by government advertising (especially classifieds for recruitment purposes). Government department advertising is organised by the **Central Office of Information** which appoints advertising agencies for different campaigns. The nationalised industries and public authorities conduct their own advertising campaigns, appointing their own agents. An example of state enterprise advertising is the British Airways Shuttle Service campaign which is described in the case study section.

If one thinks of all the departments, ministries and state-owned or state-financed industries and bodies which use advertising, the Government is a prodigious advertiser. It seeks staff, suppliers or contractors; promotes immunisation, anti-smoking and road safety campaigns, rent rebates and pensions; announces changes in contributory schemes; and promotes the products and services of the National Coal Board, British Gas Corporation, Electricity Council, the Post Office, British Airways, the BBC and IBA, the British Transport Docks Board, the British Airports Authority, and many other state-controlled organisations.

(*j*) **Trade advertising.** Sometimes rather misleadingly termed 'trade propaganda' (see definition of propaganda in Chapter 3), trade advertising is addressed to distributors—agents, wholesalers, retailers, mail order houses, servicing firms—by the manufacturer.

The media of trade press, direct mail and exhibition are the most commonly used, but TV has been used on occasion and TV contractors offer special schemes by which retailers are told of forthcoming TV campaigns aimed at their customers.

The purpose of trade advertising is therefore to secure distribution, that is to 'sell in' to the trade. Its appeal is to the distributor's desire to sell more and make more profit. It takes place (or should take place!) prior to consumer advertising because it is folly to advertise a product which is unobtainable. Nevertheless, an objective can be to *increase* distribution of an advertised product.

The advertisements will urge the distributor to buy stocks, offering him introductory discounts, display material, co-operative advertising schemes, and telling him about the consumer advertising support. This in turn will be supported by editorial write-ups about the product and its promotion. With established products, reminder advertising will also occur, and there will be seasonal campaigns to stimulate retailers to re-stock. An excellent form of trade advertising is the big broadsheet which reproduces full-size specimens of the forthcoming press advertisements and stills from the TV commercials, and also illustrates the available display material and the stereos offered for local press advertising. The broadsheet also carries an order form so that retailers may request supporting material. This broadsheet is mailed to dealers some weeks before the launch or the special promotion, and it is one of the ways of establishing direct contact when the product is distributed through wholesalers and there is no direct representation. Otherwise, trade advertising backs up the salesman and helps to overcome the problem of the salesman's four- or six-weekly journey cycle.

The trade exhibition, to quote Hotelympia, the Furniture Exhibition, the Building Exhibition and HEVAC, is a means of both demonstrating products, new ones especially, and of meeting the distributors. Some exhibitors regard trade exhibitions as chiefly a goodwill mission, a blend of trade advertising and trade PR, and a way of introducing new lines and cementing good relations. Invitation tickets are sent to distributors and the stand often includes a private lounge and bar where distributors are welcomed and entertained.

Trade relations also include education and training, the trade being taught the uses and applications of a product, and distributor's staff being trained in selling and servicing the product. We are now impinging on PR again, and a very effective form of PR is the house journal for distributors. These external journals vary according to the trade, but their objective is generally to inform, educate and help the trade to sell the product, and this may be done by suggesting promotional ideas and by reporting methods adopted by enterprising stockists. Petrol companies publish magazines for the benefit of forecourt attendants, photographic firms issue magazines which explain the technicalities of products and materials and show how stockists are displaying the goods. Window display and other contests can be run through external house journals.

Having described some of the numerous uses and forms of advertising, at least from the point of view of the advertiser, we shall now turn in the following chapter to a closer look at the nature and role of advertising in modern society.

3
The Role of Advertising in Society

In the first two chapters we have deliberately tried to draw a broad picture of advertising, hoping that this will open the reader's eyes to its multiplicity of kinds and uses. In this way the reader can begin to understand how advertising is and can be used by all sorts of individuals and organisations for many different reasons and purposes. It is hoped that these two chapters may have helped to overcome any notions that advertising is wasteful or unnecessary, and to have revealed the sheer versatility of this communication tool. Advertising is not unlike a telephone, an instrument whose usefulness can be abused but which, when properly used, can be a boon.

3.1 Definitions

At the beginning of Chapter 1 there was a brief definition of advertising as the means by which we make known what we have to sell or what we want to buy. An even better one is that **advertising presents the most persuasive possible selling message to the right prospects for the product or service at the lowest possible cost.**

This is a professional definition. It emphasises that advertising should be planned and created to achieve the most results for the least costs. When science and art are united in the forms of research and creative skills, and supported by astute buying of media and materials, it is possible to produce and execute campaigns that contribute to business success. Not surprisingly, this businesslike definition comes from the Institute of Practitioners in Advertising, the professional body of the advertising agents, and it appears in booklets produced to explain agency services to businessmen. The definition is rightly concerned about cost-effectiveness.

The same point is made by both definitions: *the object of advertising is to sell.* But unlike the salesman who sells in a face-to-face, or even voice-to-voice, situation, advertising sells in a broadcast fashion to numbers of prospects whose identity may or may not be known, and who may be close at hand or at a distance. An advertisement in *The Sun* or *Daily Express* is just as likely to sell to someone working in a Fleet Street café as it is to a man in the Orkneys. A card in a London underground train compartment can sell to the passenger sitting opposite, but equally an advertisement in a magazine can sell to someone on the other side of the world. Advertising has this remarkable flexibility and range of operation.

The versatility and flexibility of this selling force does have to be used intelligently, but as we shall see in the chapter on market research the advertising world is well served by intelligence services. When research information is coupled with the skills offered by trained and experienced advertising men and women, there is no reason why professional advertising should not do all that is claimed for it in the IPA definition.

However, if this selling force is used in a sporadic, ill-devised and un-budgeted way, money will be frittered away and it will be pointless to say that advertising is ineffectual or a waste of money. The smallest advertiser needs to plan his expenditure, media choice, timing of insertions and copy content just as scrupulously as a big spender of a million pounds with a mass national market to woo. If anything, ill-spent money can be more critical to the smaller advertiser whose slightest effort must make all the difference between survival and bankruptcy.

Turnover and profitability can be increased through judicious use of advertising. But there is advertising and advertising, and like most things in life one tends to get what one pays for. Hundreds of pounds can be squandered on what, to be kind, may be called 'charitable' advertisements in souvenir programmes for local galas or West End premières. More can be thrown away on media of doubtful sales value such as menu covers, estate agents' maps, town guides of meagre circulation, and directories and year books of minor importance which may not even see the light of day. Obviously, there are plenty of reputable exceptions such as the official holiday resort guide and the directory which serves as the 'bible' of a trade or profession, to mention only *Advertiser's Annual*. There are, however, plenty of takers of the foolish advertiser's money. The inexperienced local advertiser may easily fall victim to rackets, *unless he has budgeted and planned his advertising and therefore has neither excuse nor surplus to spend unwisely*.

Before there is any expenditure on advertising, there must first be an assessment of the likely return, and one method or medium should be judged against another on a cost–benefit basis.

3.2   Advertising or PR?

As an example, the knowledge and expertise of the pharmaceutical in-dustry is well established as a source of information for professional medi-cal, trade and lay associations. In the modern idiom, much use is now made of video-tapes as a training aid in the methods of drug administration or in monitoring techniques. Working with the British Diabetic Associa-tion, for instance, Eli Lilly—one of the world's major suppliers of insulin—have sponsored a series of video-cassettes for diabetic education.

These programmes—twenty in all—support the medical profession in providing diabetics and their families with the opportunity of understand-ing diabetes and learning about its management. No advertising is, nor should be, permitted on such tapes, but all involved—the doctors, nurses and ancillary workers; the Association; the patient and family; and the manufacturers—benefit from the use of the cassettes and the information they impart.

The videos are thus a joint PR effort, servicing both the commercial pharmaceutical company Eli Lilly and the voluntary British Diabetic Association. The Audio-Visual Education Service of the BDA hires out or sells the tapes to members, makes their availability known through its journal *Balance* and through local branches, and supports them with programme notes. Eli Lilly are credited at the end of each video and the programme notes state 'sponsored by Eli Lilly and Company Ltd, Diabetics Unit'. Famous medical authorities such as Dr John Ward and well-known sufferers from diabetes such as Sir Harry Secombe appear in the videos.

They are shown in the waiting rooms of diabetic clinics at hospitals, and so form an excellent means of educating patients at a vital point-of-interest. But perhaps even more important, these videos help to educate friends and relatives of diabetics, the people who may not understand what the disease is all about.

Public relations is a much bigger subject than advertising but the two often come closely together. The Eli Lilly/British Diabetic Association example shows how PR techniques can be important when advertising would be inappropriate. Eli Lilly would not normally advertise directly to diabetics. Moreover, the tapes are also addressed to diabetics who take tablets and do not require insulin, so they benefit from the company's sponsorship.

The subject of PR is discussed in Chapter 13, and the bibliography lists some modern books on the subject. At this point we shall differentiate between advertising and PR by examining the well-known definition adopted by the Institute of Public Relations: **Public relations practice is the deliberate, planned and sustained effort to establish and maintain mutual understanding between an organisation and its public.**

The word 'understanding' is the key to an interpretation of PR, and this is clearly quite different from the 'selling motive' of advertising. The relationship between PR and advertising is that unless people *understand* an organisation or its products there can be no goodwill, and advertising may be a waste of money and so fail to sell. Thus, PR can have the effect of making advertising work. This is because customers are more likely to be persuaded to buy something they know about and trust. It can, therefore, be a very costly, uphill task to sell by salesmanship and advertising alone, and PR can be directed at both the trade and the consumer and so break the inertia caused by ignorance, prejudice or hostility.

A good example of this is the story of cross-channel car ferries that owe some of their present popularity to a PR campaign for Thoresen in 1964 which educated travel agents about the features of drive-on, drive-off ferries, and the location of ferry ports. As a result, travel agents throughout the UK—now being knowledgeable about these facilities—were able to give first-hand advice to their clients. And car-ferry advertising was all the more effective because of the goodwill of the well informed travel trade. The PR campaign involved taking a *Viking* car-ferry on a round-Britain voyage at the close of the 1964 season, travel agents visiting the vessel at various ports and seeing for themselves what Thoresen had to offer with a new ship, a new embarkation port, and a new route to the continent.

3.3 Propaganda Defined

Propaganda is a curious word with pleasant and unpleasant associations. To propagate means to multiply or disseminate, as when we increase the number of plants in the garden, or spread ideas and gain adherents. Propagating the Gospels, and the Nazi propaganda machine, are contrasting uses of the term. Nor should we forget that the Ministry of Information was also a propaganda machine, and that Spitfire Funds (a means of deflating the wartime economy by pretending to the patriotic civilian population that investment in National Savings would buy Spitfires!) and 'Dig For Victory' and 'Be Like Dad, Keep Mum' posters were part of its war effort. There is propaganda for cannabis (and against it), for Ulster and also for a reunited Ireland, for smoking and against smoking. Propaganda is one-sided communication.

In some respects it resembles advertising, but it is hardly the same thing if we are precise about the use of terms. Propaganda has to do with ideas, beliefs, convictions, opinions. It is not necessarily emotional and it can be perfectly sincere. To promote the idea of hygiene is to use propaganda, but to promote the sale of a brand of soap we have to use advertising. And to tell the story of the soap manufacturer or to explain how soap is made, and to teach people its many uses, we use the techniques of public relations. There are subtle but distinct and definable differences between these three forms of communication. Yet it is not unusual to hear people use all three words at different times to mean the same thing. We have already, in Chapter 2, referred to the misnomer of 'trade propaganda', a diabolical abuse of language if ever there was one!

The definition is therefore: **Propaganda is the means of making known in order to gain support for an opinion, creed or belief.**

Like advertising, propaganda is biased in favour of whatever it is promoting, whether it be Christianity, Conservatism, Communism, the RSPCA, the opponents of blood sports or vivisection, or the advocates of Women's Lib. Its objective is to win supporters, members, subscribers, donors or converts. This may involve lobbying Members of Parliament, introducing Private Members' Bills, marching on Downing Street, obtaining enquiries or causing Royal Commissions to be set up.

Often, it depends which side we are on as to whose propaganda we accept, since it is applied by all governments in peace or war, although we may be sufficiently independent to reject the propaganda of both Dr Goebbels and Brendan Bracken, or of India and Pakistan, or of those for and against capital punishment. Obviously, it is difficult to be utterly unbiased, neutral or unsympathetic, although it has been achieved by the Swiss and the Swedes, and these intellectual, environmental and sociological aspects of propaganda emphasise how propaganda differs from both advertising and public relations.

The similarities are minor ones such as use of similar or even identical techniques and media. The major difference lies in the purpose. Advertising aims to sell goods and services to the largest possible market at the lowest possible cost, always provided there is a market! Of course it would be foolish to try to sell contraceptives to a Catholic-dominated country which objected to family planning, whereas there is no problem in Asiatic countries where propaganda is aimed at limiting families to two or three children. Nevertheless, with other products—Guinness is an obvious one—the advertising does not discriminate between Catholics and Protestants, not even in Ulster. Politically-orientated newspapers are not restricted to their followers, and newspaper readers often seem oblivious to the political bias of the papers they read. Advertising is aimed at markets which are defined by occupation and social class—*social grades*—and advertisers talk about *market segments* which are divisions of the buying public. The social grades A, B, C^1, C^2, D and E are based on occupation, and the JICNARS social grading system relies on the interviewer collecting extensive information about the occupation of the person to be graded. This is dealt with again in Chapter 15. But from the point of view of the previous argument, a C^2 person has certain economic and social characteristics, and no questions are asked about race, creed or colour. This leads us to a definition of marketing.

3.4   Marketing Defined

According to the Institute of Marketing:

Marketing is the management process responsible for identifying, anticipating and satisfying customer requirements profitably. Let us consider another one from the late David Malbert, former City Editor of the then London *Evening Standard*. He said:
Marketing is producing and selling at a profit goods that satisfy customers.

Producing, selling, satisfying at a profit sums up marketing beautifully.

The modern development of this is **ecological marketing**—that is, supplying what people will buy and which we are especially good at supplying.

This involves research and development (R&D) and market research (MR) to discover what will sell. This, too, may mean creating a new product to satisfy an as yet unrealised want—this was true of television, washing machines, detergents, central heating and double glazing—or one to satisfy an expressed want such as a rodenticide, or better brakes for faster cars. Just because the market cannot demand something which does not yet exist, but could be beneficial and desirable if it did, does not mean that demand should not be created. This has to be said because advertising has been criticised—usually by parsons and teachers—for stirring up materialistic and greedy demands, for making people buy what they don't want, but is it not more appropriate to see advertising as the agent of marketing? The combination of advertising and marketing, that is making known things that can satisfy customers, has consistently expanded choice and raised standards of living. In the 30s a large number of people did not enjoy making a choice between a holiday abroad, double glazing and a sailing dinghy. It was more likely to be a choice between a new bicycle, a suit or a week at Southend. Advertising has contributed to the affluence of modern wants, and marketing is the post-World War Two means of making many of those wants possible. By this is meant the difference between booking travel tickets and hotel accommodation on an individual basis at very considerable cost and buying a packaged holiday abroad at modest cost. Advertising and marketing have made the packaged tour possible, the idea pioneered no doubt by pre-war holiday camps in Britain.

Marketing, as suggested by other earlier and limited definitions, is not only to do with the distribution of goods from maker to user. Today, marketing takes in everything from the search for a new product to after-sales service. That covers designing, branding, pricing, packaging, market research, test marketing, salesmanship and distribution. Advertising is part of the **marketing mix**, being used to persuade distributors to take the stock, and to persuade customers to buy the stock. Advertising augments the work of the salesman, both in selling in and selling out. A good description of advertising is that it is the *life-blood* of business. This is very apt because the flow of business depends on the repetition of sales so that production is maintained at optimum level. This required level of production means that full advantage can be taken of bulk buying of raw materials and other supplies, that labour can be trained and permanently employed, that machines can be run continuously, so that costs are spread over a large enough volume of goods to sell competitively while maximising profits. Marketing sets out to achieve economic business management, using advertising as its ammunition.

A shop cannot remain open if customers stay away and goods become dusty or mouldy on the shelves. The wholesaler cannot prosper if no one wants his supplies and he has to stockpile. The manufacturer has to lay off hands and cancel orders for supplies if the order book is slack. There really are wheels of industry which have to be kept turning, and advertising is the lubricant.

Advertising needs no apologist. It is as essential to industrial society as oxygen is to the human lungs. We cannot buy what we do not know exists. We are capable of forgetting what is not told us over and over again. Even the football coupon envelope repeats 'Full postage MUST be affixed'. People *are* dumb! 'Sorry, I forgot' is the commonest of excuses. And just because we bought Swan Vestas or Oxo once or last time does not guarantee that we shall ever buy it again. The modern industrial world cannot wait on the caprices of the average forgetful and indifferent individual. A man still has to ask a woman to marry him, and he still has to have intercourse (short of artificial insemination) to beget children. A manufacturer still has to woo customers, and inject the desire to make a purchase. None of these things happens of its own volition, and not everyone believes in virgin births. There is certainly no gooseberry bush for advertisers.

3.5 Marketing—Advertising—PR—Propaganda

To distinguish these four activities in practice let us now take the hypothetical example of a Government policy to overcome an acute shortage of housing resulting from a balance of payments deficit and the country's inability to import building materials. The policy is to offer financial aid to landlords and private house-owners who are prepared to convert existing large property into self-contained flats. Let us assume that a serious objection to this policy is that the roofs of such houses have so deteriorated that re-tiling is necessary but prohibitively expensive. Consequently, the Government's policy is foredoomed.

But the managing director of a servicing company whose business is property maintenance recognises that if they can find a method of renovating these old roofs without having to re-tile they can win some very worthwhile business. The company is nationally organised with regional offices, depots and suitable staff. More men can be recruited and trained if necessary, so there is no problem about capacity. Meanwhile, the market is there waiting to be satisfied: there are thousands of deficient properties and the offer of Government grants to put them right. There is actually Government *propaganda* urging property owners to repair and convert their houses, and this propaganda has been disseminated by official announcements, a booklet published by HMSO, and posters which are displayed in public places. The scheme has been given coverage in the press and on radio and TV.

So we start at the birth of a marketing scheme. The potential market is estimated and the Research and Development division, under the guidance of the technical director, is charged with finding a solution that is commercially viable. This is no simple task: it may take a year or more to discover and test an answer. The research will entail discussions with the Government's Building Research Station, a search through international technical literature, and especially an investigation into what is done about roof preservation in other parts of the world. At some point it may be decided that the plausible alternatives are:

(i) A replacement roofing material which is either inexpensive in itself, or inexpensive to lay, or

(ii) A method of treating existing tiles and slates, thus obviating the costs of scaffolding, and removal and replacement of old roofing materials.

Let us assume, for the sake of the example, that a decision is taken to investigate whether the causes of deterioration can be overcome by the treatment of the tiles or slates *in situ*.

After experiments, let us further assume that a fluid is formulated which will do all that is required, and that it has been proved successful under tests which have simulated the effects of erosion by the elements during a time-span of 20 years. Moreover, the official Building Research Station has subjected the fluid to its own independent trials, and has certified the efficacy of the formulation.

This is a good point at which to invite the advice of a marketing orientated advertising agency. The following decisions have now to be made:

(i) Whether to market the fluid so that it may be bought by house-owners and building contractors.

(ii) If so, whether to distribute through all kinds of outlets willing to stock it, e.g. builders' merchants, do-it-yourself retailers, department stores, etc., or to restrict distribution to builders' merchants. Direct sales to local authorities and to large estate and property owners are also possible.

(iii) Instead, whether to retain the monopoly of the product and develop the servicing side, the company's own staff applying the product. Or do both, sell the product and the service.

(iv) What will the product be called, or will the new roofing service be given a special name—Roofpruf or the Roofproofing Service? Or both?

(v) What container will be used for the fluid? Bottle, jar, can, drum? And in what quantities? Is it concentrated? Dangerous? Does it have to conform with any safety regulations regarding colouring, labelling, warnings, instructions? What size packs will be rational and economical for the domestic user and for the trade?

(vi) If the product is to be made generally available—and why not, the company is unlikely to get all the available work yet open knowledge of the product may well help to sell the company's service—what will be the recommended retail price, the bulk price and the trade terms?

(vii) Can the finished job be guaranteed for a given number of years, say twenty, as in the simulated trial?

(viii) How will the product and/or service be advertised?

(*a*) To what market segment(s)?
(*b*) When?
(*c*) Using what media?

    (i) Trade and technical press.
    (ii) Building Exhibition, DIY Exhibition, Ideal Home Exhibition.
    (iii) Direct mail.
    (iv) Technical data sheet.
    (v) Descriptive print.
    (vi) Demonstrations.
    (vii) Building Centre displays.
    (viii) Press read by property owners/DIY enthusiasts.

(*d*) What theme, or copy platform, will be adopted—perhaps a tie-in with the Government appeal?

    (ix) How can PR assist in educating trade and market?

(*a*) Press receptions.
(*b*) Documentary film, VHS and Betamax video-cassettes.
(*c*) News releases, pictures.
(*d*) Exclusive feature articles on successful treatments to well-known buildings, and on the application technique.
(*e*) Technical seminars in branch areas for dealers/large users, making use of the documentary film and/or video.
(*f*) Supply of technical data to works of reference such as year books which print recommended treatments.
(*g*) When a substantial number of houses has been preserved and treated suggest the topic to producers of suitable TV programmes, or supply tapes to radio and video-cassettes to TV.
(*h*) Arrange visit to a treatment in progress for journalists who specialise in property, including editors of house-buying magazines, radio, TV and—because of export prospects—the COI and external services of the BBC.
(*i*) Build a library of photographs of the treatment being applied, and of typical buildings or kinds of roofs preserved. These can be used for slide presentations and for press use.

In this brief sketch—and in practice the strategy would be planned in much greater depth and in accordance with the value of the market, the profitability and the budget of marketing and promotional costs—we can at least see the four activities operating like this:

   (i) Government *propaganda* to get property owners to adopt the policy of converting large old houses.

  (ii) The overall *marketing strategy* from R&D to guarantee.

 (iii) The *advertising* to users of the product or service.

 (iv) The *public relations* to educate property owners and so win their confidence and understanding.

We have only touched on the sales side, but in this exercise it is assumed that the company has a national sales force based on local branches. They are already selling the company's other building maintenance service and can be augmented if business expands. There is also an existing servicing organisation which, again, can be expanded if required.

This imaginary example shows the role of advertising in modern society, and the same argument applies whether it is a staple product or something highly specialised like our roofing fluid. But advertising does not stop with launching the new product or service, and this is where critics fail to understand the need for and the value of advertising.

3.6 Advertising and the Critics

There are five principal criticisms of advertising, and it is sensible to discuss them quite frankly. Are these attacks justified, or are they fallacies? They are usually made by three groups of people:

(*a*) Those who seek a political or intellectual hobby-horse, as when the Labour Party advocates taxes on advertising. It is usual to tax an income, and it is surely incongruous to tax a cost!

(*b*) Those who find it difficult or impossible to come to terms with the quantities involved in production, distribution, sales and uses outside their immediate personal experience as the buyer of one item from one shop once a week.

(*c*) Those who think it is unethical to persuade people to make purchases, because this conflicts with the free will of the individual to buy what he or she likes.

These critics are likely to make one or more of the following five criticisms:

(*a*) **That advertising is parasitical.** All you have to do is produce something worthwhile and it will sell. In the words of the famous fallacy, the world will beat a path to the better mouse-trap. It won't, for the simple reason that we are not a population of explorers. If a man makes a new kind of jam in Brighton it is highly unlikely that anyone will hear about it in neighbouring Hove unless there is some kind of publicity.

The critic will retort that he is uninfluenced by advertising, that he is an intelligent rational person who buys only what he wants to buy, and goes to some trouble to seek out precisely what he wants. This is a generalisation belied by the existence of industrial society. Advertising does influence choice and purchases as can be tested by visiting a shopkeeper some days after a product has been advertised on TV: very often he is out of stock and his excuse is 'it must have been on the telly!'

This is not to say that advertising has *forced* people to make particular choices or purchases, but it has told them very convincingly that *the choice or opportunity is there*. There is nothing to stop them from rejecting the goods at the point-of-sale. Many of us do exactly that. The advertised article looks promising, whether it be a book, a shirt or a car, but when we see it in the shop or showroom we change our minds and don't buy it. Even if it is wrapped or canned like chocolate or baked beans, we may still hesitate when confronted by the appearance, size, weight, price, value for money. And if we decide to try it we may decide not to buy it again. We are not absolutely brainwashed by advertising.

The British are apt to resent salesmanship, and to deny the success of advertising, yet if they want a job, house or car, or a nice restaurant for a celebration, they immediately resort to the advertisements. That eventually helpful or decisive advertisement may be no more than a black type entry in the telephone book, but it is still an advertisement. Equally, if they want a new assistant or secretary, or have something to sell secondhand, they turn to advertising.

It is significant that when several brands of cigarette were no longer made during the Second World War, and no advertising was required for them, these brands were so quickly forgotten that when some returned after the war people were surprised that they had in fact succeeded in forgetting their previous existence. To stop advertising a popular branded product for only a few months is suicidal. One company did convince itself that advertising was a waste of money, and after that sad experiment it took three years of intensified advertising to regain its market share.

The reader may care to prove this point by making an experiment: ask a person aged over 50 how many brands of cigarette he can remember and note how many of the following once well-advertised brands are included in his list:

Abdulla	De Reszke Minors	Robin
Ardath	Du Maurier	Sarony
Astoria	Four Square	Star
Bar-One	Greys	Tenners
BDV	Markovitch	Three Castles
Capstan	Park Drive	Top Score
Churchman's No. 1	Perfectos	Turf
Craven A	Rhodian	Victory V
De Reszke	Richmond Gem	Wills Gold Flake

Alternatively, ask someone slightly younger but over 40 how many former national newspapers he or she can recall, and check how many of the following are listed:

Daily Herald	*Sunday Citizen and Reynolds News*
Daily Sketch	*Sunday Dispatch*
Daily Worker	*Sunday Empire News*
News-Chronicle	*Sunday Pictorial*
Sunday Chronicle	

(N.B. The list includes some name changes, *The Sun* taking over from the *Daily Herald*, the *Daily Worker* being renamed *Morning Star*, and the *Sunday Pictorial* being renamed *Sunday Mirror*.)

The results of these tests may be surprising, and the person questioned may have to think very hard.

(*b*) **That advertisements are untrue or misleading.** This claim is unlikely to have any basis in fact since there are laws such as the *Trade Descriptions Acts* and the *Independent Broadcasting Authority Act*, 1973, plus the British Code of Advertising Practice and the Advertising Standards Authority which impose either legal or voluntary controls upon advertising in the UK. The remedy is to report a false claim to the local Weights and Measures Inspector, or to report any other type of advertising offence to the ASA at Brook House, Torrington Place, London, WC1E 7HN. ASA advertisements invite written complaints.

Advertising is no more perfect than anything else, and it is open to abuse by rogues, but it is not in the interests of regular advertisers jealous of their reputations deliberately to hoodwink the public. There are, of course, businessmen who are not as ethical as advertising practitioners, men who think it is smart business to depend on a mug being born every minute, but the advertising business is conscious that public confidence is essential to its success. If the public really had no faith in advertising there would be some substantial bankruptcies among advertising agencies! Unlike American banking and stockbroking at the time of the Great Crash in 1929, advertising is not a giant confidence trick.

British advertising does tend to suffer from stories we hear about the greater licence adopted by American advertising, despite rigorous Federal legislation. But as President Roosevelt discovered when trying to impose his New Deal philosophy upon unenthusiastic businessmen, even the Supreme Court may reject your perhaps naïve expectations. More recently, the Federal Trade Commission has discovered that forty well-known American breakfast cereals did 'little to prevent malnutrition', and in 1971 twenty-six of those brands reformulated their products to include at least a quarter of the daily requirement of vitamins. This investigation brought to light the fact that American breakfast cereal advertising had been falsely claiming a high nutritional value for their brands. This was certainly taking *caveat emptor* too far, and such advertising invites legal control.

Britain had her share of dishonest advertising in the days before the British Code of Standards in Relation to the Advertising of Medicines and Treatments (1948) which is now incorporated in the present Code of Advertising Practice and in the *IBA Code*. Before that Code of 1948 (pioneered by the Advertising Association) practically anything went in British proprietary medicine advertising. Pill advertisers promised to cure almost any ailment or disease, and there were firms which offered to diagnose illness by post, while among the advertisements which, before the Second

World War, provoked the vigilance of the Advertising Association were those for Simpson's Iodine Lockets and iodine impregnated shoe socks which were supposed to ward off ill-health.

But the point that has to be appreciated is that it was—and always is— the *advertiser*, the manufacturer, the businessman, the client who is at fault, *not* advertising. In most cases, it is the advertiser who makes the claims for his product, not the advertising agent who either accepts product information in good faith or rejects it because it is unbelievable, untrue or at variance with the legal or voluntary controls.

It is therefore worth considering a statement made by Professor John Howard, a lecturer who was appointed by the US Government to analyse testimony given at Federal Trade Commission hearings on American advertising, and quoted in *Campaign* (January 7, 1972). He said: 'There's a great difference between what the advertising industry calls persuasion and what many people see as manipulation, confusion and exploitation of the consumer.' *Campaign* worried further by saying: 'Of course things—as the well-worn cliché goes—are different in Britain. But are they? And if so, how different? With so many American companies operating in this country, it is surely not unreasonable to expect a few answers.'

Perhaps we should be thankful for the sales resistance of the typical Britisher!

While the advertising business is anxious to perform honestly and responsibly, intensity of competition, the fear of displeasing and losing a client, and the over-enthusiasm of a young copywriter, may provoke occasional lapses. But on the whole, the *organised* advertising business believes that advertising can prosper only if ethical standards are maintained.

Nevertheless, it would be silly to whitewash the business, and two dangers have to be recognised. When business is bad agencies may cut corners to retain clients, and media may turn a blind eye to doubtful advertisements. There is no doubt that this does happen.

In the case of agencies, what other excuse can there be for the spate of 'knocking' and 'ash canning' advertisements which agencies have been perfectly willing to produce—despite the Code of Practice—presumably to satisfy clients who will take their business elsewhere if orders to be extra-competitive are not obeyed? The sinister aspect is that most of the advertisers guilty of 'knocking' (criticising rivals) are American firms operating in Britain.

But in the case of media there is a cynical disregard for ethics when circulation and readership figures are disappointing and space is hard to sell. The harder it becomes to sell space the more willing are publishers to accept any advertising. In the media world it has to be admitted that ethics are very largely a matter of economics.

Three examples may be quoted. In the 50s, when newsprint rationing still restricted the size of newspapers and therefore the volume of acceptable advertising, some publications refused to accept *any* proprietary medicine advertising. They could afford to, Code or no Code. But to take the second example, when space was less easy to sell at one point in the 60s, newspapers (and even the *Radio Times*) accepted advertisements for the pernicious 'switch selling' racket when ancient sewing machines were advertised for £15, but doorstep sales were switched to £40 new machines. And third, most of the rackets and vice advertisements—usually in classified form—appear in small circulation newspapers and magazines which are glad to accept revenue from anyone. In other words, the rejection of undesirable advertising by publishers is sometimes related to purely business considerations of the extent to which they can afford to be an upholder of the Code of Practice, irrespective of whether it belongs to an organisation which is a signatory to the Code. In the situation which press media have suffered in recent years, sale of space is a matter of survival, and publishers' standards can be at the mercy of rogue advertisers.

The 'ethics are economics' argument can also be looked at in reverse. To trick customers is poor policy. The victim will not return his custom, nor make recommendations, and successful business does depend on the PR element of goodwill. A misleading advertisement is bad 'PR'. In some large companies advertising comes under the control of PR for the very reason that the company or its products must not suffer from the ill-effects of advertisements that are in bad taste, exaggerated, 'knocking', badly designed or not in keeping with the 'house style' or corporate identity. The latter may include the use of a company symbol, specified type face or faces, and special colour schemes.

(c) **Advertising creates false and materialistic demands for things people do not really need or want.** Indeed, it may well be asked do people need false eye-lashes or wigs; was it necessary for detergents to be introduced in competition with soap flakes; wouldn't it be better if there were fewer cars; don't all these cars mean that our towns are cluttered up with petrol pumps; are we so weak and lazy we can no longer peel potatoes; and must we eat so many sweets, drink so much beer, smoke so many cigars, feed so many cats and dogs, and go rushing off at dead of night to eat our fish and chips and play bingo in Majorca?

Well, why not?

Advertising offers us choice. Tons of potatoes are sold to determined potato peelers, and plenty of people prefer not to take packaged holidays. Lots of people slim, or are teetotallers or non-smokers. Inter-City trains must have taken a lot of motorists off the motorways. Other choices are being exercised too. Advertising is the story of man earning a living (otherwise called economics) and making his choice between scarce alternatives. Yes, even Golden Wonder potato crisps are scarce, relative to the ability of everyone to buy them. Scarcity is indicated when the 'house full' notices go up, or our stockist is temporarily 'sold out', or when we have to wait six weeks for delivery of a new car, or have to book the holiday accommodation months in advance.

Advertising offers us rewards for bending over the factory bench, the office typewriter or the kitchen sink. Why shouldn't a man who has worked all day in the boring hell of a motor-car factory respond to the invitation to 'spoil himself' or the implication that he deserves it? Isn't that what the beer ads are all about—'the taste that satisfies'—or those which offer mouthwatering soups or glamorous holiday brochures, sizzling sausages, dreamy wines or fascinating Italian and Oriental dishes in a can. He's ready to buy the sizzle. He's earned it.

Advertising also tells us about products we've never heard of before, to mention only new kinds of safety razors, ready-pasted wallpaper, paints with rock hard, unscratchable surfaces, new part works, toys for Christmas or ways of controlling softer bodies. But for TV advertising some husbands wouldn't know what their wives spent the housekeeping money on, or why they deserved more. And when we take up a new interest, it is the advertising in specialist magazines that we have never had cause to buy before which now helps us to choose and spend and acquire.

The market is never static. Very few pre-war houses were built with garages: now the housebuyer wants a double garage or at least space for a car-port, and the town house has become the answer to the density problem. Advertising goes along with these changes, and what the critic considers materialistic is a matter of improved living standards to others. Man is an acquisitive animal, but is this instinct necessarily a greedy one? We are also back to the medieval argument if modest demands and self-sufficiency are held to be superior to enriching our lives by the sweat of our brow or the exercise of our brain.

(*d*) **There's no need to go on advertising an established product.** Manufacturers would be delighted if this were true: in fact products have life cycles and need to be advertised for as long as they will survive, after which they are either withdrawn or revamped. Motor-cars are a good example, ten years being the ideal life-span of a particular model including its year-by-year modifications. Products like Swan Vestas matches, McDougall's flour, Bisto, Guinness or Heinz baked beans seem to go on for ever in much the same way, and yet they too get their 'new looks' from time to time with fresh packaging, new advertising styles and premium offers.

The Bisto packet still features the Bisto kids and the old slogan 'Ah, Bisto!' which was originated more than fifty years ago, and refreshingly they returned to replace more sophisticated TV ads in 1976. Guinness has gone through an amazing sequence of advertising styles, mostly with the one agency, Bensons, until the switch to J. Walter Thompson and now ABM who have produced a fascinating variety of lively and amusingly original commercials. Guinness advertising has had the rare effect of being liked by people who never drink their beer. But the question is: how many people who *do* drink their beer would go on asking for it if Guinness said enough is enough, we've kept the British amused long enough, and went into an Irish tizzy and stopped advertising? There is no doubt what would happen: Allied Breweries and a few others would have their own dark, tangy stout with a frothy head on the market so quickly that Guinness would have to turn Park Royal brewery into a depository.

Let us repeat the reply to the suggestion that there is no need to go on advertising an established product: just look at one of those pictures of London absolutely jammed with horse-drawn or early motor-buses. The vehicles are covered in advertisements, mostly for firms which are still advertising today. Most of the big successful firms, the ones whose products are household words, the ones we like and trust, built their sales and goodwill on advertising begun seventy or more years ago. And they are still advertising. They are the real big spenders—Cadbury's, Heinz, Nestlé and many others.

(*e*) **Advertising causes costly competition and higher prices.** If competition becomes too hot for comfort the advertisers get together through their trade associations and impose a voluntary curb. This has actually happened. In the late 30s and again in 1977 cigarette manufacturers stopped gift coupon schemes because they had become prohibitively expensive, and in the 50s certain alcoholic drink manufacturers agreed not to buy time on TV.

No advertiser is going to throw money away on needless advertising any more than it will employ unnecessary salesmen or keep running a factory whose production is uneconomic. Competition is also eradicated by means of acquisitions, mergers and take-overs.

All costs have to be budgeted and justified in a well-run company. The prevalence of competitive advertising does suggest an endless sales battle, but is this any different from the existence of rival shops in any High Street? Are competitive advertisements any different from competitive stall-holders in a market place—except in the volume of sales produced by mass advertising compared with the fewer sales obtained by the bawling of the solitary salesman? The alternative occurs in wartime when there are shortages and rationing, in the state-controlled economy of a developing country, in societies where there are insufficient goods and buying power to make choice possible and advertising necessary.

Does advertising put up prices? Is it an agent of inflation? Does it therefore tend to lessen buying-power? Would a restraint on advertising expenditure help to control rising prices? These are tempting questions, beloved of the more hidebound left-wing politicians whose economics do not seem to have advanced beyond Marshall.

There is no doubt that the customer pays for advertising. The manufacturer does not make some peculiar donation out of profits. Advertising is a legitimate distribution cost just the same as salesmen's salaries, trade discounts, packaging, guarantees, warehousing and delivery costs. Everything that happens to a product once it is made becomes a distribution cost and has to be included in the price. For example, the pit-head price of coal is less than the price of coal in London. There are anomalies as when eggs are dearer when we take the trouble to buy them direct from a farm, but the majority of prices reflect what it has cost to get them from the factory to our home. Whether we like it or not, advertising is part of the operation. It is true that at least a third of most retail prices is the cost of transfer from maker to buyer, and that includes telling the buyer that the product exists, even that it still exists.

Nevertheless, prices may not be *as low as they are* but for the economies of scale achieved by producing the volume that can be sold thanks to advertising. Nowadays, prices are subject to purchase, sales and value added taxes, and there is no longer resale price maintenance to standardise prices fairly, so that the effect of economies of scale is obscured. In the days before a Conservative Government destroyed RPM it was possible for a manufacturer to guarantee price and sell on a price that had to be maintained everywhere. Moreover, a big advertising appeal was a price cut, but only the retailer has this advertising benefit, and then it is generally used in a misleading way as a 'loss leader' with price increases on other items!

Before the abolition of RPM it was easy to see the effect of advertising on prices, the classic example being the Lyons Swiss Roll which went steadily down in price as advertising created demand. This was in the late 30s when price reductions were a notable advertising appeal. At best today, a retailer like Sainsbury will pass on the benefit of bulk purchases.

There is one example of the ability of advertising to reduce rather than increase prices, and this is when a luxury becomes a semi-luxury, when greater demand for expensive products makes it possible to spread overheads and so make the product purchasable by a larger public. The television receiver, washing machine, tape recorder and central heating are examples, and so too are foodstuffs less frequently bought in the past by the working class such as butter, fresh milk, poultry and cheese. While it is true that incomes have increased, and some families have two or more incomes, it has been necessary to promote these products, especially new ones like the broiler chicken, Cyprus sherry and packeted soup. It is perhaps hard for the modern reader, especially the younger one, to understand that for the majority of British people in the 30s a chicken was something you had at Christmas if you were lucky, whereas in our affluent world of today 'chicken and chips' is on sale every night at the local fish and chip shop! So, although all the credit cannot be placed on advertising, it has been a contributory factor in the immensely improved standard of living which has developed in Britain in the past thirty years despite economic crises. If advertising had seriously inflated prices, or inflated them at all, these social advances would not have occurred.

Again, when a pre-war motor-car cost £100 against today's £5,000 (a Ford 8 against a Ford Escort), it is necessary to balance better engineering and inflation plus tax against higher incomes and the greater ability of the general public to buy motor-cars or of companies to provide them for their staff. If all cars were still hand-built for the few they would cost much the same as a Rolls-Royce, Aston Martin, Bristol or Ferrari. A popular car is therefore priced in relation to volume production which is dependent upon market demand which is induced by, among other things, advertising. The success of the Nissan and Vauxhall campaigns supports that argument.

Advertising is a stimulant, without which production plans would not be justified and the price would be too low to permit a profit.

Probably the best and most consistent example of advertising contributing to the reduction of prices is the packaged holiday, whether at a British holiday camp, on a sea cruise or at an overseas resort with cheap air travel included. Because advertising—as we see on TV and in the press at Christmas and in the early months of the year—can produce such a multitude of enquiries and bookings it is possible to gain the advantage of air fares which are a fraction of scheduled flight fares. Admittedly, it generally means night flights, chartered aircraft and possibly older aircraft, but the prices for holidays in Spain and Majorca, Italy and Yugoslavia, and visits to the Dutch bulb fields or weekends in Paris, are extraordinarily cheap compared with the cost of a similar holiday booked as an individual undertaking with normal air fares and hotel tariffs.

The benefits of advertising are therefore part and parcel of modern society which we may or may not like. On the whole most people do benefit most of the time from most advertising. The real problem with advertising is that we cannot avoid it. Sometimes there seems to be too much of it, as when we are irritated by the 'natural break' in that exciting film on TV (which inconvenience we do not have to suffer in the cinema), but the amount of advertising is in proportion to the size of the market, its ability to buy, and the variety of products made available to it. In other words, a dearth of advertising would reflect a diminished market, weak purchasing power and a narrow choice of goods.

To take another example, when consumer goods were scarce in the shops of Communist Russia, advertising was unnecessary except perhaps to announce in the shop window that the goods had arrived and were now available. But as consumer goods have become more readily available in Russia it has become necessary to use advertising to attract customers. When, in wealthier countries, goods are plentiful it is necessary to use really competitive advertising. This does not raise prices. Advertising has not raised the prices of private houses in Britain: scarcity has done that.

Devaluation, insistence upon a favourable balance of payments, plus Common Market agricultural policy, increase the cost of meat. When the cheaper meats of the Argentine, Australia and New Zealand are not available to compete with the more expensive meats of the UK, Ireland and Europe the dearer meats have the monopoly. For many years the advertising of New Zealand meats helped to keep down meat prices because housewives were able to take advantage of low-priced produce promoted by the New Zealand Meat Producers' Board and by British butchers. Thus prices are artificially inflated by political manipulation, not because of the evil influence of advertising.

Nevertheless, in spite of the depression of the 80s Britain's three million unemployed are not 'unempayed' and the employers still recruiting are supermarket chains. People must eat. There has never before been so much advertising by retailers, mostly in the popular press and on TV. New technologies are booming, and the Royal Wedding of July 1981 gave a boost to sales of video-cassette recorders. In 1981, shops were opening everywhere, and in 1982 public libraries were joining them, to hire out films on cassettes. Meanwhile, the 80s have seen a remarkable increase in direct marketing by press ads, TV commercials, direct mail and the Oracle, Ceefax and Prestel systems. The credit card has repudiated monetarism.

To aid the economy advertising works best when there is reasonably free trade, full employment and high purchasing power, which is the hope of the industrial side of the Common Market. In those circumstances advertising works like a lubricant, and is a force for social good since it helps to maintain prosperity and to raise the standard of living.

What is the justification for this claim? Three historical eras substantiate it. The heydays of advertising were:

(i) When the industrial revolution was resulting in the mass production of consumer goods in the late 19th century and early 20th century with the USA ahead on consumer durables.

(ii) When Britain, in the 30s, changed from being a primary producer to the initiator of light industries.

(iii) When the affluent 50s and 60s coincided with the introduction of commercial TV and revolutionary new looks at marketing including merchandising now called sales promotion.

3.7   The Present and the Future

Where are we now? It is significant in 1985 that the changes in advertising correspond with social, economic and political changes. Today we see products and services on television and in the popular press which were not there only a few years ago. They range from Asiatic airlines on TV to home computers in *The Sun*. Never before have so many excellent motor-cars been advertised to motorists. There is a spate of bank, building society, insurance and investment advertising, for those in work are well paid and others have pensions and other lump sums to invest.

The face of Britain has changed, and there are growing ethnic minorities whose special needs have to be satisfied with special products, media and even financial services. Life styles are changing. Advertising reflects the demands of new interests and the growth of new service and leisure industries together with the development of direct response marketing and the use of plastic money.

The de-massification of media, especially television, places us on the threshold of both a media explosion and a media revolution. The mid-80s show advertising as the mirror of all these traumatic changes. The trend is towards demand information, to which advertisers must respond. Teletext and Viewdata are serious rivals to TV commercials.

4
How Advertising is Conducted

Few businesses are so complex or so fascinating as advertising, but by complex we mean rich in resources and not confusing or difficult to understand. Moreover, the complexities vary according to which side of which fence you happen to be on. There is no such thing as 'advertising' plain and simple. To the advertiser it means a method of promoting sales, to the media owner a way of making money out of vacant space or empty time, and to the agency it means using skills to exploit the space or time in order to promote the client's sales. Are you buying or selling advertising, seeking advice or giving it, or providing a specialised service?

Advertising is therefore an amalgam of many arts and crafts, businesses and professions which employs the services of men and women with very different training, experience, skill and temperament. The complete advertising person does not exist, so great is the division of labour and specialism. The nearest to an 'all-rounder' is the client's advertising manager and the agency's account executive, and yet each of these requires additional industrial or managerial knowledge which is not essential to, say, the artist or production man. Again, the publisher's advertisement manager may have a very slight knowledge of advertising but has to be a first-class salesman with an understanding of marketing and market research and probably some technical knowledge of the particular printing process by which his journal is printed. Thus, most advertising people have points of mental sympathy and conflict.

To understand how advertising is conducted, two analyses are helpful—one of the various facets of advertising, the other of the ways in which the advertiser may undertake his advertising. We shall then consider the interaction between three pairs of advertising people, advertiser and agency, agency and advertiser, and media owner and agency/advertiser.

4.1 The Six Sides of Advertising

It is normal to speak broadly of the three sides of advertising—advertiser, advertising agency and media owners—but a public relations consultant may form a *fourth* side since PR programmes and advertising campaigns often operate in concert, and all four are supported by the *fifth* side of ancillary services. Increasingly important is a *sixth* side, freelance services. Rocketing overheads and the emergence of 'hot shops' have resulted in the use of freelance creative services instead of employing creative staff full-time. This has made it less necessary to change agencies, since the next one may well use the same outside services! These *six sides of advertising* can be set out more clearly like this:

(a) **The advertiser**—manufacturer, importer, retailer, mail order trader, public authority, official body or department, voluntary organisation, and so on.

(b) **The advertising agency**—large comprehensive service agency, medium-size service agency, specialised technical agency, media independent or the new breed of à la carte creative agencies and those specialising in new product development, direct response or sponsorship. In the 80s, the agency world has changed dramatically since the à la carte agency buys no media, does not require recognition, and is remunerated by fees, not commission.

(c) **Media owners**—publishers of newspapers, magazines, directories, year books, timetables and other publications which carry advertisements; television, radio and cinema screen advertising contractors; outdoor and transportation advertising contractors; exhibition organisers, and others with specialised media.

(d) **Public relations consultants**—PR departments of advertising agencies, PR consultancy subsidiaries of advertising agencies, and independent consultancies. Consultancy business has boomed in the 80s, some having £3–4 million incomes.

(e) **Ancillary services** which may include:

Photographers and photographic studios.
Artists and art studios; art agents.
Models, actors, performing animals—and their agents.
Typesetters, process engravers and litho plate makers.
Printers—letterpress, lithography, gravure, silk screen, etc.
Film and video-tape makers—documentary, commercial, cartoon.
Distributors of documentary films and video-cassettes.
Ink makers.
Paper makers.
Makers of various kinds of container.
Exhibition stand designers and constructors.
Point-of-sale display material producers.
Incentive marketing, premium redemption, contest entry services.
Door-to-door distributors.
Direct mail houses, list brokers.
Electric, electronic, painted sign makers.
Working model and scale model producers.
Advertising gift suppliers—ashtrays, pens, etc.
Suppliers of audio-visual equipment and services—closed-circuit TV, video-taping, projection equipment.
Market research units—shop audit, consumer panel, field survey, opinion survey, motivation, product pre-testing, etc.
Merchandisers, demonstrators, commando salesmen.

All these different services cannot be explained in one chapter, but each will be explained in its appropriate place. Organisations and their roles and purposes are described in Chapter 5. If immediate explanation is required this can be found by reference to the index.

(*f*) **Freelance services** of copywriters, visualisers, artists, journalists, technical authors, etc., provided they are properly qualified and are not merely amateurs dabbling in the business, perhaps at cut-rates. (A typical dabbler is the journalist who pretends to offer a PR service, charging by the advertisement rate of the quantity of space he has obtained in the editorial!)

From this list it is clear that there is no shortage of expertise, and a problem is how expert is the client in selecting and buying these services? It is a neglected area of management training. Should he plump for the complete service agency which can give him everything, or should he pick and choose suppliers of services as he thinks best? The following are some of the ways in which advertisers do go about conducting their advertising:

    (i) By employing an advertising agency.
    (ii) By using the company's own advertising department.
    (iii) By using freelance services.
    (iv) By using service departments of media.
    (v) By doing it themselves, e.g. the proprietor or sales manager producing sales letters, catalogues or press advertisements.

Combinations of these methods may be adopted, although media service departments are most likely to be used by the small or occasional advertiser. The expressions 'above-the-line' and 'below-the-line' are applied to mean the five traditional media (press, TV, radio, cinema, outdoor/transportation), and non-commission-paying media such as point-of-sale material, sales promotion schemes, direct mail, print, etc., respectively. There is sometimes a division between these two, the agency handling the first and the second being carried out by the advertiser. The content of 'below-the-line' activities will largely determine the size of the advertising department.

But some companies prefer to retain total control of their advertising and do not use an agency even for 'placing' advertisements in the media. Examples are certain department stores, mail order houses, travel agents and some highly technical firms in, say, pharmaceuticals or electronics. The large retailer, with changing merchandise, prices and offers, may find it slow and inconvenient to work through a third party and so prefers to deal direct with media. Some—not all—travel agents prefer to 'go it alone' because of the critical timing on the printing and mailing of holiday brochures. Mail order traders may be principally concerned with the writing, designing and printing of a mammoth catalogue which is best done 'in house'. And some technical firms, having to employ creative staff with specialist technical knowledge who will not be found among more generalised agency staff, find it advantageous to do the rest of the job themselves.

The sixth method of 'doing it oneself' may or may not be successful according to the promotional flair of the person responsible. Some businesses have been wholly created by the wizardry of a business principal, but nowadays that is rare. Few things are worse than an amateur sales letter or news release, and their destination—the wastepaper basket—is certain.

While PR consultants will handle other PR work besides what is sometimes called 'product publicity', that is obtaining press write-ups about a product which is news in the context of certain features or journals, this form of *press relations* is an important aspect of the marketing strategy as was shown in the mock case study of a roofing preservative in the previous chapter.

All sides will use some of the ancillary services.

Media independents and à la carte agencies have introduced interesting new kinds of agency service. The media independent concentrates on media planning and media buying, operating on either a commission or fee basis. The creative à la carte agencies, being free of media planning and buying (but often collaborating with media independents), are also free of the commission system and recognition for this purpose by the media owners. This has made it financially possible for new agencies to be set up by people who concentrate on creating advertising or specialising in special areas such as sales promotion or direct response. They do not depend on commission income but charge professional fees. These new agencies reflect the advertiser's need for greater expertise and more cost-effective advertising in the sharply competitive economic climate of the 80s.

Ideally, the six sides of advertising should work together as an harmonious team if profitable advertising is to result. Perhaps this is expecting too much, if only that the advertiser is being *sold* a conflicting variety of media and services which are not always easy to evaluate, and clashes of personality may also occur because so many high-powered individuals are employed on all sides!

There are also certain problems inherent in the inability of some British businessmen to buy communication services, even to recognise their value or necessity. The failing is remarked upon by Americans who have almost made a fetish of business schools and training in management, marketing and communication. For instance, there is as yet no university chair of PR in the UK, whereas many have existed in the USA for decades. At the time of writing there are few British chairs of marketing, and while there are evening and other courses in advertising at a number of polytechnics and technical colleges in the UK there is only one centre devoted to advertising studies. This same centre (the Marketing and Advertising Department at the College for the Distributive Trades in Leicester Square, London) introduced the first ever fulltime course in PR as recently as September 1972! Perhaps management has little chance of becoming better acquainted with the use and purchase of communication techniques—except through short, intensive courses—or, perhaps, with characteristic British indifference (according to the astonished Americans!) it does not want to. Cranfield, however, is pioneering a PR-orientated MBA.

These criticisms seldom apply to American-owned companies operating in Britain, or to the American and European supra-national companies which straddle Europe, or to Scandinavian companies whose market is the world. The excuse or apology of the British businessman may simply be a question of size and the fact that for too long he enjoyed preferential treatment in Commonwealth export markets.

The challenge of Common Market conditions—where he has to meet the competition of Philips, Siemens, Fiat, Renault, IBM, General Motors, Indesit and others—will shock him into expediting not merely long-wanted investment in industrial modernisation, but investment in marketing skills. In a chapter on 'how advertising is conducted' it is therefore coldly realistic to understand how well advertising is produced despite the antipathies between those involved, and how much it can be and—in the Common Market context—needs to be better. Europe has markets, media and advertising customs and facilities very different, and different country by country, than obtains in Britain which in many respects is isolated and unique as an advertising exercise. Two of the differences are the British facility of a *national* press, and the rigorous controls related to our commercial television which do not exist on the continent.

There does seem to be a chasm in modern management training in all these respects. Better understanding of agency procedures could mean lower advertising costs, while appreciation of the value of PR to every facet of a business could, among other things, contribute enormously to industrial peace. In the Common Market situation, both are vital.

These are not idle or kite-flying comments but are borne out by the dismal findings of three important surveys into agency–client relations carried out in recent years by Scientific Advertising and Marketing, Pace (of Manchester) and the Unilever agency, Lintas. The first two are discussed in detail in another book by the writer, *Advertising Today*, while the Lintas survey is featured in the chapter in this book on the advertising agency.

For the purpose of considering the conduct of advertising let us now try to sit on three of the fences and examine some problems, weaknesses and desirables in each rather different situation. The deficiencies of business management are taken into account in the following three check lists of successful relationships:

4.2   Advertiser and Agency Relationship

How can the advertiser work efficiently with the advertising agency? How can an effective partnership be woven with an outside service, probably located some distance away from the advertiser's headquarters?

(*a*) **By learning what an advertising agency is and how it works** before seeking and appointing one. The Institute of Practitioners in Advertising publishes explanatory booklets.

(*b*) **By making sure that the executive responsible for liaison with the agency has a working knowledge of advertising.** If not, he should be instructed to undertake training at evening class or by correspondence school. Anyone responsible for dealing with an advertising agency should have passed the Institute of Marketing Diploma examination or hold the CAM Certificate in Communication Studies, The LCCI Group Diploma in Marketing if not the CAM Diploma in Advertising. Anyone less qualified may be a liability to his firm and an embarrassment to the agency.

(*c*) **The agency should be accepted as a means of augmenting the company's marketing department,** not as an outside firm which is not to be trusted with confidential information. In other words, an advertiser should not appoint an agency unless that agency is to be trusted with company secrets. This is critical because the agency cannot work in a vacuum, and it may have to plan a year or more ahead when new products are at a development stage or company policy is tentative. It is important that the agency should be able to attend early discussions about new products and policies. This implies that the appointment of an agency should be for at least three years, which further implies that the onus should be on the advertiser to invite agency services rather than on the ability of the agency to pitch for the business at a competitive presentation which may well be illusory. Appointing an agency should not be regarded as Leap Year for agents.

(*d*) **In buying agency services the client should make sure that he understands how the agency will be remunerated.** We shall return to this topic again, but for the moment the point is made that there are several methods by which agencies are paid, remembering that primarily **the agent is (in effect although not legally) the agent of the media owners** who pay commission to those whose credit-worthiness they 'recognise'. But some suppliers do not pay commission (e.g. printers) and the agency adds a percentage to print bills. In any case, the majority of agencies nowadays add a supplementary percentage to increase media commissions from the meagre 10 per cent of the trade and provincial press or the inadequate 15 per cent of the nationals and TV to a uniform $17\frac{1}{2}$ per cent.

Alternatively, some agencies prefer to dispense with the commission system so far as the client is concerned, rendering net accounts and charging an overall fee based on a percentage of the total sum spent with the agency. 'Unrecognised' agencies, since they receive no commissions from the media owners, have to charge a fee anyway. It should be noted here that agencies are recognised by the media owners for the purpose of commission: it does not indicate that they are any better than 'unrecognised' agencies, nor has it anything to do with membership of the Institute of Practitioners in Advertising. Creative à la carte agencies do not require 'recognition'.

So, the client needs to know what he is paying for. This is important because the false idea may exist with the new or smaller advertiser that it costs nothing to use an agency. It is true that the media owners pay for a lot of services which the advertiser would have to pay for himself—the services of the account executive, media planners and buyers, and the production staff, for instance—but artwork, camera-ready copy and other materials have to be paid for in addition to space and time. 'Production costs' must not be overlooked, whether or not an agency is used.

(*e*) **An appropriation or budget should be agreed in such a way that the client understands how 'extra' costs may be incurred.**

Extra costs are liable to result from two causes:

(i) The inability of management to know what it wants until expensive creative and production work has reached a stage of near completion when alterations are costly in both time and materials. This sort of unbusinesslike extravagance occurs where management is unable to make decisions at an early stage, when copy is still in typescript and not yet committed to metal, film or plate, and when the artwork is no more than a visualiser's rough impression. Such time-and-money-consuming and temper-fraying extravagance may also result from the arrogance of management which merely wants to show its authority.

A typical agency lament is that clients always know what they want when it is too late, which expresses a fine contempt for the client. Usually it is deserved, but it can be avoided. After all, management doesn't change the design of the new office block when the contractors are working on the fourteenth floor, but they will exercise their privilege to rewrite copy at the proof stage, and afterwards complain about the bill and eventually make 'excessively high production costs' one of their excuses for changing the agency. *Most agency changes derive from client inefficiency* which is unfairly blamed on a frustrated agency. An agency is usually as good as the client makes it or allows it to be.

(ii) Changes or additions to the advertising campaigns are a second cause of extra costs. In expanding companies such amendments may be inevitable, but if there is frank discussion between client and agency contingency funds can be included in the appropriation. In this way it is possible to avoid cutting back on a campaign in order to include something fresh, the first campaign suffering to the extent of perhaps failing to achieve its sales objective.

(*f*) **The client should be forthcoming with information of value to the agency in looking after the client's interests.** Again, appreciation of agency working helps here. The marketing, advertising or product manager should initiate a flow of information to the agency. The agency should receive the following *as a matter of course:*

(i) The annual report and accounts.

(ii) Copies of all news releases issued by either the company PRO or by the PR consultant.

(iii) Invitations to all company functions such as sales conferences, managers' meetings, product trials, press conferences, Christmas parties, etc.

(iv) Copies of internal and external house journals.

(v) News of all price changes, including trade terms and promotions.

(vi) Information about changes in distribution methods.

(vii) Samples of new packages, sizes, materials, containers, stuffers.

(viii) Changes in specifications, formulations, components, materials, finishes, casings, colours, etc.

(ix) Samples of new or changed products.

(x) Documentation such as order forms, guarantees, service manuals.

(xi) Copies of research reports, including useful statistics on enquiries, keyed replies to advertisements, and conversions into sales.

(xii) Information about changes in key personnel, and important new appointments.

(xiii) News about R&D work and information about prototypes of new products.

(xiv) Details of production or other problems affecting advertising, including trade disputes in or outside the firm, and difficulties over imported parts or materials.

(xv) Proposed legislation likely to affect the client.

(xvi) City matters such as a private company going public, a new share issue, or an acquisition, merger or take-over.

(xvii) Trade association matters liable to affect advertising.

If this list seems formidable it should be remembered that not every item applies to every client, and that with the exception of regular items such as house magazines most of these 17 items will occur only occasionally. The annual report, and statistics on advertising returns, are yearly affairs; Stock Exchange matters are infrequent; and information about changing personnel can be filed so that telephone calls are not made to people who have left the staff and contact reports are sent to the right personnel.

These 17 points reflect once again the need to take the agency into the client's confidence, regarding it as an ally, as virtually part of the organisation. Yet it happens that agencies are permitted to produce advertisements for products which are not in production, or not available from retailers, because of a breakdown in elementary communications, production not informing marketing, and marketing being unable to inform the agency.

This erratic state of affairs can exist with a manufacturer whose catalogues contain scores of items, some of which may be stocked by one shop, some by another, while not all of them are in regular production. An advertising agency is expected to work in this wonderland of managerial confusion. Agencies which give marketing advice do try to rationalise their client's marketing and production procedures, but in industries as diverse as fancy goods, stationery supplies, confectionery, insecticides and proprietary medicines such chaos is more of an everyday experience than one would seriously expect in these days of computerised inventory control.

Incidentally, from bitter experience, women's feature editors will not write about products unless they have guaranteed national distribution, and the problem of stocks and stockists applies even more critically in press relations.

The chief reason why agencies are so ill-informed is that it never occurs to some clients that the agency *should* be informed. Such reticence is not always a question of security: it is more likely to indicate a lack of understanding of management communication, otherwise known as PR. A good flow of useful information—of *information sharing*—results when the client has a conscientious advertising manager who sincerely appreciates that by keeping the agency constantly 'in the picture' the best possible agency service will be forthcoming. A lot of needless mistakes can be avoided and much more enthusiasm can be inspired when agency personnel are encouraged to feel that the client is aware of their existence. Agencies and clients are often located many miles apart, and absence does not make the heart grow fonder in this sort of relationship. Sight of the house journal can make all the difference: so can the phone call when the caller says 'I thought you ought to know . . .'

But one word of warning: the ability of the agency to cope with so much information or to participate in client activities will of course depend on the size of the account!

4.3   Agency and Advertiser Relationship

What is the reverse of the coin? How can the agency achieve good relationships with the client? We have highlighted some of the problems and some of the faults on the client side, but how well do agency personnel understand how industry and commerce is run? What are agency shortcomings?

(*a*) **The account executive should permit the client to visit the agency,** inviting him behind the scenes, allowing him to attend plans board meetings, and establishing a working relationship between the client and the creative team no matter whether they are full-time or freelance copywriters and visualisers. The client will usually be the advertising manager, but managing directors, marketing managers and sales managers should not be excluded from such visits.

Some agencies find it extremely difficult to allow the client past the front man and the board room; some agency staff feel they are fenced off from the client. This attitude and predicament can only be harmful to agency–client relations. Intimacy is best experienced between the smaller agency and the client. A very happy relationship can be built up between the local businessman and the local agency, and it is possible that clients may be able to do better business with a nearby agency than one in London or a major provincial city. But that is a generalisation, and so much depends on people and their ability to get on with other people, which is not the most outstanding of British virtues! Perhaps the reason for so many poor agency–client relationships has to do with the well-known inability of Englishmen to talk to one another in railway carriages. The Common Market should change all that.

(*b*) **The agency should have a simple system of paperwork**—job sheets, job numbers and contact reports—which make instructions and communications easy and, most important, which make accounts simple to understand. No meeting or telephone conversation should go unrecorded without a contact report which clearly states decisions with identified responsibilities for further action.

(*c*) **The account executive should understand the structure of the business world,** and so appreciate how clients run their businesses, including offices, retail shops, factories and warehouses. They should be able to read a balance sheet and comprehend board room procedures, the roles of company personnel, the production techniques and workshop practice, the channels of distribution and the trade union complex. Ideally, an account executive should be a graduate in economics, marketing or business management who has spent two years as a trainee in the agency before dealing with clients. The CAM syllabus covers business organisation, while the Social Science interdisciplinary syllabi of the Open University go much deeper into topics of relevance to the account executive, so there is no lack of training facilities, and no excuse for ignorance about the world in which the client operates. But advertising is a young man's world and the businessman must be forgiven his scepticism about the nice, self-confident young man from the agency who seems to descend from an ivory tower and have little idea how companies are run. True, the advertising business is complex enough, and the businessman may be ignorant about the advertising world, but the account executive with industrial and business knowledge will be welcomed and many of the barriers of communication will then be down.

(*d*) **The agency should be able to interpret the client's policy,** and produce advertising that presents the company or its commodities to the right market, at the same time establishing a correct impression or image of the organisation. There is a PR element here in advertising which can be destroyed or distorted if too-clever gimmickry is allowed to intervene. For examples, advertisers such as Players, Cadbury's, Shell, Stork, Ford, Nestlé, British Airways, Omega, Grundig, Van Heusen and Volvo have all established images which it would be foolish to ruin because an agency failed to recognise the value of the publicly held correct impression of the organisation or its policy, products or services. Of course, if the image has to be changed, that is another story, as has been seen when a passenger shipping line switches to holiday cruises or when a firm well known for cooking fats diversifies and markets tinned meats.

There is nothing more disastrous than the agency which insists on trying to sell the client ideas which are foreign to his company's image, and which management knows will be detrimental to its carefully nurtured reputation. There is obviously great risk of upsetting images when agencies make presentations to obtain new business, and if they are making these presentations in competition with other agencies they may be imperfectly briefed or have made inadequate investigations. Opportunity to service the account may be lost on this question alone.

(*e*) **Agency personnel should always be punctual for appointments.** A perpetual complaint from clients is that the account executive is a bad timekeeper, whether they are telephoning him first thing in the morning or expecting him to arrive for a meeting. Trivial though this may seem to the London commuter who is always at the mercy of the vagaries of public transport, unpunctuality is treated as a cardinal sin by out-of-town clients who walk or motor to their offices and are never late.

As an extreme example of this, the writer once had to deal with a client who called advertising meetings for 9 o'clock on Monday mornings, which meant that the account executive had to sacrifice his Sunday afternoon to stay overnight in a hotel close to the factory. Not to do so would have been considered a mark of discourtesy and the account would have been lost.

Against this must be reckoned the earlier opening and closing of factories compared with city offices, and the seeming unreasonableness of the out-of-town client has to be considered against the working hours with which he is familiar. Many factories are deserted by 4.30 p.m. when the agency staff are still working at 6 p.m. or later.

(*f*) **The agency should endeavour to have each account serviced by an account executive who is compatible to the client.** This is a tricky business, an exercise in psychology very often, one account executive proving a tremendous success with one client but failing utterly to get on with another. The delicate process of finding the right man to deal with a particular client can be one of the small nightmares of agency administration. The difficulty is all the greater if the appointment of the account executive comes after the agency directorate have won the account and then the client finds he is being serviced by not merely a stranger but an inferior. Clients resent being fobbed off with underlings, and it is best if the account executive is present at the original negotiations. If the account executive is not engaged by the agency until after the account is gained, prior meetings are not possible. A further problem is that the agency may well have gained the account because the client managing director got on with the agency managing director, but in the event the advertising manager and the account executive will have to work together. Agency appointments are usually made by top management.

(g) **Agency staff should never accept the client's approval of copy or proofs as being the 'last word'.** Clients may be unused to meticulous syllable-by-syllable, comma-by-comma proof reading, watching out for alternative spellings of names, and double-checking prices and specifications. Consequently, they are capable of overlooking typewriting or typesetting errors. It could therefore be dangerous for an agency to 'take the client's word for it' for he will surely blame the agency if errors are spotted after the work appears in its final form. So, the wise agent will re-check all copy and proofs, and 'nurse' the client, especially if the client has no professional advertising staff. In any case, it pays to double-check everything, and to query anything that incurs the vaguest suspicion of inaccuracy. This is one of the prime responsibilities of the good advertising man or woman.

(h) **The agency should familiarise the client with legal and voluntary controls.** There are many laws and voluntary codes relating to advertising of which the client is unaware, and the agency should try to explain them to clients. In this way ill-feeling may be averted when the agency has to adopt a professional attitude to the client's expressed wish to be more competitive than is permitted or advised. A gentle programme of education may be necessary with some rather truculent clients, and this can be done by sending them copies of the various Codes, especially the British Code of Advertising Practice, together with the *Trade Descriptions Acts*, the *IBA Code of Standards and Practice* and the annual report of the Advertising Standards Authority. The monthly ASA investigation reports could be enlightening! It may be necessary to do this because otherwise clients may think that the agency is adopting a prima donna attitude and is just resisting outside ideas.

4.4 Media Owner and Agency/Advertiser Relations

Owners of media include publishers, TV, radio, cinema, exhibition, outdoor and transportation advertising contractors.

(a) **Media owners should be forthcoming with statistical information about sales, readers, audiences and attendances.** There are still a few publishers who refuse to give audited net sales figures. Equally, not every exhibition promoter will give authenticated numbers of visitors. Both advertisers and agents are entitled to know what they are paying for. In publishing there are two sets of figures which influence the purchase of space—**circulation** (number of copies sold or, in the case of controlled circulation journals, distributed against proven demand), and **readership** (estimated number of readers per copy together with other information obtained by means of a readership survey). The number of copies printed may have no relation to those either sold or read. Not for nothing does the advertising world regard 'publishers' statements' as 'publishers' lies'!

(*b*) **While advertisement managers are bound to seek every opportunity to increase revenue, they should avoid annoying advertisers with 'blackmail' schemes** such as features where the advertisements can be of very slight value to anyone, readers or advertisers. The worst example is probably the feature about a new building, store or hotel with supporting advertising from contractors, subcontractors and suppliers. While the feature may delight the proprietor of the new premises, the appeal for advertising support is nearly always a nuisance and a waste of money from the point of view of the advertisers. The welcome exception is when the feature is of genuine advertising value, as when a topic of reader interest is treated seriously with good editorial and it provides advertisers with an excellent market place: such features might be on gardening, holidays or home improvements.

(*c*) **Proofs should be submitted in good time,** not when it is practically too late for corrections. The habit of late submission of proofs has probably developed because the majority of advertisements are complete blocks or artwork which will not be altered at the proof stage. Nevertheless, there are still some paper-set advertisements, some may have different addresses for separate editions, and there is always the risk that the wrong advertisement may be inserted by mistake.

(*d*) **Special editions, supplements and features should be planned six months ahead** at least so that they may be considered when campaigns are being planned. For example, a boiler manufacturer will need to know which newspapers and magazines are likely to publish features about central heating, so that they may be included in the annual appropriation and media schedule to form a complete campaign. This information will be required twelve to fourteen months before publication, since a campaign starting in January and running to December will be finalised by October of the previous year, the planning having commenced in the summer. The *Financial Times* announces an annual programme of features, and so do other newspapers and magazines which run regular or seasonal features or special numbers. *Advance* publishes feature information monthly.

(*e*) **Advertisement managers should understand that PR is different from advertising,** and that a report, picture or article about a firm or its products will be printed by the editor on its merits as reader interest. It is *not* a form of free advertising. An advertisement in the same issue may be desirable, in order to give additional sales information or to provide a coupon for further details, but it may not be necessary, it may not fit in with the planned campaign, and it certainly should not be inserted as a kind of 'thank you' for the editorial.

The impression can be created that but for the ad. there would be no editorial and *vice versa*, one nullifying the other. The advertisement manager will be wiser to approach the firm *after* the editorial has appeared, perhaps armed with evidence of reader interest. He needs to understand that there is a world of difference between advertising which is planned and controlled and publicity which results from any public announcement, good, bad or indifferent.

(*f*) **Instructions should be followed carefully,** and the make-up watched at the paste-up stage so that embarrassing juxtapositions are avoided. Care must also be taken to see that ads containing coupons do not back up so that one coupon cancels out another.

(*g*) **New advertisers should be given advice on how best to use the medium,** it being a short-sighted policy to coax an inexperienced advertiser into taking too much space or time. A really skilful advertisement manager will show the advertiser how to profit from advertising. Then, the advertising will grow with the business and both media and advertiser will benefit. To this end, media owners have service departments to help in the production of effective advertisements.

However, the media owner may have to deter a businessman from booking ads which (because of the pulling power of the medium) are almost certain to produce orders in excess of the ability to supply. There have been actual cases of this happening. A blanket offer produced in one week a demand equal to the mill's annual production, while the offer of a home decoration booklet produced such a response that thousands of extra copies had to be printed at a cost which seriously upset the campaign budget. It is a wise precaution to limit published offers.

A number of offers, ranging from direct response marketing offers to free gift or premium offer schemes, have provoked criticism because the advertiser was overwhelmed by demand. Delays, complaints and apologies harm the reputation of both the advertiser and the medium. Wise media advertisement managers will check to see that the advertiser has adequate production capacity or delivery resources to supply within a reasonable time, say 28 days.

These check lists are by no means conclusive, but this chapter has been presented in this way so that the reader may gain an insight into the quite different roles and responsibilities of these three distinct and sometimes contrary sides of advertising. By comparing these check lists it is possible to see how advertising is conducted by each of the three sides in relationship with one another.

4.5 Relationships with Customers

In Chapters 5 and 25 will be found information about Codes which spell out how advertising seeks to protect its own good name by applying voluntary restraints upon undesirable and misleading advertising. Because TV advertising goes right into the home where the audience can comprise the whole family, TV commercials are subject to legal controls. The public are also protected by statute law, examples being listed in Chapter 25.

4.6 Does the Small Trader Need an Agency?

Once a trader requires the creative work of artists and copywriters he needs outside assistance. It may only be the occasional sign- or ticket-writer, or an imaginative author to compile his sales letters. Such specialists exist in most parts of the country, running small studios or undertaking freelance work. If the trader advertises regularly it may pay him to call in a local advertising agency. Most local agents have developed from art studios and so creative talent is usually basic to them. Media planning and buying is something else they can offer, and the trader may welcome advice on whether to use press, TV, radio, outdoor, transportation, cinema, direct mail, sales literature, exhibitions and other media which may be available in the locality. In this sense, the advertising agent's services are not unlike those of an insurance broker's.

If a good working relationship can be developed, the small trader will benefit enormously from his association with a conscientious and creative local advertising agent. This is because it is all too easy to dabble in wasteful advertising only to become disillusioned and unwilling to take proper advantages of a valuable tool.

Alternatively, local media owners can help the small trader through their service departments, as already mentioned. This is very true of TV contractors as well as newspaper publishers. Not only do these departments help the advertisers but they help themselves by ensuring the professional appearance of the advertising carried by the medium.

As an example of the value of service departments, a furniture dealer was assisted in the production of TV commercials to the extent that over a period of two years he built up a chain of shops in the same TV area, making the one commercial promote the same goods in an increasing number of outlets.

4.7 Profession or Business?

Is advertising a profession or a business? The answer is a bit of both, since advertising is professional in the sense of trained skills and because advice is given and yet it is also a business because services and commodities are being sold in a commercially competitive fashion. Nevertheless, there are rules and regulations as will be seen in the next chapter which describes the organisation of advertising.

The advertiser wants the best bargain for his money, the agency wants to boost its billings, and media owners want to increase their revenues. All three are possible. And all three are competitive. Skill in advertising management lies in finding a balance between these somewhat conflicting mercenary aims. The advertiser will succeed in business if he conveys the most compelling message to the largest number of buyers at the least cost so that sales are achieved. The agency will retain—or gain—clients according to its ability to satisfy their trading targets. The media owners will succeed provided the media satisfy the needs of advertisers and agents can be convinced that their clients can be so satisfied.

In such a battle-field it is not surprising that harmony is improbable, that clients will seem to be restraining expenditure, agencies will seem to be trying to expand client usage of their services, while media will always appear to be selling empty space or future time to anyone who will buy it whether it will profit them or not. And there are some media owners or contractors who will sell advertising space on anything not otherwise occupied such as clouds in the sky, litter-bins, taxi-cab seats, the undersides of aircraft wings, menu covers, shopping bags or deck chairs at the seaside. The small trader has to beware of really dubious or downright fraudulent attempts to take his money, among the most vicious being the offer of attractive discounts for the prompt payment of bills for advertising he hasn't even booked!

5
How Advertising is Organised

In this fourth edition extensive amendments have been made to this chapter, and some new organisations have been added. This fairly early chapter serves as a source of reference wherever initials such as IPA, NPA, ITCA or ASA are found in the text. This chapter also tells much about the historical development of the whole communications industry including marketing and public relations. It shows how the modern communications industry is organised, in both its own and the public interest. Some forty organisations are described in alphabetical sequence.

THE ADVERTISING ASSOCIATION, 15 Wilton Road, London SW1V 1NJ. Telephone: 01-828 2771. Founded 1926.

Constituent organisations

Advertising Film and Video-tape Producers Association
Association of Free Newspapers
Association of Independent Radio Contractors Ltd
Association of Market Survey Organisations
Association of Media Independents
Association of Multi-Media Proprietors Ltd
The British Direct Marketing Association
British Printing Industries Federation
The Cinema Advertising Association Ltd
The Communication, Advertising and Marketing Education
    Foundation Ltd (or its successor)
The Direct Mail Producers Association
Incorporated Advertising Management Association
The Incorporated Society of British Advertisers Ltd
Independent Television Companies Association Ltd
The Institute of Practitioners in Advertising
The Institute of Sales Promotion
International Advertising Association (UK Chapter)
The Marketing Society
The Market Research Society
The Newspaper Publishers Association
The Newspaper Society
Outdoor Advertising Association

Periodical Publishers Association Ltd
Post Office
Proprietary Association of Great Britain

The Advertising Association is a federation of constituent organisations representing advertisers, media, agencies and services. It aims to ensure that everyone with a view or a voice in advertising—participants, supporters and critics—should understand the role of advertising in society and the economy, and the part it plays in creating prosperity and employment. Through a number of liaison groups, the Association maintains contact with specific audiences, such as government and politicians, trade unions, the media and consumer groups. Its International Working Party monitors EEC legislation and co-ordinates industry activity in putting the British case on marketing matters.

Aims

The main aims of the Association are as follows:

(*a*) To promote confidence in advertising.

(*b*) To establish that responsible advertising is an essential factor in the marketing of goods and services, and in the economic life of the country.

(*c*) To demonstrate the efficiency of the service that advertising can give to Government, industry and the public.

(*d*) To safeguard the common interests of those engaged in or using advertising by the promotion of common action and the support of protective measures.

(*e*) To persuade officials and legislators in the UK, Europe and elsewhere to remove or modify regulatory provisions adverse to the interests of the advertising industry, and industry generally.

(*f*) To encourage in all milieus a continuing improvement in standards and efficiency in communications, of which advertising is a part.

The AA organises a major conference every two years. It publishes works based largely on the Research Committee, and the Statistics Committee produces a quarterly survey of newspaper advertising expenditure in addition to its *Quarterly Forecast of Advertising Expenditure*. The quarterly *International Journal of Advertising* is published for the AA by Holt, Rinehart and Winston. *The Marketing Pocket Book* is a comprehensive collection of advertising and marketing statistics.

Information Services

External enquiries amount to some thirty a day, totalling well over 8,000 in the year, by telephone, letter or personal visit. The largest number come from the educational field—school children, students, teachers and academics. Numerous requests come from the business world, including the larger advertisers, agencies and media owners: and also from Government departments, the general public and overseas visitors.

THE ADVERTISING STANDARDS AUTHORITY, Brook House, 2–16 Torrington Place, London WC1E 7HN. Telephone 01-580 5555. Founded 1962.

At the Advertising Association Conference in May 1974 the Rt Hon. Mrs Shirley Williams, MP, Secretary of State for Prices and Consumer Protection, and the late Mr John Methven, then Director-General of the Office of Fair Trading, urged that the self-regulatory system of controlling abuses of advertising should be made more effective and better known to the public.

However, to work more effectively and more openly, more money was required than that provided by the Advertising Association. For this purpose ASBOF (see below) was created to raise funds independently by means of a surcharge on media purchases. This money was needed for larger premises, more staff, an advertising campaign addressed to the public and inviting written complaints, and the publication of information such as the regular ASA Case Reports. These reports are now available free of charge and report complaints and the decisions and actions taken. The old confidentiality about investigations has gone, and the press review ASA Case Reports so that there is extended publicity.

In January 1980 Davidson Pearce Ltd were appointed advertising agents, and a new advertising campaign was launched. A survey showed that the campaign succeeded in achieving additional awareness of the ASA, moving up from 31 per cent to 46 per cent. The advertisements also increased both the number of complaints received and the proportion of well-founded complaints. The slogan 'If an advertisement is wrong, we're here to put it right' was used. A typical headline read IF YOU FIND AN ADVERTISEMENT UNACCEPTABLE DON'T TURN THE PAGE: TURN TO US. Advertisements appeared in the national press and on posters. These advertising campaigns have continued, some advertisements displaying pages from the British Code of Advertising Practice.

Nearly 8,000 complaints are handled annually of which about a third justify investigation, and about half of these are upheld. Those not pursued are outside the Code, concern TV or radio, are inadequately detailed, have been investigated already, or there is no case to answer. A new edition of the Code was published in late 1984.

The British Code of Advertising Practice is constantly being revised and extended. In 1981, for instance, there were additions or amendments concerning collectibles; recruitment and vocational training; self-defence courses; smoking deterrents; rheumatic and allied pains; toothpastes; consumer credit and hire advertising; consumer investment advertising; and claims for vitamins and minerals.

To avoid contravention of the Code a free advisory and pre-publication service is available from the CAP Committee's Secretariat. Advertisers and advertising agents can discuss prospective advertisements which might possibly offend against the Code.

The membership of the Council is now more independent than in the early days of ASA, and the chairman is appointed by ASBOF instead of by the Advertising Association. At the time of writing membership of Council comprises:

Chairman: Lord McGregor of Durris

Members: Dame Josephine Barnes, DBE, FRCP, FRCS, FRCOG, Consulting Obstetrician and Gynaecologist, Charing Cross Hospital and Elizabeth Garrett Anderson Hospital (President BMA 1979–80). M. C. J.

Barnes, MA, Marketing Consultant and formerly MP for Brentford and Chiswick 1966–74. Lady Elizabeth Cavendish, MVO, JP, Deputy Chairman of the North Westminster Petty Sessional Division. E. G. Court, Chairman of IPC Magazines Ltd until 1981. Professor The Revd. D. R. Dunstan, MA, DD, FSA, Emeritus Professor of Moral and Social Theology in the University of London. A. M. Fisher, MA, Advertising and Market Research Adviser to Unilever in the UK until 1983. The Baroness Lockwood, Founder Chairman of the Equal Opportunities Commission. Patricia Mann, FIPA, FCAM, Head of External Affairs, J. Walter Thompson Group (UK). A. E. Pitcher, FIPA, FCAM, President of Ogilvy and Mather Ltd. Rachel Waterhouse, CBE, PhD, Chairman, Consumers' Association.

THE ADVERTISING STANDARDS BOARD OF FINANCE LTD, 608 Grand Buildings, Trafalgar Square, London WC2N 5HN. Telephone: 01-839 2762. Founded 1974.

When it became clear in 1974 that something had to be done quickly to make the Advertising Standards Authority better known and to enlarge it so that it could cope with the expanded work which publicity would provoke, the basic needs were for:

(*a*) More staff and therefore more accommodation.
(*b*) More publicity.
(*c*) A way of raising money to pay for the staff, accommodation and publicity which would leave the ASA independent. (Until now the ASA had been financed by the Advertising Association, which—from its origins as the National Vigilance Committee, through its years of running the Advertisement Investigation Department, and since it represented the industry as a whole—had been its natural parent.)

So ASBOF was formed to be the sole source of finance for an independent ASA. It was set up by all the advertising trade associations jointly, and ASBOF has no control over the ASA's day-to-day activities, merely an overall financial control since the ASA obviously cannot plan to spend more than ASBOF can collect. ASBOF is also the body responsible now for the appointment of the chairman of the ASA, after consultation with the Department of Prices and Consumer Protection (or other equivalent Government department) and with the Advertising Association. The ASA is therefore not burdened with the task of collecting funds to maintain itself: that job is done by ASBOF which in turn is assisted by its supporting trade associations to explain the system to its members.

The Council of ASBOF is made up of representatives of the Advertising Association, Association of British Directory Publishers, Association of Free Newspapers, Association of Media Independents, British Direct Marketing Association, Cinema Advertising Association, Direct Mail Producers Association, Incorporated Society of British Advertisers, Institute of Practitioners in Advertising, Newspaper Publishers' Association, Newspaper Society, Outdoor Advertising Council, Periodical Publishers' Association, Scottish Daily Newspaper Society and Scottish Newspaper Proprietors Association. It will be noticed that the broadcasting organisations are not represented since ASA is not concerned with radio and television advertising, their Code being incorporated in the *Independent Broadcasting Act, 1973*.

The principle behind the ASBOF Surcharge Scheme is that the surcharge should be paid by the advertiser, the surcharge being 0.1 per cent of gross media rates. The definition of advertising coming within the scope of the surcharge scheme is 'Press advertising (except classified lineage and semi-display) plus Outdoor, Cinema and Direct Mail advertising in the UK'. Also excluded is advertising for medicinal products promoted to the medical, veterinary and allied professions and supplied on prescription.

However, direct collection from thousands of advertisers would have been impractical, and a system of collection through advertising agencies and media owners has been devised. There are now some 1,200 'collectors'. For this purpose, the media have agreed that their rate cards should contain a statement that their gross rates are subject to the 0.1 per cent surcharge, and the media associations granting recognition to agencies have made collection of the ASBOF surcharge a condition of recognition. This means that the surcharge has become an accepted part of the space-buying contract. In the case of direct mail advertising, the Direct Mail Services Standards Board makes conformity with the ASBOF surcharge scheme a condition of granting recognised status to direct mail companies.

ASBOF receives the money every quarter from advertising agencies who collect the surcharge from their clients (or receives it from media where advertising is placed direct).

This method of financing an expanded and widely publicised self-regulatory system was set up with the approval of the Minister for Prices and Consumer Protection and of the Office of Fair Trading. It came into force on January 1, 1975, and by the year 1982–83 the annual total of surcharge collected exceeded £1¼m.

THE ASSOCIATION OF FREE NEWSPAPERS LTD, Ladybellegate House, Long-smith Street, Gloucester GL1 2HT. Telephone: 0452 26561.

The Association of Free Newspapers was established to bring credibility to free newspapers carrying its stamp of professionalism, through accepting the best possible trading standards, and being committed to the principle of free newspaper publishing.

The Association has in membership more than 260 free newspaper titles, distributing between them more than 12m. copies weekly—around half the total published nationally.

Criteria for membership of the Association include verified (*see* **Verified Free Distribution**) or certified distribution figures, clear definition of areas covered, dated rate cards and acceptance of the Code of Advertising Practice.

All this, together with an internal disputes procedure, enables the AFN logo to be carried as a badge of professionalism with its accompanying guarantee to advertisers.

The stated aim of the Association is to 'uphold the standards and interests of free newspapers and their proprietors . . .' Activities of the Association include the organising of an annual conference, the provision of speakers for organisations, assistance with research into free newspapers for television, radio and newspaper articles, the publication of a regular newspaper and the maintenance of a database on MediaTel—the specialist supplier of media information on Prestel.

The Association maintains close links with Verified Free Distribution Ltd, set up to monitor the circulation claims of free newspapers.

THE ASSOCIATION OF INDEPENDENT RADIO CONTRACTORS LTD, Regina House, 259–269 Old Marylebone Road, London NW1 5RA. Telephone: 01-262 6681.

This is the trade association for the 42 commercial radio companies (*see* Chapter 19) operating under the franchise of the *Independent Broadcasting Act, 1973*. It represents the collective interests of its corporate members and is involved in labour relations, where AIRC negotiates national agreements covering the terms and conditions of employment of full-time and freelance employees, and also contract artistes and musicians. AIRC also represents the interests of its member companies regarding advertising and marketing by, for instance, administering the Agency Recognition procedures, advising on terms and conditions of business and recommending submission procedures. Copy control of advertising is handled by the joint AIRC/ITCA Secretariat. AIRC administers the contract for the industry's research into audiences, JICRAR, which is currently held by Research Surveys of Great Britain Ltd.

AIRC has a wholly-owned subsidiary, the Radio Marketing Bureau Ltd, at the same address (telephone: 01-258 3705), which promotes independent radio as an advertising medium to major advertisers and agencies.

THE ASSOCIATION OF MAIL ORDER PUBLISHERS, 1 New Burlington Street, London W1X 1FD. Telephone: 01-437 0706. Founded 1970.

This is an Association of firms engaged in selling books, magazines and gramophone records by post. Its principal aims or tasks are:

(*a*) To put forward the views of the members in general matters affecting the industry. This occurs in several different ways: for example, when the government of the day has legislation in mind, or when new directives are in draft in the European Economic Commission, or again when there are points to be negotiated with the Post Office or the Advertising Standards Authority. The Association is represented on the Code of Advertising Practice Committee, and belongs to the CBI. The Association is available for consultation by members on questions affecting their legal position. The Association also has links with those departments of local government responsible for enforcement of laws regulating trade.

(*b*) To supervise the operation of the Code of Practice. This is carried out by the Mail Order Publishers' Authority, a body separate from the Association. The general public is free to send complaints to the Authority about the treatment they have had at the hands of member companies; provided the complainants identify themselves and make a written statement of their complaints the Authority will investigate. The Code itself, which all members undertake to follow as a condition of joining the Association, was reissued in 1977 with the approval of the Director General of Fair Trading. The latter publishes a report on the working of the Code after discussion with the Authority and with other agencies.

Membership comprises full members, associate members and affiliates. The first two categories consist of mail order publishers and the difference is mainly one of size. The affiliates consist of firms providing services in support of the publishers: for example, advertising agencies. All full members are automatically represented on the Executive Committee, while associates are represented by two persons, and affiliates by one. They are elected annually.

Achievements. In its 10 years' existence, the Association of Mail Order Publishers has performed effectively as trade organisation and lobby. AMOP claims a string of successes in negotiating with Government departments, consumer agencies, legislators and other interested parties. Perhaps the best indicator of what has been achieved comes in comparing the conditions of mail order and direct mail in this country with those in other countries of the EEC. Although operators may at times feel hampered and hamstrung, the industry is a lot freer than they are, particularly in the fields of privacy, use of premiums, and wholehearted commitment to the principle of self-regulation.

Publications include bulletins, occasional papers, the quarterly *AMOP News*, and functions.

THE AUDIT BUREAU OF CIRCULATIONS LTD, 13 Wimpole Street, London W1M 7AB. Telephone: 01-631 1343. Founded 1931.

Membership is tripartite—about 2,900 in all, of which 2,600 are publications and the rest are divided almost equally between advertisers and agencies. The Council is divided 50/50 between publishers and advertisers/agencies. Thus more than 2,600 titles now give ABC figures every six months, and this number had doubled in the past ten years. Exhibition attendances are also certified.

An ABC figure is an audited net sale figure based on an average number of copies sold per day, week or month as the case may be over the preceding six-monthly period prior to June 30 and December 31. The Bureau issues audit forms, return of net circulation forms, and a certificate stating the circulation after scrutiny of the return. The actual audit is conducted by the publishers' own accountants. Net sales means '*copies bought by individuals either at the full price or at a lower price . . . all bulk sales to organisations and companies which then distribute them free must be excluded*'. There are special regulations concerning 'controlled circulation' journals which have to declare the number of copies individually requested, company requested and non-requested. There is close co-operation with *British Rate and Data*, which publishes ABC figures, and no circulation figure can be claimed as being ABC '*until such time as a signed certificate from the Bureau has been received by the publisher covering the audit period concerned*'.

The significance of the ABC is that advertisers and their advertising agencies are informed of the actual number of copies of newspapers and magazines which are sold or reliably distributed against requests. Before the ABC was set up—and in the case of publications without either their own or ABC audited net sale figures—the only figures known were often vague statements based on the number of copies printed. In the days when newsprint was cheap the number of returned unsold copies was sometimes higher than the number actually sold, and some highly spurious 'circulation' figures were quoted by publishers who were happy to sell advertisement space at grossly inflated rates. The ABC was created against severe opposition from the publishers, and was the creation of the Incorporated Society of British Advertisers, based on the American Audit Bureau of Circulations founded in 1914. As the ABC says in its booklet *Knowing Your ABC*, '*The newspapers and periodicals guarded their circulations like secrets of state. . . . There was no way of finding out whether an advertisement appeared in 5,000 or 50,000 copies.*' (See references to controlled circulation journals, pages 20 and 50).

These first organisations provide an insight into the history of advertising for we have been able to refer to the Advertising Association battling with unscrupulous advertisers while advertisers—through ISBA and the ABC—were battling against unscrupulous publishers! The opportunity occurs here to reiterate that advertising itself is but an innocent tool. No apology has to be made for the stupidity, vileness, avarice or incompetence of particular bad *advertisers*, and in that respect it is possible to understand why Labour politicians want to chastise them along with the so-called 'vermin' of the opposite party! But no apology has to be made for *advertising itself* which Russell Chapman in the 30s, the AA (with its AID) throughout, and the ASA and CAP Committee more recently have been at pains to defend from those who would abuse it. Labour made fatuous misuse of advertising with its ill-starred Forgotten Men campaign, which rebounded with ironic and disastrous effect. It is significant of the blindness of 20th-century party politics in Britain that Labour advocated a tax on advertising when what they really meant was that business follies should be taxed. There is a difference between taxing a waster and a winner!

THE BRITISH ASSOCIATION OF INDUSTRIAL EDITORS, 3 Locks Yard, High Street, Sevenoaks, Kent TN13 1LT. Telephone: 0732-459331. Founded 1949.

Membership is open to men and women engaged in various ways in the production of house journals and other media of internal communications. The Association has defined a house journal as '*a publication issued periodically, and not primarily for profit, by an industrial undertaking, a business house, a public service, a trade union, the armed forces, or an incorporated organisation, membership of which consists mainly of people engaged in industry, business, commerce or public service*'. There are nearly 1,000 individual members in categories of Fellow, Member, Associate, Honorary Fellow and Honorary Member. All applicants engaged in industrial editing may be admitted as Associates. Persons engaged in work allied to industrial communications may be admitted as Affiliates. Full membership may be obtained by taking an examination.

Aims

(*a*) To develop the skills and promote the interests of members.

(*b*) To provide the means for a regular exchange of ideas and experience between members, not only in connection with house journals but in the wider field of modern communication techniques in general.

(*c*) To provide courses in industrial editing for members and those seeking membership and to encourage the provision of such facilities by other education bodies.

(*d*) To provide facilities for entrance to membership by written examination.

(*e*) To work for the improvement of communication in industry and particularly of all types of house journal.

(*f*) To work for the recognition by managements and other governing bodies, employees, and the various associations of both, of the importance of effective communications, including house journals, to good human and industrial relations.

(*g*) To establish and maintain friendly relations with other organisations concerned with the work and interests of house journal editors.

(*h*) To provide whatever services are feasible to meet the requirements of the membership.

Activities include a monthly newspaper, a twice yearly magazine, an annual convention, an annual house journal competition, visits, lectures and social events.

BRITISH DIRECT MARKETING ASSOCIATION, 1 New Oxford Street, London WC1A INQ. Telephone: 01-242 2254. Founded 1976.

In April 1976 this organisation replaced the British Direct Mail Advertising Association, placing greater emphasis on direct response mail order. There are corporate members representing mail order and direct response advertisers, non-mail order direct mail users, individual and overseas members. Many service companies, e.g. advertising agencies, mailing houses and computer bureaux are also members.

The new body was set up to fight discrimination against the mail order industry and to defend its image and good name.

There is a Council of 20 members, two of whom must be individual members, representing all sectors of the direct marketing industry. It organises Direct Marketing Day (October), BDMA Conference (May), monthly Working Lunches, and, with the Post Office, the Direct Marketing Awards. The Telephone Marketing Congress (February) is organised in conjunction with British Telecom.

There is a phone-in Legal and Trading Standards Advisory Service.

All members undertake to obey the CAP and Sales Promotion Codes and guidelines have been published for telephone marketing. The BDMA Code of Practice and guidelines on lists and telephone marketing has been revised in consultation with the Office of Fair Trading.

Publications include *BDMA News* (4 per year), *Troubleshooter* and 'Work in Progress' bulletins.

BRITISH EXHIBITION CONTRACTORS ASSOCIATION, Kingsmere House, Graham Road, Wimbledon, London SW19 3SR. Telephone: 01-543 3888. Founded 1913.

Originally called the National Association of Exhibition Contractors, the present name was adopted in 1979. Member companies carry out work associated with all aspects of the exhibition industry, from standfitting to floral display.

Aims

(*a*) To provide an effective voice in representing the interests of its members, and to bring the experience of the member companies to the attention of exhibitors and organisers for the common good.

(*b*) To encourage and help its members to improve their professional competence as leaders in the field of exhibition contracting.

(*c*) To provide an information service to its members and in particular to represent employers on the two National Joint Councils for the industry.

The Association is governed by a Council consisting of a president, vice-president and up to ten elected members of Council. There are eight specialist committees. Exhibitors are protected by the BECA Code of Conduct to which members must adhere.

BROADCASTERS' AUDIENCE RESEARCH BOARD, Knighton House, 52–56 Mortimer Street, London WIN 8AN. Telephone: 01-636 6866.

BARB replaced JICTAR in July 1981, ending the controversy which had existed as a result of conflicting television audience figures produced by different research surveys. JICTAR had used a system of automatic electronic meters attached to TV sets in a representative sample of homes, with viewers completing diaries for each quarter-hour period. The BBC had conducted street interviews.

The BBC and ITCA worked together from 1975 onwards to set up a single system of TV audience research. Their first objective was to produce a method of audience measurement which would provide a common data base of adequate reliability and acceptable cost.

The broadcasters' efforts were at first unsuccessful, but they were encouraged to persevere by the report of the Annan Committee, published in February 1977. This recommended that television audience measurement should be obtained by a combined system so that resources could be released to enable more attention to be directed to research on the reactions of audiences to the content of programmes. With this recommendation the BBC and ITCA concurred, and in 1978 they were able to announce agreement on the way these aims should be achieved.

The essence of their agreement was that, for audience *measurement*, they would adopt the system of electronic meters attached to a representative sample of television sets, supported by diaries recording the personal viewing of members of the household: this was the system in use for ITV under the auspices of JICTAR—it has now been adjusted to take account of the needs of the BBC and has now been modernised by the introduction of electronic methods of recording personal viewing as well. For audience *reaction* research, they agreed to use the mechanism of the BBC Daily Survey, adapted to provide for the needs of both television systems.

To give effect to this agreement, the BBC and ITCA set up BARB Ltd, a company in which they have an equal share. The board of the company contains representatives of both partners and works through a director and a committee structure with which, on the measurement side, the IPA and ISBA are associated. The committees can call on the necessary technical research and engineering advice when required. The research company which carried out audience measurement for JICTAR, namely AGB Research Ltd, was appointed for the next two years and has subsequently been re-appointed for a further five.

With the creation of BARB the opportunity was taken to introduce a few changes, notably improved techniques to monitor the viewing of second sets in people's homes, which was becoming increasingly important in the audience as a whole, as well as nearly doubling the sample size in Wales, and making technical adjustments to cover the different viewing habits of the public as between the alternative television channels. The information produced is available to the broadcasters and to those who subscribe for it, the latter including the advertisers and advertising agencies.

BARB issues monthly, in addition to information on hours of viewing and the share of each channel in the total, tables showing the figures for the ten most popular programmes over the five channels. It is considered that figures for a month have more meaning and value than those for a week, but weekly lists are also released of the most popular programmes on each channel, together with material for the separate regions.

The BBC Broadcasting Research Department, which is responsible for the Daily Survey, conducts and analyses experiments devised by broadcasters on both sides of the industry. The BRD is the contractor to BARB in this sphere and meets the needs of all television broadcasters. The research involves personal in-home interviews with a sample of individuals, involving the placing of a diary questionnaire to be completed by the respondent during the following five days. This diary contains questions inviting both overall and specific comments on BBC and ITV television programmes viewed during this period. The IBA is closely involved in planning and execution in this field, since it operates its own audience appreciation survey, and makes a substantial financial contribution to the work.

CAM SOCIETY, Abford House, 15 Wilton Road, London SW1V 1NJ. Telephone: 01-828 7506.

After operating for 16 years as the Society of Members of the Advertising Association on behalf of those who had passed the Advertising Association examinations and chose to take up membership, the CAM Society superseded the SMAA in 1972. The change was made because the CAM Education Foundation had taken over the Advertising Association's examination function together with that of the Institute of Practitioners in Advertising and the Institute of Public Relations. In 1977 the Society was integrated into the CAM Education Foundation.

Membership of the CAM Foundation (MCAM), is open to those who were former members of the SMAA, MIPA's (by examination), those who successfully complete the CAM Diploma and MIPR's (by examination). Thus all members of the Foundation hold the CAM Diploma. Some, with advertising and public relations qualifications, may in fact hold two diplomas. The CAM Foundation is therefore a federation of those in advertising and public relations who are professionally qualified by examination, as distinct from being elected members of professional bodies.

THE CINEMA ADVERTISING ASSOCIATION LTD, 127 Wardour Street, London W1V 4AD. Telephone: 01-439 9531. Founded 1979.

The Cinema Advertising Association is the trade association of cinema advertising contractors in the UK and Ireland. Formerly the Screen Advertising Association (founded in 1953), the new name and trading style were adopted in September 1979.

The CAA's primary *aim* is to promote cinema as an advertising medium, and to conduct research into the cinema and its audience. In 1980 the CAA commissioned and published the first of a series of in-depth audience studies through Carrick James Market Research. This study forms the basis of Chapter 22. The CAA continues to provide audience data based on Government statistics and special analysis of JICNARS data.

Its role is partly one of a watchdog, acting to ensure that professional standards are met and maintained by the cinema advertising industry, and it performs this aspect of its work in two ways. It is responsible for vetting all commercials prior to their screening in cinemas, in order to ensure that they do not make unfair advertising claims or offend against public taste. It ensures that cinema advertising conforms with the British Code of Advertising Practice. The CAA is one of the member organisations of the CAP Committee. It is also responsible for conducting regular checks to ensure that cinema advertising bookings are screened under optimum conditions from the advertisers' point of view (i.e. prior to the main feature film with the house lights down).

The other purpose of the CAA is to educate and inform and to provide advertisers and their agencies with an up-to-date guide to the cinema medium and the unique advantages it has to offer.

CODE OF ADVERTISING PRACTICE COMMITTEE, Brook House, Torrington Place, London WC1E 7HN. Telephone: 01-580 5555. Founded 1962.

Although the first edition of the present Code was published in 1961, under the auspices of the Advertising Association and supported by 17 organisations, it succeeded the *British Code of Standards in Relation to the Advertising of Medicines and Treatments* which was first issued in 1948 and to some extent was based on the earlier Code of the Proprietary Association of Great Britain which had conducted an approval scheme for the advertisements of the proprietary medicine industry. The CAP Committee therefore represents two things: a simplification of the previously over-complicated advertising control system, and a code which embraces all advertising. Moreover, the Code covers many areas of advertising—e.g. knocking copy, inertia selling and switch selling—which are not covered by the *Trade Descriptions Acts*. Despite numerous laws in relation to advertising, voluntary controls—or 'guidance'—remain necessary to maintain the proper use and good name of advertising.

The composition of the CAP Committee is interesting since it includes the broadcasting trade bodies, and is more broadly based than ASBOF. This is because the CAP Committee aims to promote the highest standards of advertising in all media even though advertisements on television and radio are the responsibility of the Independent Broadcasting Authority. The membership of the committee consists of representatives of 21 advertising organisations.

The copy panel consists of five sections and is available to meet every week. Each section has six members, five from the advertising industry and one an independent member of the ASA Council. The sub-committees are: Chairman's, Financial Advertising, Health and Nutrition, Mail Order and Sales Promotion.

The chart on page 68 shows how the self-regulatory system is organised, and sets out the relationship between the ASA and the CAP Committee.

Sales promotion is a sensitive area and the Sales Promotion Monitoring programme conducts purchasing trips to provincial centres. For example, in a year some 1,000 individual promotions may be investigated to see whether they conform to the British Code of Sales Promotion Practice. One result of these investigations has been the publication of Guidance Notes on Promotional Packs.

THE COMMUNICATION, ADVERTISING AND MARKETING EDUCATION FOUNDATION LTD, Abford House, 15 Wilton Road, London SW1V 1NJ. Telephone: 01-828 7506. Founded 1969.

The CAM Education Foundation is an educational charity launched as a collective attempt by trade associations and professional bodies to devise an effective, integrated system of education and training in the related fields of communication, advertising and marketing.

However, references made in this section are subject to possible revisions and restructuring recommended by the Planning Committee which superseded the original secretariat at the end of 1984.

The CAM Certificate in Communication Studies requires passes in six subjects chosen from Marketing, Advertising, Public Relations, Media, Research and Behavioural Studies, Communication Practice and Business and Economic Environment. Certificate holders, or others with prescribed exemptions (e.g. Distinctions in same LCCI subjects) may take examinations for a CAM Diploma for which a pass is required in three subjects or five for an Honours Diploma. Diploma subjects are Consumer Advertising and Marketing, International Advertising and Marketing, Industrial Advertising and Marketing, Advanced Media Studies, Market Research, Marketing Strategy, Management Resources, PR Strategy, PR for Commercial Organisation, PR for Non-Commercial Organisations. (*See* Fig. 5.2 on page 71.)

In the UK, students may prepare for these examinations by attending evening classes or by taking correspondence courses, while CAM puts on a number of special seminars.

Aims

To promote for the general benefit of the public, the advancement of communication, advertising and marketing education at all levels and to provide education facilities, both general and specialised, for persons taking part in or intending to take part in the communication, advertising and marketing processes and generally to assist in the improvement of educational and training standards.

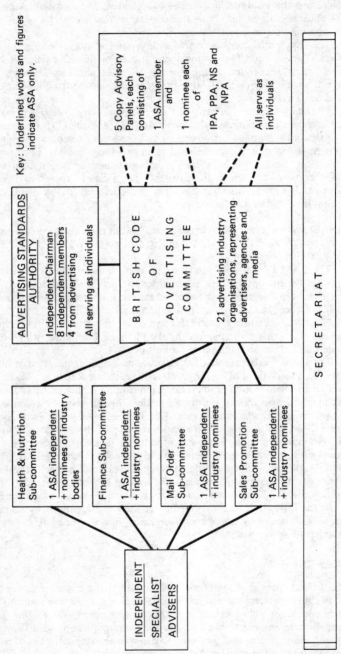

Fig. 5.1. Structure of the ASA/CAP Committee Self-Regulatory System

Key: Underlined words and figures indicate ASA only.

5 Copy Advisory Panels, each consisting of

1 ASA member and

1 nominee each of IPA, PPA, NS and NPA

All serve as individuals

ADVERTISING STANDARDS AUTHORITY

Independent Chairman
8 independent members
4 from advertising

All serving as individuals

BRITISH CODE OF ADVERTISING COMMITTEE

21 advertising industry organisations, representing advertisers, agencies and media

Health & Nutrition Sub-committee

1 ASA independent + nominees of industry bodies

Finance Sub-committee

1 ASA independent + industry nominees

Mail Order Sub-committee

1 ASA independent + industry nominees

Sales Promotion Sub-committee

1 ASA independent + industry nominees

INDEPENDENT SPECIALIST ADVISERS

SECRETARIAT

To achieve these aims, CAM sets out to:

    (i) Identify training and educational needs.
    (ii) Unify and supplement existing facilities.
    (iii) Promote liaison between universities, polytechnics, and other colleges and industrial training schemes.
    (iv) Run examinations and award certificates and diplomas, recognised as the accepted professional qualifications.
    (v) Help maintain high standards of tuition.
    (vi) Run courses and conferences and correspondence courses.
    (vii) Develop syllabuses, teaching aids and methods.
    (viii) Publish books and other literature.
    (ix) Provide the opportunity for people in other countries to gain professional qualifications in CAM fields.
    (x) Advise employers on all aspects of training.

DIRECT MAIL SERVICES STANDARDS BOARD, 92 New Cavendish Street, London W1M 7FA. Telephone: 01-636 7581/2. Founded 1983.

The Direct Mail Services Standards Board was established with Post Office support to promote improvements in the ethical and professional standards of the direct mail advertising industry. The Board runs a recognition system for direct mail agencies which adhere to the British Code of Advertising Practice and other relevant Codes, and have been scrutinised by the Board's staff. They receive from it a commission on their postage bill. Advertisers are encouraged to use agencies recognised by the DMSSB. More than 100 agencies are so recognised.

The Board and its activities are not directly visible to the consumer: the board deals mainly with advertisers and their agencies. Where consumer complaints occur, they continue to be directed to the CAP Committee, and those upheld by the ASA are referred to the Board for action if a recognised agency is involved.

DIRECT MAIL PRODUCERS' ASSOCIATION, 34 Grand Avenue, London N10 3BP. Telephone: 01-883 7229.

Members of this trade association consist of direct mail agencies which specialise in the planning, creation and despatch of direct mail advertising.

Aims

To promote the wider use of direct mail advertising and to maintain the highest standards in its creation, production and despatch.

THE INCORPORATED SOCIETY OF BRITISH ADVERTISERS LTD, 44 Hertford Street, London W1Y 8AE. Telephone: 01-499 7502. Founded 1900. Formerly the Advertisers Protection Society.

The primary purpose of ISBA was and is to protect the interests of advertisers and right from the start it set out to extract and publish true circulation figures, this leading to the formation of the Audit Bureau of Circulations in 1931. Its vigorous pioneering character has been seen in other ventures—the first newspaper readership survey in 1936, the first survey into the listening patterns of sponsored radio in 1938 (when the British listener had a wide choice of continental light entertainment programmes sponsored by British advertisers), assistance to the Government in advising on the setting up of commercial TV in 1954, and operation of the voluntary 'anti-clutter code' when nearly half a million untidy advertisements outside shop premises were either removed or resited. More recently, ISBA led the creation of the levy on advertisements to finance the expansion of the self-regulatory control system (ASBOF), thus protecting advertisers from government tax and intervention, and also defending the need for competition in TV air-time selling in the setting up of Channel 4.

The above sketch shows how ISBA has, for many years, set about the following aims:

To enable advertisers to speak with one voice and to represent members' views on advertising to Government, opinion leaders, media owners, advertising agencies and to the public.

To establish acceptance by Government and media of the freedom to advertise in all media, subject only to the law, Codes of Practice and well-established editorial policy.

To promote highest standards of advertising practice by observance of and adherence to the Codes governing advertising and sales promotion practice agreed to by the Society.

To promote and protect Members' interests through the relevant ISBA Committees which have responsibilities for all aspects of advertising.

To co-operate with all other national and international bodies concerned with marketing and advertising for the overall benefit of members of the advertising industry.

To provide information and vigilance on advertising matters of key concern to Members.

On the three tripartite media research JIC's and BARB, ISBA represents the advertisers. Internationally, the ISBA is active in the International Union of Advertisers Associations (IUAA), and in the International Chamber of Commerce (ICC).

ISBA publishes for its members a variety of reports and guides on topics such as industrial advertising, exhibitions, outdoor advertising, advertising research and overseas advertising, and a monthly newsletter with supplements covering industrial, international and exhibition matters.

INDEPENDENT TELEVISION COMPANIES ASSOCIATION, Knighton House, 56 Mortimer Street, London W1N 8AN. Telephone: 01-636 6866. Founded 1958.

ITCA is the trade association of the programme companies appointed by the Independent Television Authority, renamed Independent Broadcasting Authority in July 1972 to incorporate commercial radio. All such appointed companies (the programme contractors Anglia Television, Border Television, Central Television, Channel Islands Communications, Grampian Television, Granada Television, Harlech Television, London Weekend Television, Scottish Television, Television South, Television South West, Thames Television, Tyne–Tees Television, Ulster Television, Yorkshire Television and TV-am—16 in all) are members of ITCA and its

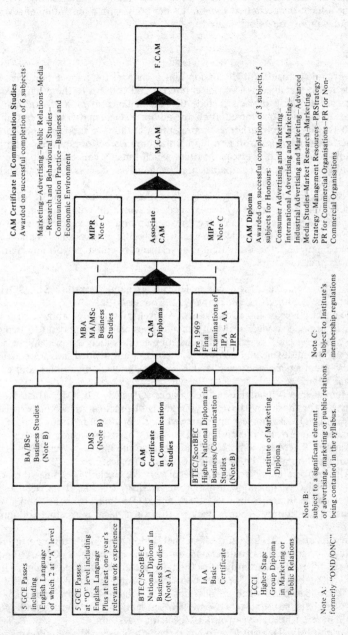

Fig. 5.2. CAM Foundation membership and entry routes

source of funds. These companies produce programmes and sell advertisement time in the permitted six minutes per hour, with a maximum of seven
minutes in any one clock hour.

Aims

To provide a forum for discussion and a channel for joint action over a
wide range of subjects of common interest and concern to the programme
companies. These subjects include the maintenance of high general standards in the industry, consultation and advice on legal matters, negotiations
with royalty-collecting bodies, representing authors, composers and publishers, and relations with and representation on other organisations, both
in this country and overseas. Matters which directly concern the business
dealings of individual companies are not, however, discussed or dealt with
within the Association.

As stated in the popular yearbook of the Authority, the work of the
Association is governed by the council, on which all companies are represented at high level. The council has set up and receives regular reports
from a number of committees to deal with specific subjects such as finance,
public relations, cable and satellite, advertising, research, performing rights
and technical matters.

INSTITUTE OF MARKETING, Moor Hall, Cookham, Berkshire SL6 9QH.
Telephone: Bourne End (06285) 24922. Founded 1911.

The objectives of the Institute are to develop knowledge about marketing, to provide services to Members and registered students and to make
the principles and practices of marketing more widely known and used
throughout industry and commerce. Activities are divided into four main
areas: Membership and membership services, education, training and external affairs.

Membership is available in four grades (GInstM, AInstM, MInstM or
FInstM) for those who have varying levels of practical marketing experience and who also possess an approved marketing qualification. Two aca-
demically approved alternative entry routes exist for senior persons in
marketing. There are some 22,000 members in the UK and overseas, all of
whom are bound by the Institute's Code of Practice.

All members enjoy a wide range of services, including a fine library,
an extensive marketing information service, free legal advice and
career counselling. In the UK, there are 36 Regional Branches and five
Industry Marketing Groups. Each of these is a 'local marketing training
centre'.

In education, the Institute offers the Diploma in Marketing, an inter-
nationally-recognised qualification rated equivalent to a CNAA first
Degree. There are currently 15,500 students studying for the Diploma in
the UK and overseas. The post-experience training arm of the Institute
is the College of Marketing, now superbly equipped in new premises at
the Cookham headquarters. Some 260 residential short courses and 160
seminars are run each year on all aspects of marketing.

A Retail Management Centre has recently been opened and tailor-made
courses for individual companies are offered by Marketing Training Ltd.

The Institute runs the National Marketing Awards, an Annual Conference and the Marketing Advisory Service.

Publications include *Marketing*, issued free of charge to members, and the *Quarterly Review of Marketing* which is issued free to students and members of the Marketing Education Group. Non-members may subscribe to these journals. Textbooks are published in conjunction with Heinemann, and the IM itself publishes a series of professional papers, surveys and special reports.

INSTITUTE OF PRACTITIONERS IN ADVERTISING, 44 Belgrave Square, London SW1X 8QS. Telephone: 01-235 7020. Founded in 1917 as the Association of British Advertising Agents and becoming the Institute of Incorporated Practitioners in Advertising in 1927, but dropping the 'Incorporated' in 1954.

The Institute came into existence as the trade association of service agencies as distinct from space brokers. With the advent of the CAM Diploma, which superseded the IPA's own examinations, a new system of individual membership was introduced in 1969 so that personal membership has been divorced from examinations. It should be clearly understood that the IPA does not 'recognise' agencies as is often mistakenly thought, this being done by the bodies representing the media owners.

The Institute of Practitioners in Advertising is the central representative organisation for UK advertising agencies. It represents the collective views of agencies (and the people who work in them) in discussions and negotiations with Government departments, the media, and industry and consumer organisations. The IPA also provides for its members a number of specialist and information services covering practically every aspect of UK and overseas advertising.

The IPA has approximately 270 member-agencies who between them handle about 85–90 per cent of all advertising placed through UK advertising agencies. IPA agencies have a turnover of around £2,500m. which their clients invest in campaigns in newspapers and magazines, TV, radio and posters, as well as in retail displays, direct mail, exhibitions, merchandising and market research.

There are something like 850 advertising agencies in Great Britain, and of the 500 or so who are not members of the IPA, most are small firms staffed by only a few people. Only those agencies which provide full services, and which are able to plan and execute an advertising campaign from start to finish, and thus satisfy the IPA's governing council of their competence and professionalism, are admitted to membership.

IPA agencies range from big multinational companies with media billings in excess of £120m. a year to medium-sized specialist agencies with services and facilities geared to industrial, financial and recruitment advertising. Few IPA agencies have media billings below £750,000 a year.

Although the majority of IPA agencies are London-based, there are well over 100 in major regional centres. These agencies are grouped in three main IPA branch areas—Northern, Midland and Scottish—each with its own honorary officers who plan and organise meetings and other events specially geared to the needs of agencies in the regions. About two-thirds of IPA agencies have overseas offices or close links with agencies throughout the world.

The IPA has demonstrated just how effective advertising can be through its Advertising Effectiveness Awards scheme, which was started in 1980 and is now held biennially. The major prize-winning papers and a selection of commended entries, each showing evidence of advertising working successfully, have been published in *Advertising Works* and *Advertising Works 2*, available from the IPA or the publishers Holt, Rinehart and Winston. The Awards were presented again in 1984.

The IPA is very active in the field of training, organising the Evening Series for Trainees for newcomers to the business, the Campaign Planning Course for more experienced young agency employees, and the Senior Advertising Programme, an eight-day residential seminar for senior agency people. The IPA Society, whose membership is open to all staff in agencies, but particularly more junior staff, organises regular meetings with speakers to discuss controversial or topical subjects. The IPA also arranges seminars and conferences on management and specialist subjects.

It publishes statistical data on agency performance, salary levels and numbers employed as well as management aids on such subjects as insurance and costing techniques, marketing and media appraisals, information on overseas markets and practical guides to everyday agency problems. Its legal service is one of the most heavily used IPA services, advising members on the legislation affecting advertising and keeping them abreast of EEC and international legislation. This service includes a regular bulletin of developments in the legal and advertising control field.

In post-war years the IPA has made a notable contribution to the production of independent surveys of media readerships and audiences—that is, independent of the media owners. As a result, the IPA sponsored the *National Readership Survey* in 1956, this succeeding the famous *Hulton Readership Survey* which has pioneered this form of research in earlier post-war years. Instead of being produced by only one publisher the NRS was undertaken by the IPA in conjunction with the publishing organisations. With the further co-operation of ISBA, media research was put on a tripartite basis, and since the late 1960s there have been four Joint Industry Committees for research into newspaper/magazine readerships, radio, television and poster audiences. (These are described in a separate section of this chapter.) For the JICs, the IPA provides the secretariat except for BARB, which has replaced JICTAR and operates from the same premises as ITCA, and JICPAR which is run by the Outdoor Advertising Association.

In these ways the IPA has been able to provide its members with a statistical service in keeping with the professional needs of the modern service agency, and the IPA definition already given that '*advertising presents the most persuasive possible selling message to the right prospects for the product or service at the lowest possible cost*'. Readership research—that is, the study of readership as distinct from immediate sales, discovering how many and what kind of people read newspapers and magazines, the extent of duplication, and so on—has been invaluable in eliminating wasteful advertising. Today most schedule analysis is obtained quickly and cheaply by computer. Of course, the space or time has still to be filled with the most effective message, but here the IPA has concerned itself with training to the extent that it now has its own training scheme independently of CAM.

INSTITUTE OF PUBLIC RELATIONS, Gate House, St John's Square, London EC1M 4DH. Telephone: 01-253 5151. Founded 1948.

Membership of the IPR is individual, in the categories of honorary fellow, honorary member, fellow, member, associate and student. A full member has to be at least 26 years of age and have five years' comprehensive experience, three years' experience being acceptable if the candidate holds the CAM Diploma. Members have to sign an undertaking that they will abide by the Institute's *Code of Professional Conduct*. For election to fellowship a citation has to be presented to Council.

Aims

To enhance the status of public relations and establish high standards of professional conduct.

The President and Honorary Treasurer are elected annually, the President acting as President-elect for a year, and then as Immediate Past President for the year after his term of office. Council members are elected to serve for three years. There are standing committees—Membership, Professional Practices, Education, International, and so on—whose chairmen, together with the officers, form the Board of Management. There are also Area Groups covering all parts of the UK which have elected Council representatives. Vocational and Special Interest Groups are organised to help members with specific business interests.

Major activities include a national conference, seminars and workshops. Throughout the year luncheon meetings and other functions are organised by the Institute in London, or elsewhere by regional vocational groups.

The Institute's *Code of Professional Conduct* is strictly enforced, and is reviewed from time to time and amended to meet changing circumstances. The fact that membership of the IPR implies acceptance of this Code is a major incentive for being accepted by this professional body.

Publications include a Register of Members, a quarterly journal *Public Relations*, a monthly newsletter and professional practice papers.

The Institute is a constituent member of the CAM Foundation which is responsible for setting examinations, in co-operation with the Institute, for the CAM Certificate in Communication Studies and the CAM Diploma in Public Relations. The Foundation is also responsible for the establishment of courses leading to these examinations. The IPR makes awards to the best students in the CAM Public Relations examinations at both Certificate and Diploma level. However, changes may occur in 1985/6.

The Institute is affiliated to CERP, the European Confederation of Public Relations, of which it is the largest affiliated body.

INSTITUTE OF SALES AND MARKETING MANAGEMENT, Georgian House, 31 Upper George Street, Luton, Bedfordshire LU1 2RD. Telephone: 0582 411130. Founded 1981 in its present name.

The Institute of Sales and Marketing Management is the descendant of the Institution of Sales Engineers (founded 1966) and the Institution of

Professional Salesmen (founded 1974). The latter body changed its name to the Institute of Sales Management in 1976 and in 1979 both bodies merged. In January 1981 the name was changed to its present title.

The Institute's name has always been descriptive of its membership and changes of name have been dictated by the changing membership profile. The vast majority of early members have gained promotion and have attained senior sales and marketing management positions, thus reflecting the effectiveness of the Institute in pursuing its main purpose, which is to do all it can to ensure the professional success of its members.

The Institute is a proprietary club, owned by a specially constituted limited company, Sales and Marketing Management Ltd, not by its members, and managed by a board of directors. The directors are John Goodman, David Waller, Bill Lister and Alan Payne. The Institute's members are its 'customers' and include HRH Prince Philip, Duke of Edinburgh, and many top industrialists. Its President is the Earl Bathurst and its four Vice-Presidents are Lord John Boyd-Carpenter, Viscount de L'Isle, Lord Birdwood and Sir John Buckley.

Membership grades are fellow, member, associate and affiliate/student, depending on qualifications and experience. Members receive legal services, business leads and other services including an excellent monthly magazine, *Sales and Marketing Management*, which contains practical information and advice. Courses are organised for members.

INTERNATIONAL ASSOCIATION OF BUSINESS COMMUNICATORS, 870 Market Street, Suite 940, San Francisco, CA 94102, USA. UK Secretariat: Richard Pledger, 13 Kirkstall Road, London SW2 4HJ. Telephone: 01-674 3572. Founded 1970.

The IABC is an international organisation created by the amalgamation of three American and Canadian house journal organisations. Today, with a membership of over 10,000 in 45 countries, the IABC represents not only internal communications but the broad span of PR and communications techniques. Especially notable is the high professional standard of its conferences, seminars, publications and member services. The IABC has become a world-wide body of directors, managers, editors, educationalists, writers, audio-visual specialists, consultants and other business communicators.

The IABC seeks to build a broader understanding of the practical values of effective communication in the management of every business, industry and organisation. It aims to encourage and assist the professional development of its members through a variety of publications and programmes.

It does not compete with national institutes, yet its membership is very broad, embracing many ancillary services, and offers membership to professional people who might not be eligible for membership of other bodies, e.g. video and film producers. The IABC has 125 chapters in the United States, Canada, Hong Kong, the Philippines and the UK.

The British chapter was founded in 1979 and has an active membership, monthly workshops and other events, a monthly newsletter and a 'brains exchange'. The world annual convention will be held in Britain in 1987.

Communication World is a first class monthly magazine. There is an annual Gold Quill competition for many categories of print. Membership

is open to those who are working in some aspect of communication programmes and techniques. Accredited membership (ABC) may be gained
by examination.

INTERNATIONAL PUBLIC RELATIONS ASSOCIATION, Case Postale 126,
CH-1211 Geneva 20, Switzerland. Telephone: 22-29.28.21, Telex: 428380
CRE CH. Founded 1955.

The concept of an international public relations association originated
in November 1949 when two Dutch and four British public relations men
met in London. A provisional international committee was set up, regular
meetings were held during the next five years, and IPRA was born in
London on May 1, 1955. The IPRA Council meets biannually to administer
the affairs of the Association and to consider proposals from the six IPRA
standing committees. National corresponding Council members are appointed where there are three IPRA members in a country.

Aims

To raise the standard of public relations practice in the various countries,
and to improve the professional quality and efficiency of public relations
practitioners.

The Public Relations World Congress held every three years has to date
been held in Brussels, Venice, Montreal, Rio de Janeiro, Tel Aviv, Geneva,
Boston, London and Bombay. The 1985 Congress was in Amsterdam and
the 1988 Congress is in Australia.

The IPRA Code of Conduct was adopted in Venice in 1961, and the
Code of Athens was adopted at an IPRA Council meeting in 1965, the
latter being inspired by the United Nations Declaration of Human
Rights.

The IPRA President's award is made annually, and recipients have
included the doyen of PR, Dr Edward Bernays.

Members are individuals elected on the basis of their experience (minimum five years) in international public relations. There are more than 750
members in 62 countries.

As a result of a meeting of public relations educators in Hong Kong in
September 1980, recommendations for university-level education in PR are
being discussed by IPRA members and national PR institutes and associations throughout the world including the UK. There is an active IPRA
group in the UK.

Publications include a Members' Register with portraits of all members,
IPRA Newsletter, and *IPRA Review*, which contains learned articles on
PR practice.

JOINT INDUSTRY COMMITTEE FOR NATIONAL READERSHIP SURVEYS, 44
Belgrave Square, London SW1X 8QS. Telephone: 01-235 7020. Founded
1968.

The initials JICNARS are somewhat misleading since the letter A is
used to create a name from a set of initials—JICNRS. It is in fact the Joint
Industry Committee which has taken over the *National Readership Survey*
originally sponsored by the IPA. The constituent bodies are the Press Re-

search Council, the IPA and the Incorporated Society of British Advertisers.

The *National Readership Survey* publishes the results of just under 30,000 interviews a year. From 1984, nearly 200 national publications are included, and from time to time certain specialist magazines also. Besides questions relating to readership data, questions are also asked on ITV viewing, cinema-going and listening to commercial radio.

JOINT INDUSTRY COMMITTEE FOR POSTER AUDIENCE RESEARCH (JICPAR), 3 Dean Farrar Street, London SW1H 9LG. Telephone: 01-222 0441.

JICPAR was established in 1983 as successor to the Joint Industry Committee for Poster Audience Surveys (JICPAS). JICPAR comprises representatives of the Outdoor Advertising Association of Great Britain Ltd; the Incorporated Society of British Advertising Ltd; the Institute of Practitioners in Advertising; and the Council of Outdoor Specialists.

In 1984 JICPAR carried out a poster site classification and audience measurement project which was funded by the OAA. A central data bank was established and put into operation.

JICPAR has established a User Sub-Committee to consider detailed aspects of the Committee's functions, and a Publicity Sub-Committee to publicise the Committee's work.

JOINT INDUSTRY COMMITTEE FOR RADIO AUDIENCE RESEARCH, 44 Belgrave Square, London SW1X 8QS. Telephone: 01-235 7020. Founded 1974.

The latest of the tripartite research Committees, JICRAR is formed from representatives of IPA, ISBA and AIRC and was set up to agree a specification for and method of publication of research into the commercial radio audiences. A diary method is used to record listenership. The research itself is commissioned and paid for by the individual radio stations in membership of AIRC.

JICRAR publishes annual radio audience reports, giving audience ratings at half-hourly periods for seven days a week. It covers all ILR radio stations and gives demographic details of age, sex and social grade. The surveys are sold to subscribers by the Association of Independent Radio Contractors.

THE LONDON CHAMBER OF COMMERCE AND INDUSTRY, Examinations Board, Marlowe House, Station Road, Sidcup, Kent DA15 7BJ. Telephone: 01-302 0261/4.

The LCCI Examinations Board holds examinations at centres throughout the world in commercial and business subjects including Advertising, Marketing, Public Relations and Selling and Sales Management. The Advertising examination has been held for some 50 years. A group diploma is awarded to those who gain a pass in *either* (*a*) Marketing plus passes in two of the three subjects mentioned above; *or* (*b*) Public Relations plus passes in two of the three subjects mentioned above. These are Higher Stage certificate subjects, and Distinctions in Advertising, Marketing and Public Relations are accepted on a subject-for-subject basis for exemption from these subjects in the CAM Certificate in Communication Studies.

However, an advantage of the LCCI examinations for overseas candi-

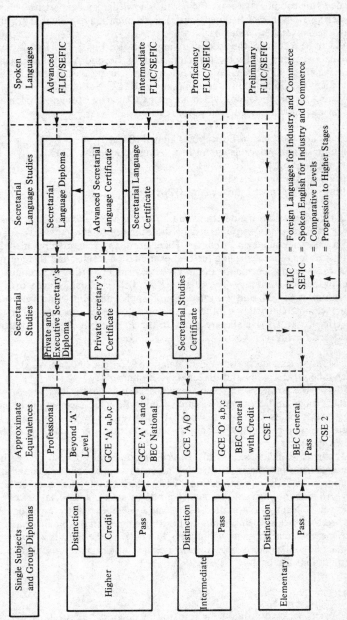

Fig. 5.3. Inter-relationship and structure of LCCI Examinations Board examinations.

dates is that the papers are not UK-orientated and there are opportunities for overseas candidates to use their local knowledge and experience when answering a number of the questions. The examinations are held in April–May and November–December.

As will be seen from the accompanying chart (see Fig. 5.3), a Distinction in the above mentioned subjects is equivalent to 'Beyond A Level', a Credit is equivalent to GCE A Level grades a, b and c, and a Pass is regarded as equivalent to 'GCE A Level grades d and e, BTEC National'.

Among the organisations which accept LCCI Certificates and Diplomas for various entry or exemption purposes are:

Business and Technician Education Council (BTEC)
Communication, Advertising and Marketing Foundation (CAM)
Institute of Export (IEX)
Institute of Marketing (IM)
Institute of Personnel Management (IPM)

LCCI publications include the annual *Regulations, Syllabuses and Timetables of Examinations* (published in the Summer of the previous year), and a quarterly magazine *Comlon*. There are many scholarships, medals and prizes for those achieving the best examination results, and there is an Overseas Awards Scheme for the top overseas student sitting the examinations in their own country. The Charles R. E. Bell scholarships are worth a maximum of £1,000, and are intended for applicants who wish to pursue higher commercial studies (other than correspondence courses) either in the UK or abroad. Details are given in the *Regulations*. Typical awards have been for university study.

THE MARKET RESEARCH SOCIETY, 15 Belgrave Square, London SW1X 8PF. Telephone: 01-235 4709 and 01-235 4894. Founded 1947.

This is the professional body for those using survey techniques for market, social and economic research, and with 4,300 members it is the largest body of its kind in the world. It is governed by a council with a chairman, vice-chairman, honorary secretary/treasurer and ten other elected members.

Membership includes not only survey practitioners but also people in manufacturing industries, advertising agencies and various academic institutions. The MRS is a professional body offering individual membership only. All persons engaged or having an interest in market, social or economic research may be admitted as associate members. After a period of two years' associate membership, full membership is attainable if the associate member reaffirms his willingness to abide by the Society's *Code of Conduct* as well as being able to satisfy certain other conditions. Diploma Examinations are held.

Aims

The Society seeks to promote and protect the interests both of its members engaged in market research and of those employing their services. It stimulates the flow of ideas and techniques between all branches of the profession, and endeavours to make the role and value of scientific market research fully understood outside the profession.

Its *Code of Conduct* covers, in addition to professional ethics, standard conditions for conducting scientific sample surveys and reporting results. The Code is continually reviewed by the council in order to cover the ever-widening field of market research activity in commerce, industry, Government and the social sciences. All members are automatically bound to observe its provisions.

Publications include the quarterly *Journal of the Market Research Society* and half-yearly *Abstracts* from published journals of articles relevant to market research, and a number of books. A very informative *Yearbook* is published.

THE NEWSPAPER PUBLISHERS' ASSOCIATION LTD, 6 Bouverie Street, London, EC4. Telephone: 01-583 8132/9. Founded 1906. Formerly known as the Newspaper Proprietors' Association.

This is the trade association of the national newpapers and the London evening newspaper.

Aims

(i) To co-ordinate the activity of national newspaper publishers, and to act on their behalf, so as to promote the social and economic interests of the national newspaper industry.

(ii) To provide such services for national newspaper publishers as to enable them to take full advantage of opportunities in the national newspaper industry.

The following services are provided to members: (*a*) labour relations and management services; (*b*) training and management development; (*c*) marketing: distribution and advertising; (*d*) newsprint; (*e*) legal affairs and Government representations; (*f*) provision of press facilities.

So far as this book is concerned, of prime importance is NPA (and also joint NPA and Newspaper Society) **recognition of agencies.** This will be dealt with more fully in the chapter on media owners, but a major factor in 'recognition' is **credit-worthiness,** since large sums of money are involved in the purchase of space and publishers have to protect themselves against possible losses incurred by defaulting advertising agencies. Agencies act as principals and are responsible in law for space purchases (and TV or radio time or any other bookings) made on behalf of their advertiser clients. This is really what 'recognition' is all about: it does not mean that an advertising agency is recognised for its proficiency.

The NPA plays a big part in industrial relations, representing the publishers in negotiations with trade unions (as when Fleet Street newspapers stopped publication during the 1971 dispute). The NPA is also responsible for arranging distribution of newspapers, both in the UK and abroad. It also operates a rota system of reporters and press photographers for Government and Royal occasions so that Ministers and members of the Royal Family are not unduly pestered, and also for sporting events where press facilities may be limited.

THE NEWSPAPER SOCIETY, Whitefriars House, Carmelite Street, London EC4Y 0BL. Telephone: 01-583 3311. Founded 1836.

Probably the oldest of all the associations connected with the communication business, the NS has only recently come to be known by its initials. The Newspaper Society was born in the offices of Britain's first advertising agency, White's. At 33 Fleet Street on April 25, 1836, many provincial newspaper proprietors attended a meeting under the chairmanship of J. M. Gutch of *Felix Farley's Journal*, an old school friend of James White.

Its members are regional and local newspapers, and for many years it was the only organisation in the UK representing the publishers of newspapers *and* magazines. Today its 262 members publish 22 morning newspapers, 76 evening newspapers (outside London), and more than 1,000 paid-for and free weekly or bi-weekly newspapers. Free newspapers are eligible for membership provided that they meet the same editorial criteria as required by the NS. (National morning and Sunday and the London evening newspaper are now represented by the NPA; general magazines and trade and technical magazines by the PPA.)

The principal objects of the Society shall be as follows:

(*a*) As a central organisation, to maintain a free press; to deal with all matters affecting the industry; promote, further and safeguard the interests of members; and promote co-operation among members in all matters affecting their common interests.

(*b*) To encourage the formation and maintenance within the British Isles of regional and local organisations to be affiliated to the Society having objects similar to those of the Society.

(*c*) To deal with all matters, whether arising nationally or locally, relating to the remuneration, hours, holidays and working conditions of employees covered by agreements between organisations of workers and the Society; when considered appropriate to conclude, vary or terminate such agreements; and to assist in the formation and maintenance of any defensive organisation necessitated by the circumstances of the industry.

(*d*) To enhance the local and national advertisement revenue of member-newspapers by promoting their use by advertisers and advertising agencies.

(*e*) To enter into and suspend or terminate when necessary agreements for the official recognition of advertising agencies; to supply confidential information to members about the financial status of such agencies and of advertisers and about advertisers and advertisements unacceptable in the interest of the public; and to encourage members to observe current codes of advertising practices.

(*f*) To develop, organise and implement further education and training programmes to meet the needs of members; to support schemes for the education and training of juniors and apprentices in any branch of the industry; and to liaise, negotiate and co-ordinate activities in all areas of further education and training with Government organisations and other appropriate bodies.

(*g*) To promote and safeguard newspaper interest in Parliament and in the adminstration and exercise of their powers by Government departments, courts of law, local authorities and other bodies.

(*h*) To take all possible action to safeguard the interests of members in relation to the laws of defamation and copyright, and to provide a central machinery by which the members of the Society may enter into combination for defending proceedings for defamation.

(*i*) To maintain the Newspaper Conference of the London editorial representatives of member-newspapers, which shall promote and safeguard the editorial interests of those newspapers and of the press generally.

(*j*) To assist in the maintenance of, and to accept as an affiliated organisation, the Guild of British Newspaper Editors, so long as its objects shall be consistent with those of the Society.

(*k*) To investigate and report on technical developments affecting the newspaper industry; and to assist members to apply such developments to their best interests.

(*l*) To inform, assist and safeguard the interests of members on matters affecting sales and distribution of newspapers; to promote the successful marketing of newspapers; and to liaise, negotiate and co-ordinate activities with other bodies with similar interests.

(*m*) To maintain a young newspapermen's organisation, the objects of which shall be consistent with those of the Society.

The Society 'recognises' 75 advertising agencies under the separate NS recognition for agencies not placing advertisements in the national press, and more than 600 under the joint NPA/NS recognition system. The Society is increasingly involved in promoting advertising to local advertisers, while the Regional Newspaper Advertising Bureau puts its emphasis on national business.

Newstime is the Society's monthly publication which is distributed to all members.

OUTDOOR ADVERTISING ASSOCIATION OF GREAT BRITAIN LTD, 3 Dean Farrar Street, London SW1H 0LG. Telephone: 01-222 0441.

Membership comprises companies who together control about 90 per cent of all outdoor advertising sites and panels throughout the UK.

The main aims are to protect and promote the interests of the members, in particular on legal, trading, planning and Parliamentary matters.

The OAA is joint owner with the ISBA and the IPA of the Poster Audit Bureau Ltd which monitors outdoor advertising campaigns to assure advertisers that their displays were on the right panels, at the right time and were maintained in a good condition.

The OAA represents media owners on the Joint Industry Committee for Poster Audience Research (JICPAR), and funds the classification and audience measurement of all poster panels belonging to participating companies.

PERIODICAL PUBLISHERS' ASSOCIATION LTD, Imperial House, Kingsway, London WC2B 6UN. Telephone: 01-379 6268. Founded 1913.

This organisation represents both kinds of periodicals—the general magazines which usually have bookstall sales, and the business and professional press which are sometimes sold on bookstalls but more frequently are distributed by post, either by subscription or by the controlled circulation method. There are some 140 member companies publishing nearly 2,000 titles and representing about 80 per cent of the total magazine market. Each year the PPA makes its Award for Editorial Excellence, open to non-members. This is the major award scheme for magazines.

More than 700 advertising agencies are recognised.

Aims

The overriding aim of the PPA is to co-ordinate, initiate and participate in co-operative work, in order to assist the profitable development of all members, protect their interests, and safeguard the freedom and well-being of the periodical press. In particular:

   (i) To provide information and advice, and to promote opportunities for members to discuss matters of joint interest.

  (ii) To maintain beneficial relationships with organisations concerned with any aspect of periodical publishing.

 (iii) To watch developments in Parliament and Government departments, and national organisations and, when necessary, to act on behalf of the interests of members.

 (iv) To influence the development and maintenance of uniform business and ethical standards and the economic effectiveness of advertising.

  (v) To maintain a system of agency recognition involving supervision of credit standing and payment of accounts.

 (vi) To help to secure for periodicals an increasing share of advertising budgets, nationally and internationally, by promoting to advertisers and agencies the collective claims of periodicals.

(vii) To encourage high and uniform standards of market and media research, auditing procedures and information presentation.

(viii) To achieve the most cost-effective distribution arrangements by post, rail, road and air at home and abroad.

 (ix) To assist members to achieve maximum sales through wholesale, retail, or subscription channels at home or abroad. To promote nationally and internationally the information and entertainment benefits of periodicals to readers.

  (x) To explore and assist in the provision of services, where it is advantageous for these to be provided co-operatively by the PPA rather than by individual members.

 (xi) To achieve maximum desirable membership for the PPA.

The repeated references to **overseas sales** are a noticeable feature of these aims. British periodicals are important exports, and they are important media for British exporters. British technical journals vie with American ones as world authorities on their topics.

PUBLIC RELATIONS CONSULTANTS ASSOCIATION, 37 Cadogan Street, Sloane Square, London SW3 2PR. Telephone: 01-581 3951 and 01-581 8023. Founded 1969.

The Public Relations Consultants Association is a trade association formed to encourage and promote the advancement of companies and firms engaged in public relations consultancy, and its members are bound by the Association's Code of Practice.

Objectives

To raise and maintain professional standards in consultancy practice.

To provide facilities for Government, public bodies, associations representing industry, trade and others to confer with public relations consultants as a body and to ascertain their collective views.

To promote confidence in public relations consultancy and, consequently, in public relations as a whole, and to act as 'spokesman' for consultancy practice.

The PRCA supports, and maintains a close fraternal relationship with the Institute of Public Relations.

Activities

The PRCA has a regular programme of activities, issues publications, carries out research into consultancy practice and usage, informs and assists its members and generally promotes the use of public relations consultancy to outside organisations.

Its professional practices, consultancy management, membership and education and training committees meet regularly.

Functions

There is a main annual conference, and other occasional conferences on other subjects. Seminars in London and the regions are held on topics of relevance. Discussion evenings include a wide range of activities related to public relations for management and their staff. There is an annual dinner with guest speakers of high standing. The PRCA participates in external conferences and meetings such as those organised by the IPR, IPRA and CAM. Constant liaison is maintained with bodies such as the CBI, Institute of Directors and Institute of Management.

Publications

The Public Relations Year Book, published annually by the Financial Times Business Publishing Ltd, includes detailed profiles on all member consultancies; *PRCA News* (monthly newsletter for members); guidance papers cover all aspects of consultancy practice and are issued and revised regularly. Booklets include *Public Relations and the Chief Executive* and *Selecting a Public Relations Consultancy*. Sets of case studies are also published.

Education

The PRCA is a full member of the Communication, Advertising and Marketing Education Foundation and through its co-operation with CAM is actively concerned with recruitment, training and education for PR consultancy personnel.

Research

Regular research is carried out and the results are published. The Association has also undertaken research into the use of PR in various sectors and on corporate social responsibility.

THE REGIONAL NEWSPAPER ADVERTISING BUREAU LTD, Grosvenor House, 141–143 Drury Lane, London WC2B 5TD. Telephone: 01-836 8251. Founded 1980.

The Regional Newspaper Advertising Bureau was formed in April 1980 as a result of a merger between the Evening and Weekly Newspaper Advertising Bureaux. The Bureau is financed by subscriptions from member newspapers and governed by a board of directors elected from its membership, which accounts for about 80 per cent of all regional newspapers—evening, weekly, morning and Sunday.

Aims

Its principal aim is to provide advertisers and agencies with information and services which they need in order to use the regional press as an advertising medium in any part of Great Britain, Northern Ireland, the Isle of Man and the Channel Islands.

To achieve this aim the Bureau presents the case for using the regional press to advertisers and agencies, and makes a considerable investment in market and data sources. It has a computerised data base with all aspects of the regional press on it, particularly rate, production and circulation data in great detail plus census information on Newspaper Marketing Areas. RNAB offers a scheduling service, and a full central booking copy and billing service. It also has a comprehensive co-operative advertising service which co-ordinates schemes both for suppliers and retailers.

Publications include *Regional Extra*, a quarterly newspaper about developments in the regional press, and a number of leaflets on colour advertising, co-operative advertising and other topics.

RNAB also organises group and individual readership surveys and maintains details about all research which concerns the regional press.

VERIFIED FREE DISTRIBUTION, 13 Wimpole Street, London W1M 7AB. Telephone: 01-631 1343. Founded 1981.

To deal with the increasing number of free publications now available in the UK, the Audit Bureau of Circulations launched a subsidiary company in 1981, Verified Free Distribution, (VFD) to certify the distributions of free publications delivered to households or available from bulk supplies. Delivered copies (newspapers, magazines and directories) receive VFD certification, bulk supplies (copies available in hotels, airlines, retail stores) receive BVS (Bulk Verification Services) certification.

VIDEOTEX INDUSTRY ASSOCIATION LTD, 1 Chapel Court, Borough High Street, London SE1 1HH. Telephone: 01-407 0270. Founded 1978.

Formed originally in 1978 as the Association of Viewdata Information Providers (AVIP), the Videotex Industry Association evolved in 1982 to identify, promote and support the broader interests of all sections of the UK Viewdata and teletext industry. As the industry grows the role of VIA expands, and its services are growing to encompass the needs of a wide-ranging membership.

These needs and the subsequent policies and activities of VIA are controlled and directed by the members through an elected Council. A team of full-time officers headed by a chief executive implement Council policies.

One of VIA's prime objectives is to act as an authoritative interface between Government Departments and other bodies, and the Industry. This has led to VIA being awarded Government contracts to promote and provide services to the industry related to export markets.

Member Services

Code of Practice. The VIA produces and administers for the industry a self-regulatory Code of Practice for Information Providers. This Code is endorsed by Prestel and to which their IPs are contractually committed.

Information. News and comment on the fast-moving and often confusing videotex scene is covered by the monthly publications, *VIA News* and *World System News*. On Prestel, *Update 808*, is the VIA's continuously updated news service about the world videotex scene. Books and pamphlets are published, and these are available free or at special prices to members, e.g. *UK Videotex Industry Directory*.

A Videotex Industry Information Service monitors the media for items of relevance to the UK videotex industry, and collects and disseminates information on all aspects of private and public Viewdata and teletext.

Conferences

A key part of the Association's activities are conferences, seminars and workshops.

6
Business and Other Users of Advertising

How is advertising applied to different kinds of business organisation? What other types of organisation use advertising? Do some tend to use public relations techniques rather than advertising?

First of all, what do we mean by a **business organisation?** Broadly speaking, there are two main groups of undertaking, those run by private enterprise and those which are subject to public control. Within these two big groups fall the following special kinds of organisation:

PRIVATE ENTERPRISE BUSINESS ORGANISATIONS

One-man businesses or sole traders.
Partnerships, including limited partnerships.
Private limited companies.
Public limited companies (now referred to as PLC, not Ltd).
Multi- or supra-national companies.
Co-operative societies.

BUSINESSES UNDER PUBLIC CONTROL

Government departments.
Nationalised industries and public authorities.
Public utilities.
Local authorities.
Social services.

A more detailed breakdown can now be given of the businesses in the private enterprise sector.

6.1   Private Enterprise Business Organisations

Sole Traders

These include small tradesmen, craftsmen and professional men and women, shopkeepers, contractors, accountants, consultants and so on.

The trading area of the **sole trader** may be geographically restricted because of the location of his shop, but that is so only if the shop attracts custom from only a limited area, or 'threshold'. A neighbourhood shop falls into that category, but nowadays with out-of-town discount stores and supermarkets we have to be careful how a local shop is defined. But a shop in a market town, or in a major shopping centre for a county or region, will have a threshold of many thousands of visiting shoppers. The neighbourhood shopkeeper must rely on window displays, door-to-door leaflet distribution, the telephone and perhaps an advertisement in a local tenants' association magazine. By contrast, the shop with a substantial clientèle from surrounding neighbourhoods can use the local newspapers, posters, transportation, cinema and the broadcast media. This shopkeeper may still be a sole trader such as café proprietor, bookseller, radio dealer, pet shop or tailor.

Now, supposing he can also sell by post? Or supposing there is not enough local or regional trade? This could apply to a dealer in foreign stamps, coins, antiques, pictures or first editions. There are also mail order traders who deal entirely from home, an office or warehouse and have no retail premises at all. In fact, it is quite extraordinary what is marketed in this way: ladies' exotic underwear may be seen advertised in newspapers published hundreds of miles away from the trader's address which appears to be a private house. Similarly, distributors of contraceptives advertise in free sheet local newspapers issued in towns some distance from the source of supply. It is not merely shyness that makes people buy intimate products by post for they also enjoy the convenience of shopping from their armchairs.

Sole traders, small though they may be, can nevertheless exploit advertising as the principal means of doing business. Whether they sell second-hand cars, have a drive-in garden centre or operate a private detective agency, advertising links them with their markets. Much of their trading skill depends on clever and diligent use of advertising, and this cleverness relates to media planning and scrupulous budgeting just as much as to creative ideas. Often, there is very little creativity, advertisements being paper set or run-on as classifieds.

Partnerships

Similar remarks apply to partnerships except where professional rules forbid advertising or specify the form in which announcements may appear, as with the display of architects' names while building work is in progress, or 'business card' advertisements in directory-style features. Doctors and dentists are bound by professional strictures and are limited to name-plates or their names on doors or windows. Estate agents and auctioneers must obviously advertise their client's properties and so attract buyers, and they are regular users of poster, press and direct mail advertising.

Private and Public Companies

Private companies are usually family businesses where the principal shareholding is in the hands of one person or a small group of individuals. The reason for this is probably that, apart from the personal interests, large capital is not required. But when money is wanted for development, or when the business is so successful that it pays to sell shares to the public, the company may 'go public'. Following a share issue, with the usual double-page advertisements in the *Financial Times* and *The Times* setting out the prospectus with its company history and trading prospects, the shares become 'quoted' on the Stock Exchange and may be purchased by anyone. This does not mean that all the shares are freely available on the market, otherwise there would be more take-overs than there are, and so large blocks of shares usually remain with some large shareholders. However, because of the broader spread of share ownership the board of management is usually less dominated by family or entrepreneur interests, and it is less easy for individuals to possess a majority shareholding, except when a take-over bid occurs and a majority holding is sought in order to gain control of the company.

Thus, public limited companies—those quoted on the Stock Exchange—are usually larger and consequently liable to grow larger through amalgamation or acquisition. The tendency is for companies to link together in amalgamations or groups, either horizontally where like businesses join together or vertically where a company makes itself self-sufficient by owning sources of raw materials and supplies. Combines may be headed by holding companies which own shares in subsidiaries. There are also holding companies that own a variety of companies which operate in their own names.

Most of the motor-car giants are **horizontal** companies, owning companies which make different kinds of vehicles. A food company which owned its own plantations overseas, its own shipping, and all the means of processing, packing and distributing would be a **vertical** company. A company which owned hotels, dairies, a furniture factory, an airline and a plastics factory would be a **holding** company or a **conglomerate**.

Multinational or Supra-national Companies

These international organisations are familiar in the fields of chemicals, foods and electronics, to mention only Unilever, IBM, ITT, Philips, General Motors, Coca-Cola, General Foods and Air Products. They straddle continents with international businesses. The computer and office equipment firm, IBM, has a series of factories in Europe, each of which produces at least one complete piece of equipment and also produces components for all the others.

Co-operatives

These fall into two groups. There are the 'Rochdale Pioneers' type which are owned by the members on the principle of sharing profits according to the value of purchases, the retail co-operatives having adopted savings stamps in place of the 'divi'. Then there are the agricultural co-operatives which offer farmer-members privileges in buying stock, machinery and supplies, and assistance with the marketing of produce. The London Co-operative Society belongs to the first type (supported by productive, wholesaling, banking and insurance societies), while SCATS (Southern Counties Agricultural Trading Society) is representative of the second.

Co-partnerships

These offer profit-sharing to employees, an idea frequently canvassed by the Liberal Party. Kalamazoo, the Birmingham business systems firm, is a co-partnership. So is the John Lewis Partnership.

6.2 Businesses Under Public Control

Government Departments

Government departments conduct the Government's business and while this may not be commercial—that is, conducted at a profit—the policies, actions, schemes and facilities of the Government (as distinct from party politics) do have to be 'sold' to the electorate. Occasionally, an item may actually be sold at a profit, as in the case of the *Highway Code*, but generally speaking the Government is not 'in business'. Publicising Government services and activities calls for the commercial techniques of advertising in order to make known or promote premium bonds, rent rebates, new NHI contributions and benefits, road safety, training schemes for nurses, plus all the hundreds of official appointments handled by the Central Office of Information, Civil Service Commission and other official agencies.

The advertising of official appointments has grown with the expansion in Government activities such as Mr Gladstone's introduction of competitive entry to the Civil Service. White's, London's oldest advertising agency, was involved in producing publicity for Government lotteries about 1800. Charles Lamb was the copywriter! For the first 120 years of its existence, White's was the sole advertising agent for the War Office, Admiralty, HM Commissioner of Prisons, and it also handled the Colonial Office and the Crown Agents. Eventually much of this work was lost to other agencies when it was put out to tender but Whites Bull Holmes (now part of Lopex) still handles advertising for the Crown Agents and in postwar years has increased its work for local authorities.

The Central Office of Information, which has its own creative departments, acts as a huge group advertising department for the various Government departments. Just as the advertising department in a commercial group puts out much of the work to advertising agencies, so does the COI.

Public Authorities—Nationalised Industries—Public Utilities

Labour and Conservative Governments have differing views on whether publicly owned businesses should make a profit, that is to say compete with private enterprise. Ironically, Labour tends to expect a nationalised industry to serve the public interest in a profitable fashion, whereas more recent Conservative Party policies have seen nationalisation as something for unprofitable industries which need to be run in the public interest. There are certain political contradictions which make it very difficult for those trying to run public authorities. Appointed by the Conservatives, Labour's Lord Robens showed that the National Coal Board could make a profit. Similarly, Lord Beeching showed the Conservatives how to rationalise the railways but he was unacceptable to the succeeding Labour Government. By contrast, Rear-Admiral Slattery, as BOAC's chairman, challenged a Conservative Government to decide whether it wanted a profitable airline or merely a flag-carrier. Conservative Government policy in the 80's has been to hive off profitable sections of nationalised industries, or to sell shares to the public, e.g. Cable and Wireless. In the circumstances of continual conflict, the promotion of public enterprise must be a joyless task.

Nevertheless, public authorities and public utilities are in business, whether they be airlines, railways, road haulage, airports, seaports, or steel, gas, electricity, coal, sugar, and the postal services. Often they not only have to pay their way but repay Government loans. Consequently, they have to operate as efficiently as private enterprise: why should the taxpayer have to subsidise losses? In the public interest—sometimes in the interest of overseas prestige, defence or export trade—these industries may be subsidised by writing off losses or by favourable financing facilities which would not be available to privately owned concerns. Whether the efficiency mentioned above is to be measured by performance or profit is something the taxpayer and the politician may argue about.

The fact is, however, that the state airline British Airways uses advertising like any commercial firm, and does so exceedingly well. British Airways has earned praise for the beauty of its aerial photography in TV commercials, and it has excelled with striking bulletin board outdoor advertisements. British Rail has vigorously promoted both its Inter-City express trains and its Sealink car ferry services. Recruitment advertising for the Armed Services and Police has been lively and original. British Steel has shown us new uses for steel. British Transport Docks Board and the Port of London Authority have used advertising to pioneer the new container ports. And the Electricity Council and individual electricity boards, and the British Gas Corporation, have made expert use of advertising to sell their fuels, products and services.

All in all, state advertising forms a very large proportion of national advertising expenditure, and those who are liable to criticise advertising should remind themselves that they are, as members of a democratic society, just as much involved in advertising as any big businessman.

Local Government

Local government advertising depends on the type of authority, whether it has any trading departments, and also whether it needs to attract outsiders to occupy offices and factories, or as residents, tourists and holiday visitors. There are five broad reasons why a local authority is likely to engage in advertising:

(i) To attract applicants for jobs.
(ii) To attract trade for:
    (*a*) its own enterprises
    (*b*) the town's private enterprises.

(iii) To attract investments.
(iv) To attract residents.
 (v) To attract industry and commerce.

All kinds of staff from town clerks to temporary snow clearers are sought by advertisements. In fact, a local authority has a constitutional duty to make public announcements. Advertising is also used to raise funds for LA projects. Some authorities have special trading activities which require promotion, and these may be a bus service, a civic airport, or catering facilities. Some authorities are of historic interest, others are spas or resorts, and advertising may have to compete with that of packaged tours abroad. In Blackpool the transport department has sponsored the famous illuminations to promote passenger traffic which in turn has given the resort a late season attraction. Other towns seek residents, while still more seek tenants for office blocks and factory estates.

Advertising is therefore a valuable aid to hundreds of LA's, although some of them are slow to appreciate that it is a specialist function requiring a suitably competent official. Surprisingly there are still large authorities with populations of a quarter million or more which do not have a PRO or publicity manager, bits of jobs being scattered among other officials as different as the entertainments manager and the mayor's secretary.

One usually finds that a Conservative-dominated council resists such appointments whereas the opposite is true where Labour holds the majority. For many years the London County Council and then the Greater London Council was dominated by Labour—with Herbert Morrison as its revered architect—and it maintained a large publicity and information section. When control fell to the Conservatives the election promise was to cut the publicity and PR services. In the event they were found too vital and valuable to tamper with, for the incoming council had to explain its new policies and actions to the people of London, especially in connection with housing, education and roads.

In local Government it is not sufficient merely to appoint an ex-journalist to act as an information officer, working mainly between the council and its committees and the press. One of two types of qualified person is required, either a PRO to communicate local Government services to its various publics or a publicity manager to promote trading services or the town's attractions. Most seaside resorts are well served by able publicity officers, but certain other inland authorities have been reluctant to spend ratepayers' money on communication services.

There is, however, one area where PROs and publicity officers have been found essential and this in the *development corporation*.

Social Services

Under this very broad heading there are educational, hospital, ambulance, fire, police and other public services which use advertising for recruitment, enrolment or educational purposes. Universities, polytechnics and technical colleges make dual use of advertising to attract both teachers and students. The police and the fire services are making increasing use of PR techniques, one of the most successful being the BBC's *Crimewatch UK* television programme.

From this analysis of users of advertising it is clear that not all of them are industrial or commercial concerns run by private enterprise, and that some non-commercial organisations are nevertheless concerned with trade. After all, HMSO bookshops are excellent suppliers of maps, books, brochures, magazines and picture postcards quite apart from statutes, white papers, green papers and blue books. We have already referred to the *Highway Code*, a best-seller running into millions of copies and retailed like a paperback novel.

Since we have thought it necessary to touch on a few aspects of PR in this book—and this was inevitable when commenting on public services—this is an appropriate place in which to explain that one of the reasons why PR is a subject bigger and even more complex than advertising is its use by every kind of non-commercial organisation. These bodies may use a little advertising but only for limited purposes such as recruiting staff, announcing statutory or constitutional obligations, promoting events or publications, or when seeking members or donors. Much of their communication work is informative rather than persuasive, employing PR instead of advertising techniques.

The following organisations, therefore, may use mainly PR techniques:

Government departments
Royal commissions
Professional societies
Trade associations
Employers' federations
Trade unions
Public utilities
Charities, benevolent societies
Special interest voluntary
    associations
Sports clubs
Local authorities
Youth organisations
Religious organisations
Universities and colleges of
    further education
Friendly societies and contributory health schemes
Police forces
The Army
The Navy
The Royal Air Force
Fire brigades
Hospitals and clinics

Part 2: The Advertising Sextet

7
The Advertiser, Advertising Manager and Advertising Department

In Chapter 5 there were several references to tripartite operations which united the three main sides of advertising—advertisers, advertising agents and media owners—but in Chapter 4 we showed that there are three additional sides—that part of PR which is linked with advertising, the numerous ancillary services upon which advertising depends, and freelance services. In this second part of the book we shall devote a chapter to PR—but merely as an introduction to its administration—and a chapter on ancillary and freelance services.

This part of the book, therefore, deals with the 'advertising sextet' but also includes chapters dealing with the planning of advertising expenditure and a separate chapter on the major ancillary service of market research.

7.1 The Advertiser

But for the advertiser there would be no advertising sextet. He is the tail that wags the dog. If he does not buy print, artwork, agency services, advertisement space, air time or outdoor sites and exhibition space, the advertising industry is depressed. This runs right through the economy and is a barometer of the nation's economic stability and prosperity. Some advertisers, like Cadbury and Heinz, go on for ever, but many others fail and disappear. The need for advertising varies, come boom, come recession, reflecting society. In the 80s airlines and retailers engage in fiercely competitive advertising, local breweries have returned, people shop without shops, and computers are consumer products. A curious thing about the 80s recession has been the intensity of advertising for expensive goods. The advertiser is therefore very important.

This book discusses advertising at all levels, and before going on to discuss the advertising manager and the advertising department, let us first consider that the buyer of advertising, in all its many forms, may be a sole trader, a business proprietor or executive, a branch manager or works manager, or a sales manager. In other words, he may well be an individual without an advertising department and special staff. He may be an occasional advertiser as when staff are being recruited, or he may be a regular advertiser like a local shopkeeper who takes a regular weekly space in the local press, displays posters on local buses, or takes time on local radio. He may be capable of producing his own advertisements, or he may use a

freelance copywriter and designer, or take advantage of the service department of the media. One way or another, he buys and creates advertising.

Alternatively, he may be the client of either a local or a national advertising agency—and still have no advertising department. The job of working with the agency, and of buying various ancillary services (which are
described in a separate chapter) may be that of the proprietor, a director
responsible for marketing, or of an executive who incorporates advertising
in his many tasks. The latter is often the case with marketing, commercial
and sales managers. Many industrial companies, producing only a small
amount of advertising, work in the ways so far described.

However, when advertising is a major part of the distributive function
the company will have at least an advertising manager. In some companies
the advertising manager will have a substantial department, and work will
be divided between the department and the agency. A few company departments are virtually advertising agencies and handle the entire promotional task. It is therefore impossible to be absolutely precise about the
way companies do or should conduct advertising: each company evolves
the kind of service best suited to its special business needs.

7.2 The Advertising Manager

One of the many organisations not included in Chapter 5 was the **Incorporated Advertising Management Association** whose membership consists of 'persons responsible for advertising, publicity, sales promotion,
marketing and public relations of commercial, public and other undertakings'. For the purpose of this chapter such a broad definition of 'advertising
manager' is very helpful because he may, in fact, be a business proprietor,
director or executive who has to wear several hats. He may be called
advertising or publicity manager, but equally he may be a sales or marketing manager who includes advertising as one of his duties. And it is becoming increasingly common for public relations officers (or managers),
communication managers and public affairs managers to embrace advertising. This latter development is particularly true of industrial companies
whose advertising expenditure is a minor part of the total communication
budget.

The practice ranges from an industrial/consumer servicing company like
Rentokil where, under the marketing director, the emphasis is on PR and
advertising is mostly directed towards consumer services and products, to
a mainly consumer product company like Brooke Bond Oxo where the
marketing manager directs the advertising with the assistance of brand
managers each handling two brands, the PR being the separate responsibility of the public relations manager. Guinness have separate
advertising and information departments, with advertising predominating
by far as our case study shows. British Oxygen have a public relations and
marketing services department of which advertising forms a part. The deciding factor is the *need* of the organisation. Obviously, a company which
has great need of both advertising and PR will tend to have separate departments, but if one need is greater than the other it will tend to dominate.
Advertising obviously dominates when a mass market is being sought, but

even BP and Esso have adopted a PR approach with their corporate TV commercials.

So, without confusing the issue further, this chapter will refer to the *advertising manager*, meaning the person responsible for advertising, whatever title he may happen to have in this or that organisation.

As a means of explaining in broad terms how advertising is conducted (Chapter 4) a check list for a good advertiser and agency relationship was introduced. Now we shall look more precisely at the work and duties of the advertising manager.

Main Types of Advertising Manager

Despite the proliferation of titles and 'hats', there are three distinct classifications:

(*a*) The advertising manager who is chiefly an administrator who acts in liaison with advertising agents and other outside services.

(*b*) The advertising manager who leads a creative department which may or may not use an advertising agency. Divisions of duties between department and agency will be described later.

(*c*) The brand or product manager who is responsible for the total promotion for one or more brands or, as in Reckitt Colman, for particular groups of products such as foods, household goods and pharmaceuticals.

Responsibilities of the Advertising Manager

(*a*) To work closely with those responsible for shaping future policy whether it concerns new or modified products, rationalisation or diversification, changes in distribution methods, or entry into new markets or market segments. In other words, it is unlikely that a company will go on making and selling the same product in the same old way, and the advertising manager—because of his need to plan six months or a year ahead—must have the confidence of those in the board room, drawing office or laboratory who will influence his future work. He should also be able to contribute to future developments.

He may become involved in setting up product pre-tests and test marketing exercises to decide whether the product, the marketing strategy or the advertising media and techniques are likely to be successful or are capable of improvement or amendment. This involvement in initial research may result in the abandonment of the proposed new product, and usually 50 per cent of products test-marketed never go on the market. In a large company, the advertising manager will work with marketing and market research executives: in a smaller company he will be responsible for initiating research himself.

(*b*) To interpret the company policy to advertising agents and other outside services so that their work is produced in accordance with this policy. This is a delicate operation, a matter of clear communication to others who do not have the benefit of his intimate inside knowledge gleaned over a period of time. Unless he is able to convey his company's requirements in easily understandable terms, time, money and patience can be wasted on producing unacceptable campaigns, copy, layouts, photographs, drawings, print, films, exhibition stands and so on.

(*c*) To determine the appropriation, or advertising budget, and to make allocations for different media and purposes. How this may be done is described in the next chapter which examines many different ways of arriving at the sum to be spent on advertising.

(*d*) To control expenditure. With monies spread over a diversity of campaigns, media and techniques, the advertising manager has to be a master of budgetary control.

(*e*) To co-operate with the advertising agency. This is absolutely essential, and it is a very good saying that an advertising agency is only as good as the client allows it to be. Agencies are not miracle workers. While their ingenuity must be encouraged they cannot work in a vacuum, and the advertising manager must be responsive in feeding his agency with all the facts, samples and other background material on which the agency can go to work. The advertising manager also has to remember that agency personnel are not always in direct contact with him, but have to work through departmental heads and the account executive. In the agency there are a lot of people 'down the line' who need to be helped to understand properly the account and the product or service. Works visits, invitations to sales conferences and social functions, and regular supply of the house journal can all help to foster good agency relations.

(*f*) To control the production of all other advertising material not handled by the agency. Some agencies will be asked to handle everything required by the client and at the other extreme agencies will handle only the booking of space, time and sites. The majority of service agencies will plan campaigns, do the creative work, buy or rent media, and produce and deliver the finished advertisements. They will do this for the traditional above-the-line media, these being the press, outdoor, TV, radio and cinema. Below-the-line items such as exhibitions, films, direct mail, point-of-sale, print, competitions, premium offers and other forms of sales promotion are mostly handled elsewhere, either within the advertising department or through specialists in these areas. Sometimes the agency will farm out such work to specialists, but it is more likely that the advertising manager will work with his own producers of these below-the-line items. (The distinction is between types of advertising on which agencies receive commission and those on which they do not but would have to charge a service fee for the time involved.)

(*g*) To control or undertake 'product publicity', that is press relations for his products. He may have his own press officer or use the services of a PR consultancy. If his company has a separate public relations department, he will work with this department.

(*h*) To assess the results of advertising, doing this where possible by means of (i) *keyed* replies to advertisements; (ii) conversions from enquiries to sales; (iii) shop audit results showing shares of the market held in relation to advertising expenditure; (iv) forms of recall research to determine how well members of the public read (or saw) and noted advertisements; and other methods.

These eight responsibilities indicate something of the breadth of the advertising manager's job. It calls for a liberal education, business experience and sound training in advertising. A glance at the subjects listed in Chapter 5 for the CAM Certificate and Diploma examinations will now show their relevance to the all-round knowledge required by the competent advertising manager. The cry today is for cost-effectiveness and he has to know what he is recommending, buying or criticising.

7.3 The Advertising Department

Having just considered the general responsibilities of the advertising manager we can now take a detailed look at the specific operations which fall under his direct control and thus gain a valuable insight into the working of the advertising department.

Whether the advertising manager uses an advertising agency, buys from a variety of suppliers and freelance workers or carries out on-the-spot operations in his own self-sufficient department, the following are likely to fall within his control:

(*a*) **Press advertising.** This may be divided into three kinds: (i) consumer or user—to promote sales; (ii) recruitment—to fill jobs; and (iii) trade—to sell to distributors. He will be concerned with the right choice of media, based on past results, circulation and readership data; the size, frequency and timing of insertions; copy and layout content; production costs and quality of reproduction. He will scrutinise the **media schedule** produced by the agency, questioning the merits of the chosen media and the sizes, positions and dates, and he will either accept or amend the total expenditure so that it fits in with his total appropriation. As the insertions appear, he will be vigilant to see that he gets value for money, watching to see that good or correct positions are occupied, that in the newspapers his advertisement does not suffer from 'show through' from advertisements on the reverse side, and that in gravure printed magazines correct colour reproduction is achieved. If the advertisements produce replies these will be counted and charted to record and check results from different publications, on different dates, in different positions, or with different copy. He will work closely with the agency, complaining or praising, providing essential reactions, results and information so that the agency can perform proficiently.

(*b*) **Outdoor advertising.** Similarly, the advertising manager will work either with the agency or with contractors to secure the most suitable sites, and he will have to approve bookings, designs and printings.

(*c*) **Television advertising.** Here he will be interested in six aspects of the medium: (i) the selection of TV areas; (ii) approval of the storyboard(s) for prospective commercials; (iii) the air time schedule; (iv) viewing the finished film or video tape; (v) making sure that as a result of audience ratings he has achieved satisfactory viewing; (vi) the effects on sales as revealed by continuous research techniques such as consumer panels or shop audits. He will also be able to view the commercials critically in his own home and see how they compare with others shown at the same time. Moreover, since this is such a universal medium, he will be made very conscious of what those close to him think of his advertising!

(*d*) **Radio advertising.** While there are obvious similarities between his associations with TV and radio advertising, there is one big difference (apart from lack of vision) and that is cost. If a sponsored show is broadcast, the cost of artists' fees and production can be high; if it is a vocal spot or a disc jockey show the cost can be low. If, in illiterate countries, radio is used, it must be remembered that in a vocal society speech must be apt and to the point. British independent local radio offers commercial breaks like TV, and it may pay a vigilant advertising manager to listen in and note the ingenuity of radio commercials.

(*e*) **Cinema advertising.** For advertisers in the UK this regrettably dwindling medium may have special uses as described in Chapter 22. He will need to appreciate its special values in certain areas, such as audiences on cruise ships, while in developing countries the mobile cinema is an important medium. If he is using TV he will find a double use for his expensive colour film sessions.

(*f*) **Direct mail.** He may use the services of a direct mail house, or be organised to create, print and despatch his own mailings. This will depend on the frequency with which he uses the medium, and the economies involved. A mail order trader, needing instant control of his promotion, will probably handle everything himself, building his own mailing lists from resources such as enquiries and orders. The distinction should be made here between mail order as a form of retail distribution and direct mail as an advertising medium. It is easy to confuse the two, but a mail order trader or direct response marketer may not necessarily use direct mail, and direct mail may not necessarily seek to sell things by post.

(*g*) **Exhibitions.** He will be responsible for knowing what exhibitions will be held at home and abroad, and for recommending those in which his company should participate. Popular shows are booked from year to year, certainly many months in advance, and he must plan sufficiently in advance to secure the most desirable sites. From then on he will be responsible for design and construction of stands, agreeing what shall be shown, and arranging supporting PR, print, samples and staff. He may also be involved in other people's exhibits. For example, those furnishing the houses in the 'village' at the *Daily Mail* Ideal Home Exhibition offer concessions to firms willing to supply materials and items.

(*h*) **Print.** While advertising agencies are equipped to design and buy print, this is often one of the major tasks of the advertising manager. He may have an inplant print shop, or deal with outside printers specialising in different classes of work. Catalogues, data sheets, price lists, instruction manuals, stuffers (leaflets that go in packs), packaging, showcards, order forms, stationery—all these and many more items may have to be designed, produced and stocked. He may also be responsible for requests and distribution for printed material. Some very large organisations sell copies of posters to collectors, or have a special department to deal with school projects, instances of each being Guinness and the British Steel Corporation.

(*i*) **Point-of-sale material.** Not all of this will be print, since it can include working models, wire stands, balloons or canvas banners. Knowledge about supplies, alternative ideas and costs together with buying skill are required here. Point-of-sale material is costly and must not be damaged in transit nor wasted because dealers are inundated with material they do not have space for. Yet products need to be displayed, and cabinets have to be devised and placed. In-store promotions need background materials. Advertising campaigns need to be supported by window bills, dummy packs or display outers from which products may be dispensed on shelf or counter. The needs vary from product to product, retail outlet to retail outlet. What is required for insurance policies will be very different from that ideal for promoting packets of soup. If the reader takes note of the display material to be seen in a confectioners, a supermarket, a hardware store, a building society office and a bank, he will see how the styles of point-of-sale material differ.

(*j*) **Sales promotion.** Here we go a stage beyond point-of-sale, and consider the special aids to promoting sales, perhaps stimulating sales of a product whose life-cycle is sagging. It involves in-store promotions and sampling demonstrations, prize contests, money-off offers, banded packs, premium offers, free gifts, cross-couponing offers, High Street redemption and charity schemes which help the retailer to sell out and restock, thus maintaining production flow and sales volume. It will be the advertising manager's job (although in big firms it may be a specialist executive who handles this work) to seek new ideas, obtain quotations for supplies, organise and supervise, whether the company runs occasional schemes or a regular series of promotions.

(*k*) **Films.** He may have to produce and distribute two kinds of film, advertising and documentary. Some may be used in public cinemas or on exhibition stands, others distributed to private audiences. Again, outside services are likely to be used unless the company has its own film unit, or the film is made by a sponsor such as the Central Office of Information for overseas use in cinemas or on TV. He will need to understand the use of films and video-tapes, the audience for whom they are intended, and be able to appreciate treatments, scripts and rushes when he is asked to approve them.

(*l*) **Trade advertising.** Keeping wholesalers, retailers and agents informed about new products, trade terms, advertising campaigns and promotional material calls for direct mail, trade press and trade PR efforts. Dealer conferences and works visits may have to be organised. Video-cassettes and Prestel pages can be important.

(*m*) **Dealer co-operative schemes.** The supply of free stereos or artwork, or part payment of advertising costs, are ways of encouraging stockists to conduct local advertising. Such facilities may be announced by trade advertising (*l*) and then undertaken as a service to stockists.

(*n*) **Showrooms and display centres.** Some companies maintain public showrooms in city centres, and it will be his job to see to their proper use, supplying display materials and perhaps organising events and special attractions. Customers may be invited to receptions, demonstrations and audio-visual shows.

(*o*) **Window-dressing services.** A number of tobacco, confectionery and toiletry firms maintain a permanent window display service, shops being visited and windows set out at regular intervals. The advertising manager will have to maintain vehicles, staff and display materials for this purpose.

(*p*) **Organising sales conferences.** Because of his organising ability, and the need for films, slides, video-tapes and artwork for presentations, the advertising manager may well be asked to help the sales and marketing executives with various internal assemblies.

(*q*) **Export advertising.** Either through the home advertising agency, or through advertising agents in overseas sales territories, and in conjunction with the export sales manager, the advertising manager will be responsible for a completely new and different range of trade and consumer/user advertising services. He will also have to deal with translators, perhaps know one or two foreign languages, and work with printers who are specialists in foreign language typesetting.

(*r*) **Sponsored events.** Many sporting events—horse races, air races, one-man yachting feats, athletics, motor races, horse jumping events, and major international events like the Olympic Games and World Cup football, need the financial support of philanthropic backers. When this can be combined with publicity and goodwill, it comes within the span of advertising and PR. Other sponsorships may embrace musical concerts, art shows, books, scholarships and research grants.

(*s*) **Press relations.** This is more properly the preserve of a fully integrated public relations department, but not every company is enlightened to that extent, and many an advertising manager—often with scant understanding of the difference between what fills the advertisement and the editorial columns—has to conduct press relations and issue news and pictures to press, radio and TV. This is more fully explained in the companion book, *Public Relations Made Simple*, by the same author.

(*t*) **House journals.** Both internal and external house journals—private magazines not issued for profit—are rightly the responsibility of the public relations department and require editing by BAIE standards. Nevertheless, in smaller firms this task may well fall to the advertising manager, or the house journal editor may be on his staff. The external house journal, addressed to dealers or to users, customers and other outside readers, is replacing the absurdly lavish external magazine, and can work very hard in promoting a company's relations with stockists, customers or users such as specifiers. A typical example is the magazine presented to airline passengers. Nowadays, many large companies not only print house journals, but produce video-tape versions for playback on VCRs and domestic television sets. The electronic newspaper is used by other firms who produce 'pages' which can be called up on television sets equipped to receive Prestel.

7.4   How Are Advertising Managers Appointed?

There may be four reasons for the choice of an advertising manager.

(*a*) His knowledge of advertising, probably gained in an advertising agency, and supported by training and professional qualification, that is the CAM Certificate or better still the CAM Diploma.

(*b*) His knowledge of the industry, gained either in the same or a similar company. This knowledge may be either advertising or technical, perhaps as a technical author.

(c) His knowledge of management procedures since he will be responsible for budgeting, budgetary control and policy interpretation.

(d) His knowledge of marketing, possibly gained on the sales side, or through marketing studies or brand manager experience. Agency experience may be helpful here once again.

Ideally, with a large advertiser, he needs to combine all these attributes. Some employers will expect a degree or at least BEC qualifications as well as professional ones. Membership of the IAMA will denote experience as an advertising manager.

It happens that when there is an excellent agency–client relationship, the client invites the agency account executive to join his staff. This can turn out to be an excellent arrangement, beneficial to both sides if the former relationship is maintained, with the advertising manager now working for the company he already knows well yet continuing to work with former agency colleagues.

But there can be danger in the situation where an agency is implicated in appointing an advertising manager for a client. Two things can go wrong. If he is an agency 'plant' he may resent his sponsorship and indebtedness, and seek a change of agency in order to regain his independence and personal integrity. Or, he may be so much in the agency's pocket that he fails to satisfy the client who wants someone more company-minded and more independent of the agency.

From these two paragraphs the value of good agency–client relations is doubly apparent, and more will be said about this in the chapter about the agency when we shall look at the Lintas survey on the decision processes in the selection of an advertising agency.

8

What Influences Advertising Costs?

8.1 Who Pays for Advertising?

Before discussing the cost of advertising and the factors which influence its cost, and before going on in the next chapter to discuss ways of arriving at a budget of advertising costs, let us face up quite frankly to the perennial question: who pays for advertising? The answer to this question is one of the keys to the determining of expenditure on advertising.

In any business there are only three people, or groups of people, who can pay for running a business and making a profit. They are the investors (and they include both the bank which permits an overdraft and the supplier who provides credit), the businessman who may use his own capital plus the income he earns, and those who buy his goods or services. If the business fails, the investors fail and in effect pay the bills through their own losses; if the business succeeds everyone profits and everyone is satisfied. Only if the businessman sells at a price higher than his costs is it possible for him to make a profit. His costs include his selling effort, which may mean renting a shop, hiring a salesman or advertising in the local newspaper (and these promotional expenses can be multiplied according to the size of the business). If he is to recover these costs *and* make a profit they can come from only one source, the customer who pays the price for the goods or services.

If the product sells easily, the cost of promoting each unit is slight. But if it is a new, a costly or a difficult product to sell, the advertising cost per unit will be high.

Assuming that products or services are sold, the cost of advertising is borne by the buyer. However, if the goods remain unsold despite monies spent on advertising, the cost of advertising reverts to the producer or distributor who has failed to make the necessary sales and so pass on or recover his costs plus a profit. Even if he sells off the goods at a reduced price, and forfeits the profit, he is still seeking to recover his costs.

This has to be said because a false idea exists that the cost of advertising is taken out of profits. There are even some businessmen who delude themselves to the extent that they speak of spending on advertising 'what they can afford', as if it were a sacrifice, donation or something they could avoid, when in fact, to make a profit, they cannot afford not to advertise— or at least adopt some form of persuasive sales-promoting action.

But this is not to say that advertising is an unjustified part of the price.

It is an old chestnut to say that a certain product costing a fraction of a penny to produce is sold at an exorbitant price of, say, ten pence. It costs a lot to distribute products, and advertising is a distribution cost. *The price of advertising may be the difference between enjoying a product and not having it at all.*

8.2 The Advertising Appropriation

An ideal advertising budget—called the **appropriation**—is one which produces the greatest result for the least expenditure. This is implied in the reference in the IPA definition to 'lowest possible cost', with the further implication that effective, economic expenditure calls for expert advice.

But it is not easy to be either ideal or expert in this business of mass sales communication. There are so many imponderables, and it would not be facetious to include the weather. A few years ago there was such a wet summer that posters on the hoardings were ruined. A vicious winter, making the transportation of fuel impossible, could lead to power cuts (as during the miners' strike in 1973) so that television advertising suffered small audiences and diminished effectiveness. Guinness once inserted an advertisement in Sunday newspapers with wording to the effect that Guinness was good for you when it was nice weather for ducks. Obligingly, that Sunday was a soaker! Strikes have robbed advertisers of editions.

Textbooks on this subject usually offer a familiar set of methods for arriving at the appropriation, but these methods tend to be academic and it is doubtful whether many advertising people consciously debate which one to apply. They may well use one or the other method because it happens to be convenient to their type of business. They may be unaware of any other way except their own. It may be rule of thumb and hit or miss, but only to a degree as we shall see. In most methods there is a blend of common sense, experience, flair and statistical evaluation.

Thanks to the data available from JICNARS, BARB, JICPAR, ABC and other reliable sources, much of the one-time gamble can be taken out of mass consumer advertising. Advertisers can thank ISBA for much of this. It is, however, rather less possible to minimise wastage with industrial advertising if traditional media are used. And it is very difficult in the case of the small or local advertiser who may have to use a disproportionate amount of advertising to achieve his objective, but again this is a matter of trial and error, experiment and good judgement. A lot depends on what you are selling to whom, and also how cleverly you exploit the resources available to you. A local shopkeeper could send out a hundred tatty duplicated sales letters and get nowhere; a more enterprising person could make one significant announcement on local radio and sell out by lunchtime.

So, before launching into an analytical study of the ways of assessing the advertising appropriation—and we shall examine a far bigger variety of ways than has ever previously appeared in an advertising textbook—let us first of all think about a general assumption. Then let us consider an actual example. After that, let us face up to the imponderables which make budgeting far from being an infallible arithmetic exercise.

A General Assumption

It is generally true that the cost of advertising per product unit is in proportion to price. The advertising per unit of, say, toothpaste is minute compared with that for a motor-car, and it costs more per unit to promote an unknown product than a well-known one. Profit margins, or 'mark ups', follow a similar pattern. All this is relative to turnover. This assumption should not be confused with the total sum spent on advertising: the toothpaste manufacturer will spend more *in total* than the motor-car manufacturer because of the difference in volume of sales represented by regular repeat purchases by a very large number of people.

An Example of an Actual Appropriation

While the following example may be untypical it does have meaning for the new advertiser whose business can grow as a result of judicious advertising.

The company in our example retailed a certain do-it-yourself product and decided to market a service for those who could not do-it-themselves either because they did not want to or the job was beyond them. As a try-out, a modest advertisement was placed in a middle-class national newspaper, and it was repeated from time to time. The new servicing department consisted of only three people, who were kept fully occupied in response to this modest advertising. Gradually, the advertising was stepped up, work flowed in, more men were engaged and trained, and branches were set up in strategic parts of the country. The whole process was like a staircase, each step being an extension of advertising resulting in an extension of business. The original retail product lent goodwill to the service, and customer satisfaction with the service produced recommendations. There is a clear element of PR here which was supported by educational activities about the nature of the work and its benefits.

Once this business was operating on a national basis, the advertising was reviewed very carefully; this was necessary, because a variety of newspapers and magazines was being used including many regional papers in support of local branches. It was possible to relate keyed replies to media, and further to evaluate business against enquiries. By this means, publications which had failed to draw profitable business were eliminated from the schedule. Thus, the appropriation moved from **what was considered necessary** to attract business (a target or task method) to **that sum which could be shown to actually produce business** (a percentage of previous turnover method).

A short list of economic media was compiled, and sufficient insertions were booked each month to produce the volume of enquiries and resultant business necessary to augment recommendations and other sources of new business and achieve the sales target for the year. The sales target itself was increased year by year, which in itself implies that it was achieved each time! The system was kept sufficiently flexible to permit deletions or additions as media also changed. And to be fair, credit must be given to management for its attention to research and development, and to its financial policy of acquisitions of other companies with additional products, techniques or services. The sales graph of this company rose like steps of stairs. Eventually, in order to finance overseas expansion, the company went public and the new issue was generously oversubscribed during the late 60s when the stock market was severely depressed. In the 80s the company's share price reflects success.

8.3 Seven Imponderables Concerning Advertising Appropriations

However prophetic the advertiser tries to be, some influences are bound to be beyond his control. The following are some examples:

(a) The variety of media.
(b) The variety of appeals.
(c) The variety of techniques.
(d) Imperfect knowledge of the market.
(e) Imperfect knowledge of the competition.
(f) Unpredictable rival promotions.
(g) Unpredictable politico-economic conditions such as inflation and unemployment, social changes, new life styles and acts of God.

There are doubtless many more imponderables but these seven are sufficient to set us thinking realistically about the handicaps to fixing budgets. Can anything be done to reduce their detrimental effect, thus helping to justify the place of advertising in the marketing mix? This consideration matters whatever the size of business, and becomes more critical as the business happens to be smaller, more specialised or more localised. By this is meant that the larger business with the larger expenditure is likely to benefit from the snowball effect of mass advertising. Those with more specialist products and markets may be faced with the dilemma that even maximum advertising expenditure in certain media—say a whole page each month in the main trade journal—may be ineffectual. The latter is a common dilemma with 'secondary suppliers', that is with firms which supply components (as in the electronics and motor-car industries) whose advertising can be quite small yet extravagant if the wrong media or tactics are employed.

This problem is worth examining before proceeding to a detailed study of the seven imponderables.

Some industrial advertisers, carefully relating advertising expenditure to potential sales, may arrive at a sum which will buy a certain number of insertions (plus production costs) in trade or technical journals. Yet that spread of advertising may be inadequate, lacking **size** of space, or **regularity** of insertion and volume of **appearance** to have worthwhile **impact** and **result**. (With large consumer campaigns the media planner will seek at least 80 per cent coverage of the market, and this is often highly unlikely with the sums usually spent on industrial advertising using traditional media.)

What are the alternatives? Different media, say print and direct mail? Possibly. It may be that traditional above-the-line advertising is too expensive to be economic in this case, and other marketing techniques have to be explored. Perhaps it will be better to use technical salesmen who can set up travelling exhibits, demonstrations and seminars for potential customers. Perhaps the more educational techniques of PR, using technical feature articles, an external house journal for specifiers and users, or a documentary film or video-tape distributed to invited audiences and taken to sales presentations to prospects, will be more economic and productive.

Looked at in this context, some—not all, of course—trade and technical press advertising may be doing no more than subsidising these journals and ensuring their existence, which may be important to the industry. But it has to be said when expenditure versus results is under the microscope that some advertising agencies, confronted by a technical or industrial account, can see no farther than press advertising.

Not surprisingly, industrial advertising tends to be handled by advertising agents not over-inhibited by the commission system, conscious of the client's value-for-money problem, and relinquishing commission-paying media and operating on a time-sheet and consultancy fee basis. Alternatively, it is handled in its entirety by skilled industrial advertising managers or, thirdly, if PR approaches are adopted, the work is handled by a PR consultancy. The commission system is explained in the next chapter.

Such moves away from traditional media (press, TV, outdoor, radio and cinema) have also been made by firms selling to the mass consumer market as may be observed by the extensive use of premium offers, banded offers, free gifts, contests, money-off offers, sampling and other sales promotion schemes.

Now let us look at the seven imponderables:

(*a*) **The Variety of Media.**—Any advertiser is faced with an incredible choice of media. With their media planning and buying expertise, this is where advertising agents come into their own, and their services may be engaged for this reason alone. Britain is favoured by a large national and regional press with journals covering every specialist interest. More than that, the press is an ever-changing medium which has to be known and understood. But for the small trader, whose volume of advertising may not yet justify use of an agent, the variety of media may be bewildering. The proliferation of media, and advertising propositions put up by plausible salesmen, not only encourages profitless spending but the scattering of advertising over too many different media too thinly to be effective. *Benn's Press Directory* lists 10,000 UK publications.

A common sense approach to media selection can be gained by noting that national campaigns are mostly restricted to a **small, carefully chosen group of complementary media.** The consumer may first see the product on TV, then see local stockists advertising in the local press, and finally spot point-of-sale material in a shop window. A media sequence is thus achieved, and an example of this particular sequence is the building society which advertises in the national press and on TV, promotes its branches in local newspapers, and makes good use of branch premises and window display material.

In the place of TV another advertiser may use the press or posters. And choices may be made within the great variety of press media—say, between national newspapers, general magazines and women's magazines. Or a combination of TV and poster (very popular with brewers) or press and poster (as with cigarette firms) may be used. Weight and concentration of advertising is preferable to placing advertisements here, there and everywhere.

The small trader, with his limited budget, will do better by placing an advertisement in the same place regularly so that maximum impact is achieved. This may be on the backs of local buses, or in the local newspaper, or on local broadcast media. Consistency pays. With this discipline, the temptation to indulge in useless and wasteful advertising is trounced.

There are rare exceptions when **saturation advertising** may be adopted by the very largest mass-consumer market advertiser, although it is more usual for them to alternate between primary media. It is interesting to watch the tactics of big advertising. Commercial TV has attracted a greater variety of advertisers in recent years including expensive rather than mass market items, for instance, perfumes, airlines, motor-cars and computers. With the banning of cigarette advertising from ITV, the hoardings have become a major medium in conjunction with whole-page full-colour ads in the national press.

The chapters on media in Parts 3 and 4 will help to distinguish between the special values of each medium, but the small trader also has to contend with classes of media which seldom concern the big advertiser.

Media to be Avoided by the Small Trader

(i) Unknown directories of doubtful distribution, some of which are never published.

(ii) Guide books and maps of doubtful distribution, especially those with contracts extending over several years or editions with no opportunity to change the copy.

(iii) Blackmail requests to advertise in souvenir brochures or newspaper features as a supplier or sub-contractor, unless such advertising support promises to be truly beneficial.

But having uttered these warnings, there is still a multiplicity of media which can be valuable to *some* traders, to mention only programmes, menu covers, telephone directories, litter-bins, display panels in post offices, local magazines, street maps, timetables, delivery vans, deck chairs, taxis—in fact, anything with a vacant space capable of being filled with advertising! Each needs to be approached on a strict cost–benefit analysis. A lot of penetrating questions need to be asked, for the innocent trader will be bombarded with wondrous advertising propositions. He may even be tempted to claim a discount on an invoice for an advertisement that he has never ordered, this being a particular form of the 'directory racket'. He should certainly instruct all staff that only he books advertisements, and that no one must sign any forms, not even to say that a *directory entry* is correct!

As a quick guide, it is fair to say that one gets what one pays for. The dearest medium fetches its price because of the audience it commands. So, although we may be confronted by what appears to be a bewildering array of media, many of them are irrelevant if we have a specific market clearly in mind. London cinemas have used the London Underground in this way.

(*b*) **The Variety of Appeals.** It is said that, if asked, six different advertising agencies could put up six different advertisements for the same product, and all would be good. This is true.

Let us take a central heating system and try to think of six different appeals.

(i) The boiler is so well lagged that there is no heat loss and all the heat is transferred to the radiators.

(ii) It uses the cheapest fuel.

(iii) Installation is easy, cheap and causes little disturbance.

(iv) In the summer it can be converted into an air-cooling system.

(v) There is a low-interest hire-purchase system of payment.

(vi) The heating units in each room are unobtrusive, e.g. underfloor or skirting.

Or an ice cream may be taken as another example:

(i) Entirely new flavours.

(ii) Does not melt so quickly in hot weather.

(iii) Special packs for table use as sweets.

(iv) Premium offer.

(v) Money-off offer.

(vi) Big prize competition.

Which appeal shall we use, bearing in mind that we are in competition with other firms? We need to be different, original, compelling and competitive.

We may have to use some form of research to find out—a consumer panel, copy-testing or test marketing.

And if we take some of the psychological appeals which can be introduced into copy and presentation, we can start with the instincts and the emotions, or the biological and social drives, and find a whole range of appeals. Those already discussed are in line with Rosser Reeves' **unique selling proposition** where the appeal is directed through some special plus quality in the product. The USP has been superseded by the concept of emotional buying triggers, the appeal being made to biological and social (inherited and learned) social drives, the modern psychologist's version of McDougall's instincts, emotions and sentiments. Other appeals are based on the findings of motivational research which searches, usually, by means of clinical tests or group discussion techniques, for hidden, unknown buying motives.

From this brief sketch it is possible to see that choice of appeal is an imponderable at the outset of budgeting, since it can influence media choice, volume of advertising and its effectiveness. Some advertising appeals have seemed right to their creators, only to prove a costly flop in practice. **The appropriation may have to include the cost of research to discover the best appeal,** followed by copy-testing, and ultimately other research such as reading and noting tests to test the reaction after the ad has appeared. Dealer audit or consumer panel research may be used to test the share of the market achieved or the kind of people who are buying the product in what quantities how often.

Selecting the right appeal can be a means of reducing the volume and therefore the cost of advertising necessary to achieve the sales target. Research to this end is therefore a good investment. Weight of advertising is not everything. Of course, it goes without saying that few things help cut the cost of advertising so much as a good product, or a good reputation. Rentokil spends remarkably little on advertising because 60 per cent of the business comes by way of recommendation. When goodwill is high—and that is PR working at full throttle—little advertising expenditure may be necessary, Marks & Spencer being the supreme example of this even if their stores are colossal self-advertisements.

(*c*) **The Variety of Techniques.** We are discussing a business which offers a truly amazing abundance of techniques. We can write, draw, print, photograph, film, act, speak, animate, sing, illuminate, reflect and—in the last resort—go so far as to subliminate our message. (Subliminal advertising—showing a few moving pictures which register on the mind without being accepted by the eye—is illegal in the UK, *Independent Broadcasting Authority Act, 1974*.) The advertising practitioner is able to choose by elimination, or by his ability to combine several techniques within one medium. For example:

Press—direct-mail—poster: writing, drawing, photography, printing.
Radio: writing, acting, speech, sound effects, music.
TV—cinema: writing, acting, speech, sound effects, music, movement, cartoon, film.
Newscaster: writing, movement, illumination.

It may be decided that a particular technique is essential, and this will determine not only the medium but either the cost or what we can get for a given sum of money. Some media achieve a purpose better than others. TV is clearly excellent if a product demands visual presentation, and more so if it is demonstrable. Detergents score here.

(*d*) **Imperfect Knowledge of the Market.** Market research, and test marketing, can reduce uncertainty about the market, but the majority of new products still fail to succeed, and even successful products suffer from the whims of fashion or are the victims of **product life-cycles**. (A motor-car, for example, usually has a life-cycle of ten years and large-scale production is generally based on that assumption.) There are few certainties about markets. The bottom can drop out of any market, as with fashionwear where production is necessarily on a cautious scale. No manufacturer can control his product's destiny absolutely. Conversely, products with no apparently exceptional merit can sometimes rocket to record sales because of a fad, as when it is taken up by a popular personality. The Anthony Eden hat was an example in the 30s although no one seemed to copy Harold Wilson's raincoat in the 60s! The Royal Family tended to make corgi dogs popular, and Beatle hair styles had their vogue. And when the Prince of Wales started going hatless in the 30s, hat manufacturers got very worried. Today, Princess Diana inspires hairstyles, hats and fashions.

The businessman has two alternatives:

(i) He can start cautiously, reinvesting his profits and growing bit by bit like the firm in our example on pages 108–9.

(ii) He can plan sales and production at an optimum level and invest in an immediate conquest of a viable market.

The first method is suitable for a labour intensive service company where the greatest investment is in human skill, but where the investment has to be in capital intensive tooling, research, machinery and materials the business must begin with a certain take-up of production followed by a sustained demand. A variation on the first method is where the product is first of all sold in a **zoned market**, and is then extended to adjacent markets until eventually the national and later on export markets are developed. An example of this was St. Ivel *Gold*, first launched in Wales and the West.

Imperfect knowledge of the market tends to invite a 'suck it and see' policy which seems oddly unbusinesslike in these days of computerised marketing techniques, yet it is astonishingly common to highly successful businesses as diverse as Cyprus sherry shippers, double-glazing manufacturers, unit trust managers and kitchen furniture makers.

The **zoning method**, mentioned above, is certainly one way in which a rational approach can be made to an unpredictable new market. Zoning, that is selling to a confined geographical or distribution area, and then gradually expanding to a larger area, has been made possible by the incidence of powerful regional media—press, outdoor, broadcasting—so that it is not necessary to launch products in daily newspapers or weekly and monthly magazines. In this convenient fashion, a manufacturer can concentrate advertising, sales, warehousing, delivery and distribution and gain from all the economies which must result if all his lines of communication are comparatively short and inexpensive.

In a region such as the south of England, where Television South transmits from two locations, one in Kent and the other in the Isle of Wight, it is possible to take East Sussex and Kent as one zone or West Sussex and Hampshire as another. Mosaic Cyprus Sherry made its début with a modest launch on the original Southern Television from the Dover transmitter.

With the 42 stations of independent local radio it is possible to use this economical medium for zoned campaigns. Radio stations cover smaller areas than TV regions while having the advantage of low production costs which are ideal for an experimental or localised campaign. Moreover, the radio may succeed in reaching a large local audience more economically than local press advertising.

(*e*) **Imperfect Knowledge of the Competition.** Although it is possible to gauge the performance of competitors' products by subscribing to dealer audit surveys which give regular market share rankings for competing brands of popular commodities, and by studying the published analyses of the month-by-month advertising expenditures and promotional schemes of rival advertisers, much remains a mystery about competitive activities.

For instance, a campaign may be planned in total ignorance that one's chief competitor is planning a bigger and better one, or that a product is about to be launched that will make yours obsolete or redundant. The budget that seemed a perfect calculation could prove to be the miscalculation of all time. Perhaps this is why new motor-cars are no longer timed for the Motor Show.

But this is the gamble of the entrepreneur and the nature of capitalism.

Knowledge of competition must be imperfect in a free economy, except where it has been eliminated by monopoly, and the only true monopoly is a nationalised industry like coal, gas or electricity, and even then these are rival fuels! In these circumstances one has to aim to capture a realistic proportion of the market. A new soft drink set out to gain 12½ per cent of a zoned market. In an overcrowded market that objective seemed ambitious, but the firm justified its estimate of the quality appeal of the product. In the event, they took 15 per cent, and went on to become a national brand leader.

(*f*) **Unpredictable Rival Promotions.** In the 'below-the-line' battle of premium offers and cross-couponing, sales promotion resembles all-in wrestling. Perhaps this is why some companies adopt one of the following tactics:

(i) They cut traditional advertising in favour of sales promotion.
(ii) They have permanent schemes such as picture cards, trading stamps, gift coupons or premium offers that call for long periods of collecting as with table-ware and crockery.
(iii) They have a continuous series of six weekly promotions.

Food producers—e.g. Eden Vale, McVitie—are among the most consistent users of 'below-the-line' tactics, with teas and coffees not far behind. To these must be added the uses of regular devices such as reusable containers or returnable bottles which encourage repurchase as with beers and soft drinks.

With sales promotion schemes care has to be taken to avoid either disappointment through delay in sending premium goods, or because demand exceeds supply and credit tokens are substituted. Some schemes have proved costly to advertisers who failed to forecast demand for an offer, and in honouring the response had to exceed their budget.

The problem here is how to evolve an outstanding promotion and to support it thoroughly, the classic example of this being the Esso Tiger campaign, which was a mixture of traditional advertising, point-of-sale display, gimmickry, give-aways and actual sales of 'tiger tails', and there was even a book written about it.

(*g*) **Unpredictable Politico-economic Conditions and Other Events.** Changes in taxation, or in Government, price increases of raw materials, unfortunate climates of opinion, the results of an official investigation, war or rebellion, a Suez, Vietnam, Rhodesia or Northern Ireland, devaluation or unemployment, a Post Office or miners' strike, all such influences may be unthinkable and unpredictable when deciding on an advertising appropriation. Often, they are so untoward that allowance cannot be made for them. One just does not know where fate or man's idiocy will strike next.

Examples have been the cancer reports, the thalidomide tragedy, reports on cyclamates, reports of the Monopolies Commission and changing interest rates.

From being a negative sales appeal in the past—as expressed by General Motors in the USA in the 30s—safety factors have become much bigger sales appeals in these days of motorway madness and the efforts of Ralph Nader. From time to time there are varying political attitudes to the products of Japan, Italy, Russia and South Africa which may be unpredictable according to world events. Until fairly recently we did not expect to find goods from China or Korea in British shops. Cheap holidays in the USA were unthinkable. We might have holidayed in Poland.

It is a swings and roundabouts guessing game that confounds the most ardent marketing astrologist, and it is worsened by wars, civil wars, epidemics, floods, pestilence, drought, crop failure, strikes and unemployment. Faced with disasters and dilemmas as remotely unconnected as simultaneous civil war in Ulster and Bangladesh, or the simultaneous Rolls-Royce collapse and the Post Office strike, it is a wonder that business survives the constant assault of external affairs. Yet it is in this very state of doubt and chaos that the advertising manager has to sit down and seriously decide the sum of money most likely to be sufficient to finance the advertising ingredient of his marketing mix. He is not allowed to complain that his task is impossible.

8.4   Uncertainties of the 'Marketing Mix'

Finally, and assuming that his estimate is not far out, the advertising manager has still to contend with the vagaries of the **marketing mix** itself, for his expenditure will succeed only in so far as it combines with the other ingredients. Moreover, it has to be assumed that the other ingredients in the marketing mix are as well budgeted, planned and executed as the advertising. As a reminder of these further elements here is a list of them:

(i) The product must be right for the chosen market segment.
(ii) The product must be correctly priced, named and packaged to appeal to this correctly judged market segment.
(iii) The field sales force must be efficient and in sufficient number to conduct the shortest necessary journey cycle and to service the trade as well.
(iv) Distribution must be efficient, whether through wholesalers, own shops, appointed agents, all possible outlets, mail order traders or door-to-door salesmen.
(v) Instructions, guarantees, after-sales, spares and replacement services must be efficient.
(vi) At all levels of communication—staff and dealer relations, customer education and relations—there must be continuous PR activity.

Thus, however thoroughly we budget the advertising money, the success of the expenditure will be enhanced or weakened by:

(a) External forces over which we have little control and
(b) Other marketing influences which also need to be budgeted, planned and executed by other executives with equal rigour. The closer the advertising manager can work in concert with his colleagues the better. In the smaller organisation he will, of course, be responsible for the lot.

We have not exhausted our preliminary considerations, and before turning to the choice of methods of fixing the appropriation we should next consider the extent and the limitations of its **coverage**. The appropriation is not just a sum of total media expenditures.

Items such as the following have also to be included:

(*a*) Photography, retouching, prints; filming, location expenses, actors, music, prints, distribution; artwork, models.
(*b*) Typesetting, process engraving, camera-ready copy.
(*c*) Sales literature.
(*d*) Sales promotion schemes.
(*e*) Competition prizes, administration, judging.
(*f*) Postage, stationery and other direct mail costs.
(*g*) Advertising agency fees.
(*h*) Public relations consultancy fees.

And to be utterly realistic, an advertising manager should also cost his salaries and proportion of office overheads, although this is not always done. It is necessary if any comparison with agency or consultancy costs is to be made.

The appropriation should include all forms of advertising which, in this discussion, can be sub-divided into

(i) **trade** or distributor advertising and
(ii) **user or consumer** advertising.

This again may be divided into **above-the-line** and **below-the-line** as already explained on page 42.

8.5 The PR Budget

It is a mistake—frequently made due to misunderstandings about PR—to include PR in the advertising budget. The further error is sometimes committed of counting PR as a below-the-line expense. This often happens in advertising agency budgets when anything below-the-line is regarded by them as of secondary importance, if only that it is not commission paying! Of course, a percentage can always be added onto below-the-line activities, but this does not properly compensate for time.

When PR is restricted to product publicity news releases, these confusions are understandable but not forgivable. But as suggested in the sketch of the marketing mix, PR can contribute to many stages of the marketing strategy. Moreover, as will be shown in the chapter devoted to PR, it is a management function which serves an entire organisation, not only the marketing division.

The sensible way to budget PR is to plan a complete programme for the whole organisation, the PRO being directly responsible to the chief executive, and the allocations from this separate budget being made to the production (including staff), the financial and the marketing functions of the business. In those organisations where advertising is not a major marketing cost, the advertising may actually come within the PR budget.

Unfortunately, there are a lot of 'chicken and egg' arguments about the respective roles and responsibilities of advertising and PR. Provided it is properly understood that PR is neither a form of nor a part of advertising there is really no problem for, as already shown, PR can play a bigger and more varied part in the marketing mix than advertising, important though that is, while PR concerns the total communications inside and outside an organisation which are quite beyond the more specialist task of advertising.

In this book reference will be made to PR because it has a close affinity with advertising. **The advertising appropriation can be a waste of money if the PR has been neglected.** An advertising campaign can fail to produce enquiries or sales if:

(*a*) the product is unknown or misunderstood; and
(*b*) the manufacturer lacks the goodwill of distributors, and/or prospective customers.

The classic example of (*a*) was the abortive launch of New Smoking Mixture cigarettes containing a substitute for tobacco so that smokers would not risk suffering from cancer. The product failed, in spite of massive advertising, and millions of packs had to be withdrawn from the market. Among other mistakes, the manufacturers had assumed that because there was such a substantial anti-smoking lobby the product would sell, forgetting that non-smokers would not smoke even NSM! This disaster could have been averted had the smoking market been educated about the product so that it would have been welcomed when launched at the right time.

Understanding and Goodwill are Prerogatives of PR

In budgeting PR costs in relation to the advertising campaign, one vital difference must be clearly understood if outside consultancy services are being used. The PR consultancy, since it is not buying space or air time, does not get paid by media as is the case with the advertising agency. This means that the income of the PR consultancy is derived from the sale of professional labour or time. Every minute spent on the client's account has to be paid for by the client, and that is the basis of the fee. After that, materials and expenses are also charged, but **the prime cost of a PR consultancy service is the expenditure of time**. This time is usually charged out at an hourly rate which recompenses the consultancy for salaries and overheads and provides for profit. To operate at a profit a PR consultancy has to have an income roughly treble its expenditure on all kinds of salaries from the office junior to the managing director. One of the first charges is therefore the cost of talking to the client, and the client has to understand this, because when dealing with an advertising agent he does not have to pay for the time spent on his behalf by the account executive, media planners and buyers, production staff and others. Buying PR consultancy services is similar to buying those of any other professional adviser be he lawyer, doctor, architect or accountant.

8.6   Fee Charging Advertising Agencies

The above remarks are true if the agency bases its remuneration on the commission system. However, some years ago some agencies adopted the more realistic service system whereby they were paid according to the volume and quality of the work. This is the way most professionals are paid. Since the changes in the agency recognition system brought about by the *Restrictive Trade Practices Act, 1979* we have seen the emergence of non-media buying and therefore non-commission receiving à la carte creative and specialist agencies which can only charge fees, just like PR consultancies.

9
How to Budget Advertising Expenditure

9.1 Seventeen Ways of Assessing the Appropriation

Having surveyed some of the problems which beset the advertising manager when trying to determine how much to spend on advertising we now move on to study and compare some of the possible methods of assessing the appropriation. We promised that we would look beyond the small set of methods which have appeared in previous textbooks, and the following 17 methods (with variations of title) will be discussed:

(a) Arbitrary, rule of thumb or intuitive.
(b) Percentage of previous turnover or 'historic'.
(c) Residual of previous year's surplus.
(d) Gross margin.
(e) Percentage of anticipated turnover.
(f) Unit, case, sales ratio, sales volume or standard cost.
(g) Competitors and competitive advertising.
(h) Comparison with total product group advertising.
(i) Elasticity.
(j) Target sum, cost of exposure, task approach, objective.
(k) Corporate evaluation.
(l) Ideal campaign.
(m) Marketing model or operational research.
(n) Cost per head of population.
(o) New product investment or pay-out plan.
(p) Build-up.
(q) Composite or eclectic.

(a) The Arbitrary Rule of Thumb or Intuitive Method

By 'arbitrary' is meant that the sum is not based on any exact calculation but is what the advertiser is prepared to spend, 'what he can afford', or what he thinks will do the job. Perhaps it is a rough guess based on past experience—a blend of hunch and experience. It is a pretty vague and unbusinesslike way of spending money, and it is more common than it should be. All too often one hears—usually at client–agency meetings—the words of amateur wisdom 'we have looked at the figures and we can afford to spend only so much on advertising', as if advertising was an afterthought, some sort of ill-afforded luxury. What sort of figures have they been looking at—their bank overdraft? Such crystal ball methods are not worth taking seriously.

The fact that there are 16 more methods need not depress the reader after such a poor start, nor need they frighten him into wondering how he can possibly make the right choice. Two things will emerge, first that some methods suit some organisations better than others, and secondly that in practice it may be sensible to combine several methods. That is the final composite method which is worth keeping in mind as we proceed.

(b) Percentage of Previous Turnover or Historic Method

If the appropriation is based on previous turnover at least the aim is to do as well as before, but it is not very ambitious or forward-looking. It is virtually medieval in its lack of enterprise, but there is the further danger that if trade was bad during the previous year this unfortunate trend can be worsened by reduced expenditure in the following year.

A reasonable variation, however, is the **historic method**. The advertiser spends the same amount from year to year—not a higher or lesser sum according to the previous year's results—making adjustments to cover changing costs. This suits a business such as an hotel, motor-coach company or retail shop which is unlikely to expand its trade, has a limited capacity, and repeats much the same volume of trade year after year. It follows the same pattern as expenditure on other items such as redecoration.

(c) Residual of Previous Year's Surplus

Hardly worth taking seriously, this is nevertheless a method adopted in all seriousness by 'businessmen' with less than necessary faith in advertising. Moreover, it makes nonsense of the fact that it is the purchaser and not the manufacturer or distributor who pays for advertising. Advertising is not paid for out of profits but out of price. It is an on-cost. This economic fact escapes those who pretend to spend on advertising 'what they can afford'. Yet in this method the appropriation is based on what remains after profits have been taken from the previous year's turnover.

At first glance it looks ridiculous and one dreads to think of the firm's prospects following a lean year. But there is some merit in the idea of ploughing back profits in the form of future advertising. This is no different from any other investment of increased income. It can be applied to a growth industry, and it can be mellowed by judicious calculation of how much of the residual should be applied to advertising. But it does follow that cautious principle of only spending what is in the kitty, and its avoidance of speculation or application to a sales target does not promise much growth.

Alternatively, the 'residuum' may be assessed from the **anticipated surplus**, cost and profits being forecast. This is better and more flexible, and is favoured by some large advertisers. Nevertheless, it still suggests an appalling attitude of mind towards the job of advertising. Surely, as only one of many distribution costs, advertising should take its rightful place as one of **the calculated contributors to the gaining of gross profits?** This method is discussed more fully in the name of the gross margin method.

(d) Gross Margin Method

The gross margin method takes advertising as a percentage of the residuum *after* production and distribution costs have been deducted from income. Thus, if total sales = £A and production and distribution costs = £B, £A − £B = £C, the latter representing the balance or gross margin. Advertising is taken as a percentage of £C, and so is directly related to gross profit. As sales increase, the fixed costs are spread more economically, leaving a larger proportion for division between advertising and net profits, the opposite applying as sales fall. However, the percentage of £C − overheads may be adjusted if the sum available for advertising falls below the effective optimum. That is to say, profits may be invested in promotion to bolster up declining sales.

The fallacy of this method is that it makes a special thing of advertising, making it dependent on a residuum actually existing. In other words, if the gross margin holds nothing to cover fixed costs there will be no fund for either profits or advertising! It is therefore fallacious to divorce advertising from other expenses included in the distribution costs accepted under £B. Advertising does not belong to the gross margin any more than do the costs of warehousing, delivery services, field salesmen and trade terms. The method is back to front, and overlooks the primary contribution which advertising has to make to the total sales effort. It seems to regard advertising as a luxury to be indulged in only if there is money to spare. It belongs to the irrational 'what we can afford' philosophy which cannot be taken seriously as businesslike budgetry. Its frequent use suggests either a poor understanding of the value of advertising in the marketing strategy or (which is by no means impossible with some industrial advertisers) that advertising is the wrong means of communicating with the market.

The gross margin method is clearly useless for a new product requiring a heavy initial investment in advertising. For such a product the break-even may not occur in the first, second or even third year of trading, and eventual success will depend on investment in advertising. Promotion of a freshly styled newspaper by a new owner would require the sort of investment which fell within the target or task method.

(e) Percentage of Anticipated Turnover Method

Looking ahead at anticipated sales is more progressive, and so our fifth method is rather more realistic, provided the sales target is a good forecast. But if the forecast is wrong—maybe thwarted by one or more of those imponderables such as a strike or war—the advertising appropriation will also be wrong. It may be too late to recover or adjust, as British motor-car manufacturers found after Japanese makes had earned reputations for reliability, and had won a substantial percentage of the British market. This method also invites increased expenditure in good times and less in bad times, a contradiction since it should be easier and less expensive to sell in good times and vice versa.

(*f*) Unit, Case, Sales Ratio, Sales Volume or Standard Cost Method

Various names are given to what is best known as the **unit percentage** method, which is usually applied to repeat purchase consumer goods. The price per unit totals percentages representing every production and distribution cost plus profit. It can be applied to a bag of flour, a tin of paint or a litre of petrol, or even to a complete saleable item such as a motorcar. If the manufacturer then plans to produce and sell a given quantity of units the available fund for advertising is easily calculated. Should sales exceed the planned production, and it is economic to extend production and distribution, the advertising expenditure is spread over additional units. Conversely, if the take-up of a limited production capacity occurs before the conclusion of the campaign, it may be possible to contract the campaign, thus reducing the advertising cost per unit.

There are weaknesses in this seemingly ideal system since it rashly assumes stability in the economy and presumes that proportionate costs, including advertising, will remain constant. It makes no allowance for the need to increase advertising expenditure to meet rising costs, increased competition or a diminishing market. The mail order trader, for example, has had to raise his prices to recover the continually increasing cost of postage. The retailer has to recover increases in rates and electricity. And so it goes on. Such a method can work only if budgets are short term or seasonal, but an annual budget could be underestimated.

The unit volume or sales volume method implies cutting advertising expenditure as sales fall, and while it may sound correct to spend less on selling less there are optimum levels at which advertising expenditure can be too low to be effective to sell even a reduced volume. This can be illustrated by the example of a theatre deciding to advertise only one week in four because the show is playing to 25 per cent capacity. Apart from the qualities of the show, a cause could be **insufficient advertising** and the result of applying the sales volume method could be to deprive the theatre of business in three out of four weeks. Here, the 'unit' is a seat at a performance.

(*g*) Competitors and Competitive Advertising Methods

Here are two somewhat similar methods used for different reasons.

When we are uncertain about the weight of advertising necessary to promote a product it may be useful to study the MEAL Digest statistics on current advertising expenditure. In so doing we must remember that rivals may have had the advantage of a build-up of advertising impact over a number of years. How do we catch up? Greater expenditure, a novel appeal, different media, or a novel marketing tactic? We *may* have to spend more than an established rival if we seek to gain a similar impact, unless our new product is so superior that it is an instant winner. **What competitors are spending** will at least be an indication of the probable minimum expenditure necessary to sell that kind of product. But it must not be taken for granted that rival firms are efficient spenders.

While it is sensible for a newcomer to take cognisance of the sums which other firms appear to find necessary to spend to maintain their existing shares of the market, there is also the situation where rivals attempt to match each other's spending. This 'pound-for-pound' **competitive advertising**—like war—is pointless and uneconomic. In the end its futility leads to trade association agreements to desist, or amalgamations to eliminate uneconomic competition.

In this oligopolistic situation, forecasting becomes warped by circumstances because of the essential interdependence of a few very big companies upon each other. They can be so mutually interdependent that, as in the case of the Society of Motor Manufacturers and Traders, membership is dependent upon support for certain Society-sponsored exhibitions only, other events being proscribed under penalty of fine. Or the competition can be so intense that there is an escalation of promotional costs—rather like an armaments race—which defies sensible budgeting. But even alleged business rivals tend to meet at golf courses, West End clubs or round the trade association table and, as with wars, peace terms and economic stability are sought and eventually found by sworn enemies.

This is interesting because the lay consumer is apt to criticise the heavy expenditure on advertising by rivals (which is obvious on TV), and to imagine that such competition and such expenditure inflates retail prices. (There is a difference between advertising being part of the price and being a disproportionate part which inflates the price.) There are—as shown above—economic forces at work. If there is insufficient advertising the product will fail to sell and the consumer's choice will be reduced, and if there is excessive advertising the manufacturers will club together to minimise costs when they threaten to get out of hand and eat into profits. Equilibrium results in a maximum variety of choice, and for this privilege (and the privilege of entrepreneurs to profit by the supply of choices), the cost has to be met in the price. But the cost is not only advertising: it is every distribution cost once the product is made.

(*h*) Comparison with Total Product Group Advertising Method

Using the **comparison method**, an advertiser in a product group assesses the total expenditure of all the firms in that group, probably using the estimates published by MEAL Digest, and also those of Nielsen or other dealer audit units. Such a product group might be all makers of toothpaste or razor blades, typewriters or pickles. This total figure of product group advertising expenditure per year is then divided by the number of producers according to their market shares, the calculation suggesting what each firm should be spending. (It will be found, no doubt, that actual expenditures do not agree with calculated proportional expenditures, but it must be remembered that the product group total is not necessarily an ideal figure. Probably, it will be too high as in a saturated market where advertisers can only take sales from one another and not expand the market.) However, by this process a member of the product group—and especially a newcomer to it—can work out what he should spend to achieve a particular share of the market, or perhaps a larger share of it. Again, this process can reveal whether the extra advertising cost required to increase sales is in fact worth while.

This comparison method is a sophistication of the previous study of competitors' advertising, relating competitors' advertising to market shares and the average cost of gaining a certain share. It goes beyond taking competitive advertising as a yardstick since it looks at the *total* expenditure of *all* members of the product group, rather than that of a firm doing a comparable volume of trade.

(*i*) Elasticity Method

This method follows the influence of supply and demand curves. The profit is compared with previous advertising expenditure to give a ratio between profit and expenditure. The ratio of the average cost of the extra unit of expenditure on advertising is compared with the average return in increased profit. This calculation will reveal the limit beyond which advertising expenditure is uneconomic.

Such a method is feasible only when advertising is the chief form of promotion, as with retail store or mail order trading, and is an over-simplified form of budgeting when there are the numerous distribution and promotional costs normally experienced by a manufacturer of consumer goods.

(*j*) Target Sum, Cost of Exposure, Task Approach, Objective Method

Here we have four variations of the **target method** which has won approval in recent years. The objective is determined and the cost of advertising to achieve it is then estimated. However, the slightly different names given to the method have to do with the kind of objective sought. Is it a volume of sales, number of prospects, or weight of media coverage?

The businessman may say to the agency: 'What will it cost to use advertising to sell two thousand computers?' The agency plans board will consider the project, and the account executive will be given figures so that he can tell the client that if such-and-such a campaign is mounted the cost will be £X000. Meanwhile, the computer manufacturer may have sought quotations for achieving his sales objective by some other means. He may reject the agency scheme and decide to use sales promotion techniques only. If it is this sort of industrial product, he may prefer to spend the same or maybe a smaller sum on industrial films and technical seminars for prospective buyers.

But a quite different use of the target method may be to ask the agency what will it cost to reach the national mass housewife market. Usually, 80 per cent coverage is the accepted target, and achievement of this target is the media planner's objective. He is aided by the statistics made available by the media research conducted by JICNARS into press readership, and BARB into TV audiences.

Slight differences in the target and task methods are that the first method may mean planning an appropriation against cost of media to achieve the sales target, while the second method may refer to the cost of completing a given task.

The principle of these methods is the reverse of those already discussed. We have an objective—a sales volume, a stated number of desired enquiries, a specific number of presentations of an offer to the same prospects, and with such a target or task we now set out to discover what will be the advertising cost. We can examine and compare this or that form of advertising campaign, or sales promotion or perhaps PR. The merit of the method is its soundness in obeying the management precept that action must be preceded by definition of objectives. It is also flexible, and expenditure can be adjusted to meet events.

Mention was made above of PR, although PR is not an alternative to advertising. However, there are times when the target is more likely to be reached using PR tactics. A good example of this is the charity appeal. And if, strictly speaking, that is not commercial, a different example is an exhibition which can be difficult to advertise because of the want of continuity over a short period of time. With exhibitions, PR can be most effective if—as happens with the Motor Show, Boat Show and Chelsea Flower Show—the opening day is highly newsworthy, meriting coverage on, say, *News at Ten*. Cornhill and Canon have adopted sponsorship.

The **task approach** offers a slight modification of the more long-term target method, although the two terms are often interchangeable. A task can be something very specific such as launching a new product or boosting sales in a slack sales area, meeting exceptional competition, or overcoming something which is inhibiting sales. The task method may be applied to regions, a very big advertiser planning regional TV and outdoor advertising according to the task involved.

For this **special task** a sum of money has to be estimated which is believed capable of doing the job. Instead of saying we are prepared to spend so much for this special purpose we ask what will it cost? This is a positive approach, **assuming that a successful result is possible.** The more arbitrary method discussed in (*a*) could be a forlorn hope. But if the sum needed to win success was prohibitive it would be wise to forgo the attempt. There would be no point in literally buying sales, unless sheer brutal domination of the market was the objective. With the task method there can be a 'go/no go' point of decision.

(*k*) Corporate Evaluation Method

Almost identical to the target method is the **corporate evaluation** way of reviewing market research and corporate planning when determining what to spend on advertising. Taken to its logical conclusion, this method follows the **marginal utility theory.** Overall corporate objectives are achieved if marketing objectives are also achieved, the marginal expenditure of an extra £1 on advertising being matched by an equal or less than proportionate increase in profit.

(*l*) Ideal Campaign Method

Not unlike the task method this is one which firmly places the initiative with the agency. Using its campaign and media planning skill, the agency produces a fully costed scheme which it offers to the client as the most effective advertising mix for a given purpose. The obvious snag is that unless the agency has an inkling of the client's ceiling, it can produce a wonderful scheme at a prohibitive price. Although it is often said that agencies, and not clients, should propose appropriations, it is better if this is a joint affair with full and frank disclosure of costs on both sides. There is a saying in PR that PR is as long as a piece of string, and this is applicable to the ideal campaign or quantification method in advertising.

(*m*) Marketing Model or Operational Research Method

This is an excellent method for the advertiser who wants to see the value of larger or smaller investments in advertising. It lends itself to the needs of the mail order trader who wishes to cost promotions in relation to prospects and market share for each commodity he handles. This will also influence his buying, which in turn may involve quantity discounts. Thus, a scale can be created showing the different buying, advertising, packing and posting and overhead costs for different quantities resulting in a certain net profit. This begins to look like the unit method except that it is really the other way round since advertising costs do not go up or down according to sales, but sales are related to the injection of advertising.

There is no guarantee that the model will give precise results. It is only an abstraction. Meanwhile, the method is subject to the variables already remarked upon in the previous chapter. Nevertheless, on a probability basis of past experience, the figures on the scale can be adjusted from past knowledge and continuous current experience. This has to be said because the same advertisement can produce different results when placed in different issues and/or different positions in the same publication. The cause of the varying results may be utterly unpredictable and, as said before, it may be nothing more than a change in the weather. It is difficult to sell swimsuits on a wet day and umbrellas when the sun is shining. Fortuitous circumstances affect advertising results just as they do share prices or votes in an election.

The model under discussion may look like this:

Expenditure on advertising: £50,000—sales £$\frac{1}{2}$m.
,,   ,,   ,,   £75,000   ,,   £$\frac{2}{3}$m.
,,   ,,   ,,   £100,000   ,,   £$\frac{3}{4}$m.
,,   ,,   ,,   £125,000   ,,   £$\frac{7}{8}$m.
,,   ,,   ,,   £150,000   ,,   £1m.

The figures can be any that the advertiser cares to project according to his business experience and needs. The marketing model method may be useful to the user of frequent, short, isolated campaigns, such as entertainment promotions or store events, seasonal holidays or mail order sales, which make swift adjustment possible from one requirement to the next. It lends itself very well to direct mail advertising, as used for book and record clubs, and the cost of sales letters, sales literature, envelopes and postage can be reckoned according to the size of the mailing list and the size of the mailing calculated to produce a given quantity of enquiries or value of sales.

Models are fashionable in the social sciences, and it may be thought that advertising is too imprecise for the building of models to forecast expenditure. But models are rather like algebra, a shorthand to rationalise thinking by abstracting the essentials. Just as a London Underground map is not geographically accurate, but is a stylised presentation of routes (or a model) it is helpful in giving the traveller information and directions. A marketing model can therefore inspire more methodical planning of advertising appropriations, and this sort of charting should not therefore be discarded as being pseudo-scientific. Models also make possible the use of computers so that answers, and alternative schemes, can be produced rapidly and accurately.

One particular model, using a computer, is known as the simulation linear programming model. Data are fed in about media and consumer characteristics and the desired market share to produce a linear relationship between the variables. It requires—as with all computer practice—absolutely accurate input information, which may be hard or costly to obtain quite apart from the expense of programming. The result will be as scientific as it can be—a computer is no master mind, only an electronic calculator of given input—and can take no account of such refinements as creativity or imponderables such as external influences except in so far as anticipated influences may be given values which can be fed in. The computer may be better kept for calculating reasonably known factors such as media costs, circulations, readerships, readership duplications and so on where answers are valuable because the time consumption may be impractical if the sums had to be performed manually. The computer is used by agencies for this aspect of campaign planning.

The distinction may be made between **empirical** and **theoretical** models. The former is based on market intelligence, the latter on historical data. In a saturated market an empirical model takes account of competitive activity and advertising expenditure can be flexible to maintain market shares. The theoretical model is a more deliberate form of the percentage of past sales (historical model) already discussed, the percentage being calculated rather than declared in an arbitrary fashion.

(*n*) Cost per Head of Population Method

This refers to the 'population served by the advertiser'. If it is wished to increase the market share the advertising cost is worked out on the basis of the cost per customer to be gained. If the entire market is, say, one million of which the present market share is 50 per cent (half million) and the present appropriation is £½m., the cost per head is £1. To gain another 10 per cent means increasing the appropriation by £100,000.

This sounds simple but is specious if purchases per individual are unequal. But if purchases can only be a single unit, say a lawn mower or a refrigerator, this method can be realistic. In other words, while it does not satisfy the demands of the manufacturer of repeat purchase goods it does suit the advertiser of consumer durables and other products or services which are mostly limited to a solitary purchase which may or may not be repeated or replaced. Customers may only ever buy one central heating system in a lifetime whereas even some expensive products—cars, hi-fi sets, houses, small boats or cameras—may be replaced. But having made the distinction, it is still possible that the marketing aim may be to convert more people to taking photographs and making their first camera purchase, and a firm like Kodak could expand film sales in this way, using this formula for costing an advertising programme to that end.

In a sense, the cost per head of population method is another kind of target method, except that it is specifically related to prospects. This means that it can be applied to a market of potential students for, say, a correspondence school, or enrolments for a book or record club, or donors to a charity. It is a very personal system. It can also be applied by the producer of a specialised line such as a slimming aid who aims to sell to more overweight people.

(*o*) New Product Investment or Pay-out Plan

This is another product investment scheme whereby advertising is related to initial development and subsequent growth in succeeding and, hopefully, successful years. It is best explained with a table of figures.

	Year 1	Year 2	Year 3	Total
Sales (£'000)	100	110	120	330
Advertising (£'000)	20	15	15	50
Advertising/ Sales ratio	20%	13.6%	12.5%	15%

Such a scheme is suitable for the launch of a new product when heavy initial expenditure is necessary in the first, and sometimes in the second, year.

(*p*) Build-up Method

Yet another variation upon the target method is this one which begins with allocations to various media and then compiles these sums into a total appropriation. The method is useful when specific media service precise purposes. A mail order trader may use the press to attract new customers, direct mail to gain further sales from previous customers, and catalogues, price lists, samples, order forms, sales letters, Freepost envelopes and other print to complete sales. The appropriation or total budget is a balanced collation of these related costs, the size of the mailing list and placing of press advertising controlling the print quantities and costs.

There is nothing hit or miss about such a plan, but flexibility lies only in injecting further funds into press advertising (or mailing to an extra prospect list) if response is disappointing, but this will erode profits if prices have been fixed to cover the original advertising budget.

Again, the allocations may be by products or departments, or possibly divisions or companies in a group. Perhaps some of the previously described methods may have to be adopted in certain cases. Here, the importance of the method lies in giving proper weight to special items or sections, rather than taking an overall sum and then parcelling it out to various claimants for advertising support. It is not unlike the departments of a local authority or the central Government presenting their estimates to the treasurer or Chancellor of the Exchequer who then produces the final budget.

(*q*) Composite or Eclectic Method

Fixing the appropriation has been discussed at length, not to suggest that it is complicated but to emphasise that **while it pays to advertise it also pays to make a painstaking study of spending.** That is why we have presented here what is probably the largest collection of methods ever to have been brought together in print before. In the end we may decide that the best way to arrive at the appropriation is to make an eclectic approach. This, our seventeenth method, may be termed the **composite** or **eclectic** method. It calls for consideration of a blend of calculable influences and recognition of some of the imponderables. All these factors can be compiled to form a model such as the following:

  (i) Past sales.
 (ii) Anticipated sales.
(iii) Production capacity.
 (iv) Market conditions—economic, political, sociological.
  (v) Selling problems of product, e.g. high price, unfamiliarity.
 (vi) Efficiency and strength of the sales force.
(vii) Efficiency and adequacy of distributor network.
(viii) Seasonal fluctuations and seasonal campaigns.
 (ix) Regional fluctuations—including effect of local competition.
  (x) Appropriate and available media, and comparative costs of reaching the market with effective impact and continuity to match possible demand with optimum productive capacity.
 (xi) Trends revealed by market, media, advertisement research and any other data.

An analysis of these 11 factors (which may vary slightly from organisation to organisation) will give the most thorough approach to determining the appropriation. Working backwards now it will also be possible to discover the percentage of turnover that is devoted to the single distributive cost of advertising, and the following year this 'percentage of previous turnover' is available for repetition or adjustment in the light of the previous year's results and consideration of the other items.

Forecasting the advertising budget resembles any other form of economic forecasting. The shorter the term the more readily can allowance be made for the influences over which one has no control. In a world of unpredictable disaster and strife, it is obviously foolish to have obstinate ideas, and even more irresponsible to adopt a haphazard attitude to this subject.

Cost effectiveness has become as important to the one-man business as it is to the big concern which can afford to take advice from management and other professional consultants. The small business is by no means an uneconomic unit, the supreme example being the housewife and her housekeeping money and shopping list who can be thoroughly economic, for unless she buys things 'on tick' she balances her budget every week. Ì, small, or smaller, businessman needs to plan his spending against the greatest expectation of the greatest reward. His problem is no different from that of the giant corporation or the conscientious housewife. This chapter has therefore taken a very keen look at advertising expenditure because budgeting is the first thing to get right before tackling any other aspect of advertising or, for that matter, selling in general.

It is possible to arrive at conclusions that the cost of advertising is so great that the inflated price will inhibit sales: conversely, advertising may be unproductive at any price and some other means of communicating with the market may be more profitable.

To take two final examples: encyclopaedias have met the first difficulty, resulting in the adoption of high-pressure sales gimmicks which have provoked justifiable criticism; while press advertising for services used by the majority of industries has proved both prohibitive and unproductive compared with the PR techniques of feature articles and seminars with speakers and films. In between these extremes advertising has time and again proved to be the cheapest and most successful means of making known goods or services in order to sell them.

Advertising is not a cure-all but well used it can, like the Double Diamond beer slogan, 'work wonders'.

9.2 Special Departmental and Seasonal or Feature Appropriations

Some classes of advertiser make good use of advertising by sub-dividing their total appropriation according to products, departments, weeks, months or seasons. Or, by adopting a task-method approach to each sub-division, they can arrive at a total expenditure, rather like the build-up method. However, a manufacturer of a range of products must be careful that his sub-divisions do not result in individual budgets each of which is too small to be effectual. A **composite** advertisement for several allied products can gain greater impact, and such advertisements are likely to be **larger and to command better positions.**

Department stores apportion their appropriations between departments, e.g. soft furnishing, drapery, menswear, hardwear, china and glass and so on. They also allocate for seasonal and shopping events such as Christmas gifts, January sale, spring fashions, summer sale and autumn fashions.

Supermarkets divide their expenditure between different classes of merchandise, e.g. cereals, drinks, biscuits, dairy produce, confectionery or toiletries.

Holiday trade advertisers concentrate their expenditure at the turn of the year and the first weeks of the New Year. This is because package tour operators require deposits, and these are available out of Christmas bonuses.

British holiday resorts are able to make minute budgets work like big advertising by taking small spaces together in holiday features, the collective effect having such impact that a mere three centimetre single-column advertisement in a January holiday feature is the equivalent of a larger isolated display advertisement.

ail order traders can make tiny weekend bargain square
do the work of much larger and more expensive spaces,
appear in a collective market place of lots of small display
all making bargain offers.

This shows that the small advertiser can make his money go further or
do a 'big advertiser' job if the appropriation, timing and media selection is
well thought out. He can really make advertising work for him. And nowadays, with broadcasting as well as press, outdoor, transportation, cinema
and direct mail, his advertising can be technically on a par with that of the
national advertiser.

Many a High Street shopkeeper, with just one shop or a string of
branches, can boost business if he plans along these lines. As one example
of this, let us take a hardware trader and see how he can make consistent
hard-selling use of advertisements in his locally available media. A regular
month-by-month campaign can be devised like this:

January	New Year sale
February	Garden seeds
March	Spring-cleaning aids, curtain systems
April	Decorating materials, garden tools, crockery
May	Insecticides, fertilisers
June	Lawn tools, weedkillers
July	Holiday goods, picnic baskets
August	Deck chairs, garden furniture
September	Rose bushes, spring bulbs, bulb bowls
October	Alarm clocks, clothes driers, heat units
November	Electrical goods, Christmas gifts
December	Christmas decorations, Christmas flowering bulbs in pots, last-minute gift ideas

This is just a rough guide, and other ideas will be suggested by the range
of stock carried and the trader's own experience of month-by-month
demand which can vary from one locality to another. But the list set out
above does imply that many traders can conduct profitable advertising if a
regular series of topical customer-orientated advertisements is planned and
costed against skilful buying and desired turnover and profits. After all,
this is exactly what big city stores do with their combined personal shopper
and mail order trade. The same system can be adopted by Bill Smith with
his men's outfitters or Mary Jones with her fancy goods shop in any High
Street in any town.

10
The Advertising Agency Story

10.1 What is an Advertising Agency?

An advertising agency is a team of experts, appointed by clients to plan, produce and place advertising campaigns, but literally acting as the agents of the media which pay commission to those agents which are 'recognised' for their credit worthiness, and legally acting as principal.

The agency clearly occupies an anomalous position. Although the advertiser appoints the agency to do its work, the agency is responsible for all the bills it incurs, and the bulk of its income is received from the media owners. Ludicrous though this system may sound, it works very well and although changes are constantly under discussion no one seems very willing to dispense with the 'commission system', although agencies do organise their income in a variety of ways. For instance, clients may be charged net for space, and then charged a fee. But because 75 per cent of agency income is derived from commission on the purchase of space, air time and other media this does not mean that the agency is biased towards the media which pay it best. Its loyalty is to the client. All this will become plainer as this chapter proceeds.

10.2 History and Development of Advertising Agencies

The first British advertising agencies were one-man space-broking businesses, the agent being paid a commission on the advertising space he was able to sell for a newspaper or magazine. He was not unlike an insurance broker, except that he had no specialist knowledge. He merely hawked vacant space to those he could induce to buy it. He knew nothing, and did not have to know anything, about creative advertising. Press advertisements had appeared as early as 1666 in the *London Gazette*, proclaiming the merits of coffee, chocolate, tea and other delights in somewhat flamboyant terms. These were the days of small circulation political sheets, the 'coffee house newspapers'. Early advertisements were little more than classifieds. Type was of uniform size. There were no display faces or illustrations. Sometimes the message consisted of the same line of 7-point type repeated for so many inches down the page. More ambitious advertisements appeared in the *Tatler* in 1710.

Advertising agents came about with the growth of Government advertising during the Napoleonic wars, when money was raised partly by lotter-ies—presumably the origin of Spitfire Funds during the Second World War! Next, creative advertising agencies emerged when space-selling became more competitive, and services had to be provided (out of the commission) to get the business. The greater demand for advertising coin-cided with mid-19th-century development of mechanical production of popular goods, urban development, limited liability companies, railways, the promise of the Great Exhibition of 1851 and the growth of the new mass consumer market.

The first advertising agents really began to appear at the beginning of the 19th century. James White, with the aid of his school-friend Charles Lamb, set up the first London agency in 1800. He combined his job of clerk in the treasurer's office at his old school of Christ's Hospital with that of agent for provincial newspapers at 22, Warwick Square 'in the shadow of St Paul's Cathedral.' White's was a comparatively creative agency since Lamb was employed as a freelance copywriter on Government lottery advertisements.

In those days provincial newspapers were like country bankers—there were no national newspapers or national bankers. Although *The Times* made journalistic history by reporting the Battle of Waterloo with probably the world's first war correspondent, it was the *London Times*. Popular, national newspapers like the *Daily Telegraph* and the *Daily Mail* did not arrive until 1855 and 1896 respectively.

Another of the earliest advertising agencies was Reynell and Son of London, established in 1812. The abolition of the advertisement tax (and there was no Labour Party then!) in 1853, and the removal of stamp duty from newspapers in 1861, gave fresh incentive to both the sale of space and the use of advertising.

While there were several large agencies in London between the two world wars, many were fairly small. The space-booking was now conducted by **contact men,** a term which has died out as agents have become professional practitioners. The creative side consisted very largely of **wordsmiths** who cudgelled their brains to invent slogans. The need for this creativity has returned during the past decades with the advent of commercial television and its jingles. Among the memorable slogans of the 20s and 30s were the following, some of which are still familiar:

> *Guinness is good for you*
> *Don't be vague, ask for Haig*
> *It's sprung on springs* (Berkeley chair)
> *Ah, Bisto!*
> *For your throat's sake smoke Craven A*
> *Bovril prevents that sinking feeling*
> *That was Shell, that was*
> *Friday night is Amami night*
> *Let me be a father to you* (Bennett College)
> *I'm getting Younger every day*

Many of these slogans appeared on the 'poor man's art gallery'—the hoardings—and they characterise the inventiveness of agencies in this era when there were no statistics or copy-testing techniques, and the only judge of an agency's proposals or work was the client. The agency could not support its proposals, ideas and media schedule with figures or findings. It just had to be very clever.

And by the style of much of the advertising in the 20s and 30s the chief criterion was **did it make the client laugh?** Much of it was very funny indeed to quote only the Pears Soap poster which showed a dirty old tramp writing a letter which began: '*since using your soap I have used no other*'. Any member of the public could have a good laugh simply by walking down the High Street, which wasn't bad psychology in days of depression and unemployment. It might be a real tonic in modern times of inflation and unemployment.

American advertising developed rapidly in the 30s and 40s as its economy climbed out of the Depression with the assistance of Roosevelt's New Deal and the profitable boost exerted by the demands of the war in Europe. Already in advance of the old world with the early provision of automotive, electrical and electronic products, and having a market equivalent in size to the Common Market, advertising pranced ahead and explored the realms of marketing and market research, merchandising and public relations. Market research outposts were set up in Britain shortly before the outbreak of the Second World War, notably A. C. Nielsen, while American industry had been investing in UK plants and markets for some time so that agencies like J. Walter Thompson were also encouraged to move into Britain.

During the six years of war British advertising stood still while American pushed ahead. Very few British firms had anything to advertise during the war years, the outstanding example being Van den Berghs who advertised non-existent Stork margarine in order to retain their investment in this brand leader. Agency chiefs now headed the information and propaganda departments of ministries, continuing to sloganise and often learning PR techniques which they transplanted into PR consultancies after the war, Government advertising appealed to the home front with *Dig for Victory*, *Be Like Dad, Keep Mum* and *Is Your Journey Really Necessary?*, the latter being borrowed from the title of a stage farce.

Post-war Labour Governments clung to controls and rationing, and this included newsprint control so that publications had a restricted number of pages. This led to people buying more than one paper—a whole sheaf on Sunday and Sunday newspapers were excellent advertising media—while the provincial dailies were favoured by advertisers who could not buy enough space in the nationals. Pre-war continental radio advertising, save for Radio Luxembourg, had disappeared. The general magazines—*Picture Post, Illustrated, Everybody's* and *John Bull*—were in demand by readers and advertisers alike, and with sales exceeding a million they made economic use of colour gravure printing and cheap but shiny super-calendered paper. The new detergent Dreft had to be launched entirely by poster because of the dearth of space in the national dailies. Cinema advertising filled some of the gaps, and British films were attracting big audiences. Television was still a rich man's pleasure. ITV and the renting of sets, and council house skyscapes of TV aerials had yet to come. There was no British commercial radio.

A number of things happened almost simultaneously, to the joy of the agencies. Labour went out of office. Controls began to vanish. New products came on the market. Everything went colourful—motor-cars, paints, plastics, kitchen utensils, carpets *and* advertising. The gravure printed general and, particularly, women's magazines were ideal media for all the new post-war colourful products. The removal of building permits reintroduced speculative building, and new houses needed new products. Magazines like *Ideal Home*, and of course the *Daily Mail Ideal Home Exhibition* and the *Festival of Britain* in 1951 were in the vanguard of newly released consumer demand.

The advertising agency responded with the concept of the *modern service advertising agency* which had borrowed American techniques (if it wasn't actually American owned) and was able to offer the advertiser every possible service including marketing, market research and public relations. Some made the mistake of trying to provide extra services without extra charge, not realising for example the costliness of performing PR. They thought PR was just postage and stationery and overlooked the major element of labour.

Sir Edward Hulton, owner of *Lilliput*, *Picture Post*, *Farmer's Weekly* and *Housewife*, was the catalyst of the 50s when he pioneered readership surveys, and for the first time agencies were given an estimation of readership beyond the net sales already provided by the Audit Bureau of Circulations and the audited net sales issued independently by Lord Camrose's Amalgamated Press and *Daily Telegraph*.

Next came the boom in the trade and technical press, with many new titles and eventually controlled circulation journals which commanded much deeper penetration into specialised markets because they did not rely on subscriptions. Industrial advertisers had so many new products and services to offer other industries and the wholesale and retail trades that advertising predominated over editorial. Some magazines like *Homefinder* had very little editorial, while in *Architect's Journal* a thin core of editorial was wedged between pages of advertisements. Here was an open door for the now growing technique of press relations, and new product features and PR-inspired or supplied technical articles literally filled the gap and serviced editors who not only needed to inform their readers but had the revenue from advertising to provide extra editorial pages.

After the war there had been a spate of institutional or prestige advertising, mainly in *The Times*, *Sunday Times* and *The Observer*, and this was largely how advertising agencies saw PR, but press relations was a technique which called for a new breed of PR practitioners and consultants whose attributes were writing for the press and organising press events.

Television made its greatest impact with the Coronation of Queen Elizabeth II in 1953, while live events such as show jumping also attracted viewers. The real growth in receivers and audiences came with commercial TV in 1955. And this made new demands upon advertising agencies, again learning from America where sponsored television had existed for several years, benefiting from experience gained in both Hollywood film-making and sponsored 'soap opera' radio.

Television wrought other changes too. So great was its impact that it had an effect upon mass consumer product sales never previously experienced with advertising. It also had a big effect upon leisure habits. And it provided instant reportage of news and events. The advertising money that went into TV had to come from somewhere else, and as circulations of some journals slipped, and as cinema audiences melted away, other media were less preferred to TV. Advertising agencies had to keep pace with these trends and apply themselves to more impactive advertising. Moreover, they became armed with statistical ammunition which made media schedules far more critical than had been possible only a few years earlier. Agencies became masters of media planning and buying and of dramatic creativity. It became possible to reach the mass consumer market by a few well-proved routes, using a limited number of media the maximum number of times. For example, national press advertising campaigns could be mounted in the *Daily Mirror* and the *Daily Express* and nothing else. Newspapers like the *Star*, *News-Chronicle*, *Sunday Chronicle* and *Sunday Empire News* went to the wall. All four general magazines mentioned earlier folded. Yet a brand new women's magazine, *Woman's Realm*, was able to fight its way into big circulation figures and big advertisers' media schedules.

This is but a sketch of an ever-changing scene but this has been the world of the advertising agency, and to its credit it has shown remarkable resilience and flexibility in accepting all these demands upon its skills. In more recent years, when inflationary costs and a depressed economy have produced new difficulties, the agency has responded by rationalising its structure, finances and methods of doing business.

One of its strengths has been the **Institute of Practitioners in Advertising** which—especially since the 50s—has supported its members with services such as the National Readership Survey and culminating in the Joint Industry Committees for press, radio, television (now BARB) and poster research, while giving support to training and education of agency staff through the CAM Education Foundation. The IPA has been described in Chapter 5, and the reader is reminded here that of the 700 'recognised' agencies some 270 belong to their professional body, these IPA agencies conducting 90 per cent of the advertising business in the UK. In addition to supporting the British Code of Advertising Practice, IPA agencies also follow their own professional code of practice for the conduct of the agency side of advertising.

IPA members do not handle competing accounts without the consent of both parties, and often the problem is overcome by separating competing accounts between a parent agency and an associate or subsidiary agency so that the account is still 'kept in the family'. But of course accounts do change hands, they are known to be 'loose', and that clients are 'shopping' for a new agency, and the competition then becomes intense.

Although billings may run into millions of pounds, profit margins are small. Agencies have to buy with most of the money they handle, and they have to pay their bills more promptly than they are paid by a good many clients. This calls for the ability to give three months' credit while having sufficient cash flow to pay bills in one month. If a client goes bankrupt or if an agency loses a major client, the agency may easily become a financial casualty.

Top 20 Agencies

The following is taken from the annual table published each January in *Campaign*. The figures are for 1982–83:

Ranking			Total Billings in £m.	
1983	*1982*		*1983*	*1982*
1.	1.	Saatchi and Saatchi	134.00	114.00
2.	2.	J. Walter Thompson	126.50	108.00
3.	3.	D'Arcy-MacManus and Masius	98.00	90.00
4.	4.	Ogilvy and Mather	95.00	83.00
5.	6.	Allen Brady and Marsh	76.76	65.11
6.	5.	McCann-Erickson	74.10	72.36
7.	7.	Leo Burnett	72.30	64.70
8.	9.	Young and Rubicam	66.50	58.85
9.	8.	Foote Cone and Belding	62.50	60.80
10.	13.	Boase Massimi Pollitt	61.50	48.10
11.	10.	Dorland Advertising	60.40	54.00
12.	11.	Collett Dickenson Pearce	58.36	52.95
13.	18.	Benton and Bowles	55.13	37.01
14.	16.	Davidson Pearce	55.00	39.76
15.	12.	Ted Bates	54.36	48.81
16.	—	Lowe Howard-Spink	53.40	
17.	14.	Geers Gross	51.00	41.00
18.	19.	Doyle Dane Bernbach	49.20	34.00
19.	17.	Grey Advertising	46.60	37.20
20.	15.	SSC and B, Lintas	41.26	40.40

N.B. The above are the top 20 out of 300 service agencies listed in the annual *Campaign* service. At the same time, *Campaign* listed details of 28 media independent and two directory agencies. No 1982 figures appear for Lowe Howard-Spink because it is a merger between Lowe Howard-Spink and Waseys.

11
The Advertising Agency—How it Works

11.1 Changed 80s Scene

In the last few years there have been revolutionary changes in the British agency world, accelerated by the Office of Fair Trading interpretation of the *Restrictive Trade Practices Act, 1976* when it was extended to cover services. Previously, agency recognition entitled agencies to receive standard rates of commission from members of recognising bodies. Recognition by the Newspaper Proprietors Association, for instance, guaranteed a commission of 15 per cent on media purchases from national newspapers. But in 1979 the OFT ruled that this was a restrictive, monopolistic and therefore illegal practice. The dilemma was resolved by the recognising bodies (NPA, NS, PPA, ITCA, AIRC) recognising agencies for their credit worthiness and adherence to the British Code of Advertising Practise, and leaving commission to negotiations between agencies and media owners.

The essential factor of recognition remained. It endowed no professional status, but simply ensured that agencies had the ability to pay their debts promptly.

But it also changed the agency scene. Media independents—agencies which specialised in media purchasing—had already arrived but now they became even more important. In 1981 the Association of Media Independents came about and by 1984 it had a dozen members and a total billing of around £300m.

Before the OFT ruling stopped the monopoly of the commission system it was extremely difficult to set up a new advertising agency. Since most income was derived from commission on media purchases it was vital to be recognised, but the media owners would recognise only those agencies which has a certain volume of business from a minimum number of clients. About the only way to comply with this was for agency principals to break away from an existing agency, taking clients with them.

Today, we have an array of **creative agencies**. Just as the media independents offer no creative services so the new à la carte creative agencies—modern versions of the hot shops of the 70s—offer no media planning and buying services. Thus, they do not require recognition because they do not depend on commission income, their income being produced by fees.

Yet another change has occurred, although this has been a slow change over a period. Some agencies have 'gone public' and their shares are sold on the Stock Exchange, either among the listed shares like Saatchi and Saatchi which are very high-priced, or more modestly on the unlisted securities market of 'over the counter' shares. In their glossy annual report for 1983, Saatchi and Saatchi, with 13 years of continued growth, reported double audited billing of £603m. for their world-wide group of agencies, and pre-tax profits of £11m. Having entered the United States market, Saatchi and Saatchi (in March 1984) forecast that results were 'well up to forecast'.

In the 80s the British advertising agency business ranges from the mighty Saatchi and Saatchi to many very successful creative or specialist agencies which are very small by comparison but nevertheless highly successful.

Yet another change, which can only be mentioned here, is that whereas in the past PR had mainly prepared the market for advertising, or paralleled advertising, it was now replacing advertising at the point where traditional advertising (especially on TV) was ceasing to be cost effective. The big American-owned international PR consultancy Burson–Marsteller was the leading proponent. Meanwhile a number of large companies were adopting tactics such as sponsorship rather than traditional advertising. The trend took off with Cornhill's sponsorship of test cricket in 1978, and culminated in Canon's record £3m. sponsorship of League football in 1983.

11.2 Merits and Demerits of Commission System

There are three points of view, those of the advertiser, advertising agency and the media-owner and the agency is caught in the middle of an anomalous situation.

From the advertiser's point of view, the commission system is very convenient and very economical. Provided he is spending enough on media advertising the agency will earn sufficient commission to provide the advertiser with full advisory, administrative and supervisory services ranging from the work of the account executive to the buying of space, airtime and materials. The advertiser has to pay the price of media and creative or production work. Moreover, the advertiser is able to enjoy a share of a highly qualified team which it would be uneconomic for him to employ full-time.

Advertising agencies have long thrived on deriving most of their income from commission on space and airtime bookings, and for a large agency, usually with large volumes of repeat advertising requiring no extra creative work, the commission system guarantees a high volume of income. However, the commission system means that financial success depends on volume rather than quality of advertising, and the agency has no means of earning directly according to its ability like a barrister, doctor or architect. It remains, literally, a 'ten percenter' or whatever the rate of commission is.

It is a perfect situation for the media owner. He can restrict his efforts to a limited number of customers, both in selling and in account collection. He can demand very prompt payment—however dilatory clients may be in paying their agencies—and so 'recognition' virtually means recognising agencies with a three months cash flow.

Third, the media can protect themselves handsomely by passing the buck to agencies to see that both they and their clients comply with the British Code of Advertising Practice.

The commission system is therefore a relic of the past, and the OFT ruling has opened up possibilities which promise to make advertising agencies both more professional and capable of being paid what they desire to earn.

Even so, a number of variations on the straight commission system have been in operation for a number of years, these being:

(*a*) Traditional media commission only, plus charges for work and materials such as artwork, TV commercials, blocks, print, etc. Typical of large consumer accounts.

(*b*) Fee plus commission, a basic service fee being paid by the client and the agency taking commission from the media. Typical of medium-sized consumer durable and industrial accounts.

(*c*) Flat fee only. This method applies particularly to technical accounts where commissions are negligible (because of low rates in technical journals and minimum rates of commission), or where there is virtually no above-the-line advertising. The work may consist of sales literature, catalogues, packaging, exhibitions and displays.

(*d*) Cost plus fee. Here the client pays for the cost of work done together with a fee for agency facilities, overheads and profits. The work is charged 'at cost'.

(*e*) Cost plus. Somewhat similar to the fourth method above, a percentage being added to the cost of work done, this percentage covering overheads and profit. The work is charged 'at cost'.

(*f*) Commission credited. An increasingly popular method, and really the grand compromise with the commission system, this method consists of a fee from the client from which is deducted commission received from the media. Thus the client pays a fee over and above the gross media rates, and the agency loses nothing by rebating part of the commission. This retains the media commission system without the advertiser getting everything for nothing, while the agency enjoys a more professional and less of a 'ten percenter' role.

11.3 Types of Agency

The following are the main types of advertising agency which exist in Britain in the 80s.

(*a*) Full service agency. This is the traditional advertising agency, generally concentrating on above-the-line advertising but offering a full service including marketing and market research, and being equipped to handle television advertising. Typical full service agencies are J. Walter Thompson, Ogilvy and Mather, Saatchi and Saatchi-Garland Compton, and Allen, Brady and Marsh.

(*b*) Media independents. As already mentioned at the beginning of this chapter, an innovation has been the arrival and development over the past decade of agencies which devote their skills to media planning and buying.

They do not plan complete advertising campaigns, nor create or produce advertisements. They are recognised by the media owners but they do not rely entirely on commission for their remuneration. A number of payment systems are applied which reflect the complicated nature of modern media, particularly with the great variety of new broadcasting media, to mention only independent local radio, Channel 4, TV–am and Oracle teledata. Some media independents charge an agreed percentage of the media spend, some a share of agency commission and others a fee based on workload and volume (there can be combinations of commission and fee). This flexibility enables clients to buy the best media at the lowest cost.

(c) À la carte agencies. Once called 'hot shops', the à la carte, alternative or creative agencies, buy no media, do not therefore require recognition because credit-worthiness in respect of media purchase does not apply, and they concentrate on campaign planning and creativity for which they charge fees. Thus, a client can use a media independent and an à la carte agency, and get the best of both worlds. Moreover, they are not agents of the media, and not necessarily concerned with media advertising. They may undertake *ad hoc* jobs such as pack design, a corporate identity campaign, production of TV commercials, or the design of an exhibition stand. But equally, they may create entire advertising campaigns, especially for new product launches, and use a media independent for media planning and buying purposes. The important thing is that they are independent creative agencies, free of the recognition restrictions which made it very difficult, for financial reasons, to set up new agencies.

In addition to the specifically creative agencies there are many other kinds which offer specialised services, these being:

(i) New product development agencies. Starting at the very birth of a new product, these agencies contribute to the whole process of new product development and its launch on the market. This can include product design, packaging, pricing, distribution, sales training, marketing research, test marketing, and the planning and creation of the sales promotion and advertising. A more thorough service is offered than when a general service agency is asked to prepare advertising for a new product, a big advantage being the experience gained from specialising in solving the problems of new product development.

(ii) Direct response agencies. Direct response marketing is the modern face of mail order trading and goes beyond the work of direct mail houses to embrace 'off-the-page' direct response advertising, direct mail and catalogue selling, mail drops, and new forms of direct response marketing such as offers on commercial TV with phone-in orders, use of credit and charge cards, and computerised recording of orders.

(iii) Sales promotion agencies. Sales promotion will be discussed in Chapter 24, but here we have agencies which devise competitions, premium offers, High Street redemption schemes, in-store demonstrations, cross-couponings and charity promotions. The latter has become very popular, tokens printed on the pack having a charitable donation value. It is necessary to create original schemes which will boost sales, especially of fast moving consumer goods such as one finds in supermarkets.

(iv) Sponsorship agencies. These fall half-way between creative advertising agencies and PR consultancies, using the techniques of both. They work in collaboration with the representatives of interests seeking sponsors and companies willing to act as sponsors, bringing the two together in harmonious partnerships. Major sponsorships such as those of cricket, football, tennis, golf, motor sport, marathons, snooker and table tennis are organised in remarkable detail by these agencies, of which West Nally and CSS Promotions are leaders. It is not just a case of awarding cash prizes and trophies but of ensuring that the sponsor gains the greatest possible rewards in media coverage and achievement of specific advertising, public relations and marketing objectives.

There are also other specialist agencies, often small or medium-sized, which may be recognised if they are involved in media purchase. Many of these may be recognised by only the Periodical Publishers Association if they do no newspaper advertising, or by the ITCA and AIRC if they buy airtime.

(v) Poster agencies. Poster advertising may be used irregularly, and may not be handled by service agencies. Over the years various poster agencies have come and gone, but the object is to offer a site booking service coupled with the planning of economic campaigns to gain maximum coverage of required poster audiences.

(vi) Industrial agencies. These are usually medium-sized service agencies handling technical accounts such as electronics or computers, and having copywriters and artists skilled in the creativity required by clients.

(vii) Studio agencies. Again, these may handle mainly technical accounts, but the design and production of promotional print may predominate over even trade and technical press advertising.

(viii) Overseas press agencies. As the name implies, these agencies specialise in the preparation of international advertising, including translations, and they are experts in the press of other countries. They handle export campaigns.

(ix) Recruitment agencies. Recession has reduced their number, but these agencies place both classified and displayed advertisements for clients seeking staff. It was with this type of advertising (for the Government) that our first agencies were set up in the early nineteenth century.

(x) Financial agencies. They place advertisements such as those seen in the *Financial Times* and *The Times* for new share issues, and other financial advertisements announcing company results, or during take-over bids.

(xi) Radio and television agencies. These agencies specialise in the selling of airtime and/or writing scripts for radio commercials or producing TV commercials.

(xii) Telephone selling agencies. Yet another new development has been the setting up of agencies to provide campaign facilities for telephone selling and telemarketing, a form of direct response or retailing without shops distribution.

Many of the specialist agencies above are independent companies. However, a number are subsidiaries of the big full service agencies which have moved with the times by exploiting opportunities for new agency services for their existing clients, or for those who do not require the services of a large general agency conducting mainly above-the-line mass media advertising.

11.4   How Do Agencies Work?

This question is best answered in two ways: how does the team operate as a team and how do the individuals within the team operate as individuals?

When we speak of the agency as a team it is clear that various specialists must come together to plan, create and execute advertising campaigns. But this is done in different ways, with different nomenclature, mainly to suit the kind of accounts serviced by the particular agency.

Some agencies operate the **plans board** system, the board being a committee of departmental heads. Typical members will be the account executive (or agency representative), the media planner, marketing manager and creative director. If TV is being used there may be separate representatives for press and TV planning. The PR manager or consultant may also be present. This board or committee will meet to receive news of a new assignment, meet again with preliminary ideas, and gather to consider the final scheme for presentation to client. They may go on meeting as other needs arise. They may meet regularly. In some agencies these agency leaders will get together at four o'clock in the afternoon and go on talking until mid-evening, while in another agency the plans board may take a working lunch with beer and sandwiches. Dependent on the closeness of relations with the client, and the calibre of the advertising manager, these meetings may also be attended by the client who can guide the agency towards an acceptable scheme. It is ideal when agency representative and advertising manager can present client top management with a joint scheme.

Other agencies have a **review board** which works rather differently, a campaign being criticised by agency personnel who have had nothing to do with its planning and creation. It is possible to have a plans board for the first stages, and a review board for the last stage before client approval is sought.

But some agencies have nothing so specific, and there are merely meetings or conferences of those involved at different stages. In a small agency, the principal will call together members of his staff to report on the progress they have made so far.

Reverting to large agencies, it is also common for them to operate the **creative group system**, each group being responsible for one or more clients. The group will be led by either copywriter or visualiser according to which man or woman is the better all-round planner. This system is ideal when a new product—a new motor-car is a very typical example—requires the concentrated effort of a small team over a period of several months.

How the plans board and the creative group systems work can be illustrated by their handling of a TV campaign.

In the first case, some three meetings of the plans board will be held over a matter of four to six weeks. Present will be a director, the account executive, creative director and air-time planner. At the first meeting, the available finance will be discussed, at the second meeting the individual agency specialists will present documents setting out their ideas, and at the third meeting schedules will be ready spelling out number, frequency and timing of commercials together with a proposed shooting script and storyboard. The storyboard resembles a strip cartoon, sketches showing the sequence of the action. Once client approval of expenditure and ideas has been gained, the creative group head discusses the scheme with one of the agency TV producers. The producer—perhaps guided by client wishes—will appoint the production company and film director and become involved in approving the casting of artistes. There are therefore two stages, the plans board being responsible for the creative strategy and the producer for translating this into actual film or video-tape.

Under the **creative group system**, a more intimate team of specialists will produce ideas which, when approved, will be given to the producer to execute. The reader may see small difference between the two methods, but it is this: the plans board operates for the whole agency and all accounts in that the same agency heads will be present, whereas with the creative group method there can be many of these groups operating independently and simultaneously. The plans board suits the medium-size agency, the creative group is really a development of the plans board and suits the big agency.

Already a number of job titles have been mentioned, and a description of the roles and functions of agency personnel will explain the division of labour in agencies. Obviously, the smaller the agency the more individuals have to be jack of all trades, the larger the agency the greater the specialisation. In a very small agency, one man may write and design advertisements, mark up the type faces and buy the settings and blocks, or organise litho and gravure artwork. But in a big agency a copywriter, visualiser, layout man, typographer and production man will handle each stage of the work.

11.5 Agency Personnel

The **directors** may be responsible for certain functions such as finance or the creative side. Most agencies are partnerships or private companies and directors are usually specialists with working roles. **Account directors** control groups of **accounts**—the agency name for clients. This agency use of the word accounts should not be confused with accountancy. Under each account director will serve a number of **account executives**.

In pre-war days the account executive was known as the **contact man** while the tendency is now to call him the agency **representative**. He is the liaison between client and agency. He has to understand what the client wants and what the agency can do. The best account executive (or representative) is usually a graduate who has been given an all-round training in the agency for about two years before specialising. His job is not unlike that of the technical sales representative. He may not be concerned with seeking new business but more with servicing and keeping clients. He is the person the client will see most frequently, and by whom the agency will be judged. Although employed by the agency, he has also to see himself as an extension of the client's advertising department. Trying to ride two horses at the same time is the real measure of his ability. Not surprisingly, account executives tend to gravitate to the client side of the business and become advertising managers, although it is also true that industrial and technical agencies tend to be made up of ex-advertising managers who have set up agencies. The efficient account executive is therefore able to win the acceptance and confidence of the client so that he is given all the facts he needs, and is also able to win the regard of his agency colleagues so that they produce for him the campaigns which will please the client.

In the 50s the **marketing manager** became an important agency executive, but as clients set up their own marketing departments this service became less required and some agencies rationalised their organisations by dispensing with their own marketing manager. While it is very necessary for all agency personnel to be marketing-conscious—bright ideas must sell—the agency marketing manager tends to fulfil one of two purposes. Either he provides an opposite number to the client's marketing manager, or he provides an extra service for the client who does not have a marketing manager. Most large advertisers have a marketing manager or director to whom advertising, product or brand managers—and sometimes PROs or press officers—report. His role in the agency, and on behalf of the client, is to study and make recommendations about the market segment to which the advertising is to be directed, or about new markets, or about distribution methods, packaging, pricing and product presentation, and to recommend market research where necessary. There may also be a **market research manager** who will buy research services from the companies which specialise in different classes and techniques of research, interpret reports produced in this way, and also study and make use of the vast quantity of statistics which are produced by Government, trade associations, universities and other sources.

The **media planner** and **media buyer** (combined as **space buyer** in the smaller agency) evaluate and plan or haggle and buy accordingly. In big agencies, separate sections will deal with the press and TV. Media planning has developed with the provision of statistical data about readers and audiences, social grades, programme ratings and cost per thousand (net sales, readers, housewives, etc.). Campaigns can nowadays be calculated on a slide-rule or by computer. And the media representative has to bring with him statistical arguments for buying his space, not a buttonhole, a smile and a free drink.

Skill in gaining maximum impact with costly television advertising can depend on just when and where the commercials appear. The contracting companies—e.g. Thames, Granada, Anglia, Television South—supply agencies with advance information about forthcoming shows. The sharp-witted media planner or air-time buyer will search for opportunities for his client's advertisements to appear in advantageous breaks. He may have *carte blanche* to get the highest possible audience ratings. This is how a lively agency gets the greatest mileage out of the appropriation, and supported by good media intelligence (which is the responsibility of the sales offices of the TV companies) it can make advertising work extra hard for its clients.

Advertisement rates vary according to the regional audience size, and only a large national advertiser can afford to network throughout the U.K. But cost is relative to the size of market and volume of business sought. What may seem expensive could be economical. According to the BARB Establishment Survey of TV Homes, December 1980, the networked commercials covered almost 20 million households. However, it should be remembered that those 20 million households, although they can be multiplied to accept more than one viewer in many households, have to be divided among a number of channels (at least three), alternative forms of viewing, radio, and no viewing at all. Consequently, an audience of 15–20 million is the sort of large audience any extremely popular programme is likely to attract.

JICTAR (and the JICTAR Top Twenty and Top Ten Charts which used to be published in the press, often contradicting the audience measurement figures of the BBC!) was replaced by the research services of the Broadcasters' Audience Research Board (BARB). As explained in Chapter 5, BARB combines ITV and BBC audience research.

National and area Top Tens are published weekly, and are produced by Audits Great Britain (AGB). Here is an example of the National Top Tens for the four main channels, together with audience figures, followed by an example of a single ITV area, London, with its TVR rating. These statistics are for the week ending March 18, 1984.

	Individual viewing (millions)
BBC 1	
1. Jim'll Fix It	12.00
2. Some Mothers Do 'Ave 'Em	11.25
3. That's Life	10.95
4. Dallas	10.15
5. A Question Of Sport	10.10
6. Hannibal Brooks	9.95
7. Dynasty	9.85
8. Top Of The Pops	9.75
9. Diana	9.70
10. Holiday	9.65

BBC 2	
1. Best Of Paul Daniels	5.75
2. Long Weekend	4.95
3. Sands Of Iwo Jima	4.50
4. Call My Bluff	4.25
5. Forty Minutes	3.65
6 = Treasure Houses	3.45
6 = Tucker's Luck	3.45
8 = Charlie Brown	3.40
8 = Marti Caine	3.40
10. Horizon	3.35

ITV	*Originating programme company*	*ITV areas*	*Individual viewing (millions)*
1. Duty Free	Yorkshire	All	16.65
2. Coronation Street (Wed.)	Granada	All	16.35
3. Minder	Thames	All	16.25
4. Coronation Street (Mon.)	Granada	All	15.75

5. This Is Your Life	Thames	All	15.35
6. 3-2-1	Yorkshire	All	13.65
7. Fresh Fields	Thames	All	13.40
8. Shroud For A Nightingale	Anglia	All	12.50
9 = T. J. Hooker	ITV	All	12.20
9 = Live From Her Majesty's	LWT	All	12.20

Channel 4	*Individual viewing (millions)*
1. Ice Castles	3.20
2. Treasure Hunt	3.15
3. Cheers	2.95
4. An Audience With Joan Rivers	2.80
5. Brookside (Wed.)	2.60
6. Brookside (Tue.)	2.45
7. Love, Sidney	2.15
8. Bewitched	2.00
9. The Lady Is A Tramp	1.90
10. The World At War	1.85

London	*Originating programme company*	*Screened by*	*TVR*
1. Minder	Thames	Thames	32
2 = Duty Free	Yorkshire	Thames	29
2 = Coronation Street (Wed.)	Granada	Thames	29
2 = This Is Your Life	Thames	Thames	29
5. Jim'll Fix It	BBC	BBC 1	27
6 = Coronation Street (Mon.)	Granada	Thames	26
6 = That's Life	BBC	BBC 1	26
8. Fresh Fields	Thames	Thames	25
9 = Some Mothers Do 'Ave 'Em	BBC	BBC 1	23
9 = 3-2-1	Yorkshire	LWT	23
9 = Boat Race	BBC	BBC 1	23

The television viewing rate (TVR) is the percentage of individuals viewing the programme out of all those individuals in homes with sets capable of receiving ITV transmissions from that area. The calculation is the average audience throughout the programme. A practical example of the application of TVRs will be found in the Brooke Bond Oxo PG Tips case study at the end of this book.

The **copywriter** may work under a **copy chief**, but the copywriter may be a member of a creative group or be a freelance who is commissioned by the copy chief. Copy has two meanings in printing, publishing and advertising. All material for printing may be called **copy**, as with the **copy date** by which a publisher wants advertisements. In this sense copy may consist of a complete metal plate of the advertisement, or a layout accompanied by typewritten wording and original blocks of the artwork, or typewritten wording and artwork such as drawings, photographs or colour transparencies. All these combinations are copy to the printer. But in advertising a more precise meaning is that **the copy consists of the wording**. The copywriter writes the words. However, he will probably also think up the general theme and presentation of the advertisement which will be interpreted by artists. The old idea of the copywriter sitting in one room writing the words, and the layout man or visualiser sitting in the studio and fitting them into his design, is almost extinct. In any worthwhile agency, it is realised that there must be fusion between copywriting and its presentation.

The copywriter has to be a very talented person able to work in the different media of, say, press, poster, television or radio. He has to be able to coin the slogan or jingle that has universal application, or write competition rules that meet the gambling laws.

The **creative director** will combine the talents of writing and art to produce complete advertisements, and this may mean bringing together or directing creative groups, or buying outside freelance and studio services. He is the conductor of the advertising orchestra, and the partner of the more administrative and businesslike media planners and buyers. Under the creative director will come the copywriter already described, and those who design and possibly those who instruct printers.

The **visualiser** is an artist who can rapidly produce rough ideas which are variously called **scamps**, **scribbles** or **visuals**. With these roughs the visualiser is able to interpret the copywriter's ideas and show a variety of ways of presenting them.

The **layout artist** (who may be the visualiser) produces designs which closely resemble the printed advertisement. He 'lays out' the copy and pictures, usually producing a drawing of exact measurements which typesetter, engraver, platemaker, paste-up artist and printer can follow.

The **typographer** (who may also be the layout man) is an artist in type who not only knows the hundreds of different type faces but knows for which sorts of work particular type faces are most suitable. Having selected the faces he then specifies their sizes and weights, and also instructs the printer about spacing, according to the printing process. A good typographer can make an advertisement not only attractive and original, but legible and a pleasure to read.

The **finished artist** draws or paints the final artwork, and much of the artwork in advertisements is produced by famous artists who also undertake commercial work. The **scraper board artist** is a specialist at producing a drawing—often based on a photograph—which by means of lines, dots, stipples and cross-hatchings will gain clear and bold reproduction in newspapers.

Progress chasing is essential if many separate jobs are to culminate in a complete, approved advertisement delivered on time. The **production manager** heads a department of **production assistants** who are responsible for buying typesetting, original blocks, stereos and electros for letterpress printed advertisements and print, and for supplying text and artwork for photogravure and offset-litho printed publications. It is also his job to organise the work-flow so that copy and artwork, proofs, corrections and final copy are achieved according to a timetable which he establishes once the presentation to client has won approval for the campaign to be executed. For greater convenience in the larger agencies there is a **traffic controller** who directs this work-flow, much of which requires duplicate copies of instructions and orders being distributed among the departments which need to be informed.

Finally, the **finance director** or **accountant** will control the despatch of bills to clients, supported by vouchers issued by the **voucher clerk**. Vouchers are copies of journals containing the actual press advertisements, and sent to clients as proof of insertion. Reference was made earlier to the extended credit which agencies may have to offer while being responsible for quick payment of their own accounts to media and suppliers. To overcome cash-flow problems one or two special systems are used. If it is a small account, or one producing little or no commission income, the agency may ask the client to deposit funds in a pool held by the agency—which is not unlike the PR consultancy which charges fees a month or quarter in advance—while other agencies invoice clients with space accounts at the time of insertion and not after accounts have been received from the publishers. Again, if an advertiser makes large regular expenditures the agency may be so cautious as to book not more than one week ahead and demand payment before making further bookings. Even so, in the case of one mail-order trader, this proved ruinous for an advertising agency since one week the trader went bankrupt and left the agency liable for payment of several whole page advertisements in the national press. The agency failed too.

Money problems are heightened by credit squeezes and the inability of banks to permit large overdrafts, the result being that firms simply borrow off their suppliers by extending credit. For businesses like advertising agencies this behaviour means one of two things: drop the slow-paying client or go out of business. In taking on new clients, agencies need to be as strict about credit-worthiness as the media owners are when granting agencies recognition.

11.6 Agency Paperwork

Important to the efficient and profitable running of an agency is its paper-work system, and a few brief recommendations will now be stated. It will be seen that some of these are as helpful to clients as they are to agents.

(*a*) Whenever fresh work is started for a client it should be given a **job number** prefixed by the code letters allotted to the client. Thus, if a photographic session is booked for Jones Brothers Ltd, the job may be identified as, say, JB101. This procedure is most important because several people in an agency may be responsible for ordering materials and supplies for a client. Sometimes it is done under pressure, by word of mouth, over the telephone, through a secretary or an assistant. Unless given a job number it will be impossible to identify the account when it comes in weeks later, the client will never be charged, and the agency will be the loser.

(*b*) Details of the job, and the job number, should be entered on a **job sheet** produced with duplicate sheets, each sheet being a different colour for, say, creative, media, production and finance departments. Traffic control can then distribute the job sheets to their respective departments. This raising of job sheets ties in with the ordering, which should be confirmed by letter of instruction or contract and bearing the job number. Ideally, suppliers should be told not to accept an order which does not bear a job number which they must then repeat on their invoices to the agency.

(c) The **agenda** for the agency–client meetings should be drawn up by the account executive, items being identified by their job numbers.

(d) After the meeting (or even after a telephone call or a casual meeting) a **contact report** should be written at once. The report should state who attended the meeting, when and where it was held and its purpose and the distribution list. The report should follow the pattern of the agenda and state as briefly as possible what happened or what decisions were taken concerning each job-numbered item. On the right-hand side of the sheet there should be a vertical rule, setting aside in the right-hand margin a column in which responsibilities can be set out against the initials of the person on either client or agency side who has to take agreed action. If this contact report is presented within 24–48 hours it is possible to clear up any misunderstandings and get agreements, decisions and responsibilities determined beyond doubt. This may be called a **call** or **progress** report.

(e) **Invoices** can be paid by the agency on the basis of job-numbered information and instructions, and **invoices** can be rendered by the agency which both recover job-numbered outlays and charge for job-numbered work with which the advertising manager is familiar. Thus, accounts are likely to be accurate and beyond challenge.

11.7 Should Clients Change Agencies?

There is clearly merit in an agency–client partnership which becomes richer over the years by its mutual sharing of confidences and knowledge. It can take three years for an agency to reach a proper level of efficiency in dealing with a client's advertising, yet this is the very point when some firms decide they must find a new agency. The following are some of the reasons why clients do seek such a change:

(a) Client–agency management got on well before the appointment was made, but liaison is then handed over to an account executive previously unknown to the client. The client feels fobbed off with a substitute as if the agency regards his account as a minor one, which perhaps it is! Nevertheless, the resentment rankles and persists until sooner or later an excuse is made for ending the contract.

(b) There is a change of client personnel and with it a 'new broom' attitude which is fatal to the existing agency. Perhaps the new marketing director or advertising manager wants an agency he happens to know and likes or used to work for.

(c) The agency does not understand the account, and mistakes occur because policy decisions are not interpreted to agency personnel. A fault here may be that agency personnel never have a chance of meeting the client and discovering the policy at first hand.

(d) The agency may have got into a rut, and being devoid of new ideas deserves to lose an account which it may have been taking for granted.

(*e*) There may be disagreements over charges and account rendering. This may result from the agency farming out work, imposing an on-cost, and expecting the client to pay two outside profits. The client says if the agency cannot do the work inside with its own staff he may as well buy direct himself or use a more comprehensive agency with cheaper services.

(*f*) Agency staff tend to change fairly rapidly. It is a young person's business, and experience can be gained only by moving around. In industry, people are more apt to devote a lifetime, or at least a long time, to employment with one firm. The client may become disheartened by agency staff changes and seek another agency without understanding that agency staff changes are inevitable.

These are but a few of the reasons why accounts change hands. Human rather than business reasons predominate, and often the reasons seem unfair and irrational. But they are not unlike the reasons why we stop buying petrol at a certain garage, change our barber or swear we'll never eat in that restaurant again. Very largely, it is a matter of human relations and that often means a lack of clear and regular communication. Disenchantment is not always necessary.

Some of the above reasons are taken from the surveys carried out by Scientific Advertising and Marketing Ltd (since renamed Interad Ltd) in 1967, and by Pace Advertising and Print Services Ltd in 1969. From a survey conducted by Lintas Ltd in 1970 into the decision processes in the selection of an advertising agency it is interesting to quote two tables. One indicates the reasons why agencies were **short listed** and the other the reasons for the eventual **appointment**. Then we shall look at the key people in the decision process.

Why Advertising Agencies are Shortlisted

After visiting agencies and discussing their services and other clients, clients put agencies on the short list because of:

1. Creativity.
2. Experience.
3. No conflict.
4. Reputation.
5. Size.
6. International.
7. Management.

'It should be noted that before taking into account the kind of criteria described above . . . the most important factor in getting on the short list is that the agency must be known. There was *no* evidence that advertisers made deliberate effort to seek out previously unknown agencies. The reasons given for short listing agencies and for finally appointing one show an expected degree of agreement.'

Reasons for Appointment

1. Understood problems.
2. Creative.
3. Management.

4. Ability.
5. Compatibility.
6. Presentation. Other accounts. Success.
7. Small agency.

'The fact that the agency was demonstrably able to understand the client's problems and related its skills to those problems came out as the most important reason for making the appointment.

'In the course of the study we also collected rather more impressionistic data about the kind of evidence sought by advertisers in assessing agencies and perhaps the findings here can best be illustrated by a number of verbatim quotations:

> '*We looked at their accounts, and the accounts they had lost and gained.*'
> '*The work they had produced for other clients.*'
> '*I knew them personally.*'
> '*They already work with us on other accounts.*'
> '*Recommendations of people I know in the advertising business!*'

Key People in the Decision Process

The survey indicated that 'Among the 48 advertisers who had appointed an agency in the three years prior to the interview, it was clear that the final say as to which agency to appoint split almost equally between those where it lay with the group, e.g. the board of directors, and where it was an individual decision of one of the senior directors.'

These were:

Chairman/managing director.
Marketing/sales director.
Special committee.
Board of directors.

Only in a small number of cases did the advertising manager have authority to appoint the agency.

Advertisers' Requirements and the Criteria of a Good Agency

In this section of the study all 165 advertisers were interviewed, that is including those who had changed their agency in the three years prior to the interview. All 165 advertisers were required to rank in terms of their importance the twenty-one criteria already identified from the Pilot Study by which an agency could be judged. Each criterion was rated on a four-point verbal scale from 'essential' through 'very important' to 'fairly important' and 'not important'. These were then given values of 3, 2, 1 and 0 and mean scores were calculated on this basis for each attribute. The following mean scores resulted from this procedure.

	Mean score
1. 'be creatively lively'.	2.7
2. 'able to produce original, creative ideas'.	2.7
3. 'really interested in the client's problems'.	2.7
4. 'have a top class management team'.	2.5
5. 'high level of understanding of your marketing problems'.	2.5
6. 'have a very high calibre of personnel'.	2.5
7. 'flexible in meeting client's changing requirements'.	2.4
8. 'practical consumer orientated creative approach'.	2.3
9. 'progressive in its outlook'.	2.3

		Mean score
10.	'use research intelligently'.	2.2
11.	'have an outstanding media department'.	2.0
12.	'have a wide range of experienced personnel'.	2.0
13.	'give personal attention to client at senior level'.	1.9
14.	'have a clearly defined approach to marketing'.	1.9
15.	'allow client to deal with the people who do the actual work'.	1.8
16.	'have a systematic approach to new product development'.	1.3
17.	'agency should be growing and expanding'.	1.3
18.	'experienced in your type of market'.	1.2
19.	'have facilities for producing below-the-line material'.	1.0
20.	'uninterested in winning advertising awards'.	0.7
21.	'a world-wide organisation'.	0.6

'From this it will be seen that the most important criteria in agency selection were its ability to be able to produce original creative ideas; the interest which it demonstrated in the client's problems; and the quality of its management. . . . Once again, the importance of creativity is demonstrated, but the constant reiteration by respondents of the importance of creativity must lead us to ask whether "creativity" is not some kind of halo description which is merely another way of saying "I like the agency".'

These extracts are taken from the paper which Gerald de Groot, research director of Lintas International Advertising, presented to the 1971 congress of the European Society for Opinion and Marketing Research held in Helsinki. He subsequently made use of the findings of the Lintas survey at *Campaign*'s one-day conference on *How to choose an advertising agency* held in London in December 1971.

We began this two-chapter study of the advertising agency with an historical survey, and if we conclude with the Lintas comments on the advertiser's demand for creativity this does seem to be the historical justification for the existence of the advertising agency, at least from the point of view of the advertiser. Nevertheless, while agencies may try to be statistical, scientific and businesslike, to preen themselves as professionals, it is after all the ideas, the showmanship, the gimmickry, the mystique of the fabulous, unreal, imaginative, creative agency world that the advertiser is after. He can buy and sell but he cannot create. He is no poet, writer, artist, photographer—no, he is a man of brass. Originally, ideas were needed for the early press, for the walls of railway stations, and the sides of horse-drawn buses. Come the dreary 20s and 30s and it was fun ads—*Bovril Prevents That Sinking Feeling* and *My Goodness, My Guinness*—that won his favour and today, with the insatiable appetite of television and its high standards of film studio sophistication, creativity rules again.

In other words, the value of the advertising agency lies in its success in providing the magical blending of mind, words and pictures, colour, action and sound which is quite beyond the balance sheet dullness of the businessman. He is the perpetual child at the circus.

The development of commercial radio in Britain presented yet another demand for creativity, whether provided by traditional or specialist agencies. The success of commercial radio from the points of view of station contractors, advertisers and listeners depends upon the extent to which creative advertising, as well as good programme material, makes it an economic proposition. Perhaps no other medium is capable of driving away its audience through unimaginative advertising than radio. There have actually been complaints from listeners about too strident commercials!

Relevance of Surveys Today

Although the surveys quoted above were conducted some years ago their relevance to developments in the agency world are interesting and obvious.

Whether it be in the success of the top 20 agencies listed at the end of the previous chapter, or in the successful emergence of the specialist media independents and the à la carte creative agencies, media buying and creative skills predominate as the chief assets of an advertising agency.

12
Ancillary and Freelance Services

12.1 What Services are Available?

Such is the variety of work carried out by both the advertiser's own advertising department and the advertising agency that many specialist services have to be employed from time to time. Some may be used every day, others only when a particular need arises. Either way, it means that advertising managers and agency personnel require a sound knowledge of these facilities so that they can be skilful buyers. For example, an imperfect knowledge of printing techniques can easily lead to an unexpectedly large bill because overtime costs have been incurred. Or, photographs may turn out to be disappointing because the buyer of photography has not understood that most photographers are specialists in certain kinds of work and he has commissioned the wrong man. Frankness between buyer and seller is always advisable so that the supplier knows what is wanted and the customer knows what he is getting.

12.2 Twenty Services Described

The following are some of the ancillary and freelance services that are available. They will be found classified and listed in *Advertiser's Annual*, and freelance services are advertised in *Campaign*.

Typesetters.
Process Engravers.
Stereotypers.
Art Studios.
Art Agents.
Design Consultants.
Photographers.
Retouchers.
Film and Video-tape Producers.
Printers.
Display Producers.
Exhibition Stand Designers and Constructors.
Direct Mail Producers.
Freelance Copywriters and Visualisers.

Translators.
Market Research Services.
Outdoor Advertising Agents.
Door-to-door Distributors.
Public Relations Consultants.
Merchandiser/Sales Promotion Services.

Some of these services may be bought direct by the advertiser, but all of them can be bought by advertising agencies. It is not uncommon for the advertising agency to handle 'above-the-line' media advertising (and the services directly linked such as the first three on the above list), and for the advertiser's own advertising department to handle 'below-the-line' work. But the small advertiser, having no agency, will buy direct as and when he needs a photographer, printer, display producer or freelance copywriter.

Typesetters. There are 'trade' typesetting houses which set printing type, either because the printer does not employ a mechanical typesetter or requires special faces which are not stocked in the printing works. Typesetters also set small lots of type as when advertising agencies require copy to be set for advertisements so that eventually they can supply complete advertisements in metal form to the publishers of letterpress-printed newspapers and magazines. Other small typesetting jobs may be those known as 'sorts', when a trade typesetting house supplies words set in special type faces, such as titles and display lines. They may also set up display faces from which reproduction 'pulls' or proofs are made on chromo-art paper and used as original artwork. Copy may also be IBM or photo-set.

Process engravers. These are 'block makers' who produce line, half-tone and combined line and half-tone plates for the reproduction of drawings and photographs by the letterpress printing process. The principle here is that the artwork has to be transformed into a metal or plastic plate on which the areas to be inked and printed are raised in relief. A line block is not unlike a date stamp or lino-cut but a half-tone block has a printing surface made up of dots which have been produced by photographing the original picture through a screen. The block, strictly speaking, is the wooden or metal mount for the metal or plastic plate, but it is common to speak of the mounted plate as the 'block'. Before ordering from the process engraver it is necessary to know whether the printer or publisher wants the plate mounted or unmounted. The mount makes the 'block' type-high so that it matches the type.

Stereotypers. A stereo is a copy, made by taking a mould of the type, blocks or complete advertisement made up of type and blocks, and such duplicates are required when the same advertisement is to appear in more than one publication. (A tougher and superior duplicate is an electrotype made by the process of electrolysis when copper is deposited on a shell-like mould of the original.)

Art studios. Few agencies or advertising departments can afford to employ specialist artists full-time, but artwork may be commissioned from studios producing particular classes of work. Lettering, scraper board and industrial artists often work in independent studios.

Art agents. Many professional artists work at home and in out-of-the-way places and they employ art agents both to find work for them and to sell their services. It is seldom beneath the dignity of the Academy painter to produce commercial art. Thus, if the art director of an advertising agency wants a picture of a horse, a bottle of brandy or of a pretty girl he will consider photography and various art mediums. If he wants a drawing or painting he will ring up an art agent and ask whether this agent represents artists capable of doing this kind of picture. Usually, the agent will come along to the agency and show the art director files of specimen drawings by several artists. The art director will select the style and artist he prefers, and terms and briefings will then be agreed.

Design consultants. These specialist artists accept commissions for house styles and logotypes, and some famous examples have been the redesigning of the liveries of British Airways and British Caledonian Airways. A corporate identity can include everything visible about an organisation and so this can be a major undertaking ranging from the decoration of aircraft, vehicles, premises and property to the design of all forms of print and including uniforms, napkins, cuff-links, ash-trays and so on.

Photographers. There are thousands of photographers, and most of them are best at certain classes of work. In fact, some undertake only one kind of work whether it be table-top, industrial, portraiture, figure, wild life, aerial or perhaps underwater. Before engaging a photographer it is therefore important to see samples of his work. Jack of all trades photographers should be avoided.

Retouchers. It may be necessary to retouch a picture, not necessarily because it is bad but in order to obtain the best possible reproduction, bearing in mind that in the course of plate-making for all printing processes there is bound to be a loss of quality. The retoucher—usually a very fine artist—can enhance highlights, remove unwanted backgrounds or reflections and possibly add lettering. To do this he must know the eventual use of the artwork, preferably the kind of publication in which the picture will appear. Retouchers may be on the staff of the art studios mentioned above, or they may work independently.

Film producers. Advice on film-making may be obtained from organisations such as Cygnet Ltd, Bushey Studios, Melbourne Road, Bushey, Herts. There are, however, two kinds of film and two kinds of film-making. There is the commercial which runs for a matter of seconds, as shown on cinema and TV screens, and there is the non-advertising or PR documentary which averages about twenty minutes. The two kinds of film-making are studio and outside location, although some films may contain both indoor and outdoor sequences.

A comparatively new development has been the production of videotapes, and these are widely used on TV. They can also be made for sales conferences, for which a film would be an excessively costly undertaking. It is also possible to transmit VTR by Post Office land-line so that audiences may view an event at a distance from where it is taking place. Thus, an overflow audience can view an event or performance on a giant Eidophor screen in a different building. It is also possible to hold a press conference in central London for an event that is taking place hundreds of miles away. One of the best examples of this 'narrowcasting' technique has been the simultaneous holding of Billy Graham meetings throughout

Europe, Billy Graham conducting his meeting in one centre and film and sound being transmitted to audiences in other countries. Today, many large firms have their own video studios or equipment, but there are specialist video production companies. Industrial work uses the Sony Umatic system, but this can be transferred to VHS and Betamax tapes.

Printers. Mention of printing processes concludes the chapter on press advertising in the media section. Quite apart from the different printing processes, printers are rather like photographers in that according to their equipment and their experience they tend to specialise in kinds of print work. Therefore, in buying print it is wise to ask for examples of work done, and before placing an order the buyer of print should satisfy himself that the right printer has been found for the job. This decision may be complicated when dealing with a printer's representative who is selling for a group which aims at offering a comprehensive service. However, generally speaking, there are those that do jobbing work such as stationery and others which print newspapers, some which specialise in posters and still others that print books. There are flexographers who print on delicate materials, and thermographers who produce print resembling die-stamping. A lot of questions need to be asked of eager print salesmen. There are no standard print prices, and quotations will vary according to process, size of machine, location of works, speed of operation, drying methods and extent of make ready.

This is a fascinating world and printing is a major craft. The art of working with the printer is one that can be immensely beneficial to the print buyer, and it implies working methodically and co-operatively with the printer, appreciating his skill and not making impossible demands.

Display producers. These are firms which design, construct and print all kinds of display aids, mainly for point-of-sale. Again, firms tend to specialise, one in wire stands, another in scale or working models, and yet another in showcards, cut-outs, mobiles or signs.

Exhibition stand designers and constructors. Two services are combined under this heading, although usually they are two separate individuals or firms. A designer will produce an idea supported by an artistic impression or a model, and if this is accepted by the exhibitor either he or the exhibitor will commission a firm of stand constructors to actually make the stand to the agreed design.

Direct mail producers. Direct mail producing houses possess libraries of mailing lists, and will undertake the writing of sales letters, design of mailing pieces and the addressing, filling, sealing, franking and posting of the finished job. Different producers may offer special lists or services, or their own style of mailing shot.

Freelance copywriters and visualisers. Freelance creative staff are frequently used by advertising agencies so that they are able to call on a variety of talent, or use those writers and artists who are best suited to particular campaigns. Equally, the advertising manager—or the small advertiser—can employ freelance creative staff. For instance, the small trader will find that it will pay him to have his sales letters written by an expert: amateur sales letters can be very bad indeed! Sales letter writing is a special technique.

Translators. A mistake in translation can be a disaster, and a big problem can be to find a translator who is familiar with current idiom or the jargon of a particular industry. Ideally, the translation should be made by a native of the country whose language the work is being translated into, and this may require having the work done abroad. Advice can be obtained from Chambers of Commerce and the Department of Trade and Industry. So here is an ancillary service of some importance which must not be undertaken lightly. It is a chastening experience to commission a translation in the UK, and then see how it is rewritten by a native in the country where it is to be used! Time needs to be allowed for such checking.

Market research services. The variety of market research techniques is discussed in Chapter 15, and once again there are research units specialising in different techniques. Research firms are listed in *Advertiser's Annual*, and the Market Research Society Yearbook contains a directory of research organisations and their specific services. These services may include field surveys, consumer panels, omnibus surveys, dealer audits, in-hall and in-theatre tests and discussion groups, to mention only a few. Most research organisations tend to be selective in both techniques and kind of client, the latter consisting, for example, of consumer, industrial and financial clients.

Outdoor advertising agents. Because there is irregular use of outdoor advertising by clients, most advertising agencies limit themselves to the creative side and place bookings through a jointly owned poster booking agency. Commission is split 10 per cent to the poster agency, and 5 per cent to the placing agency, with some surcharges for the user.

Door-to-door distributors. Here we have firms which deliver mail-shots, premium offers, samples and other promotional items, either on a general door-to-door basis or more selectively according to the assignment. Economies are possible as when two or three items for different users are delivered at the same time. This is sometimes called 'direct advertising' as distinct from 'direct mail' which is posted. Mail-drops are made to selected addresses.

Public relations consultants. While a whole chapter—the next one—has been devoted to PR, the outside PR consultancy service has a place in this array of ancillary services. Advertising agencies seldom have their own PR department (but the larger ones do own subsidiary consultancies) and so they may recommend the use of a PR consultancy. Again, the advertiser may wish to engage a PR consultancy in addition to the advertising agency, taking either a continuous or an *ad hoc* service. Moreover, most PR consultancies specialise and their services may be used for assistance with an exhibition, to produce a house journal, to run a press relations service, or because advice is needed on financial PR.

The Public Relations Year Book, published by the Public Relations Consultants Association (see Chapter 5) in co-operation with the *Financial Times*, gives detailed information about PR consultancies, supported by features on PR practice.

Merchandiser/sales promotion services. Under this very general heading must come all kinds of marketing services including those which run incentive schemes for salesmen, provide commando corps of salesmen to support regional campaigns, supply merchandising staff who will arrange shop displays or give in-store demonstrations.

There are also promotion agencies which undertake complete campaigns such as a competition with point-of-sale displays and supporting literature, a complete below-the-line programme.

The Institute of Sales Promotion has its own Code of Practice, runs courses and examinations, and provides its members with standard rules for competitions. Reference to these rules may be seen on the entry forms for sales promotion prize contests.

In this chapter we have discussed 20 ancillary and freelance services. To these may be added many more such as Xerox copying, floral services, caterers, girl agencies which supply models, demonstrators and saleswomen, window dressing services, and suppliers of visual aids and display equipment. The advertising business sustains a variety and wealth of services of all kinds.

13
Public Relations

Public relations has been defined in Chapter 3 (see p. 24), the roles of the IPR and the PRCA will be found in Chapter 5, (see p. 75 and pp. 84–5) and several references have been made to the omnibus nature of PR in relation to the total communications of any organisation, commercial or otherwise, combine or sole trader. In this chapter two aspects only will be discussed:

(a) *Public relations and advertising*, and
(b) *PR administration and services*.

13.1 Public Relations and Advertising

The layman—and even the businessman—may take the broad view that any *favourable* commercial reference is an advertisement. They are quite jealous when, in a BBC news bulletin, it is announced that British Leyland has sold its ten millionth bus to Tristan da Cunha. It does not occur to them that this is legitimate news. It is not advertising, although it is publicity which, being the inevitable good or bad outcome of publication, is hardly the same thing.

If a politician is exposed in a corruption scandal, or a famous pop singer is arrested on a charge of smuggling drugs, there will be publicity in the media. But while each may have maximum impact, neither of these news reports will be an advertisement.

The distinction between an advertisement and a PR news item—or any news item—is this: an advertisement is a controlled announcement issued how, when and where its author wishes, provided he pays the price for occupation of the space, time or site, and provided the announcement does not offend voluntary codes or the law. Moreover, an advertiser has the right to be conceited and biased in his own favour. He is entitled to say 'Bloggs Baked Beans Are Best' as boldly, as loudly and as often as he likes, provided he keeps the peace.

But no matter whether a newspaper or magazine be biased for or against the Government, blood sports, immigration, women's lib or pacifism, it will spurn any news story from a PR source which is biased in its own favour.

Public relations—of which advertising is a part if we regard PR as total communication to every public of an organisation—will not succeed if it tries to put words into the editor's mouth. It must not comment in its own favour. The difference between writing advertisement copy and a news story is that the superlatives are left out of the second. No editor will print a story saying 'Bloggs Baked Beans Are Best', at least not without a snide aside 'so the makers claim!' 'Bloggs Baked Beans Are Best' is a **legitimate puff** in the legal sense, but it is a meaningless generalisation otherwise. But PR news stories must never be puffs, and there is no worse insult to a PR practitioner than to deride him as a 'puff merchant'. Historically, in the days of coffee house newspapers, 'puffing' was the art of advertising.

No, the editor will want to publish facts, and they must be facts of interest to his readers. Every story must be judged by its reader interest— in other words will it help to maintain or increase readership? PR people do the favours, not editors. The beans are of a certain kind in a particular sauce. They are packed in a certain kind of container. The can holds a particular quantity. It is a food that can be served in a particular quantity. And so on and on. These are *facts*, unembellished, advertising nothing because they influence no action. Facts can merely inform, perhaps arouse curiosity for more facts, but they cannot advocate or persuade. A maintenance manual or a technical data sheet instructs or specifies. It does not sell. Nor does a news release.

Public relations deals in information, and it is nonsense to try to distinguish between 'information' PR and 'promotional' PR.

The point of this chapter is to emphasise that **advertising can fail if the organisation, product or service is not understood,** and so PR can be very important in a marketing operation.

For example, if it is believed that flying is dangerous people will neither book seats on flights nor send freight by air. All the advertising in the world will not convince people otherwise. Nigeria Airways suffered this PR problem when their VC-10 crashed and Nigerians mistrusted their airline until they were eventually convinced of its efficiency. Conversely, following the crash of a DC-10, the confidence publicly expressed in the aircraft by Sir Freddie Laker, and public confidence in him, helped to persuade passengers to continue flying on the DC-10. Every airline flying DC-10's benefited from this confidence.

There is no doubt that advertising works better when prospects know what you are talking about. This is very true with new things, whether they be a jumbo jet, a garden insecticide, a sewing machine or the pill.

The *Daily Mirror* devoted a whole page of editorial to descriptions of every form of contraception, its application and source of supply. But that was not a free advertisement for the London Rubber Company, or for every reader's local chemist or barber's shop. Nevertheless, this fortuitous *information* may have made more sense of the tortuously innocuous advertisements that one sees published or displayed for such essential everyday products.

When Rentokil introduced their damp-proofing system—now so successful that rival firms have entered the business—it was almost condemned out of hand by sceptics. For 18 months a PR programme was mounted to prove by example and education that the system worked. Part of this was a treatment at Gloucester Cathedral which was written up in the building and architectural press. This PR programme culminated in a press conference at which the *Financial Times* science correspondent stood up and said 'I don't believe it, but if Rentokil say it works it must work!' Since that time the advertising of this service has also worked.

13.2 The Image

What the *FT* man really meant was that such was the reputation of the company, such was the *image* of Rentokil, that he could not doubt what appeared to him to be scientific nonsense. This is a splendid example of what the PR practitioner means by this much abused and misunderstood word image. **By image we mean a correct impression.** Not a concocted one, not an improved or polished one, but a true idea of a policy, product or service.

In this busy complex world most of us have garbled notions about lots of things. This is inevitable. The PR practitioner tries to put this right by creating in our minds an idea that is free of our inhibitions, prejudices, ignorance and misunderstandings. Sometimes the image changes with the times. In recent years shipping companies like P & O have had to change their image from passenger ships to cruise ships. Woolworth have changed their image from 'threepenny and sixpenny bazaars' to retailers of much higher-grade merchandise including furniture and electronic organs. Harrods have sought to lose their old 'dowager duchess' image, and become more proletarian.

Even though the attempt may be made from time to time, even though advertisers try to employ PR practitioners for this purpose, it is not the place of PR to cover over the cracks and whitewash an organisation whose reputation has been tainted by malpractice. In the Rentokil example there was no point in trying to foist on an unwilling public a service about which there was doubt: its efficiency had to be proved. It is a pity more companies do not follow this example: there would be fewer public complaints about break-downs in mechanical goods whether they be motorcars or domestic appliances, the buying public having to endure the role of guinea pig.

13.3 Press Relations

Press relations implies good relations with the press, and that means helping the press to publish material which sells papers. The managing director who says, 'I want this in the *Financial Times* tomorrow morning' is not practising press relations but press piracy. Press relations can succeed only when a service is provided for the press. This means supplying news, pictures, background information and features in a journalistic form in time and while it is still news. All communication media—press, radio, television, teletext—are included under this heading.

The reader may retort with some indignation that it is not his business to help the media make a profit—surely they do that well enough out of his advertising! The point is that *if* the reader wants his organisation and its activities, policy, personnel, products or services reported, and reported accurately, he must take the trouble to understand the how, what and when of media requirements. When he serves the media *first* he succeeds in incidentally serving himself, but if he seeks only his own advantage he will fail to serve either himself or the media. This is the elementary criterion of press relations.

Foolishly this criterion is generally ignored. Consequently, PR is derided by the media. Consequently, 70 per cent of news releases—being obvious puffs or stale or misdirected news—are discarded practically unread. Consequently, the news agencies fill two huge plastic bins with useless news releases every morning because the authors will not confine themselves to the **hundred words** that news agencies require. The reason is that the majority of writers of news releases have never ever learned how to write a news release. Strangely, many of them are ex-journalists—but many more of them are businessmen and marketing, sales and advertising executives who do not know the difference between an advertisement and a news story.

13.4 How to Write a News Release

First, collect all the relevant facts—try to prevent the editor's having to ring up for important details which are not in the story—and then check them to make sure that they are absolutely correct. The onus is on the writer to make sure that he issues nothing that is incorrect. Unlike the media he has the time and the opportunity to get the story right. This in itself is good press relations. He will become trusted and his material will be sought after if he establishes a reputation for reliability. Having assembled the facts the news story should be written in the following way:

(*a*) **The headline** should not be clever but should identify what the story is about. It is unlikely that the headline will be printed, editors preferring to be original or to write headlines that fit the space.

(*b*) The **subject** should be in the first three words, and preferably in the first. Many rejected news stories suffer from the defect that the subject is buried in the third or fourth paragraph. The writer must also decide what exactly *is* the subject. A story about an airline could have as its subject the name of the airline, the kind of aircraft or the route—which subject is news? If the company name is the subject it should be presented as simply as possible—IBM rather than IBM (United Kingdom) Ltd. The full name can come later. And if the company is part of a group, don't drag in group references in the first sentence, no matter what the company secretary insists.

(*c*) The **opening paragraph** should summarise the main points of the whole story. It may be all that will get printed.

(*d*) The **development** should follow in paragraphs which give the facts in a logical sequence such as (i) advantages, (ii) applications and (iii) specifications.

(*e*) The **final paragraph** should give the name and address of the organisation, and the source of any additional information or material such as price lists, data sheets, samples or demonstrations.

(*f*) The story should bear the name of the **author**, and be **dated**.

(*g*) There is no need to use an **embargo** unless the media are privileged to receive the story in advance, as with an annual report or a copy of a speech that is to be made.

13.5　Presentation of a News Release

(*a*) The **heading paper** should be distinct from ordinary business letter-heading, but should not be so designed and worded that it looks like an advertisement. The best news release headings are neat and simple, possibly stating **News** or **Information** at the top so that the story predominates, the name and address and telephone number of the sender being printed distinctly but discreetly at the foot of the sheet. Very few news release headings follow this basic requirement. The worst come from advertising managers who insist on claiming—on a news release heading!—that their company is the biggest manufacturer of this or that. Only one colour is necessary, the most common being red or blue which may be a good reason for choosing something different such as black. The only purpose of the heading is to provide a means of sending the story and saying where it has come from. A neat company logo like that of Dunlop or Heinz may be used.

(*b*) The first paragraph should **not be indented**. All succeeding paragraphs should be indented. This is followed by most newspapers. Other 'secretarial' styles should not be used.

(*c*) **Subheadings** should not be used—the editor will create them, thank you—unless the story refers to more than one item and subheads help to identify them. But it may be better to write separate stories about each item.

(*d*) **Capital letters** should be restricted to proper names such as surnames, company names, geographical places and very important ranks such as the Queen, President, Prime Minister or Archbishop. Titles such as chairman and managing director do not need capital letters, nor do materials such as steel or polystyrene. Nothing should be completely in caps.

(*e*) Nothing should be **underlined**. Underlining means set in italics.

(*f*) **Figures** (except for dates, prices or measurements) should be spelt out one to nine, then set out in numbers, but to avoid confusion large numbers are best spelt out—twenty-one thousand—or clearly expressed such as one million or £1 million. Or £1m.

(*g*) **Abbreviations** should not be spattered with full points. A.B.C., B.Sc(Econ.), I.P.R. and P.R.C.A. should be presented as ABC, BSc(Econ), IPR and PRCA. At a glance, the reader will see that without the full points less space is occupied and the initials are more legible.

(*h*) All copy for the press should be **typed** on a machine with upper and lower case characters—not italic or all capitals—and the work should be double spaced on one side of the sheet with equal margins of about 1½ inches or 4 cm. This will permit the editor to add his printing instructions (or amendments) between the lines and in either margin.

(*i*) **Continuations** should be clearly stated at the foot of the incomplete copy and at the top of the following sheet. Write 'More'.

(*j*) The **length** of a news story should be the minimum necessary to present all the relevant facts. Ideally, the story should not exceed one sheet of foolscap, A4 or quarto paper. Obviously, stories which set out to supply journalists with important background information will tend to be longer, but the average **product publicity story** need not exceed 200 or 300 words. If written as recommended above, and given genuine reader interest, it may well be printed word for word as it stands, even given that great accolade of the professional news story—the byline of a staff journalist who accepts your story as his own work!

Throughout, the expression **news story** or **news release** has been used. We do not speak of 'hand-outs'. Nor, when media are not limited to the press, should we speak of 'press releases'. Strictly speaking, a 'press conference' should be called a 'news conference' if a mixture of media are invited. However, it seems difficult to find an alternative for 'press relations' or 'press officer', although 'information officer' may be used.

13.6 Feature Articles

Another form of press work, often of lasting value, is the exclusive signed feature article which may be produced by a staff writer to whom facilities have been provided, or written by a PR practitioner. If written by the PRO or PR consultant articles should *not* be produced speculatively. The idea should be offered to the editor of a suitable journal, and the editor should be asked the following questions:

(*a*) Does he like this idea?
(*b*) If so, how many words would he like?
(*c*) Does he require illustrations and if so what kind and how many?
(*d*) When is he likely to publish the article?
(*e*) When does he want copy?

All this can be set out in a letter. There is no need to buy the editor an expensive lunch or drown him in gin.

Once the editor has 'commissioned' the article—which will be supplied 'without fee'—the writer must honour the agreement and keep to the agreed deadline or copy date. The value of the article may be perpetuated by buying reprints from the publisher.

The PR practitioner often knows of article material which is unknown to editors and can offer a valuable press relations service of mutual benefit to the editor and to the sponsoring organisation. Such articles should be published on their merits, and do not need supporting advertising *unless*, and only unless, an advertisement can offer some additional information—such as a coupon offer of a catalogue—but normally one should not be blackmailed into buying needless advertisement space. Such advertisements can be refused on the grounds that they are irrelevant to the planned advertising campaign. Advertisement managers will, of course, try to sell space to firms which are mentioned in the editorial, but it is really zealous salesmanship taken to the point of shortsightedness. A good feature article should be independent of advertising.

It is quite likely that the magazines and newspapers in which PR stories, pictures and articles appear will be entirely different from those on the advertising media schedule. For example, a clock manufacturer may advertise in popular national newspapers which seldom print his news releases, but the news releases may well be accepted by women's magazines in which he never advertises.

13.7 Photographs and Photo Captions

Editors frequently complain about the quality of photographs issued for PR purposes. The chief complaints help to provide a check list of editorial photographic requirements:

(*a*) Pictures should be suitable for publication in the journal to which they are sent. The *Financial Times* does not want dolly birds nor straight product shots. Trade magazines want interesting newsy pictures, not typical industrial record shots. For letterpress newspaper reproduction, sharp big-subject pictures are necessary, otherwise small detail will be destroyed by the coarse half-tone screen and the poor quality newsprint which encourages the ink to spread. But litho-printed journals want detailed pictures.

When ordering photographs it is therefore vital to explain to the photographer exactly what is to be photographed and how the picture will eventually be reproduced. Few photographers are equally good at photographing every kind of picture, and they need to be engaged according to their special skills. A studio photographer is rarely a good action photographer, and the man who specialises in photographing children is unlikely to be a first class photographer of racing pigeons. Unfortunately, very few photographers will admit this, yet editors maintain files listing scores of specialists, and so do art buyers in advertising agencies.

(*b*) Prints should be glossy but unglazed, and preferably on double weight paper. Editors naturally like as big a picture as they can get. However, if a picture is being distributed by post to many editors two things have to be remembered: (*a*) cost and (*b*) the risk of damage in transit. The safest practice when mailing photographs to the press is to use nothing larger than a half-plate print. If pictures can be hand-delivered, whole plate prints will be appreciated.

The reason why editors like large prints is so that they can 'crop' them, that is cut away unnecessary parts to achieve a more artistic or dramatic composition. But if this dramatic composition is achieved on the negative, cropping becomes unnecessary and the smaller half-plate print is all the more acceptable. A good deal of cropping derives from the speed with which news pictures have to be taken with little regard for composition. Working in sympathetic collaboration with the right specialist photographer, the PR practitioner can obtain well-composed, interesting, newsworthy pictures which will enhance the editorial columns of newspaper or magazine.

Let us take two examples to demonstrate how this can be done.

Suppose the subject is a new teapot. For a catalogue it could be photographed sideways on, a straight record shot. For a product publicity shot, the teapot could be turned to a more interesting angle, photographed from a higher angle, or a woman's hand could be holding the handle and pouring tea into a cup.

For the second example, suppose we wanted an interior picture of a factory. A record shot might take in a large area, but for PR purposes the camera could peep over an operative's shoulder at the job he was doing, or if more of the factory had to be in the picture the workman could occupy the foreground. With factory pictures the photographer should never tell an operative to turn from his or her work and grin into the camera.

(c) If the picture consists of people they should be asked to stand close together, and a more detailed and dramatic effect will be gained by taking from head to waist rather than full-length figure shots. If there is a small group, as with a presentation, subjects should be closed up so that the picture does not contain a vacant space in the middle, a fault that easily occurs when photographing two people shaking hands. Most formal groupings make very dull pictures. Few things are more uninteresting than a full-face portrait, yet this is the sort of picture most editors receive with an announcement about a new appointment or promotion.

Remember (unless a special arrangement has been made) that editors want *black and white pictures.* But *colour slides* are wanted for TV news stories.

More advice could be pursued: *the message is make PR pictures worth printing!* To see how not to do it ask any editor to show you what he has received this week, or pay a visit to the press room at an exhibition centre such as Olympia or Birmingham. Bad photography is where most money is wasted in PR, and not on gin and tonics which went out of fashion with professional PRO's a long time ago.

Captions—Why They are Necessary and What They Should Say

Bad as many PR photographs generally are, their worst and most common and most incomprehensible failing is their lack of caption. When captions are supplied they are more often than not oddly uninformative. Even more remarkable, the source is seldom revealed.

Every illustration submitted to an editor *must* bear a caption which explains what the picture shows. The caption should be brief but fully informative. If people are in the picture they should be clearly and accurately named from left to right. The caption should be well attached to the print, not dangling from it so that picture and caption are easily separated. It helps to rubber-stamp the back of the print with the name and address of the sender—*not* the photographer. The best captions have printed headings stating the name, address, telephone number and negative number, the actual caption details then being duplicated on the vacant space below or above the printed identity of source.

All pictures issued for PR purposes must be issued **free of copyright,** and this means that the sender must *own* the copyright. The mistake is sometimes made of stating on rubber stamp or caption that the picture is the copyright of the sender, but this invites the editor to reject a picture on which he presumes he will have to pay a reproduction fee. Nor should the sender plead for acknowledgement or for a cutting of the reproduction.

13.8   News Conferences, Receptions and Facility Visits

A news (or press) conference is an informal assembly, perhaps called at short notice, so that a statement may be given to reporters and questions answered. A news (or press) reception is a more formal and organised occasion when there is a programme of activities such as demonstrations, speeches and perhaps the showing of a documentary film, videotape or slide presentation supported by hospitality which may include a bar and buffet. A facility visit entails taking a party of reporters on a visit to a distant location or on a demonstration ride, flight or voyage.

In organising these PR events the following points should be considered very carefully:

(a) Does the *news content* of the occasion warrant bringing busy journalists and others from their offices to your venue? Would not a news release suffice? It is a fallacy to believe that the press come only for the beer.

(b) Is the **date** sufficiently advanced to allow your guests to print the story? As a general rule, early in the day, early in the week, early in the month, and an early enough month are excellent guide lines. It all depends on whether the story is intended for tonight's, tomorrow morning's, this week's, next week's, or next month's newspaper or magazine. If it is intended for the women's press they are planning six months ahead and need copy at least three months in advance because of photogravure printing.

(c) Is the **venue** easily accessible? London journalists often find themselves invited to two or three events occurring simultaneously. If the venues are not too far from Fleet Street it may be possible to cover all of them, so the convenience of the press is a point to keep well in mind.

(d) The **press material** should be slight and simple such as a brief news release and a well captioned picture, supported by a sample if that is feasible. Elaborate press packs, loaded with irrelevant items such as a picture of the chairman, catalogues, price lists, sales leaflets, picture postcards, free gifts, house journals and company histories are definitely not wanted. The ideal press material can be stuffed in jacket pocket or handbag.

But if more elaborate material is absolutely essential, there should be an assistant on duty who will undertake to have bulky material hand-delivered or posted to the journalist. If there is, for example, a choice of pictures they should be displayed and guests can then be invited to request prints which can be despatched as required.

It is not very hospitable to thrust a heavy press pack into the hands of guests as they arrive—they do need hands with which to write and handle cigarettes, drinks and food. Nor is it wise to place press material on chairs. The distribution of pictures and information should be strictly controlled and this will ensure that it stands the greatest chance of being used. On press facility journeys it is extremely foolish to distribute heavy press packs at the beginning of a journey, but better to supply a brief itinerary or background information on the outgoing journey, and to supplement this with further information—if required—during the day or on the return journey. Unwanted and irrelevant press material will be unceremoniously deposited under seats and lost!

These remarks may seem like common sense, but there seems to be a fetish that a specially designed and printed press kit must be produced, and that it must be packed with every conceivable item. All the press want and need are the essential unadorned facts which seldom need occupy more than one piece of paper. Sometimes as much as £10 is spent on a useless press pack which the majority of journalists will lose as soon as is decently polite.

Press packs become even more pointless in the press rooms of exhibitions where perhaps between one and four hundred exhibitors are supplying press information. The simple, clear, single sheets of paper will disappear into journalists' pockets; the cumbersome expensive press packs will have to be dumped by the luckless exhibition organisers when the show closes. The press do not come to exhibitions armed with suitcases; in fact, they seldom carry brief-cases. How not to conduct press relations can be learned in one short visit to an exhibition press room.

13.9   PR Administration and Services

The majority of PR practitioners are employed on the full-time staff of organisations, and a very large number of these are with non-commercial organisations such as central and local Government, voluntary bodies, social services and educational establishments. An increasing number of industrial and commercial companies are engaging their own PR personnel. Sometimes these PR practitioners are concerned with internal and external communications of every kind, but more often they are associated with the marketing side of the business. Much depends on the kind of business, and the importance that top management places upon PR.

Outside PR services may be engaged through the following PR units:

(*a*) The PR department of an advertising agency.

(*b*) The PR subsidiary of an advertising agency, operating independently and under a very different name in most cases (e.g. J. Walter Thompson and Lexington, Brunnings and Leedex, Foote Cone & Belding and Welbeck).

(*c*) An independent PR consultancy—that is, one having no financial association with an advertising agency.

Names and addresses of consultancies, and sometimes lists of their clients, may be found in *Advertiser's Annual, Hollis Press and Public Relations Annual* and *The Public Relations Year Book*, and a directory is published in *Campaign* once a year.

Some PR consultancies specialise in classes of work such as financial PR, publications and house journals, exhibitions, or particular industries. Some handle consumer goods, others industrial. A few offer counselling services, that is studying the communication problems of an organisation and making reports and recommendations only.

14
The Media Owner or Promoter

For the sake of simplicity those in the media business have been referred to in this book as 'media owners', but to be strictly accurate we should also refer to 'media promoters', since a direct mail house does not own any media, poster contractors rent sites on buildings and vacant land, while exhibition organisers have to hire halls for events which they own in name only. Media consist of almost anything which can be used to convey an advertising message. It may be a deck-chair on the beach, a cloud in the sky, or the side of a vehicle. In other words, it is often anything unused which could very well be utilised by an advertiser, if he can be shown the value of it and is willing to pay a price. Parking meters are a recent medium.

In most cases the media owner is concerned with two functions and sometimes, but not always, two sources of income. In the first place he does something that attracts an audience, and in the second he sells the presence of that audience to advertisers. A football club attracts a crowd, and the perimeter of the pitch is sold to advertisers; the cinema-goers, theatre-goers or concert-goers congregate as an audience and the screen, safety curtain or programme becomes an advertising medium; or a medium of information or entertainment—radio, television, press—can be offered cheaply or freely to listeners, viewers and readers if the costs can be subsidised by advertisers interested in reaching these people.

Media owners are therefore very similar to advertisers in that they have something to sell and have to adopt normal selling methods with sales managers (advertisement managers), sales representatives and all the supporting advertising and sales promotional techniques. Their 'product' is empty space or future air time or vacant sites whose value is determined by their potential audience. It is important to understand this because although media owners are very much part of the advertising scene they are not of the advertising business like the planning and creating agencies. A media representative need not know anything about advertising, but he does have to know how to sell. The advertising value that he puts upon his commodity is that of the salesman, not the advertising man. There is therefore a natural conflict of interest between the media owner and the other two main sides of this tripartite business of advertiser, agency and media owner. There is a simple buyer and seller situation.

It is also important that this be understood because it may be thought that advertisement managers and media representatives are merely order takers, waiting for the agencies to book space, air time and rent sites. True, the media planner and the media buyer can plot a campaign without any help from the media owner, but to survive hard selling is still the task of the media owner's sales department.

14.1 How Media are Promoted

The sales department of most media organisations is headed by an executive known as an **advertisement manager.** To remember the distinction, it may be said that an **advertising manager** buys space and an **advertisement manager** sells it. In small publishing houses, editor and advertisement manager may be the same person, but in a large publishing house the two sides of editorial and space selling are often poles apart. Some editors scarcely admit that advertising exists, some advertisement managers regard the editorial as the space between the ads. In other publishing houses the two work very closely together. In some—newspapers which run special features to attract advertising—a special editorial section is run as part of the advertisement department.

In commercial television, advertisement managers are called sales managers, and normal sales management titles are used.

Display and classified advertising is usually handled by separate advertisement managers. Displayed classifieds—for staff recruitment, estate agents and various traders—come under the classified advertisement manager if they appear in the columns of 'smalls'.

Advertisement rates are related to sales, readership or audience figures and, of course, 'what the traffic will bear'. Generally speaking, a cheap rate means a low audience figure, as when newspapers offer bargain rates for insertions on Bank Holidays or television companies offer package deals including time on Sunday afternoons when one half of the audience is sleeping off Sunday lunch while most of the others are taking a 'constitutional'.

The media owner does not therefore have one rate for a column centimetre, a page or thirty seconds air time no matter when and where it occurs. If more people read page one than page two, if more people watch TV between seven and nine o'clock or listen to radio at 8.30 a.m. than at 3.30 p.m., then higher and lower rates will be charged accordingly.

The following are some of the terms used to depict varying value, just like theatre seats in the stalls, circle and gallery:

Special position means that the advertisement will occupy a position on a page of special interest such as the front page, leader page or women's page.

Run-of-paper on the other hand means that the advertisement may be placed anywhere at the publisher's discretion.

Solus position implies that there is no adjacent advertisement. Large supersite outdoor advertisements occupy isolated or solus sites often decorated with gardens and given extended visibility by means of floodlights. A single advertisement on the page likewise enjoys a solus position.

An **island site** at an exhibition is one that is open to visitors on all sides, and clearly has advantages over more confined sites.

Facing matter means that the ad is not buried in an advertising section but is next to editorial. **Next matter** means the same thing.

Series rate means that there is a discount for booking a given number of insertions simultaneously.

The **single column centimetre** (sc cm) has replaced the old single column inch (sci) as the unit of vertical measurement of advertisement space, although the sci may be retained in those countries where metrication has not been introduced.

All these details are set out on the media rate card, and current rates appear in *British Rate and Data* (*BRAD*) which is the space buyer's monthly bible.

The media owner also has to provide mechanical and copy date information, and in planning an advertising campaign it is essential to know the different requirements of journals printed by the three major printing processes, letterpress, lithography and photogravure. While an advertisement may be inserted in some newspapers at a few hours' notice, it will be a few weeks, and perhaps months, in the case of women's magazines and weekend colour supplements which are printed by offset-litho or photogravure.

It is therefore an important aspect of media selling to keep advertisers and agencies aware of opportunities to reach readers and viewers, of production requirements and of deadlines.

While it may be thought that the statistical information used by the media planner in his choice of media is mainly to his advantage, it can also be exploited by the advertisement manager. He will study readership and audience surveys and seek to attract advertising from firms which can benefit from the fact that he has the largest number of weekend gardener readers or the largest number of A–B readers who might have a swimming pool constructed in the garden. Likewise he will calculate the cost-per-thousand rates which are advantageous to him—the *Daily Moon* may be able to offer the lowest cost-per-thousand spinsters under 22 years of age, which may be an ideal market for advertisers of engagement rings, transistor radios or padded bras.

Service Departments

Many media owners try to encourage and develop new advertisers by offering a service department. This may mean giving advice on how to produce a TV commercial, placing posters on the outside of a bus for the advertiser to see, or writing and designing press advertisements.

Supplements and Features

Enterprising advertisement managers will naturally try to increase sales and one method is to organise special features and supplements, an editorial being published as an inducement to advertisers who wish to be associated with the theme. Some of these are excellent, others are a waste of advertisers' money. Some are blatant attempts to exploit a certain situation, others are respected annual reviews which are of great reader interest and therefore great advertisement value. The advertiser needs to pick his way carefully through this particular jungle. But no advertiser should feel obliged to take space, and if there is any element of blackmail the advertiser is advised to keep out. Obviously, it is well worth while for a fuel or appliance company to take space in an important feature on central heating, but quite unnecessary for a supplier to congratulate a trader on opening new premises. The first is an excellent bringing together of reader and advertiser, the latter is little short of a racket. Unfortunately the trader is often too flattered to realise the imposition he is placing upon his suppliers.

14.2 How Media Promote Sales

Having taken a general look at some of the ways in which media owners promote sales of space, time and sites, let us now examine more specifically the range of sales-promoting material and activities which may be used to create revenue.

(*a*) **The rate card,** which is reproduced in *BRAD*.

(*b*) **Sales letters** announcing special numbers, features, supplements and composite pages. The latter consist of market-place features which bring together like advertisers such as holiday resorts, horticultural firms, mail order traders, property or educational services. These sales letters may be accompanied by *dummy pages* showing the available advertisement spaces surrounding the editorial.

(*c*) **Promotional folders,** often lavishly produced, and sometimes designed as a wallet to carry a specimen copy of the publication.

(*d*) **Specimen copies** of special issues, mailed to advertisers and agencies to demonstrate the success of the publication. Some mammoth issues have been sent out in specially made boxes, and the cost of postage has been a sizeable item in the promotion.

(*e*) **Maps of circulation areas,** and the extent of penetration into a region, are favourites with provincial newspapers.

(*f*) **Research material** is made available, the more elaborate surveys being sold which tends to enhance their value.

(*g*) Any firm gaining an **editorial mention** may have a specimen copy of the journal mailed to the advertising manager by the advertisement manager. This is commonly done, and is somewhat self-defeating. *It indicates that the advertisement manager doesn't know the difference between PR and advertising*. There is no reason why the advertising manager should feel favourably disposed towards a newspaper or magazine just because its editor prints a news story, picture or article about the company. In fact, it is quite likely that advertising will appear in one group of journals and PR material in another.

(*h*) **Reader service enquiry schemes,** whereby readers do not have to clip coupons but can make requests for literature on one coupon or card returned to the publisher, enable the advertisement manager to prove the pulling power of his journal. There is a danger here that having been invited to fill in the application coupon or card some readers will greedily ask for many items. Is this wasteful or not, or does it give the advertiser an even better chance of getting his literature into more hands? In the holiday business, where full-colour brochures are expensive, requests are nowadays limited to four or six items.

(*i*) Controlled circulation magazines supply **breakdowns of the classes and numbers of readers** to whom copies are distributed.

(*j*) **Exhibitions** are run which are not only profitable ventures in their own right but help to sell space in the sponsoring publication. Examples are:

Business to Business Exhibition (*Sunday Times*)
Ideal Home Exhibition (*Daily Mail*)
Hotelympia (*Caterer and Hotelkeeper*).

(*k*) Media owners take **stands at exhibitions,** e.g. *Homefinder*, at the Ideal Home Exhibition, and *Heating and Ventilating News* at HEVAC.

(*l*) Television companies issue **brochures** to sell package deals, or holiday advertising at Christmas which is linked with press media, especially *TV Times*, or to convince advertisers that there is a summer audience.

(*m*) Exhibition promoters issue **brochures** supported by **plans** of the exhibition site with stand spaces drawn out and numbered.

(*n*) Direct mail houses issue **catalogues** listing the categories for which they hold mailing lists, and stating the numbers of available addresses.

(*o*) Publishers issue **advance programmes** of special numbers, the *Financial Times* providing an annual list.

(*p*) **Novelties,** such as miniature issues of newspapers or magazines, are occasionally used as special gimmicks.

(*q*) **Specimen campaigns** are planned and costed for advertisers, sometimes in combination with other media.

(*r*) Transportation contractors supply **brochures illustrating** the use by advertisers of **different positions** outside and inside vehicles and about premises. They also give **specimen costs** for using different quantities of posters or cards in each situation or position.

(*s*) Outdoor advertising contractors supply **statistics** about the poster audience, and the cost of gaining maximum coverage of marketing areas throughout the country.

(*t*) **Reprints of trade press articles** about the medium are mailed to advertisers and agencies.

(*u*) **Advertisements** are placed in the trade and business press; transportation firms advertise on their own vehicles; and individual television companies show commercials on their own behalf. Similarly, billposters take their own medicine and advertise their services on their own sites.

(*v*) **Collective or co-operative advertising** is conducted by the media owners' own promotional bureaux such as RNAB.

From these 22 items alone it will be seen that there is very vigorous promotion of advertisement media, and that space, time or sites are sold just like any other product.

14.3 Agency Recognition

This has been mentioned in Chapter 5, which outlines the roles of media organisations which grant agencies 'recognition', and the nature of the commission system was described in Chapter 11 on how the advertising agency works.

The agency recognition system has changed to comply with the Office of Fair Trading ruling of November 1978 that, under the *Restrictive Trade Practices Act 1976*, the old system of stipulating a fixed commission was monopolistic. The various media owners' organisations now recognise advertising agencies for their credit-worthiness and adherence to the British Code of Advertising Practice. Agencies now negotiate their own discounts from the media, and seek remuneration from their clients in various and sometimes competitive ways.

Commercial television companies operate the ITCA system of agency registration and credit listing procedures. The following is quoted from guidance notes published by the ITCA:

Agency Registration and Credit Listing Procedures

The ITCA Agency Recognition Committee has been replaced by the ITCA Agency Registration and Credit Listing Committee.

The procedures of the ITCA Registration and Credit Listing system are as follows:

(*a*) a credit listing system for agencies has been introduced;
(*b*) a registration system has been introduced whereby agencies not credit listed may be registered by ITCA.

ITCA no longer maintains a Commission Register. Payment of commission is now a matter for the individual companies. Details of the proposed new procedures are as follows:

1. Credit Listing

The following are the revised credit procedures for agencies seeking credit facilities and for currently credit listed agencies:

New Applications for Credit Listing. An agency applying for credit and not already credit listed by ITCA must meet the following minimum requirements:

(i) if the trading period has been less than six months, provide a statement from the auditors giving the date of the agency's incorporation and the exact date when trading commenced.

(ii) provide evidence that the Company is legally constituted.

(iii) in the case of companies having an issued fully paid up share capital of at least £20,000 (the total shareholders' funds being in excess of this amount) provide either:

(*a*) audited accounts, the year of which should not be more than three months before the date of application and a Statement of Solvency (incorporating a cash flow forecast) signed by its directors and auditors dated not more than three months after the year end of the last audited accounts.

or

(*b*) audited accounts the year end of which should be not more than six months before the date of application which provide evidence that the agency meets the following criteria:

(i) *Debt: Equity Ratio*. The ratio of debt to shareholders' funds should not exceed 1:1. Debt is defined as the total of loan capital, long and short term loans and overdrafts.

(ii) *Shareholders' Funds*. At least £500,000 (excluding intangible assets such as goodwill).

(iii) *Net Current Assets*. At least £250,000.

(iv) *Profitability*. The agency to have earned profits in the last two accounting years. The criteria for shareholders' funds and net current assets were determined at January 1, 1980 and will be reviewed annually and linked to the retail price index.

Notwithstanding the foregoing requirements, the Agency Registration and Credit Listing Committee reserves the right in addition but not by way of limitation to require the completion of a Statement of Solvency which deals with a period of at least one year from the date of application, as a prerequisite to granting National Credit Listing.

Notwithstanding the foregoing requirements, the Agency Registration and Credit Listing Committee may require personal guarantees by the directors where:

(*a*) an agency wishes to obtain credit listing, or;

(*b*) suspension or withdrawal of credit facilities are being considered, or;

(*c*) the Agency Registration and Credit Listing Committee is not fully satisfied that an agency meets any or all of the criteria for credit-worthiness.

2. Registration

An agency which is not credit listed by ITCA may apply to the Agency Registration and Credit Listing Committee for registration as an agency whose details will be recorded in a list ('the Register') which will be maintained by ITCA to which an individual television company may refer for guidance. In assessing whether an agency is eligible for registration, the Committee will have to satisfy itself that the agency complies with all relevant legislation relating to television advertising for the time being in force, namely Sections 8,9,37(3) and Schedule 2 of the *Independent Broadcasting Authority Act, 1973*.

An agency will not be registrable unless it agrees to abide by the Independent Television Code of Advertising Standards published by the Independent Broadcasting Authority for the time being in force and all other enactments having a bearing on the content of commercial advertising on Independent Television.

15
How Market Research Aids Advertising

Like public relations, market research is a subject on its own worthy of a separate book. Here we shall take an introductory look at the applications of market research techniques *before, during* and *after* advertising campaigns.

How can research help in the finding of a copy platform, the selection of media, or in making a choice between alternative press advertisements, posters, packages or television commercials?

How can research help us to find out the effectiveness of advertising during the run of a campaign?

How can we check the success or failure of a campaign after it has finished?

Can advertising be made scientific and not only creative, despite the demand by advertisers for creativity—as shown at the end of Chapter 11.

The answer is that much of the risk and gamble can be taken out of advertising by using one or more of the many techniques available to the advertiser.

15.1 How Market Research is Conducted

Investigations can be initiated by either the advertiser or the agency, and media owners will be happy to give evidence of reader service enquiries. Very big advertisers have their own market research departments, so do large publishers, while most of the big agencies have subsidiary market research companies. There are also many independent research organisations. Some of these units use more than one research technique, others specialise in, say, shop audits, consumer panels, industrial research or opinion surveys.

It is possible to conduct the same enquiry by two different methods and get two different answers, as occurs with election-time opinion polls, or used to happen with TV audience surveys. The point is that research does not produce **facts,** only **tendencies.** Statistics can be interpreted in various ways. But the inexactitude of market research does not condemn it. Moreover, we are dealing with the social sciences, especially psychology, sociology and economics, and these are full of contrary schools of thought. There are 'schools' in market research too! Nevertheless, market research may be regarded by the advertiser as a form of insurance.

15.2 Social Grades

Campaigns may be addressed to 'C¹–C²' housewives, or a magazine may be said to have an 'A–B' readership. What do these strange symbols mean? It is a rather mercenary way of classifying or stratifying people according to occupation, interests and social background. The former expression 'socio-economic groups' has given way to 'social grades'. By grouping people in this way it is possible to organise research surveys that seek or gain information from people of either sex, different ages and different occupation brackets. Readership surveys are a good example, making it possible to discover what sort of people, as well as how many people, read various newspapers and magazines. Again, given this information, media can be selected according to the classes in the community to which the company aims to sell. Here, then, is use of scientific methods to eliminate wasteful advertising, and to make every pound spent work as hard as possible.

The following table (revised 1984) is based on the *Social Grading on the National Readership Survey* by Donald Monk of Research Services Ltd, published by JICNARS, 44 Belgrave Square, London, SW1. Respondents are placed in these grades as a result of searching questions into the precise job of the head of the household. This is more realistic than the former method of grading people by their income, although this is still used for some surveys, and overseas where such information may be more relevant.

SOCIAL GRADES

A	Upper Middle Class	The head of the house-hold is a successful business or professional man, senior civil servant, or has considerable private means	About 3% of total
B	Middle Class	Quite senior people, not quite at the top.	About 13% of total
C¹	Lower Middle Class	Tradesmen, non-manual workers, 'white collar' workers.	About 22% of total
C²	Skilled Working Class	Usually an apprenticed worker, 'blue collar'.	About 32% of total
D	Semi-skilled and Unskilled Working Class		About 20% of total
E	Those at lowest level of subsistence	Pensioners, casual workers, those dependent on social security	About 9% of total

It tells the advertiser of mass market goods, for instance, that the mass consumer market consists of 77 per cent of the adult population. These are the people who watch commercial television—hence the popularity of the medium for detergents, beers, confectionery, margarine, petfoods, package holidays, petrol and toiletries. Many of these products are also bought by the other grades who also watch television. Thus, TV is a more universal medium for today's staple products than any single newspaper.

Before going further, the rest of this chapter will be easier to follow if some of the basic jargon of market research is defined.

The **sample** is a number of people large enough to be representative of the whole **population** (or **universe**) relevant to the enquiry. The population is the **total number of people (e.g. all school teachers or all motorists) who, as said above, are of value to the enquiry.** The number of people in a sample may vary from as few as a dozen in a discussion group to 30,000 for the JICNARS national readership survey.

The size of sample will depend on the simplicity or complexity of the questions and the number of characteristics that exist in the population. By **characteristics** we mean different things or kinds of people who must be represented in sufficient numbers so that their opinions, preferences or motives are discovered. In a survey of motorists it might be necessary to go beyond sex, age and income and include owners of different kinds of vehicle, and different purposes for which the vehicles were used. Size may also depend on the degree of accuracy that is required (where this can be calculated) or the amount of money that can be spent.

As an example of cost and accuracy, it is cheaper but usually less accurate to use a **quota** rather than a **random** sample. This somewhat misleading expression 'random' should be clearly understood: it does not mean that interviewers go out into the street and interview anyone at random. It is actually very precise and its accuracy can be calculated mathematically, whereas the quota sample is subject to human bias. A better name for random is **probability,** as we shall see from the following definitions.

A quota sample is made up of quotas or agreed numbers of people falling within age, sex and social grade groupings. The interviewer will be instructed to interview so many people of each type, and they are found by observation and questions. Thus, inevitably, a certain degree of error in selection can occur. But with the random sample no such human error can happen because the interviewer is given actual names and addresses and at least three attempts must be made to contact the members of this provided sample. The names and addresses are taken at random, usually by the process of selecting every n'th name from the electoral roll or a membership list. (The **random walk** method may be used in developing countries, where lists do not exist, and houses are visited at intervals, say, every tenth house in a street.) The probability is that a cross-section of every kind of person in the universe will be discovered, the method working on the law of averages.

So that interviewers do not have to travel long distances between one address and another, large surveys use a stratified random sample which reduces the national random sample to names and addresses within scientifically selected polling districts.

The **questionnaire** is the document containing both questions and instructions which the interviewer has to complete for each respondent interviewed. A **diary** is a document which a respondent completes at home to show purchases made or programmes watched or listened to. Questionnaires need to be designed by experts, and this is where the psychologist enters into market research, devising questions, their kind and their sequence so that answers are obtained easily, simply, accurately and without causing offence.

Depth interviews are those conducted without a formal questionnaire, questions being answered freely and the interviewer writing these down verbatim, or recording them on a tape. ·

Opinion research seeks attitudes or shifts of opinion, and questions usually require 'Yes', 'No' or 'Don't Know' answers. Most market research invites **preferences** for this or that product, package or advertisement, while **motivational research** uses clinical tests—rather like intelligence tests—to identify the natures of the persons forming the sample, and then to reveal their hidden motives. With motivational research the respondents are usually unaware of the reason for the enquiry and so their answers are unlikely to be biased.

Some research is *ad hoc*—single complete enquiries—while other surveys—e.g. national readership survey—are *continuous*. Further examples of continuous research are **consumer panels** on which housewives are recruited and asked to submit regular reports on their purchases, or the panel used for the BARB TV audience research (using both meters to record programmes received and diaries to complete about programmes watched). Consumer panels are also used to test new products. Another form of continuous research is the **dealer, retailer, shop** or **store audit panel** of shopkeepers who are regularly visited by representatives of a research company who record stock received and stock unsold to discover sales for each brand at each shop. From the total figures it is possible to issue reports showing the share of the market held by each brand. Succeeding reports can be compared to reveal trends.

Finally, there is **desk research** which consists of the study of existing or published data ranging from internal reports to those published by the Government, trade associations, universities, banks, publishers and other organisations. It is not always necessary to undertake original research. A wealth of statistics is available from Government agencies, based on census figures, taxation, import duty, motor licensing and other sources. The Department of Trade and Industry, the Department of the Environment and HM Customs and Excise are all excellent sources of data of value to the advertiser.

15.3 Market Research Applied to Advertising (Before)

Motivational and other forms of research may be used to find a copy platform, and this survey may take the form of a discussion group.

Alternative advertisements may be presented to a sample of potential customers, and evaluations made of what was remembered, liked or had a sales promoting effect. This can be done with TV commercials, members of the public being invited to a film show in a hall or private cinema. A number of films are shown, including the one or ones under test, and a measure is taken of the shift in brand awareness as a result of seeing the new advertising. Press advertisements can be **copy-tested** by asking members of the public to look through a folder containing a mixture of advertisements. Questions are asked to learn what respondents recall about each advertisement, and in this way the strengths or weaknesses of certain headlines, slogans, pictures or offers can be measured.

The **split-run** technique may also be used to determine the response to different advertisements. The term originated from publishing where the print run of a publication was divided between copies carrying one advertisement and other copies carrying another advertisement. Response is easily checked by replies to a coupon offer, although other methods can be adopted if there is separate geographical distribution. This can be done with a television company like TV South which has two transmitters, and different commercials can be transmitted to different audiences who can be tested next day for recall.

Test marketing can also be used to decide whether the right appeal or the right media are being used, assuming that a national campaign is simulated by using media such as TV or posters—but seldom press—which are typical even in a miniature campaign.

Direct mail campaigns can be tested by sending out **trial mailings** to test response to alternative appeals or offers, and mail order traders may also test alternative prices in this way. More people may buy at 58p than 62p, or vice versa.

Media research also aids the advertiser, and certainly helps the agency to plan campaigns and to justify schedules. Audited net sale (circulation) figures are supplied by the Audit Bureau of Circulations, while readership data is available from JICNARS. Other readership material is available from publishers, to quote the *Financial Times* and IPC surveys. Publishers of provincial newspapers also supply statistical details of their coverage of local markets. Information about audience figures for the previous week's programmes on commercial television are published by BARB. JICPAR and the poster industry offer data on 'opportunities to see' and 'adult site passages'. JICRAR conducts surveys of commercial radio audiences, and figures for cinema advertising are based on entertainment tax returns. One way and another it is possible to work out cost per thousand figures for reaching most media audiences.

15.4 Market Research Applied to Advertising (During)

While a campaign is running there are several research opportunities for checking its effectiveness. Using dealer audit research, it is possible to use a certain medium in one town or area and not in another control district. Sales can be checked one against the other, having first taken an earlier base period to establish a norm.

Or reading and noting tests can be applied following the appearance of press or TV advertisements, each element of the advertisement being checked and given a rating. Thus so many per cent of men and so many per cent of women recalled the headline, the company name, the picture, the free offer, the copy in the box and so on right through the advertisement.

Or replies can be counted for each insertion of an advertisement which is 'keyed' differently for each appearance, the key being either a necessary part of the address or a coding printed on the coupon.

Advertising expenditure by rivals can also be checked by subscribing to the reports published in MEAL Digest.

15.5 Market Research Applied to Advertising (After)

The effectiveness of a campaign is often best checked by the numbers of enquiries, bookings or sales received, and these can be converted into cost-per-reply and cost-per-conversion figures which will reveal the most economical media. Holiday and direct response advertising relies on this method of evaluating the pulling power of media or appeals, but it cannot be applied to advertising which directs buyers to the point-of-sale. But here, continuous research of either the dealer audit or consumer panel kind should reveal whether the advertising increased sales or, which can be important too, whether it maintained them.

There are **omnibus consumer panel surveys** which combine the enquiries of different clients which may or may not be long-term, and advertising effectiveness can be checked by **piggy-backing** on one of these postal or interview surveys for a month or more.

Enquiries are sometimes carried out in the field with questionnaires to find out reactions to advertising, or the **discussion group** method may be used provided the small group is representative of the market.

The advertising world is therefore fortunate in having so many research facilities available to it. Many of these services have been derived from marketing research proper, and of course the advertiser can gain valuable information from product research which can later be applied to the advertising campaign. It may be the name of the product that has been researched, and names for new magazines, teas, soft drinks, motor-cars and so on are frequently researched before being adopted. Brand and model names are vital aspects of any advertisement.

In the dispute between Granada Television and the Ford Motor Company over the use of the name *Granada* it was said in evidence by Ford that they had chosen the name after 'extensive market research in six European countries as well as in Britain and without it ever crossing their minds that anyone would associate the car with the Granada Group'.

Finally, it must be said that although market research can be helpful it offers no guarantees. More than one form of research may be needed, such as a combination of readership survey to pick the right schedule and copy-testing to eliminate the wrong appeal. But because people say they like an advertisement this cannot be taken as proof of their intent to buy. Research can only rule out the improbabilities and indicate the probabilities. But a strike, war, thunderstorm or rival advertising campaign could evaporate all our expectations! This is the lot of both entrepreneur and state planner.

Part 3: Advertising Media

16
Media Evaluation

The most brilliant and original advertising ideas will be wasted if they are not presented in the right place at the right time to the right people. The football pool advertisement on the sports page early in the week, the holiday advertisement in the Sunday newspaper in January, the detergent commercial on peak-hour ITV, the Underground carriage card offering jobs to secretaries, and the poster on the back of a bus for windscreen wipers—all these are examples of carefully planned use of media.

Media (plural of medium) supply the vehicles for advertising messages, carrying them to the right readers, viewers, listeners or passers-by. They are a study on their own, and in advertising agencies there are media planners and media buyers who are highly experienced experts. Conversely, the media owners exploit the advantages of their media in order to sell air time, space or sites. Media are subject to intensive buying and selling activity.

16.1 Relative Costs of Media

A frequent error is to misunderstand the cost and value of media, maintaining that one 'cannot afford', say, television advertising. It is really a question of *need*, not *cost*. Media costs are relative to the size and penetration required of a particular market. The widow with a room to let may find that a card placed in her front window will produce an acceptable lodger. But if few people walk down the street, and there is inadequate penetration of her market, she will need to place a small classified advertisement in a local newspaper, or put a card in a shop window. But she does not need a 16-sheet poster in the High Street, nor even a spot on radio, let alone a colour commercial on TV. It is therefore nonsense for an advertiser to say, 'I can't afford TV. It's too expensive'. What he really means is that TV is the wrong medium for him, that it appeals to the wrong market, or he does not need the volume of business that TV might bring him. Even so, some firms have found that with inexpensive slides and use of less popular viewing times it is possible for TV to work for smaller, regional advertisers. Many a big advertiser has started in a small way: Mosaic Cyprus Sherry began with a modest campaign on one-half of the Southern Television region.

Similarly, a cigarette manufacturer may spend thousands of pounds on a whole-page ad in full colour in national morning newspapers, whereas a Scottish holiday resort may get a record demand for guide books from a number of 3 centimetre single-column ads. in several newspapers, the whole campaign costing a fraction of the rate for only one of the cigarette advertisements.

The weekend bargain square ads are another case where a relatively modest expenditure in big media produces a very profitable return, but this sort of small space advertising would be useless for a beer, detergent, margarine, hair shampoo or a small cigar.

16.2   Above-the-line Media

The expressions above- and below-the-line are used in advertising to distinguish between two classes of advertising. They are quite artificial divisions which may not occur to the advertising manager who has to decide which media will best carry his sales message to his market. But in the agency world, the distinctions are meaningful, even to the extent of adopting a superior attitude towards below-the-line advertising.

Above-the-line is also known as media advertising, and this refers to the five traditional media of press, TV, radio, outdoor and transportation (mostly posters), cinema and radio. These are the media for which agencies have to be 'recognised' and from which they receive commission on the purchase of space, air time and sites. These media represent the typical advertising agency world and the bulk of their income.

16.3   Below-the-line Media

These are the media which normally do not allow commission, and the advertising agency has either to add a percentage as a handling and profit charge, or charge a service fee for the time spent on making use of the medium. Consequently, agencies may farm out such work to specialists such as direct mail houses, producers of display material and specialists in sales promotion. Or the advertiser may deal direct with these specialists, including printers and exhibition stand designers, film-makers and package designers.

Six principal media come under the heading of below-the-line, these being direct mail, point-of-sale, sales promotion, exhibitions and sales literature.

Mistakenly, public relations may be listed under below-the-line, but this occurs only when an agency may be referring to product publicity support, although this can be complementary to an advertising campaign.

16.4   Media—Six General Considerations

In succeeding chapters each of the media will be discussed and in this introduction it is necessary to consider the overall evaluation of media in general so that the most successful choice can be made. Then, within the chosen media, it becomes necessary to make more specific decisions concerning individual publications, sites or regions; timing; volume and frequency; and such value-for-money considerations as rate versus coverage. The most essential general considerations are likely to be the following:

Frequency

How often does the medium appear, or how frequently can changes be made? Newspapers are printed daily—morning and evening—and weekly—Sundays and weeklies. Magazines are published weekly, fortnightly, monthly, bi-monthly and quarterly. The frequency with which an advertisement can be repeated or the copy can be changed will affect different advertisers according to what they are selling. A cinema proprietor has to promote changes of programme so that monthly publication is useless, but a monthly magazine may be suitable for a motor-car which is constantly on sale. Posters are usually changed every 13 weeks, so that this medium is best suited to popular repeat purchase goods, the poster acting as a reminder on the way to the point-of-purchase. An exhibition may be held annually or biannually, and as we have seen with the Motor Show it may cease to be the best time to launch a new car, although many products are first introduced at shows. Direct mail is very flexible and letters can be put in the very next post, or timed to arrive on particular days.

Thus media selection becomes a fascinating exercise, a medium being picked because of its precise value or rejected because of its limitations. It is no use wishing to use a certain medium just because we happen to like it. We may wish to make our flight to New York on Concorde but if the flight times are inconvenient we shall have to choose another aircraft, perhaps another airline. So with the choice of media.

Penetration

How can we penetrate the market most thoroughly or how can we reach the greatest number of potential customers? Shall we use the morning, evening, weekly or Sunday newspaper? Shall we use a magazine that is bought by readers or one that is sent to them free? Shall we reach housewives at the kitchen sink by means of radio or in the armchair with TV, and which is likely to have the greater impact and so penetrate the home market for washing-up liquid? Shall we reach more doctors, and appeal to them more effectively, by a direct mail shot in their morning post or though an advertisement in the *Lancet* which they may read at their leisure?

Here we can truly see the importance of correct decision making, and that the success of a campaign will depend on a blend of creativity and media planning. The two are inseparable and weakness in either department can destroy the other.

Circulation

This applies to the press, and a publication may be judged on two counts, whether it has an audited net sale at all, and what that net sale is in comparison with its advertisement rates and in further comparison with the net sale and rates of rival publications. There is no honest reason why a publisher will not submit to the auditing of his sales, except that he is ashamed of them, which means that he may be charging an excessive rate for space.

Attendance at exhibitions can be placed under this heading, too, and certified attendance figures are now being given by promoters. However, this is a controversial topic, because it may be more important to know the calibre of the visitors rather than their numbers, this being especially true of business and trade exhibitions where admission is by invitation ticket rather than turnstile ticket purchase.

Circulation should not be confused with **readership.** Circulation means the number of copies sold after deduction of free copies, returns and other differences between the total number of printed copies and the total number sold at the full price. The circulation of controlled circulation journals is audited on the basis of requests for copies.

Readership

One person may buy a copy but there is likely to be a secondary readership by others. A magazine is passed round the office, read by the family, or given to the neighbours. A newspaper may be read by all the family. Small circulation newspapers like *The Times*, *Financial Times*, *Journal of Commerce* or *Lloyd's List* may have substantial readerships in offices, clubs, waiting-rooms and other places frequented by likely readers. That is the **quantity** aspect of readership which will usually show that the readership figure is anything from three to fifteen times greater than the circulation figure.

There is also the **quality** aspect. What kind of people read the publication? What sex, age, income, social grading statistics are available? For most large circulation newspapers and magazines such data can be obtained from the National Readership Survey conducted by JICNARS, but we have to rely on publishers' statements if we want to know who reads the more specialist and technical press. In the latter case there may be a discrepancy between the readers aimed at by the editor and those who actually read the journal. Nevertheless, it is possible to differentiate between the readers of say the *Chemist and Druggist*, *Chemical Age* and *Chemical Communications* in that they are aimed at retail chemists, industrial chemists and research chemists respectively. The *Benn's Press Directory* gives this kind of information, but only an impartial readership survey will give a breakdown of the **profile** of a journal.

Profile

The profile of a newspaper or magazine is the proportional breakdown of its readers into the social grades known as A, B, C^1, C^2, D and E as described more fully in Chapter 15 and as revealed in the JICNARS readership survey mentioned above. Having selected the market segment for the product or service which is to be advertised it then follows that media must be selected which will reach the largest number of people in the segment to produce the greatest sales at the lowest cost.

The profile can also be the breakdown of the readership into, say, architects, civil engineers, town planners and builders for a construction industry magazine, or into university, polytechnic, secondary and primary school teachers for an education journal. It is interesting that it has been possible to split *The Times Educational Supplement* to form a second weekly, *The Times Higher Educational Supplement*, the two having quite separate profiles.

Primary or Support Media

Media selection implies narrowing down the choice, and the art of media planning is often to produce a schedule containing the fewest necessary media to reach the market most effectively. The advertising is not scattered hither and thither, impact being achieved by concentration and repetition provided this can be directed at the maximum number of potential buyers. It may be more economic to exploit the largest section of the market than to attempt to reach pockets of possible buyers on the periphery of the main market. Thus, a clock campaign was aimed at C^1–C^2 women who, research showed, bought clocks as gifts, although clocks are bought by men and both men and women from other social grades are also clock buyers.

The choice will be narrowed down to primary media which will gain the initial and most powerful impact. This may be women's magazines or TV for one product, the *Economist* and the *Sunday Times* for another, and maybe radio for another. Different media suit different products or services. One medium may be taken as primary, or two or more which are complementary to one another, such as TV and *TV Times*, may be combined as first-choice media.

Secondary or support media will then be used to perpetuate the message and help to continue the campaign to the point-of-purchase. Typical combinations may be TV, posters and point-of-sale display for a food product, or trade press advertising and direct mail for a technical one, or local press, bus advertising and window-bills for a retailer's campaign.

Here it will be seen that each medium has a specific job to do. One medium on its own may prove a failure because it needs the support of other media at different stages of the advertising approach. If we take the food product once again, the housewife may see the TV commercial at home, during the evening, sitting relaxed with her feet up. She is not going anywhere and in any case the shops are closed. Next morning she does not jump out of bed intent on rushing to the grocer's to buy the new soup. She has the family breakfast to see to. And because she shops only once or twice a week it may be a day or two before she does enter the grocer's shop. But each night she sees the commercial again, reinforcing her interest, desire and intent. On the day she goes shopping, and probably on other journeys on previous days, she sees posters for the new soup. Finally, at the shop she sees window-bills, display outers, special offers, sales promotion or other support media which clinch her intention to try the product. Throughout there is a progressive use of media from the moment of original awareness to that of actual sale, and there may be yet another inducement on the pack to encourage repeat purchase.

16.5   Media Choice and the Product Life-cycle

The product life-cycle theory suggests that products follow a five-phase process of development, success and decline. First, there is investment in research and development; then the product is pioneered on the market; a period of rapid growth follows if the product is popular; and then there is a stage of maturity, after which sales will decline. The time-scale will vary between the extremes of a primary product such as coal and a short-lived craze that comes and goes in a matter of weeks. Media choice may depend on the stage of the life-cycle that the product has reached, and this may bring about a reversal of what are primary and support media. Sales promotion predominates in the situation when intense competition threatens to bring about decline, and the product is given 'shots in the arm' to sustain sales. Or the product is modified or given some new additive so that it can come back and fight once more for its market share.

There is also the situation when a motor-car is nearing the end of its typical 10-year life-cycle (including annual titivations), production is proceeding on the new model, but dealers still hold stocks of the old car. There is suddenly a spurt of promotional activity to sell the surplus old models, and this is done *before* the new car is announced. If the campaign is too successful orders are easily switched to the new car. Press advertising, direct mail, special offers may be used to clear the decks.

The product life-cycle theory may not apply to every product, and there has been some criticism of it on these grounds. What, we may ask, is the life-cycle of Guinness, which has been brewed for well over two hundred years! Yet even Guinness is subject to the decline in beer sales. Nevertheless, there are clearly products which do become superseded in time, and the media used for a launch may be unsuitable either to maintain sales or to rescue them.

There are three sophistications of the product life-cycle which are also of interest in advertising and public relations.

First, there is the **recycled PLC**, which applies to the long-lived product which suffers no decline but has periodic market challenges. These threats are met by injections of product modification. Second, when one product is replaced by another (as with motorcars), there is the **leapfrog effect**. And third, there is the very interesting **staircase** effect where the life-cycle continues to take off from the point of maturity as new uses and markets are discovered. Nylon is the classic example. From a substitute for silk in stockings, it went on to synthetic textiles, ropes and fishing lines, golf clubs and so on. Another example is the passenger shipping line which met the competition of the aeroplane by developing car ferries, cruise ships and container ships.

17
The Press

Why, despite the advent of commercial TV, does the press remain the major advertising medium in Britain? Why is it likely to remain so despite the introduction of commercial radio? Why does Britain enjoy the rare phenomenon of a national press?

One reason is its remarkable resilience and flexibility. Newspapers and magazines come and go, change name and style. Some seem to go on for ever, either increasing in influence or diminishing. Those which lose status, circulation and revenue may be kept alive by subsidy, successful publications in the group making up for the losses on less successful ones which the proprietors wish to succour.

The revival of the provincial weekly press, and the arrival of new evening newspapers, was the result of the greatest innovation in newspaper production, the web-offset-litho printing machine. With this process it became possible to have presses in strategic parts of the country which, because of the speed of printing, could print a number of different newspapers. At a time when many local newspaper proprietors could not afford to replace outworn letterpress machines, Woodrow Wyatt's import of the American web-offset machine was a life-saving act for the British provincial or—as it is now called—regional press.

There are also historical, economic, geographical and sociological reasons for the importance of the British press as an advertising medium, and for the existence of a national press.

(*a*) In Britain many millions of people exist in a compact geographical area with an elaborate network of road, rail, sea and air communications.

(*b*) This large population consists mainly of big urban populations, many in huge conurbations.

(*c*) Production is highly industrialised and has been for more than a century in most cases. This has required mass markets, again made possible by urbanisation and communications. Mass production calls for mass distribution and mass media.

(*d*) A high standard of living has resulted, justifying the proliferation of press media to cover every possible subject. This further assists distribution.

(*e*) The standard of literacy is high and there is virtually none of the lost-literacy found in developing countries. The demand for reading matter is nation-wide.

(*f*) Britain has a single language, Welsh and Gaelic being of minor importance, but an immigrant press has emerged. Publications, therefore, can be printed in large quantities in one language common to all.

No other country in the world enjoys this combination of advantages. Moreover, English is understood in a very large part of the world, including a great deal of northern Europe, so that British publications have international circulations. This is probably the greatest single asset that British manufacturers have in the Common Market. There are more than 10,000 British publications.

The press succeeds when it does what no other medium can do. General interest picture magazines could not compete with television. Mass market newspapers with too small a circulation could not compete with the minimum number of dailies necessary to reach the bulk of the mass market. Before the IPC empire was set up there were too many rival publishers producing women's magazines with inadequate circulations, and there is today a minimum of titles with big circulations. Best of all, the press can provide a transportable medium—which can be enjoyed practically anywhere—containing detailed information which can be retained if desired. The sheer convenience of the press, to sum up the three points made above, is its chief characteristic. And that makes it an excellent advertising medium, always provided it reaches enough of the right people at an economic price. That economic price results from a comparison with the effectiveness per pound spent on any other medium.

It is interesting to see how mail order clubs have regular insertions in *TV Times*.

Moreover, the press has certain specific advantages over all other media. It is still by far the cheapest way of reaching a very large number of people, and it is the most effective and economic means of reaching large numbers of scattered and unidentified prospects. At little or no extra cost, copy can be changed at short notice, and different copy (e.g. branch addresses) can be inserted in regional editions. A major advantage is that press media offer the opportunity to include coupons so that immediate response can be stimulated. This makes the press a primary medium for mail order traders, book clubs, record clubs, insurance companies, horticultural suppliers, unit trusts, football pool promoters and others who have no comparable means of reaching their market. For some, radio may be an alternative, but preferably national or networked radio, not local. For others, direct mail can provide similar, often better, spread of sales information, but direct mail requires known prospects. Answers to press advertisements may provide mailing lists of enquirers and customers for future direct mail shots.

A London stamp dealer placed a six centimetre single-column advertisement in the Saturday mail order section of a national daily newspaper, and built his business on that solitary insertion. Response to his offer of British Christmas-issue first-day covers brought him his regular clièntèle for future first-day covers and other philatelic services which he developed.

A new household service was launched with an 18-centimetre double display advertisement in the *Daily Telegraph*, and from a three-man department a national business was founded that has now become international and, moreover, copied by many competitors. Twenty-five years later, it continues to seek new business through press advertising, using mass circulation media such as the *Radio Times*.

When a new cash-and-carry warehouse organisation sought to attract custom to its 54 self-service depots the agency recommended a single whole-page colour ad in the *Daily Express*. These depots had a turnover of £40m. a year. The £10,000 ad boosted the weekly trade by 17 per cent. Such was the power of one well-placed insertion.

The intelligent user of press advertising can exploit the reader's selectivity, accepting that readers are unlikely to read every word of every advertisement. Nevertheless, the newspaper or magazine with its wide-ranging readership is likely to attract response from a sufficient number of people to make the expenditure worth-while. To take another instance, a Sunday newspaper may have a circulation of some millions, but a thousand requests for a brochure will be a wonderful success for an advertiser who has spent only a few pence on each enquiry. To achieve this kind of economic return it is necessary to take only the minimum amount of space and, if the advertisement is small, to see that it is included in a market place of advertisements for like products or services.

An analysis of the UK press will help to show the variety of press media that are available to all kinds of advertiser, large or small, national or local.

17.1 Newspapers

National Daily Morning Newspapers

The *Daily Express, Daily Mail, Daily Mirror, Daily Star, The Sun, Daily Telegraph, Financial Times, Guardian, Morning Star* and *The Times*, together with the sporting dailies, commerce and shipping journals, and the licensed victuallers' daily, the *Morning Advertiser*.

London Evening Newspaper

The *Standard*. (Its circulation area covers the Home Counties with fringe circulation some distance farther off, but a number of new evening papers have been competing for the peripheral circulation areas.)

Weekly Colour Magazines

The *Sunday Telegraph, Sunday Times, Scotsman, Mail on Sunday, Observer, News of the World*, and other photogravure or offset-litho printed colour magazines supplement the normal letterpress-printed newspaper.

National Sunday Newspapers

News of the World, Observer, Sunday Express, Mail on Sunday, Sunday Mirror, Sunday People, Sunday Telegraph and *Sunday Times*. (The *Mail on Sunday* and *Sunday Telegraph* are the rare exceptions of new post-war national newspapers. Several Sunday newspapers have been closed in the past 20 years, and two have changed titles.)

English Regional Morning Newspapers

Their dwindling number includes famous papers, to mention only the *Liverpool Daily Post*, *Birmingham Post* and *Yorkshire Post*.

English Regional Evening Newspapers

Some 60 provincial evenings remain, but no English region outside London can now boast of more than one title. Whereas the regional mornings tend to have a business readership, the evenings are popular family reading. By the introduction of women's interest features, these papers have achieved a take-home readership which has in turn increased their value as advertising media. Many of these papers are among the very best produced newspapers in the UK, enjoying circulations in excess of 300,000 nightly. It should be remembered, however, that the expression 'evening newspaper' is something of a misnomer, since racing editions appear in mid-morning, followed by lunchtime editions. They might better be called all-day newspapers!

English Regional Weeklies including bi-weeklies

There are three classes of weekly newspaper, the suburban paper to be found in large cities such as London and Manchester; the town weekly with a circulation fairly restricted to an urban area; and the truly regional weekly which is read in towns and villages in a geographical area which may contain two or three counties. These regional weeklies may have localised editions, as with the *Kent Messenger*, *Chester Chronicle*, *Warrington Guardian* and other series.

English Regional Sundays

Three exist, the *Independent* in Plymouth, the *Sunday Mercury* in Birmingham and the *Sunday Sun* in Newcastle.

Scottish, Welsh, Northern Ireland, Channel Islands and Isle of Man Newspapers

Scotland has important newspaper publishing centres producing morning, evening and Sunday newspapers, these being Glasgow, Edinburgh, Dundee and Aberdeen, and there are also numerous Scottish weeklies. Welsh dailies—one morning and three evenings—are to be found in the three principal cities of South Wales, Cardiff, Newport and Swansea. In the north, North Wales editions of Liverpool and Manchester papers cover the area. Belfast is the publishing centre of morning, evening and a Sunday newspaper. The Isle of Man has no daily newspaper but does have four weeklies, but Jersey and Guernsey have their dailies and weeklies, one of each in each island. Most national campaigns will include at least one Scottish daily and one Northern Ireland daily in their newspaper schedule.

17.2 Magazines

These are best broken down into five groups. If the reader wishes to familiarise himself more thoroughly with titles and readerships covered he is advised to study works of reference such as the *British Rate and Data*, *Benn's Press Directory*, the *PR Planner* or *Advertiser's Annual*. The five groups are: (*a*) Special interest; (*b*) Trade; (*c*) Technical; (*d*) Professional; and (*e*) Regional.

Special Interest Magazines

The remarkable thing about the British periodical press is that almost every conceivable interest has its own journal. This makes it possible for advertisers to direct advertising at very precise markets such as bee-keepers, electronic engineers or gatherers at the nineteenth hole.

Women's magazines, both weekly and monthly, form the largest single group of special interest magazines.

A medley of not-so-specialised magazines may be lumped together under the heading of 'general interest' magazines and these include such diverse titles as *Country Life*, *The Listener*, *Men Only*, *Private Eye*, *Punch*, *The Spectator* and *What's On In London*. Really specialised ones cover religion, investment, motoring, sailing, do-it-yourself, CB, pets, riding, films, music and very many other interests.

Trade Magazines

These have been separated on purpose because trade, technical and professional journals are often referred to erroneously as the 'trade press'. Trade magazines are read by distributors—wholesalers, factors, mail order traders, retailers, agents, importers and exporters. Examples are *The Grocer*, *British Baker*, *Newsagent* and *Games and Toys*. Through these magazines the manufacturer can announce new products, advertising schemes, sales promotion offers, display material, co-operative schemes and so on, using both advertising and editorial columns.

Technical Magazines

Distribution of these journals is mainly to those in manufacturing but could include service engineers and those in service industries like heating and lighting, refrigeration and air conditioning. Advertisements will be for equipment, materials and services.

Professional Magazines

Teachers, doctors, lawyers and other professionals are the readers of these journals which differ yet again from trade and technical ones. Occasionally, a magazine will be so broad-based that it covers all three interests, and *Campaign* is one that is read by people in all branches of the industry and profession.

Regional Magazines

These fall into three groups: glossy magazines that have revived the style of the *Tatler*; county magazines that devote themselves to historical and environmental, cultural and development interests; and trade, commercial and industrial magazines published by chambers of trade, business organisations and similar local bodies, a good example being *Midlands Industry and Trade*. To this group may be added the localised farming journals such as those of the NFU county committees.

17.3 Directories, Year Books and Timetables

A large number of reference works such as *Kelly's Directories*, the *Rose Society Annual* and *ABC transport guides* form another press medium. *Advertiser's Annual*—the 'blue book' of the advertising business—is a valuable desk aid, but lesser annuals may serve as little more than mailing lists for direct mail campaigns. It depends who you are and what you are selling. If your prospects are likely to be frequent thumbers-through of a certain book it could be a first-class medium for your kind of advertising. The important thing about a directory is that it should be as complete as possible in its information and this means that initially all entries must be free, paid entries being quite additional. A directory consisting only of paid entries is likely to be very unrepresentative.

17.4 House Magazines

These are private journals, 85 per cent being published internally and 15 per cent externally. Those with very big circulations—e.g. *Coal News* and *Rail News*—are useful media for popular consumer products. Among the externals there are those like the *Port of London* which circulate round the world and provide useful media for those whose prospects lie within that kind of circulation.

17.5 The Main Printing Processes

Mention has been made in this chapter of the three printing processes, letterpress, lithography and photogravure. It is important to understand how the journal is printed and what this implies in terms of black and white or full-colour facilities, copy dates and style of artwork. It is also vital to know the ways in which the advertisement has to be supplied for printing, to understand something about paper quality and how far ahead space has to be booked. For example, if a campaign is being planned in November for the New Year, it will already be too late to obtain space in gravure printed journals, especially monthlies. The *Sunday Times* colour magazine has a copy date of 50 days, and by copy date is meant the supply of the finished advertisement. A brief introduction to these three printing processes will therefore be helpful to an understanding of press advertising.

Letterpress

Still the most popular and versatile printing process, letterpress is the process whereby the printing surface is raised—in relief—just like a date stamp or a character on a typewriter. This relief surface is inked and brought into contact with the paper to produce a printed copy. The words consist of metal slugs, either of individual characters or of column widths. The pictures are either **line** or **half-tone,** the first reproducing a line drawing with a relief printing surface, the second reproducing a photograph or painting by means of dots of varying sizes according to the blackness or greyness of different parts of the picture. Typesetting and blockmaking can be done rapidly, as when newspaper printing machines are stopped and a new page is made up to report the latest news. This is one of the advantages of the letterpress process.

Lithography

Here the image is on the surface of the metal plate, and the process evolves round the principle that grease and water will not mix. The litho plate is damped and the water repels the greasy ink except from the areas of the greasy printing image. The modern litho concept is **offset** which means that the plate never touches the paper and so does not wear very quickly: it prints on to a rubber blanket which offsets onto the paper.

The basic merit of offset-litho is that the long-lasting plate makes it economic to print long runs. The football pool coupon was one of the original examples of this. With the web-offset-litho machine it is now possible to print newspapers and magazines, a reel (the web) of paper being used instead of flat sheets.

There are many other advantages, since papermakers, inkmakers, platemakers and machine makers have all contributed to improving offset-litho. These include fine screens of 120 or 150 lines to the inch (as against the coarse screens necessary when printing by letterpress on newsprint), compact four-colour machines and the use of phototypesetting. Here, no metal is used, artwork and typography being photographed for printing down on the plate from which prints will be made on the machine. It is a photographic process. However, the platemaking takes longer than the corresponding preparations for letterpress printing, and copy dates, therefore, are in advance of those for letterpress-printed publications.

Photogravure

This process can be used for fairly cheap print such as women's weekly magazines, or for the printing of postage stamps and the reproduction of works of art. It differs from the other two processes in that the printing area is recessed below the surface, in square cells which are shallower or deeper according to the quantity of ink required for different portions of the print. A spirit ink is used which is sucked out of the cells onto the paper, giving a velvety quality. But to achieve the cells, the surface of the plate (or sleeve—it is a cylinder about the size of a roll of linoleum) carries a grid or resist. The screen is usually 150 lines to the inch (but 400 for postage stamps) with the result that the edges of type tend to be damaged and imperfectly printed. Under a glass, the words on a page of photogravure print look very ragged. However, it is an excellent means of printing millions of copies of popular magazines in full colour. But the preparation is lengthy, being justified only by long runs, and most gravure-printed magazines are prepared about three or more months in advance, copy going to the printers about four to six weeks in advance. Photo-typesetting is used, and corrections cannot be made once the plate has been engraved for it is not unlike an etching and once cut it cannot be changed. But rivalling the quality of fine-screen offset-litho there is now the German *Klischograph* hard-dot cylinder system of photogravure, the printing areas being on the surface of the plate instead of being recessed. Reproduction is superb.

In the above passage the original half-tone screens have been quoted as they are more descriptive, but they have been replaced by metric screens. Letterpress printed national dailies use screens 24, 25 or 26, web-offset newspapers screen 40 and web-offset magazines screens 40–48.

17.6   Some Basic Terminology

All media have their special nomenclature, and the following terms are peculiar to the press:

sc cm—single column centimetre, the standard unit of measurement for advertisement space in newspapers, the minimum space being three single column centimetres. Magazines sell space by the page and *pro rata*. Newspapers also sell by the whole or full page, and half page.

Type area—the area of the page occupied by printing matter whether editorial or advertisement.

Bleed—to print to the extreme edge of the page, achieved by having the blocks or artwork large enough so that the paper can be trimmed to give the bled-off effect. Advertisements that bleed are charged at a higher rate.

Rate card—a postcard-size price list of space rates together with every kind of information required by the advertiser or his agent. Rate cards are reproduced in *British Rate and Data*, the monthly Bible of the media planner and buyer.

Display—advertisements that are laid out with a variety of type faces and sizes, usually illustrated.

Classified—advertisements that appear under classified headings, and usually in words only run on, not displayed.

Displayed classified, or *semi-display*—advertisements in the classified section which are not merely run on, but set out and possibly illustrated, e.g. recruitment advertising.

Run-of-paper—advertisement inserted at the discretion of the advertisement manager and charged at the basic rate.

Special position—advertisement position which earns a premium because it attracts a higher or a special readership.

Next matter or *facing matter*—advertisement position next to editorial or reading matter for which a premium is charged, making it a kind of special position.

Solus position—the only advertisement on the page.

Spot colour—a single second colour as when the brand name is picked out in, say, red.

Mechanical data—page type area, and advertisement space measurement.

Copy date—date the advertisement, whether paper set, in block form, or artwork (for gravure, litho), must be delivered.

Press date—the date of publication and not to be confused with copy date—the date of going to press.

Ears or title corners—small spaces on either side of the title or masthead at the top of the front page of a newspaper.

Voucher—copy of the publication containing the advertisement as proof of insertion.

Cover price—the retail price.

OTS—opportunity to see, another way of expressing readership figures, one OTS being one reader.

Camera-ready copy. Letterpress-printed publications require blocks of illustrations, or metal stereos of complete advertisements, but those printed by offset-litho or web-offset-litho require artwork or camera-ready copy which can be photographed for platemaking. This artwork will usually consist of pasted-down typesettings and Letraset display lines. Illustrations will be supplied separately if half-tone screens are to be applied. Colour separations will be necessary for full-colour pictures.

Space broking and **media co-ordination** are recent developments that reflect the economics and competition involved in the press advertising world. With space broking, space is bought rather like blocks of theatre seats by ticket agencies and re-sold to advertising agents and advertisers. This means buying the space at well below the rate-card price, hawking it to prospective buyers and gaining the best possible price. This helps the media-owner to off-load space that is not selling very well, and the agent or advertiser to buy space at an advantageous price. The drawback is that it may not be the space which would be bought as part of a properly planned campaign.

Media co-ordination (which has operated very well in the poster world) is an attempt to use one agency to co-ordinate media buying for different product accounts placed with different agencies, the aim being to buy media more competitively. It also permits the client's original agency to concentrate on the creative side, which is what most clients select their agents for. It is an interesting rationalising of agency resources which suits the modern need to cut overheads in expensive city centres where the majority of agencies operate.

17.7   Changes in The Press

The introduction to the 1984 edition (the 132nd edition since 1846!) of *Benn's Press Directory* reveals some interesting changes and developments in this versatile medium. Free distribution newspapers or free sheets had increased from 529 to 580. The number of paid-for regional weeklies had fallen, although some had survived by becoming free newspapers with door-to-door distribution instead of retail sales. This meant larger circulations which made them attractive to advertisers.

To quote: 'Despite this country having the largest number of home computer owners, the written word is anything but obsolete. Magazines supporting the microchip revolution dominate the new titles . . .' The *Directory* lists 322 titles under Audio Visual, Computer and Electronics, and of these 63 were launched since the 1983 edition.

Another interesting change was the modernisation of *Radio Times* which had for long had a black and white letterpress programme section with some full-colour magazine pages, and in 1984 it adopted offset-litho. However, this was achieved only after an industrial dispute during which the magazine was not published.

All IPC women's magazines used to be printed by photogravure or letterpress. The long established journals *Woman, Woman's Own, Woman's Realm* and *Woman's Weekly* are photogravure and so is the text of *Woman and Home,* but *Honey, '19', Woman's World, Look Now, True, Hers, Loving, Ideal Home, Homes & Gardens, Successful Slimming, Mother, Woman's Journal* and *Options* are offset-litho.

Media independents. Reference has already been made in Chapter 11 to the non-creative agencies, called media independents, which specialise in media buying and are recognised for their credit-worthiness by the NPA, Newspaper Society and PPA.

New formats. In recent years newspaper format has changed, in many cases from large broadsheet to the more compact tabloid. After 140 years of being a broadsheet, the *News of the World* became a tabloid on May 20, 1984. One of the reasons for the decision was to appeal to a younger readership. Another significant change in format in 1984 was the re-launch of the *Sunday Times* colour magazine in a larger version with 25 per cent increase in page size, making it a 'real magazine' rather than just a supplement. The new 'king size' *Sunday Times* magazine first appeared on April 29 and represented a challenge to other colour magazines, especially the *Observer's.* The trade press greeted the new size with 'thumbs-up' headlines.

18
Commercial Television

Note that this chapter is headed 'commercial television', for this is where British television differs from that in many other countries. It also accounts to some degree for the acknowledged superiority of British television. Commercial television means that the programmes are put on independently of the advertisers. Sponsored television means that the advertiser provides the programme in which he inserts his commercials.

In various parts of the world there are different ways of providing television out of the revenue supplied by advertisers (as distinct from the BBC method of providing television out of viewers' licensing fees). In the USA, sponsoring is common, although the cost of producing programmes has made this prohibitive except for the largest advertisers. Spot advertisements also occur.

Nigerian TV has an interesting mixture. Advertisers buy air time as in Britain and short commercial films, slides and sponsored programmes (e.g. football matches) are transmitted. In a magazine programme, some items may be regarded as informative (and no charge is made) but if the item is about, say, a new product it is regarded as a commercial. Big advertisers like Guinness and Coca-Cola sponsor give-away and sports programmes. The United Bank for Africa sponsored a twice-weekly half-hour drama series on rural life, *The Cock Crows At Dawn*. In Indonesia TV ads were banned because they aroused expectations which the economy could not satisfy, but previously all commercials were limited to two periods, interspersed with top pop records to attract viewers. In Malaysia, all TV commercials must be made there. Advertisers demand prime time spots in Zimbabwe so that there are big clusters of commercials, but in Cyprus commercials are shown at the discretion of the TV company. Malawi has no TV.

In Britain commercial television was first launched in 1955 as a result of the *Television Act* which was produced in consultation with the IPA and ISBA representing the agencies and the advertisers. Thus a second channel was provided, the BBC having transmitted TV programmes since the 30s with the exception of the war years. Commercial television therefore came about as an alternative channel, but with stringent legal requirements about who was to produce programmes and the kind of advertising that was to appear. Parliament was anxious not to have in Britain the American style of television which so many people deplored. Breakfast-time TV began in May 1983. Now that commercial television has become a major advertising medium it is possible to analyse its merits and deficiencies.

First, let us dispose of one point. Some critics object to television advertising as such, disliking the breaks in programmes (especially films) which they would not otherwise suffer in a theatre or cinema. They also object to the repetitiveness of some of the advertising and to the persistence of the appeals. To these criticisms three answers can be given:

(*a*) Without the commercials there would be no other channels providing an alternative choice of programmes. This extra choice of viewing is not paid for out of licence fees even though it is illegal to watch the commercial channels without having paid the licence fee.

(*b*) As explained in Chapter 5, where the control system is explained in the section about the Independent Television Companies Association, there is very strict control over what is shown. Scripts and storyboards are vetted at an early stage—before filming—and many commercials are checked at the double-head stage before sound and vision are joined in the married print. And all commercials are viewed for approval by the ITCA and the IBA prior to transmission.

(*c*) The medium is one of popular entertainment and information. Products advertised, especially in the peak viewing hours of mid-evening, are bound to be those which are likely to be bought by the mass public, particularly housewives. This tends to reduce the number of products or services suitable for TV advertising, and to concentrate the medium on those products or services (e.g. repeat purchase small unit items) which either require or justify frequent presentation. Production of commercials is costly, and not every advertiser will be justified in making more than one film. Moreover, much depends on the geographical location of the viewer and the extent to which he is watching the commercials of local or national advertisers. In the London area, very few local advertisers use the medium whereas the reverse is the case in the regions. Obviously, the larger advertiser will invest in more sophisticated commercials than the local firm with more limited resources.

18.1   Characteristics of the Medium

Now let us consider the characteristics of this important medium, before looking more closely at its advantages and disadvantages.

(*a*) **It is a regional medium.** Commercial TV is not a national medium, like the morning newspapers published in Fleet Street. There are 15 programme contractors who sell air time in their regions. To use the entire network—not unlike using all the evening newspapers published in Britain—would be prohibitive for all but the biggest advertisers, and even some of those omit certain channels such as Ulster or Channel Islands. But it is a flexible medium so that one can advertise where one wishes and still reach the mass audience in that area. Some advertisers launch a product in one area and gradually add areas as sales develop. In a similar way, TV is excellent for test marketing since the media for a larger campaign can be simulated in one TV region.

No other medium enjoys this special distinction of regionalism. A regional newspaper has neither the penetration nor the visual, sound and colour qualities of TV, and British commercial radio is more local without having the visual impact.

(b) **It is a home and family medium.** The sales message and the product or service demonstration or presentation is transmitted to the home and seen simultaneously by those watching. Again, there is great penetration of the market.

(c) **Viewing is effortless.** Unlike the situation with most other media, the only effort the viewer has to make is to stay awake or keep his or her eyes open. Other than the cinema, and perhaps cards in the interiors of public transport, most other media require effort which one may decline to make or be distracted from. Because the TV ads are screened during the breaks of only two minutes it is hardly worth making the effort to resist them.

(d) **There is movement.** Only the cinema can compete, but with diminishing cinema audiences movement becomes a major distinction of TV advertising. This means that the product or service can be given the realism which makes desire to purchase more readily achieved. The aircraft acquires a beauty not apparent when flying high above in the sky, or static in other forms of advertising. The expression on the child's face signifies that the foodstuff has a delicious taste. Her teeth really do look sparkling white. That kitchen does look superb, whether cleaned, decorated or fitted out.

(e) **There is reliable statistical data.** Thanks to BARB, audience figures are available every week, and it is possible to evaluate coverage, as instanced in the Brooke Bond PG Tips case study in Part 4.

18.2   The Fifteen Regional Companies

The Independent Broadcasting Authority awarded its third set of eight-year contracts to the following programme companies which have operated since January 1, 1982. Some of the contractors, and some of the regional areas, are different from those in the two previous periods.

Anglia Television Ltd	East of England
Border Television Ltd	Borders of Scotland and England, and Isle of Man
Central Television Ltd	Midlands
Channel Islands Communications (Television) Ltd	Channel Islands
Grampian Television Ltd	N.E. Scotland
Granada Television Ltd	Lancashire
Harlech Television Ltd	Wales and West of England
London Weekend Television Ltd	London (Weekends)
Scottish Television Ltd	Central Scotland
Television South West Ltd	S.W. England
Television South Ltd	South and S.E. England
Thames Television Ltd	London (Weekdays)
Tyne-Tees Television Ltd	N.E. England
Ulster Television Ltd	N. Ireland
Yorkshire Television Ltd	Yorkshire

There is now Channel 4, TV-am and the Welsh language S4C. TV-am had its early problems but with new control and personalities it had gained 57 per cent of the breakfast audience by October 1984. Moreover, the average total minutes viewed by both BBC Breakfast Time and TV-am increased by nearly 35 per cent on the previous twelve months.

18.3   Special Merits of Commercial Television

In describing the distinctive nature of the British system we have already touched on some of the advantages, but now let us weigh some of the merits against the demerits, taking five in each case.

(*a*) **TV has immense impact.** No other medium can compare with TV for its power to attract attention and interest, and in achieving these first two stages of the AIDA formula it overcomes the first two problems facing any advertiser. How does he command attention, how does he claim interest? By the use of numerous techniques, the TV commercial is impactive. The *I'd Like to Buy the World a Coke* Coca-Cola commercial was impactive even if the viewer was temporarily out of the room! Only the cinema screen advertisement has similar (or greater) impact, but only if you go to the cinema.

(*b*) **Excellent quality of production.** The majority of British TV commercials are of a very high standard of production and the Authority is very jealous of its reputation in this respect. The creation and production of commercials is the responsibility of skilled agency and professional film production teams. In fact, the film team which produces a commercial may consist of the same people who will next produce a full-length cinema film or a TV series. There is nothing amateur about filmed and video-taped commercials, although the cheaper, simpler slides must look contrastingly less efficient. Some commercials may seem extravagant with their Caribbean or Mediterranean locales, but there is certainly a richness and variety about some of the settings so that they make a refreshing change from the outworn studio sets and properties which are repeated in so many programmes. (When will they lose those prints of old aircraft and vintage cars, and that split-level interior set?)

(*c*) **Familiar, friendly voices.** Very seldom do we have to suffer the bombastic voice of an American-type salesman, but instead we have a familiar character, or voice over, which has a reassuring, even testimonial, effect. The testimonial aspect is less important here than in the press: the audience is often quite happy to see a well-liked face and hear a welcome voice. After all, it is an entertainment medium and performers are not out of place in advertisements. The performer attracts attention in his own right, adding pleasure to the viewing of the commercial. The unknown, professional presenter is often extraordinarily dull. This is a curious and significant advantage that commercial TV has over the American sponsored show where it is less credible for the performer to switch from the entertainment script to delivery of the commercial.

(*d*) **Retailers also watch TV.** Both consumers and distributors are viewers and ITV attracts more viewers than BBC TV. But the retailer may not necessarily see advertisements in different newspapers or magazines, or on outdoor or transportation sites. This bonus effect must help the manufacturer's selling-in operation. The single medium does a double job.

(e) **It is a comprehensive technique.** With its combination of vision, colour, movement, sound, timing, repetition and presentation in the home it combines more advertising attributes than any other medium. Given a product which appeals to a large market, it also produces more results more quickly than any other medium. In particular, this has been proved by confectionery manufacturers whose products rapidly sell out of shops following TV advertising.

18.4 Special Demerits of Television Advertising

Five possible disadvantages of the television medium might be summarised as follows:

(a) **Takes time to produce commercials.** Television advertising is a very deliberate medium, requiring long-term planning, the gaining of approval (both client and Authority), and lacking the flexibility of press or radio advertising. Its use is limited to those advertisers who are not inhibited by this time factor, although video-tapes are very quickly produced. But the more urgent TV advertisements, being slides, look crude by comparison with those on which thought, time and care have been lavished, whether film or tape. However, TV commercials, once made, can be repeated.

(b) **It is a transient medium.** Here we have a very genuine weakness, and efforts to eradicate it include making a commercial work overhard with insistent jingles and repeated sales messages, or by the too frequent repetition of the commercial itself. Unlike the press advertisement that can be torn out and kept, or returned to in the issue for further study, the commercial has flickered on and off in a few seconds. It may need support media to reiterate the message at another time or in a different place (*TV Times*, other publications, posters and point-of-sale for example), whereas the mail-order or coupon enquiry press advertisement can do its job immediately.

(c) **Time gap to purchasing.** There may be just time to slip out for a beer before closing time, but most products advertised on television suffer from the delay of a night's sleep before a shop can be visited. Over the weekend, this weakness is intensified. Even the advertisement in the evening or Sunday newspaper can be physically retained: the TV advertisement has to be held in the mind.

(d) **An immobile medium.** The commercial requires presence in the room, seated and watching. The housewife, motorist, teenager and others can listen to radio in many locations. Newspapers can be read in most places. Penetration of the home can be both advantage and limitation. Portable receivers help to overcome this fault.

(e) **Difficult to gain enquiries.** The television companies have sought to overcome this through advertisement features in *TV Times* and by use of telephone numbers. Even so, not everyone has a telephone, the special effort has to be made to write down the number which is nearly as tricky as writing down an address, and the convenience of a coupon is not immediately present. So, once again, the medium tends to restrict itself to typical retail purchases.

In addition to the above appraisal there is one inherent problem about television commercials which is also worth considering. Long commercials are tedious, and 15 seconds or 30 seconds are normal lengths, an exception being Woolworth. On the continent, 90 second commercials are shown and they are boring by comparison with the shorter British ones. It is very difficult to sustain a commercial message for as long as 60 seconds. Longer commercials sometimes appear on overseas stations because the rate is cheaper, and in Britain it may be said that the briefer commercial succeeds in both getting a lot across in the time and a lot for one's money.

The result of this compression of action into a fragment of time is that the film becomes a digest which is very quickly and easily assimilated. It is rather like the pop song, whose attractions are quickly exhausted, compared with the symphony which can be heard with increasing enjoyment for a lifetime.

The following is a selection of the advertisers and products who used Thames, London Weekend and TV South during the Spring of 1984. Fast moving consumer goods (FMCGs) predominated, but there were also more expensive items such as home computers, air travel, household appliances, motor-cars and financial services.

Acorn Electron computer
Air Canada
Allied Carpet Stores
American Express
Arding & Hobbs stores
Asda clothing
Austin-Rover
Avis car hire
Barclays Bank
Barratt homes
Batchelors potato saucery
Birds Eye Superwhip
Black Magic
Bonduell frozen vegetables
BP
Britelite finance service
British Caledonian Airways
British Gas
British Telecom
Brooke Bond PG Tips
Cadbury's Roses
Castrol GTX oil
Citroen
Courage beer
Chanel No. 19
Christian Dior
Comfort

Commercial Union
Contour paper tiling
Country Pride bread
Cuprinol varnishes
Dairy Crest Melbury cheese
Daz
Diet Pepsi
Dulux paint
Esso
Fairy Liquid
Feed and Grow plant mats
Ferguson TX stereo TV
Fiat Regata
Flash cleaner
Flymo lawnmower
Ford Orion
Frys chocolate cream
Grolsh beer
Guinness
Hamlet cigars
Heineken beer
Heinz Invaders
Hellmans mayonnaise
Hofmeister beer
Hoover
ICI Lawnsman
Input magazine

Just Juice
Kattomeat
Kelloggs Crunch Nut cornflakes
Kit-e-Kat
Lancome lipsticks
Leicester Building Society
Lyons Original coffee
Lyons Quick Brew tea
Maltesers
Martini
Matthews turkey products
McCain oven chips
MFI furniture centres
Michelin MX range
Mirror Group newspapers
Nationwide Building Society
Oil of Ulay
Oral-B Zendium toothpaste
Oxo
Pal dog food
Pan-Am
Pedigree Chum dog food
Persil
Post Office
Qualcast lawnmowers
Radox bath salts

Red Mountain coffee
Safeway supermarkets
St Ivel Gold
Scholl sandals
Scotch video-tape
Singapore
Smiths Crispy Tubes
Southern Electricity
Sunday Telegraph
Sussex Building Society
Suzi-Wan vegetables
Swindon
TDK AD tape cassettes
Topic chocolate bar
TWA
Typhoo tea
United chocolate bar
Vauxhall Astra
John West salmon
Whiskas cat food
Whitbread Poacher bitter
Woman magazine
Woman's Realm
Woolwich Equitable Building
 Society
Woolworth

18.5 Cable Television

At the time of writing, cable television in Britain is in an embryonic stage, unlike the USA, and the full system will not be operative until the late 1980s. In 1984 franchises were awarded to 11 companies to launch pilot schemes. Companies such as Croydon Cable Television Ltd aim to offer their first services in the latter half of 1985.

Croydon is a good example because it is an area with an identity, has a population of 316,000 and 114,000 homes and 64.7 per cent of residents are owner occupiers so that it is a stable population which makes regular subscriptions viable.

The service will be of three kinds:

(a) *Basic Service*: BBC 1, BBC 2, ITV 1, Channel 4, regional ITV; TV Croydon; TV Europe; local, national, regional Newswire; sports Newswire; Financial; community bulletin; Swap Shop (classified ads); weather; job centre; directory channel; public/educational access.

(b) *Extended Basic*: Jack-in-the-box; cable sports; music box; TV-5 (France); Sky Channel; key channel (business).

(c) *Premium Channels* (4): separate subscription channels purchased individually in addition to the Extended Basic Channel. (1) TEN (movies); (2) TEG (movies); (3) classics/cultural motion pictures; (4) family entertainment (assorted).

It is expected that 90 per cent of viewers will take the Extended Basic service, and 80 per cent will take one premium channel such as films. There is only a one-year 'window' on movies compared with three years on BBC/ITV before new films can be televised. Each month 60 films will be available on each movie channel, each being shown at different times of the day throughout the month, and some 15 new titles will be introduced each month. Monthly printed programmes will be issued to subscribers.

In the USA cable has been popular, especially with films, because of the absence of advertising. The same prejudice does not apply in Britain where commercials are limited to six minutes in the hour and are of higher quality than in the USA. It is possible that, rather like in the cinema, advertisements may become acceptable before and after films.

The possible advertising concept is quite different from that on regional and network TV where large advertisers are able to appeal to multi-million audiences. However, ultimately, the present large audience is likely to be decimated by the ability of viewers to watch or use television in numerous ways to mention only computer games, computer VDU, VCRs and time switching, video-cassettes, cable and satellite TV.

But the advertising concept is different for three reasons. Cable relies on subscriptions for 90 per cent of its income; cable will attract local advertisers who will have to pay perhaps only £25 for a spot (although production may cost up to £150); and the medium is unlikely to attract national advertisers because any one channel may be watched by only 10–12 per cent of the cable audience. Although these viewers may represent a more definable market segment, i.e. children for Jack-in-the-box, teenagers for music box and males for sports. Three areas of local advertising are envisaged, classified on videotext, local radio commercials and TV spots. There will be sponsored advertising unlike ITV.

It is anticipated that six minutes in the hour may be used for advertising, and Rank are offering an organisation to sell national time for four minutes in the hour, and two minutes for local traders.

Another aspect of cable TV will be interactive services such as home shopping, home banking, electronic Yellow Pages, local videotext, and various business-to-business (mainframe computer users), school-to-school, hospital-to-hospital and fire brigade-to-fire brigade systems.

Cable TV therefore opens up new opportunities for the local advertiser, such as the opportunity to reach selected identifiable markets quickly and visually. The system will compete with the local press, but no doubt local newspapers will become shareholders in cable companies. But like traditional TV, cable could bring about new developments in the local press, creating new interests or greater local awareness.

19
Commercial and Sponsored Radio

19.1 How it All Began

Radio advertising is the most universal of all advertising media, and first came into prominence in the 1920s. Among the earliest commercials heard by British radio audiences were the Sunday lunch-time programmes from Radio Paris when Christopher Stone broadcast his programme of British gramophone records complete with sales information. In the pre-war 30s, when popular programmes on the BBC were limited to a Saturday night variety show and Arthur Askey's *Bandwagon*, Radio Luxembourg, Radio Paris, Radio Lyons, Radio Toulouse, Hilversum and other continental stations were presenting sponsored shows not unlike the American 'soap operas'. The late John Slater, of *Z Cars* TV fame, was an early radio performer when shows were recorded in London studios and flown over to the French transmitter.

However, the Second World War put an end to these broadcasts, the BBC Light Programme and Forces programmes adopted more popular entertainment, and after the war only Radio Luxembourg resumed sponsored programmes beamed on Britain. More recently, the attempt to run 'pirate' commercial stations on ships and forts off the British coast was quashed by the *Marine Broadcasting Offences Act, 1967*. Once again, the BBC learned a lesson, realised the popularity of disc jockey pop music programmes, and created Radio 1 and Radio 2.

While radio advertising is commonplace in most other countries of the world it took 50 years for the novelty to reach Britain through the *Sound Broadcasting Act, 1972* and the *Independent Broadcasting Acts, 1973, 1974*, and the promotion of the Independent Television Authority to its new dual status of Independent Broadcasting Authority. Perhaps the greatest novelty for British audiences was daytime commercial radio since most of the overseas and off-shore broadcasting was at peak listening hours such as breakfast-time and Sunday afternoons, or late evening.

Four-and-a-half years after Capital Radio and the London Broadcasting Company first went on the air, John Thompson, director of radio for the Independent Broadcasting Authority, was able to tell a meeting of the Broadcasting Press Guild on February 22, 1977, that the total turnover of the 19 commercial stations was £14.5m. He reported that 14 million adults, about one-third of the adult population, listened to commercial radio each week, and that more than a million young people under 15 listened to commercial radio. Radio audiences tend to be most significant at times when the businessman is unlikely to be listening!

By 1984 there were 69 locations approved for ILR stations. The following are examples of some of those operating in 1984. Some are twinned (e.g. Radio Tay–Dundee and Perth). At the time of writing, 22 ILR areas were not yet operational.

Aberdeen (North of Scotland Radio)
Belfast (Downtown Radio)
Birmingham (BRMB Radio)
Bournemouth (Two Counties Radio)
Bradford (Pennine Radio)
Cardiff (Cardiff Broadcasting Company)
Coventry (Mercia Sound)
Dundee/Perth (Radio Tay)
Edinburgh (Radio Forth)
Exeter/Torbay (Devonair Radio)
Glasgow (Radio Clyde)
Gloucester & Cheltenham (Severn Sound)
Inverness (Moray Firth Radio)
Ipswich (Radio Orwell)
Liverpool (Radio City)

Leeds (Radio Aire)
London (General entertainment— Capital Radio)
London (News, information—LBC Radio)
Manchester (Piccadilly Radio)
Nottingham (Radio Trent)
Peterborough (Hereward Radio)
Plymouth (Plymouth Sound)
Portsmouth (Radio Victory)
Reading (Radio 210)
Sheffield & Rotherham (Radio Hallam)
Southend/Chelmsford (Essex Radio)
Swansea (Swansea Sound)
Teeside (Radio Tees)
Tyne & Wear (Metro Radio)
Wolverhampton & Black Country (Beacon Radio 303)

19.2 An International Survey

To understand something of the special characteristics of the medium, a brief survey of international usage will be helpful.

In very large countries such as the USA, Canada, India and Australia, where national media do not exist because of either the size of the area or the existence of many languages, the local radio station operates rather like a British regional evening newspaper. It is a medium for news, entertainment and advertising. In smaller countries, radio provides a very convenient national medium for the same purposes.

In the Irish Republic, Radio Telefis Eireann has a clever combination of sponsored/commercial radio and commercial television. When there are good listening audiences—at breakfast-time, during the morning and at lunch-time—there is radio advertising, and in the evenings there are television commercials, with rather longer 'natural breaks' than in Britain. RTE claim that 93 per cent of housewives listen to their radio regularly, and 79 per cent watch their television regularly. So in Southern Ireland, radio is the predominant broadcast medium, and that is indicative of the Irish economic situation. Television predominates in wealthy industrial countries.

On the other side of the world, Japanese radio advertising has increased more rapidly than either press or TV advertising. This was not surprising in a land of transistor radios. Moreover, with some of the world's largest circulation newspapers, Japanese press advertising is probably running at capacity.

In India, commercial radio has been successful in carrying advertising messages to people of many different languages, something which radio can do admirably because production costs are so low. The medium was well-used for the Indian birth-control campaign.

West Africa is another area of the world where radio is the leading advertising medium. More than half of all advertising conducted in Nigeria, a vast country of 80 million people, is radio advertising. In the Lagos area programmes go out in English, but in the regions the commentators speak Hausa, Ibo, Yoruba or whatever is the local language.

The box or transistor radio is very popular in Nigeria, and is to be found fitted to the walls of cafés, rest houses and shops, while large numbers of Nigerians have their own portable Russian or Japanese sets. One can listen to Nigerian 'highlife' pop music at any time of the day, interspersed with commercial spots.

In Ghana the situation is much the same, English, Ga and Ashanti being spoken by the radio commentators and the medium being the most widespread for advertising.

Similarly, newspapers have small circulations in the Caribbean countries while commercial radio is popular with both audiences and advertisers.

The chief reason for the success of commercial radio in the developing countries is, of course, that while everyone speaks some language and can be reached by the spoken word, illiteracy is still common quite apart from the economic problems of printing in different languages and distributing over great distances to scattered and largely rural populations. On a world scale radio is an extremely important medium.

In Europe, Radio Luxembourg is international, broadcasting to France, Germany, Belgium, Holland and Luxembourg as well as England. Moreover, the English service has listeners throughout Europe including the Scandinavian countries. It is a station of some significance in the context of the Common Market, having an audience of 40 million listeners. Radio Luxembourg competes with ILR by suggesting packages combining spots on ILR and Radio Luxembourg, which claims to be 'Britain's only national commercial radio station'.

Perhaps experience gained in using European radio will be turned towards network use of domestic radio (rather like cinema advertising), and also perhaps we shall have European firms, well used to radio advertising, exploiting the possibilities of selling at modest cost to English listeners! British local radio certainly lends itself to use by foreign-car concessionaires using the medium for joint campaigns with their local dealers. As said earlier in this chapter, British local commercial radio is full of opportunities for those with the will to exploit them!

19.3   Limitations of Radio Advertising

However, we should not be so carried away by the simplicity and inexpensiveness of commercial radio to the point of overlooking its problems and limitations. The first major problem lies in the precision of the script-writing. In countries with less complicated and less rich languages than English, this problem may not occur but whatever is said on British radio must be expressed so that there is no possible misunderstanding. There is no vision and word pictures are necessary. The old over-worked American exuberance is nowadays repugnant, and over-selling in place of precise explanation can cause contra-suggestion. This is a very real danger since television advertising has, on the whole, got right away from the worst type of hard-selling presenter. With television we have got used to watching but with radio we can only listen and if the voice is too insistent it can irritate.

Another danger, which Radio Luxembourg had to deal with some years ago, is that too frequent playing of top-of-the-pops records can be monotonous. This is where we are fortunate in having commercial rather than sponsored radio since the advertiser cannot control the content of the programme.

And as with television, radio is a transient medium so that it is difficult to physically retain messages. But as with television advertising a solution is the use of telephone numbers, or tie-ins with press advertising. In the latter case, radio and local press advertising can be complementary.

19.4   Attractions of Radio Advertising

One of the attractions about modern radio is the continuous news service rather than the major news bulletins at widely spaced set times. To the advertiser, the news breaks can be peak listening points when it pays to advertise.

Production costs are minimal—a pre-recorded tape or a script for the live announcement—and this facility must be a great attraction to many people who have never advertised before on radio. Even the 'smalls' can come alive with announcements for the sale of houses, secondhand cars, situations vacant or today's menu at the local restaurant.

While costs of air time remain low there will be a big inducement for quite small advertisers to use the medium. Larger advertisers will be attracted when there is independent researched evidence of audience sizes and characteristics. The existence of such data will permit station controllers to charge economic rates (like economic rents), to the detriment of the modest local advertiser, but to the satisfaction of larger advertisers who can evaluate the medium in comparison with other available media.

19.5   Audience Research Problems

But it is not easy to research local radio audiences. Radio Luxembourg carry out an annual survey, but they are able to take a national sample and conduct an intensive one-day field sample with a diary follow-up. American radio audience surveying has suffered from conflicting figures, just as ITV and BBC ratings used to differ because of the different research methods employed. How do you research radio audiences? Probably the consumer panel diary method is best. The telephone coincidental method may not work in Britain because of the lack of domestic telephones, while the meter is useless when so many radios are on cars or are transportable transistors.

19.6   Sale of Radio Air-time

Now that there are so many ILR stations it is both more economic and convenient to buy air-time from one company. Independent Radio Sales, Ltd sells air-time for ILR stations. Air-time International and Rediffusion Central Services are sales agents for overseas radio and TV stations.

Air-time Buying

There are specialist agencies such as Radio Time Buyers Ltd and Radio Time Services, but general agencies also buy air-time and have AIRC recognition.

20
Direct Mail

The medium of direct mail advertising, or postal publicity, consists of sending advertisements direct to prospects by means of the postal services. It does not include hand-delivery or 'mail-drop' door-to-door distribution of advertising material and samples.

The *ISBA Guide to Direct Mail Advertising* states that there are four basic types of direct mail campaign, the **direct**, the **informative,** the **reminder** and the **utility**.

The direct type of direct mail seeks an immediate response, an offer being made and enclosures including a catalogue or price list, an order form and a reply envelope.

Product literature may be called informative direct mail, the task being to educate the recipient about the product or service. The material may be supplied in a form which is readily retained in a file or ring binder. Technical data sheets about components are often distributed to specifiers.

Reminder direct mail follows up earlier mailings, as when the football pool promoter reminds punters who have not 'invested' recently.

Supporting material, such as calendars, ring-files for data sheets, wall charts, samples and so on are called utility direct mail.

From the descriptions of these four basic kinds of direct mail it is clear that this is a broad-based and adaptable medium which can be used by various advertisers for a variety of purposes and which can involve all manner of materials from a single sheet letter to an elaborate broadsheet. In capacity, a direct mail shot may be anything from a telegram to a parcel of literature or samples.

20.1 Distinctive Characteristics and Advantages

Nevertheless, there are certain distinctive characteristics which make the medium different from others.

First, a list of prospects is required. It is possible to mail every voter, or householder, in the land or in an area, and mass mailings have been carried out for football pool promoters and petrol companies. But they are unusual, prohibitively costly, and liable to be wasteful. Direct mail is distinguished from all other media by its direct appeal to actual people: all other media are broadcast to unnamed prospects. The ability to identify prospects is therefore essential to use of direct mail, and the greater the accuracy of the mailing list the less wasteful and the more successful is likely to be the campaign.

Second, having mailing lists (either one's own or those of a specialist direct mail agency) it is possible to be selective. Particular lists may be chosen and if required only certain names may be taken from these lists. This gives the advertiser considerable control over expenditure, and allows him to direct specific appeals to different markets. Few other media permit such precise segmentation, that is recognition of the sub-groups which form his total market. He may have six names in one group, six hundred in another and different letters can be prepared for each.

Third, it is a personalised medium. A letter is a communication between two people. The recipient feels flattered to hear from another person, especially if the letter is addressed to him as 'Mr Smith' and not 'Dear Sir/Madam' which is an abuse of the ability of direct mail to be personalised.

Fourth, mailings can be despatched at will, on a particular day, or staggered so that replies may be handled comfortably, or in series or immediately because of an urgent need to sell a slow-moving or seasonal line. Again, the advertiser is able to exercise more control than with most other media.

A further advantage is that results are easily checked by the volume of replies and the number and value of orders.

20.2   Disadvantages

The disadvantages of direct mail mostly accrue from misuse of the medium and it is one which does tempt the amateur to try his hand without realising how highly skilled is the successful use of this medium. Sales letter writing is one of the most demanding forms of copywriting, and it will pay the user of direct mail to employ an expert sales letter writer, even if he conducts the rest of the mailing operation himself.

It is also a medium which can irritate recipients if badly used. Two examples of this are the careless choice of prospects so that mailings are received by people who are unlikely to be interested in the offer, and repeated mailings of the same sort to the same prospects, as when the same people appear on different lists. Indiscriminate and duplicated mailings are both annoying and wasteful, and show lack of control of the mailing lists.

The following cynical list of 'don'ts' is worth noting, and it is borrowed from the *Direct Mail Advertisers' Yearbook* (1969–70), published by the then British Direct Mail Advertising Association. Do the following at your peril!

15 Direct Routes to the Waste-paper Basket by Lou Klein, Klein/Peters Ltd

1. Make the envelope look like a mail shot: put the company's name on it—and tell the recipient what's inside.

2. Open your letter with 'Dear Sir/Madam' or 'Dear Reader' or 'Dear Customer'.

3. Start your story with elaborate and detailed background before getting down to imparting the relevant information.

4. Assume the reader is interested.

5. Be sure to mention all other activities of your company and of its subsidiaries.

6. Use layman's terms when talking to technicians.

7. Use technical terms when talking to laymen.

8. In conceiving the piece, refer to it as a throw-away.

9. Make the message difficult to find.

10. Make the piece too big to file.

11. Use several unrelated pieces of paper and fold them into each other.

12. Don't mention the cost.

13. Ask the reader to send for more information.

14. Make the return envelope too small for a cheque, or enclose a business reply card marked 'cheque enclosed'.

15. Never test.

Let us now consider what response, actions or benefits can be achieved by means of DM since these suggest valid reasons for adopting the medium:

1. *Mail-order sales.*

2. *Subscriptions* to magazines, book clubs, record clubs.

3. *Donations* to charities.

4. *Attendance* at exhibitions and events and meetings.

5. *Amendments* to mailing lists.

6. *Reminder* of occasional services, e.g. chimney sweep, driving school, painting and decorating, car hire, catering.

7. *Investment* in unit trusts, building societies.

8. *Visit* to store to see goods promoted by the shot (e.g. a sale), to motor showroom for trial run, to sewing machine shop for demonstration, or to shop to accept free sample.

9. *Obtain a space booking* in a special number or feature.

10. *File the latest information*, as when data sheets are mailed to doctors, architects, builders, equipment manufacturers, libraries and information centres.

11. *Obtain press coverage*, a news release adopting direct mail techniques of distribution.

12. *Enrol* members in organisations, participants on courses, delegates to conferences.

13. *Purchase* of tickets in lotteries, subject to the provisions of the *Lotteries Acts, Orders and Regulations of 1963, 1975, 1976 and 1977.*

14. *Gain repeat business*, an advertisement accompanying the monthly account so that cheques may be accompanied by fresh orders.

15. *Renewal business*, not quite the same as number fourteen, the object being to renew a contract for a further period as with insurance policies for motor-cars, property, fire or accident. Also, return visit of hotel patrons.

16. *Answers* to questions posed in a market research postal questionnaire.

17. *Gain use* of enclosed samples.

18. *Accept* goods on approval.

19. *Buy* accessories or additional lines.

20. *Adopt co-operative advertising scheme* offered by manufacturer, e.g.

stock-blocks, percentage payment of local advertising costs, display material, working model.

21. *Order stocks* from wholesaler.

22. *Anticipate salesman's announced visit* or make alternative appointment.

23. *Be informed* about the manufacturer's forthcoming advertising campaign.

24. *Be informed* about a change of address, or opening of new branches.

25. *Activate* shareholders to take required action.

26. *Vote* in a postal ballot.

As will be seen from these 26 responses—and the list is by no means conclusive—direct mail can be used for purposes other than securing mail order business. The medium lends itself to all kinds of organisation and for numerous purposes, both commercial and non-commercial. In fact, the principles of direct mail can be applied to most forms of multiple postal communication such as the despatch of house journals, rendering of accounts, issue of dividend warrants and other regular mailings.

20.3 Direct Mail in the 80s

With the growth of direct response advertising and marketing, and the arrival of *Direct Response* magazine in 1980, direct mail is a primary medium for advertisers who sell by post. Among the new developments has been the selective mailing of social grade groups, the addresses being derived from the electoral roll. This has led companies such as mail-order clubs to use direct mail when they normally depended on the popular consumer press for enrolling new club organisers.

The one-piece mailing has become a technique superior to the enclosing of numerous loose items in a mailing shot, the whole being a folder complete with order form.

The medium has been enhanced by the use of word-processing and computer services whereby letters are immaculately produced and personalised, and envelopes are addressed, using easily stored, retrieved and corrected letter content and mailing lists.

The Post Office offers discounts and incentives to direct mailers, including: a bulk rebate service; a second class discount service; an incentive discount for growth schemes; a direct mail deposit system; and introductory offers for new users of direct mail. Various concessions and discounts are offered by the Post Office to encourage use of the medium and to compensate for ever-rising postage rates.

ACORN

While the A, B, C^1, C^2, D, E social grades have their uses, in direct mail the ACORN system has been applied very successfully to direct mail. The ACORN (*A Classification of Residential Neighbourhoods*) considers demographic, housing and employment characteristics, applying published census statistics to areas of households and different neighbour-

Table 20.1. 1981 ACORN Profile, Great Britain

Acorn Groups		1981 Population	%
A	Agricultural areas	1 811 485	3.4
B	Modern family housing, higher incomes	8 667 137	16.2
C	Older housing of intermediate status	9 420 477	17.6
D	Poor quality older terraced housing	2 320 846	4.3
E	Better-off council estates	6 976 570	13.0
F	Less well-off council estates	5 032 657	9.4
G	Poorest council estates	4 048 658	7.6
H	Multi-racial areas	2 086 026	3.9
I	High status non-family areas	2 248 207	4.2
J	Affluent suburban housing	8 514 878	15.9
K	Better-off requirement areas	2 041 338	3.8
U	Unclassified	388 632	0.7

Acorn Types				
A	1	Agricultural villages	1 376 427	2.6
A	2	Areas of farms and smallholdings	435 058	0.8
B	3	Cheap modern private housing	2 209 759	4.1
B	4	Recent private housing, young families	1 648 534	3.1
B	5	Modern private housing, older children	3 121 453	5.8
B	6	New detached houses, young families	1 404 893	2.6
B	7	Military bases	282 498	0.5
C	8	Mixed owner-occupied and council estates	1 880 142	3.5
C	9	Small town centres and flats above shops	2 157 360	4.0
C	10	Villages with non-farm employment	2 463 246	4.6
C	11	Older private housing, skilled workers	2 919 729	5.5
D	12	Unimproved terraces with old people	1 351 877	2.5
D	13	Pre-1914 terraces, low income families	762 266	1.4
D	14	Tenement flats lacking amenities	206 703	0.4
E	15	Council estates, well-off older workers	1 916 242	3.6
E	16	Recent council estates	1 392 961	2.6
E	17	Council estates, well-off young workers	2 615 376	4.9
E	18	Small council houses, often Scottish	1 051 991	2.0
F	19	Low rise estates in industrial towns	2 538 119	4.7
F	20	Inter-war council estates, older people	1 667 994	3.1
F	21	Council housing for the elderly	826 544	1.5
G	22	New council estates in inner cities	1 079 351	2.0
G	23	Overspill estates, high unemployment	1 729 757	3.2
G	24	Council estates with overcrowding	868 141	1.6
G	25	Council estates with worst poverty	371 409	0.7
H	26	Multi-occupied terraces, poor Asians	204 493	0.4
H	27	Owner-occupied terraces, poor Asians	577 871	1.1
H	28	Multi-let housing with Afro-Caribbeans	387 169	0.7
H	29	Better-off multi-ethnic areas	916 493	1.7
I	30	High status areas, few children	1 129 079	2.1
I	31	Multi-let big old houses and flats	822 017	1.5
I	32	Furnished flats, mostly single people	297 111	0.6
J	33	Inter-war semis, white collar workers	3 054 032	5.7
J	34	Spacious inter-war semis, big gardens	2 676 598	5.0
J	35	Villages with wealthy older commuters	1 533 756	2.9
J	36	Detached houses, exclusive suburbs	1 250 492	2.3
K	37	Private houses, well-off elderly	1 199 703	2.2
K	38	Private flats with single pensioners	841 635	1.6
U	39	Unclassified	388 632	0.7
Area	Total		53 556 911	100.0

hood types. It is linked to postal geography and 1.2m. postcodes so that direct mail campaigns can be addressed to neighbourhood groups which reflect required social grades.

In 1983, CACI Market Analysis Division, who developed the ACORN concept, used the 1981 Census figures to produce the table opposite, and these Crown and CACI copyright figures are reproduced here with due acknowledgement.

21
Exhibitions and Trade Fairs

Britain is one of the few major countries which does not have a state-sponsored exhibition centre, and this is a political calamity which is rapidly minimising Britain's influence in the sphere of international exhibitions. The foreign exhibition centres of Hanover, Geneva and other cities have advantages which flatter both exhibitor and visitor. Any examination of exhibitions as a medium must therefore consider this serious drift away from Britain of the international show, leaving British centres such as London, Birmingham, Brighton, Harrogate, Manchester and Glasgow as being almost entirely domestic centres catering for the home market. And the dwindling influence of British shows was not rectified by the creation of the new exhibition centre at Birmingham where, despite many wonderful facilities, costs are high, and smaller shows are lost in the vastness.

Bearing these limitations in mind, let us consider the kinds of exhibition which may interest the advertiser, the characteristics of the medium and some of its special uses.

21.1 Kinds of Exhibition

(*a*) **Public indoor exhibition,** of which the best known in Britain is the Ideal Home which runs for about a month and attracts more than a million visitors.

(*b*) **Trade or Business indoor exhibition,** usually restricted to ticket only admission to discourage schoolboys and irrelevant visitors, the aim being to maintain the calibre of visitor desired by the exhibitors. Examples are the Hotelympia, Ice Cream Alliance and British Toy and Hobby Fair.

(*c*) **Public and Trade indoor exhibitions** are those that attract a mixture of distributors and consumers, but which may have special days for trade visitors. Three examples are the London International Boat Show, Motorfair and the International Furniture Show.

(*d*) **Private indoor exhibition.** Two or three small firms, or a single firm, may put on an exhibition in an hotel suite or a small hall, to which visitors are invited. Sometimes this is an educational exhibition—a PR exercise—like those of the National Book League or of tourist organisations.

(*e*) **Outdoor exhibitions** of types 1–4 may be held at venues such as Crystal Palace. Outdoor exhibitions are customary in warmer countries where the weather is less hazardous. Demonstrations of plant and equipment are often more practical out of doors, and especially on site.

(*f*) **Agricultural shows,** comprising a show-ring and an exhibition of farm equipment, supplies and services. Over the years the Midland Bank has made good use of these shows, touring a caravan from which banking services are explained. The Royal, Royal Highland and Royal Welsh have their own permanent sites. County agricultural shows are held in the main farming counties.

(*g*) **Overseas trade fairs** that consist of national pavilions which each country provides and designs for the benefit of its own exhibitors. Also Joint Venture stands sponsored by the Department of Trade and Industry.

Most exhibitions are held either annually or biennially, and to get the best sites it may be necessary to book from one event to the next. A diary of future home and overseas exhibitions is published every month in *Exhibition Bulletin*.

21.2 Kinds of Exhibition Organisers

Before booking space in an exhibition it is wise to check the reputation of the organisers. There are fly-by-night operators, and it may be that a small event in an insignificant venue will not be worth the cost of designing and constructing a stand, equipping it and diverting staff from other duties to man it. The costs of exhibiting only begin with the price of square metres.

(*a*) **Trade association.** Many shows are run for the benefit of members of trade associations. The Motor Show is run by the Society of Motor Manufacturers and Traders. So, too, is the equipment side of Smithfield, the London fat stock and farm equipment show.

(*b*) **Publisher.** A number of shows are run by newspapers or magazines, e.g. Ideal Home Exhibition (*Daily Mail*), Hotelympia (*Caterer and Hotelkeeper*), and Shoe Show (*Shoe & Leather News*).

(*c*) **Trade and/or Tourist Development Boards and Campaigns.** These may be fairly large exhibitions, such as those organised in Scotland, Wales and Ulster, or touring ones like the converted buses used to promote seaside resorts which have linked together in joint enterprises as in Kent and Sussex.

(*d*) **Societies.** These exhibitions, like the trade association events, are run primarily for the benefit of their members but more as a member activity than to promote business. Those of the Royal Horticultural Society, the National Rose Society and of many similar local societies which exhibit members' produce, come within this category and may or may not offer opportunities for trade exhibits. In the case of local flower shows, they may be run by the Parks Department of the local authority.

(*e*) **Professional organisers.** A great many exhibitions are run by professional organisers as a medium for exhibitors. These firms may also handle the management of exhibitions for any of the previous kinds of organiser. Well-known firms in this field are Industrial & Trade Fairs Ltd, Mack-Brooks Exhibitions Ltd, IPC Exhibitions Ltd, and Maclaren Exhibitions Ltd. The Andrey Montgomery Group is a holding company responsible for several exhibition companies and runs the Building Trades Exhibition and Interbuild but it is indicative of the current trend that only two or three of its scores of annual exhibitions are held in the UK.

There is a British Exhibitions Contractors Association which seeks to maintain high standards of exhibition contracting in the UK. Exhibitors are demanding the equivalent of ABC figures for attendances, and audited attendance figures are being given for some exhibitions. However, such figures cannot be entirely satisfactory, depending greatly on the discipline maintained by turnstile attendants which is sometimes complicated by purchased tickets, complimentary and press tickets, exhibitors' passes, and the general ability of people involved in exhibitions to come and go as they please so that their re-entry is counted as another attendance. Sometimes a more accurate estimation of attendance value is an analysis of the people and interests covered as shown on visitors' tickets which have to be filled in by each visitor. With trade and business exhibitions what matters is who attends, not how many go through the turnstiles. With a popular exhibition like the Ideal Home, a philosophy of the more the merrier is justified but how many of the large attendance at the Boat Show are likely to buy a boat?

21.3 Special Characteristics of Exhibitions

Exhibitions are the modern counterpart of the famous marts of the middle ages, providing a convenient centre at which buyers and sellers can meet. No other advertising medium can compare with the ability of the exhibition to present actual products and services, information and demonstrators, to those who are prepared to come and see for themselves at first hand. This advantage is immediately obvious when the product cannot be put in a briefcase but even a small item can benefit from demonstration.

By being in a central place for a length of time the exhibitor can be visited by a very large number of people, sometimes more people than his salesmen can call on in a very much longer period, while these visitors will include new and unknown prospects.

An exhibition has a 'show' atmosphere, with its novelties, demonstrations, give-aways and working models and a visit to an exhibition is an enjoyable occasion, a day out even for a businessman.

Apart from the opportunity to do business—and some exhibitors sell direct from the stand or booth—the exhibition has a large PR content. There is personal confrontation between buyer and supplier, whether the buyer be distributor or consumer. This interface is important, helping to build up goodwill through human relationships. Moreover, the visitor may feel free to make comments or complaints, and the exhibitor receives a valuable feedback as when a prototype is shown and opinions are invited. There is also, of course, another important PR aspect which is all too often wasted. This is the news-value of an exhibition and the opportunities it provides for press, radio, TV and film coverage, often with Central Office of Information (COI) support, so the message of one's participation can be broadcast throughout the UK and overseas to people who cannot or will not attend.

21.4 Problems of Exhibitions

There are, however, certain problems about exhibitions but if these are reckoned with in advance and overcome, the medium can be a most profitable one. Staffing the stand may mean taking salesmen off the road: can the company afford to do this, or do the additional sales and contacts secured at the exhibitions show sufficient compensation? There may be a big print bill but can this be controlled by cautious display and by a controlled attendance? Hospitality can run up another large bill but if the point of the stand is to meet and entertain people this cost must be expected and treated as an investment in goodwill. A very serious problem is security since thieving is a notorious characteristic of most exhibitions, especially when the hall is closed for the night! And British exhibitions have also suffered from their labour troubles so that the completion of stands has been delayed by striking craftsmen.

21.5 Special Uses of Exhibitions

Why take part? Some firms exhibit simply because their rivals will be present and they feel they must not be left out. This is a poor way to plan a marketing strategy for exhibitions should be an integral part of the media mix. Let us therefore consider some of the many reasons why and how exhibitions can be used to advantage.

(*a*) **To launch a new product.** Since most visitors attend to see 'what's new this year', the exhibition provides an excellent launch-pad for a new or modified product.

(*b*) **To meet distributors.** At trade and business exhibitions, some exhibitors are content to play 'open house' to their distributors. It may be one of the few occasions when distributors from far afield meet the company directors as distinct from the local representative.

(*c*) **To demonstrate physically the sales points of a product.** This is of value when other forms of publicity are inadequate and is especially useful for machinery which otherwise can be seen only by visiting a plant where it has been installed. But it can also apply to commodities which need to be tasted, handled or in some way sampled and proved.

(*d*) **To meet prospects quickly and economically.** This is a big reason why firms go into exhibitions, especially overseas ones where the show is a quicker and cheaper way of opening up a new export market than having a salesman travel a strange market for a year. (An alternative is to travel a mobile exhibition but this is another form of the same medium.)

(*e*) **To test the market.** A few days' exposure at an exhibition may be a good market research exercise.

(*f*) **To maintain reputation and market status.** Because the exhibition throws the spotlight on an industry it may be imperative to 'show the flag' and maintain one's place in the industry. The exhibition is an ideal means of doing so.

(*g*) **To sell the product or service.** Some exhibitors make a profitable direct selling venture out of exhibitions, literally taking their shop from one event to the next.

(*h*) **To communicate a PR message.** Some less or non-commercial participants use exhibitions as PR media, communicating their story to visitors. Trade associations, professional and other societies, and Government departments and public authorities do this.

21.6　Stages in the Preparation of an Exhibition

The following is a brief summary of the steps which have to be taken by the participant in an exhibition, and is intended to emphasise the need for planning over many months, perhaps a year. It is seldom wise to rush into an exhibition at the last minute when this may be apparent to visitors and so prove a detraction.

(*a*) Check with *Exhibition Bulletin, British Rate and Data, Sales & Marketing Management*, Department of Industry and Trade, local Chamber of Commerce or one's trade association to find out what exhibitions and trade fairs are to be held during the 12 months for which advertising is being planned and budgeted.

(*b*) Obtain from the exhibition organisers their rates per square metre and for shell schemes, together with a plan of the proposed layout of the event(s).

(*c*) Having decided to take part, book the most suitable site bearing in mind special requirements such as proximity to some relevant part of the hall (e.g. main entrance or conference hall), ceiling space if the exhibit is tall, build-up time if the exhibit is complicated to erect, and access to aisles. Prepare a budget of total costs.

(*d*) Engage a stand designer, unless a shell stand is being used as provided by the promoters, and discuss the aims of the exhibit.

(*e*) Simultaneously, plan with production what products will be shown.

(*f*) Notify the PRO or PR consultants of participation so that contact can be made with the exhibition press officer, and advantage can be taken of all pre-event publicity.

(*g*) Consider print, photographic, film, model and other supplies for the stand. Get quotations, designs and put work in hand as necessary ideally with a timetable of operations.

(*h*) Engage a stand constructor to follow agreed design.

(*i*) Allocate and/or engage sales and demonstration staff, including kitchen/bar staff.

(*j*) Submit entry for catalogue, taking advertisement space if required and preparing advertisement. Keep the exhibition press officer supplied with information.

(*k*) Take out insurance and engage security services, as necessary.

(*l*) In the case of an overseas exhibition, plan all shipping requirements, and ensure that personnel have passports, visas, inoculations, currency, transportation and hotel bookings, special clothing, etc.

(*m*) In the case of a UK event, plan all travel, accommodation, parking and other requirements for personnel.

(*n*) Make sure that all supplies will be delivered on time; organise build-up schedule including provision of all services such as gas, electricity, water, telephones, furnishings, cleaning, catering supplies, photography.

(*o*) Maintain contact with press officer, supplying news releases and pictures (*not* press kits) to the press office in good time; attending press day or preview; inviting press to stand; making sure that any special publicity facilities are enjoyed such as providing a good reason why the official opener should visit the stand.

(*p*) Place advertisements in newspaper and magazine features about the event, if this is considered valuable. Arrange this with advertising agent.

During the exhibition, means of recording contacts should be organised and they should be clearly understood by all working on the stand. These means may include a box for business cards, a visitors' book, enquiry forms or cards, questionnaires and competitions.

The above check list is a simplified one, and a more specific list set out as a timetable of operations with personnel responsibilities clearly stated is recommended. Regular exhibitors may be engaged on more than one event in different countries, and the need for precise planning is even more essential. Time-consuming aspects of overseas events may range from translations and foreign-language printings to entirely different routines for the design and construction of stands. Anyone contemplating overseas exhibiting should take advantage of the advisory services of the Department of Trade and Industry. The London Chamber of Commerce and Industry is extremely helpful to its members, and in connection with large international fairs it organises intensive short language courses.

Most advertising agencies regard exhibitions as a 'below-the-line' activity, leaving most of the responsibilities to their clients and providing only some of the services such as press advertising and possibly print. However, the client may wish the agency to take over the complete job of booking space, stand design and stand construction, print, photography, displays, and press advertising, and some agencies, mostly the technical ones, are happy to do so. This leaves the client to concentrate on the exhibits and the staffing. Very large firms have their own exhibition and display departments and design their own stands. At the other extreme, the rudiments of a stand may be accepted in a shell scheme, and the space is fitted out with hired furnishings, wall decorations and a display/demonstration of the product or service.

22
The Cinema Screen

In Britain the cinema-going habit, when people often visited the cinema twice a week and there were 3,000-seater Odeons and Gaumonts, has been replaced by watching films on television at home. Today, the big cinemas are either converted into two or three small cinemas or into bingo halls. Others have closed. Screen advertising used to be classed as one of the five traditional above-the-line media. Now it is a medium of less mass appeal, although it is still a powerful medium for its more selective audience. Cinema audiences always tended to be predominantly young, but this is even truer today. The films themselves are often ones with special effects which appeal to young people.

In the developing world, the cinema flourishes, and there are both indoor and outdoor drive-in cinemas according to the climatic conditions. There are also mobile cinemas which take film shows to the more remote rural areas. In some Third World countries the mobile cinema—often no more than a screen erected on the roof of a Land Rover—is very popular with villagers. In countries where newspapers are scarce, and illiteracy widespread, the mobile cinema is an essential advertising medium.

The following information on British cinema advertising is taken from the booklet *Cinema Scene* (Summer 1981) published by the Cinema Advertising Association.

'In 1981 we stand poised on the brink of a revolutionary new stage in the development of the audio-visual advertising media. Video-cassette and video-disc equipment are fast becoming not just the playthings of the rich, but mass consumer items which will soon be found in the majority of homes. The fourth channel and breakfast television are due to make their debut within the next two years, and satellite broadcasting from Europe will follow shortly in their wake. The effect of these innovations must be to segment the audience to commercial television into smaller more selective groupings. Indeed, within the last two years we have already seen what appears to be an irreversible erosion of the majority audiences that ITV enjoyed in the 60s and 70s.

'Cinema has also undergone its own revolution in the last few years. The mass audiences of the 30's and 40's are no longer to be seen. The cinema audience of today is far more selective and concentrated within the younger age groups. Cinemagoing is no longer an everyday habit, but has become a special event—a form of leisure entertainment, which whilst being less regular, is much less taken for granted. Cinema production techinques have recognised this, and the lavish special effects, now seen as commonplace on the cinema screen, cannot be experienced in the same depth in any other audio-visual medium. Cinema premises also reflect the changes which have been seen within the industry. Continuing rationalisation and modernisation are creating a network of cinemas in the UK, far better suited to coping with the more flexible pattern of distribution required of today's film industry.

'As cinema takes its place in the 80s amongst a more fragmented, but more selective group of audio-visual media, the CAA recognises that the advertiser will require far more detailed knowledge of whom his message is reaching. To this end the CAA commissioned and published in 1980 the first of a series of in-depth audience studies through Carrick James Market Research. In addition to looking at the nature or audiences to cinema in general, this study also probed the size and shape of audiences to particular films, and groups of films. At the same time the CAA continues to provide audience data based on Government admission statistics and special analysis of JICNARS data.'

22.1 Who goes to the Cinema?

As already mentioned above, the cinema audience is a young one, and for advertisers of products which appeal to the young this makes the medium one which reaches these age groups (15–24-year-olds) less wastefully than perhaps any other medium. The cinema audience is usually referred to as a 'captive' one, and this is a characteristic which adds strength to advertising messages projected from the cinema screen.

The Carrick James Market Research (CJMR) survey, based on a sample of 2,310 individuals aged 7 years and older, showed that 48 per cent of the survey universe went to the cinema. This figure rose sharply in the prime age group.

Age	Ever go to the cinema
7–14	91%
15–17	94%
18–24	92%
25–34	83%

About one third (34 per cent) of the total survey universe had visited the cinema within the last six months, and about half of these (16 per cent) had been in the last month. But certain age groups predominate as cinemagoers as the following table shows:

'RECENCY': PROPORTION WHO HAD BEEN TO THE CINEMA IN LAST SIX MONTHS AND IN LAST FOUR WEEKS

Age	Last six months	Last four weeks
7–10	49%	11%
11–14	62%	22%
15–17	78%	44%

Age	Last six months	Last four weeks
18–24	69%	39%
25–34	50%	21%
35–44	28%	13%
45+	8%	4%

This can be looked at in another way by examining the average number of visits within the last two months for each age group:

Age	Average number of visits in previous two months
7–10	0.34
11–14	0.55
15–17	1.13
18–24	1.10
25–34	0.52
35–44	0.30
45+	0.09

The 15–17 age group emerges once again as the leading group. It is three times higher than that for the average adult (0.41 visits).

The weight of ITV viewing among the main cinema audience (7–34-year-olds) was also studied. It was found that the *light* viewers of ITV made twice as many visits to the cinema as *heavy* viewers.

22.2   Who goes to see which Films?

The data on film watching was collected in two ways. First, respondents were shown a list of 36 films, these being representations of all films on distribution but including the major releases of recent years. They were asked which of these films they had seen in the cinema during the last *two or three years*. Second, respondents were asked about all the films they had seen during the past *two months*. More than 400 different films were involved.

22.3   Age Variations in Viewing Tastes

The survey showed that there were enormous differences in audience profile for different kinds of film, the age factor being very significant as the following tables demonstrated.

7–10-YEAR-OLDS (3.6 MILLION): MOST POPULAR FILMS SEEN IN LAST 2 TO 3 YEARS

1. Star Wars	1.4 million
2. Grease	1.2 million
3. Superman	1.1 million
4. Pete's Dragon	0.8 million
5. The Rescuers	0.7 million
6. Watership Down	0.7 million
7. Bedknobs and Broomsticks	0.6 million
8. Moonraker	0.5 million

While the Disney-type films are expectedly popular in their group, films of broader interest such as *Star Wars* were seen by nearly half of the 7–10-year-old group.

When the early teenager (11–14-year-old) group was studied it was found that similar films were popular, but in a slightly different order of merit.

11–14-YEAR-OLDS (3.3 MILLION):
MOST POPULAR FILMS SEEN IN LAST 2 OR 3 YEARS

1. Grease   2.0 million
2. Star Wars   1.3 million
3. Superman   0.9 million
4. Watership Down   0.8 million
5. Moonraker   0.8 million
6. The Rescuers   0.75 million
7. Herbie Goes to Monte Carlo   0.7 million
8. Pete's Dragon   0.7 million

Because of its appeal to young girls, *Grease* takes the lead, but the Disney films are still among the leaders.

Films preferred by girls under 15	*Films preferred by boys under 15*
Bedknobs and Broomsticks	Battlestar Galactica
Grease	Moonraker
The Rescuers	Star Trek
Watership Down	Star Wars
	Superman

15–17-YEAR-OLDS (2.7 MILLION):
MOST POPULAR FILMS SEEN IN LAST 2 OR 3 YEARS

1. Grease   1.7 million
2. Saturday Night Fever   0.85 million
3. Star Wars   0.8 million
4. Close Encounters of the Third Kind   0.8 million
5. Moonraker   0.6 million
6. Superman   0.45 million
7. Revenge of the Pink Panther   0.4 million
8. Bedknobs and Broomsticks   0.4 million

Now we begin to see the emergence of more sophisticated films. *Grease* is still the leader, and another John Travolta film takes second place. Disney films have practically disappeared, but the more serious *Close Encounters* is here and the Peter Sellers comedy-thriller. But *Star Wars* stays near the top. The variety of film is interesting.

Still dominating are the Travolta films but now we have some of those restricted by certificate classification. *Quadrophenia* drew most of its viewers from this age group (79 per cent) and *Scum*, *Halloween* and *The Warriors* also drew more than 70 per cent of their viewing from the 18–24-year-olds.

18–24-YEAR-OLDS (5.8 MILLION). MOST POPULAR FILMS SEEN IN LAST 2 OR 3 YEARS
(With this hard core of cinemagoers other types of film join the order of priority, and a longer list becomes necessary.)

1. Grease	2.4 million
2. Saturday Night Fever	2.4 million
3. Close Encounters of the Third Kind	1.75 million
4. Alien (X)	1.5 million
5. Moonraker	1.35 million
6. Star Wars	1.3 million
7. Superman	1.2 million
8. Every Which Way But Loose (AA)	1.2 million
9. Quadrophenia (X)	1.2 million
10. Revenge of the Pink Panther	1.1 million
11. Star Trek	0.9 million
12. The Deer Hunter (X)	0.8 million

With the 25–34-year-olds, *Grease* and *Saturday Night Fever* stayed at the top but *Star Wars* moved higher in the list. *Watership Down* returned to the list, probably because the audience included young parents accompanying their children.

The over 35-year-olds showed a variety of tastes but again this may have been influenced by parents accompanying children rather than preference for certain films. *Star Wars* came top and Disney films reappeared, but *Grease* and *Saturday Night Fever* fell to fifth and ninth positions, perhaps for the same reason.

22.4   Variations by Class and Sex

Male and female cinemagoers showed distinct preferences. Sixty per cent of audiences were male for films such as *Apocalypse Now*, *Manhattan*, *National Lampoon's Animal House*, *Alien* and *Monty Python's Life of Brian*. Women preferred *Grease* (61 per cent) and *Saturday Night Fever* (59 per cent). Girls in the 11–14-year-old group favoured Disney films.

Social class preferences showed that ABC[1]'s preferred the AA or A Certificate films, but C[2]DE's liked horror and X certificate films. Upper social classes favoured films such as *Manhattan* and *California Suite* which were not big box office successes.

22.5   Who goes with Whom?

Few people go to the cinema alone, only 6 per cent being solitary cinemagoers, and it is only among older cinemagoers that the number is relatively high, this being 22 per cent of over 45's.

Of children aged 7–10, 61 per cent go with their parents, and 17 per cent go with other adults. Accompaniment by parent falls with higher age groups, but with 35–44-year-olds the reverse occurs, with 23 per cent going with their own children. In between, attendance is largely with a friend of the opposite sex, 50 per cent in the prime 18–24's.

From these figures it will be seen that the cinema offers a medium of exceptional interest to advertisers who sell to young people, including children. Both major contractors offer special packages restricted to 'U' and 'A' certificate film distribution. Rank Screen Advertising offer a Disney package. These packages can be attractive when increasing restrictions are being placed on advertising made to reach children—TV, for example. Another table is therefore interesting:

ANNUAL AVERAGE FREQUENCY

Age groups	Frequency
7–8	2.88
9–10	3.11
11–12	3.82
13–14	4.91
15–17	8.27

22.6 Buying Cinema Advertising

Cinema advertising time may be bought in minimum units of one week's advertising in one cinema. Commercials are screened within one reel which is shown in all performances during that week—children's matinees excepted—after the interval, when house lights are down, and before the major film. Unlike television advertising there are no commercial breaks while the film is showing.

Screentime varies between 15 seconds and three minutes in multiples of five seconds. The basic rate is for 60 seconds. Most campaigns run for several weeks. To avoid monotony an 'alternative week campaign' or 'one week in—one week out' pattern for each cinema is recommended. For regular campaigns two prints of the commercial are required for each cinema, and 10 per cent extra prints is advisable to cover breakages.

22.7 Total UK Cinema Rates

Various packages are available from the contractors, such as: ITV areas; conurbation (big population) areas; London West End; all seaside and holiday towns; and all university towns. There are also X film, children's (e.g. matinees, Disney films, and 'U' and 'A' certificate) and selected film packages. Thus, the advertiser can direct his campaign at selected audiences. It is interesting to see how the medium has reacted to the revolution in cinemagoing.

22.8 Special Characteristics of Cinema Screen Advertising

The special nature of the medium may be analysed as follows:

(*a*) Advertising films are shown in a darkened situation, usually before the main film. Unlike TV, the film is not interrupted by commercials. Distractions are minimal, there is less inclination to leave one's seat than

TOTAL CINEMA RATES

	Total number of cinemas	Total rate per week (60 seconds' cost)
All cinemas		
(excl. overlap)	1665	£31,854
ITV areas		
London	473	£11,345
Midlands	232	£4,299
Lancashire	267	£4,252
Yorkshire	194	£3,492
Central Scotland	105	£2,300
Wales and West	178	£2,598
Southern	181	£3,208
Tyne Tees	83	£1,369
Anglia	114	£2,036
Ulster	36	£680
South West	71	£1,009
Border	21	£267
N.E. Scotland	39	£640
Channel Isles	6	£152
Outside TV	4	£44
Conurbations		
Greater London	270	£7,462
Tyne & Wear and Cleveland	56	£1,031
Greater Manchester	85	£1,316
Merseyside	40	£777
West Midlands	56	£1,263
South Yorkshire & Humberside	46	£922
West Yorkshire	53	£975
Central Scotland	84	£1,958
All Conurbations	690	£15,704
London West End	77	£3,255
Holiday resorts	240	£4,141
University towns	364	£8,245

there is in the home when commercials appear. With such a truly captive audience, full attention is gained. Memorability tests have proved that cinema audiences retain strong impressions.

(*b*) The medium can be dominated by a particular advertiser since competing brands are not shown in the same sequence of commercials.

(*c*) The sheer size of the advertisement (especially on the wide screen) with its colour, sound and movement is in itself impactive.

(*d*) Campaigns can be tailored to cover any specified region, town or even individual cinema.

(*e*) Special dealer films can be used, 60-second commercials being shown on the same reel as national advertisers. Fifteen seconds can be reserved for the dealer's name, address and telephone number, with voice-over if required. Pearl and Dean make these syndicated dealer films, covering most trades.

22.9 Audience Delivery Plan

The Audience Delivery Plan (ADP) is offered by Pearl and Dean and Rank Screen Advertising, and it aims to deliver a specified audience at a fixed cost. Once a campaign is under way, the contractors will monitor the weekly attendances, and if necessary vary the weight or the length of a campaign so that the specified audience is delivered.

The advertiser gives only general instructions, e.g. the length of the commercial, the campaign areas, the campaign period, and how many people should be reached. The cinema contractors attend to all the details and ensure that the task is carried out.

The advertiser knows that the campaign will be kept under continual review, and that he will obtain the audience which he expects. A decision to advertise in the cinema can therefore be based on the fundamental values of the medium.

The advertiser must book for a minimum of one million admissions or on an equivalent scale in ITV areas. An ADP campaign should run for at least six weeks and preferably for eight or more, and it may be used in any reasonably sized TV area. Marplan are retained by the Cinema Advertising Association to produce weekly estimates of admissions which are used to manage the packages. Ten main circuits are contacted weekly, and 40 independents are contacted monthly.

23
Outdoor and Transportation Media

Because this chapter will deal with many variants of outdoor and transportation media, two points will be clarified at the onset. First, these media are sometimes described rather generally in Britain as **'poster'** and in the USA as **'billboard'** advertising although they are by no means limited to paper posters pasted on hoardings. Second, although both outdoor and transportation advertising may use similar advertisement forms—e.g. posters—they are likely to be of different size, shape, content and audience, while the sites are mostly completely different. About the only absolute similarities are poster sites outside railway, airport, seaport, bus and coach premises which resemble poster sites in the street. The chief difference, however, is in the manner in which outdoor and transportation advertisements are seen and absorbed.

23.1 Differences between Outdoor and Transportation Media

The main differences are as follows:

(*a*) Outdoor sites themselves are mostly static, except for special vehicles which take advertisements from place to place such as an aircraft trailing a banner.

(*b*) Transportation sites are often moving ones which carry advertisements over routes where they may be seen by a continually changing and accumulative audience. These sites include public service vehicles (buses, trams, trolley buses), minicabs and goods delivery vehicles, overland and underground trains, ferries and passenger ships. Airliners do not usually have displayed advertisements but they may be included in airline magazines issued to passengers or during in-flight movies.

(*c*) The outdoor audience tends to be a passer-by one which cannot absorb much detail so that the content of outdoor advertisements needs to be brief. Exceptions are the smaller billboard (the British version being a small board as used for cinema advertisements) and the information panel.

(*d*) The transportation audience, especially inside vehicles and transportation premises—stations, waiting rooms, forecourts, booking offices— is one willing to be interested, diverted and informed while waiting or travelling. Consequently, it can absorb more detailed messages, and accept them on smaller posters, cards or signs.

(*e*) In the London area (and also in other large cities such as Paris with its famous Metro and the exceptionally attractive advertisements on the Champs-Elysées and other central stations) the Underground provides a very special medium with a large audience of commuters (especially young women), shoppers, cinema/theatre goers, and tourists (both UK and overseas). This is a unique medium.

From the above remarks it will be seen that by transportation advertising we mean all kinds of advertising on or in public transport, passenger or goods, and on or in transportation land or premises.

Outdoor advertising was defined in the *Town and Country Planning (Control of Advertisements) Regulations, 1948* as 'any word, letter, model, sign, placard, board, notice, device or representation, whether illuminated or not, used for the purposes of advertisement, announcement or direction'. It includes any hoarding or similar structure used or adapted for the display of advertisements. It also includes such forms of advertisement as a doctor's nameplate.

Like radio, outdoor advertising is a universal medium and one of great value in developing countries where there are problems of many languages or illiteracy. Posters can be pictorial, conveying messages more effectively than words which have to be few in any case with this medium. In West African towns the poster is therefore an important medium for beers, cigarettes, detergents and aspirins.

In Asia the poster has been a major medium in nation-wide family planning campaigns, the message being presented in various styles to cover local languages, customs and religions.

Slogans and cartoon drawings have been used on posters to create awareness and stimulate interest in family planning in India, so that whether the slogan was comprehensible or not the point was made by the child in the small family looking happy while his counterpart in the large family looked miserable. The Western world might learn much to its advantage from these techniques. Some of the Indian family planning slogans have been these:

> *Two or three children—stop*
> *A small family is a happy family*
> *Three or two—that will do*
> *Next child not now, after three, Never*

These positive appeals also had long-term value in that they sensitised schoolchildren to the idea that a two-child family was normal and beneficial.

This example is interesting because it demonstrates the qualities of the medium which we shall now examine more specifically.

The pictorially detailed posters in Malaysia demonstrate how supersites can be used to convey sales messages to people who speak different languages.

23.2 Special Characteristics of Outdoor Advertising

(*a*) Its **widespread popular appeal** makes it a medium for goods and

services of interest to the mass market, and for this reason it complements
TV advertising as the link between home and store.

(*b*) Most outdoor advertisements are **big and dominant** so that it is a
powerful eye-catching medium.

(*c*) It is customary for the larger outdoor advertisements to remain in
position for a period of time, usually weeks, so that they enjoy both 24-
hour exposure and **long life.** The fact that the audience may see the advertisement only fleetingly is compensated by the *repetition* of viewing. This
repetition is ideal for the name-plugging or sloganising advertisement
which seeks to familiarise the audience with a brand name, sales point or
pack design. The task of the poster is often a very simple but insistent one.

(*d*) **High coverage** is achieved since 80 per cent of the UK population
live in urban areas. The majority of these people will see poster campaigns
repeatedly.

(*e*) It is a very **flexible** medium so that the advertiser can rent sites
where he needs them most, picking this or that town and selecting individual sites within each chosen locality. About half the sites change hands in
the course of the year.

23.3   Types of Outdoor Advertising

(*a*) **Hoardings.** Mostly 16-sheet or larger, these are the large sites flank-
ing the pavement which may be permanent or temporary in the case of
building operations. *Gable ends* are similar sites on the corner walls of
houses or shops.

(*b*) **Pedestrian housewife posters.** This is the name given to the 4-sheet
posters, often on vandal-proof vinyl material, on sites which architects
have introduced into shopping precincts. The sites are either flat or circular
and some revolve.

(*c*) **Bulletin boards or Supersites.** These are large solus sites consisting of
painted panels, specially built and usually well set out with gardens and
floodlights. Special versions are those which are **animated** or given a three-
dimensional effect with a cut-out figure or replica of the product, or made
to **glow** by means of a backlighted translucent surface, while the **rotary
system** allows a set of designs to be shown in rotation among the selected
sites. Bulletin boards should not be confused with the little bulletins or
notices pinned up outside public places, as when a member of the Royal
Family is ill, or when there used to be an execution at a gaol. Bulletin
boards are about the same depth as a 16-sheet poster but may extend for
27 ft, 36 ft or even 45 ft and make very impressive advertising sites.

(*d*) **Public information panels.** These are also found in shopping precincts
and on pavements, and the panels carry the smaller double-crown posters.
Similar panels are available on bus shelters.

(*e*) **Billboards.** Portable or fixed boards for double-crown or quad-crown
posters as used by cinemas, they are sometimes used for temporary announcements.

(*f*) **Signs.** These are almost a medium on their own. They range from
moving, coloured, lighted signs like the famous ones of Piccadilly Circus,
to metal plates, glass boxes and advertisements painted on walls, bridges

or any other publicly situated flat surface. They also have special uses as when contractors announce the work they are doing, e.g. landscape gardeners, heating engineers, painters and decorators, scaffolding contractors, steeplejacks, builders and civil engineers. Architects, having to follow a professional code regarding advertising, are permitted to use only a stylised announcement which may be observed whenever building work is in progress. In post-war years, with so many new estates, high-rise flats, office blocks, motorways, bridges, tunnels and docks under construction, the contractors' sign has become an important advertising medium, and where numerous sub-contractors are involved very large 'credit' signs are erected.

The **flutter sign** has been a familiar sight overseas for many years, especially in Asiatic cities. The signs consist of strips or spangles which flutter in the breeze or reflect lights at night. They have been popular with Japanese electronic firms. During the early 80s they have been introduced into Britain, familiar sites in places like Piccadilly Circus being taken over by flutter signs advertising mostly foreign products.

(*g*) **Newscasters.** Placed on high buildings in city centres or at main-line stations, these electronic signs spell out news flashes in lighted strips, interspersed with advertisements. They are not to be confused with sound broadcasting systems on railway stations—the ones used to apologise for the late arrival of your train!

(*h*) **Aerial methods.** In the UK the 1961 regulations forbid the trailing of banners overland because of the risk of distracting motorists, and some years earlier single-engined aircraft were forbidden to carry advertising over towns. Aerial advertising is confined to the seaside where holidaymakers can read banners trailed by aircraft flying over the sea. On the continent groups of three aircraft have been used to trail multiple banners (Holland), night-flying aircraft have had advertisements picked out in lights on the underparts of their wings (Germany), and advertisements have been projected onto clouds (Germany). In Zimbabwe, amplified advertisements are shouted from low-flying helicopters, a development of a wartime propaganda device. With the development of Goodyear airships we may see the airship as a large aerial communicator. Goodyear airships are used for public service announcements in the USA and on the continent, electronic illuminated messages being spelt out on the sides of the airship. Although not normally permitted in the UK, an exception occurred during the Royal Wedding in 1981 when loyal greetings were spelt out and seen by TV viewers.

(*i*) **Litter bins.** These can be seen attached to lamp-posts. They combine usefulness with advertisements which serve a double role in attracting attention to both message and bin.

(*j*) **Directional maps.** Erected in town centres, these maps provide a medium for local advertising.

(*k*) **Puppet shows.** This is an Indian medium which provides entertainment while conveying a message, and is yet another method used in the family planning campaign. One such show tells how the rich man of the village has a large family, rejects the family planning campaign, but when his wife has twins and there are complications he calls in the midwife who tells him that his wife will not survive more births. He accepts the family planning advice, and so becomes the innovator in his village.

(*l*) **Mobile advertising.** At election times, and on certain special occasions, we have **loudspeaker vans** on British streets, but overseas (e.g. Lagos) numbers of cars fitted with loudspeakers conduct mobile advertising. In Nigeria and many developing countries, the mobile or travelling advertising show consisting of a Land-Rover cinema van and maybe a band of singers, dancers and demonstrators will carry out village-to-village shows to promote products.

In Britain, taxi-cab advertising may be placed on the outside of the taxi, or inside on the tip-up seat or front bulkhead. Cab Advertising Bureau (Licensed Taxi Drivers Association cabs) and Taxi Media handle this form of advertising. Taxi Media have reintroduced exterior taxi-cab advertising which went out of favour when mini-cabs, adorned with ads, were banned from the Royal Parks. The current method is to place an advertising panel on the nearside front door of the taxi.

(*m*) **Giant billboards.** Mention of overseas uses of outdoor media invites the inclusion of the huge, hand-painted portraits of Hollywood stars which have appeared on the Sunset Boulevard.

(*n*) **Alternating panel boards.** Finally, among the more ingenious forms of outdoor advertising, are the slatted boards which move to present completely different advertisements, not unlike the Parisian night-signs which carry a sequence of advertisements within the one area of the individual sign.

(*o*) **Projected advertisements.** Very effective, these are slides projected from one building to a blank wall opposite, and flashed on and off. They are forbidden in UK streets, but may be seen in shopping precincts and inside buildings. In other countries, where they are not deemed a traffic hazard, they may be seen in the street.

(*p*) **Meter Ads.** An innovation is parking meter advertisements, the new medium conceived by Tamlint Promotional Services Ltd of Manchester. Their appeal is that people passing a line of meters see a message repeated every 15 seconds. There are 53,000 meters in the UK. National advertisers such as British Airways, P & O Ferries, Thomas Cook and Hertz were among the first users of the medium.

23.4   Poster Sizes

Mention has been made of sheet sizes, and this is because the various multiples of quad, 4-sheet, 8-sheet, 16-sheet and so forth are based on the double-crown poster which measures 508 mm wide by 762 mm deep (20 in. by 30 in.). A 16-sheet is therefore 3048 mm by 2032 mm (10 ft by 6 ft 8 in.). A bulletin board or supersite, consisting of painted panels, is not quite so deep and the measurements are 9 ft 6 in. deep by 27 ft, 36 ft or 45 ft.

23.5   Special Characteristics of Transportation Advertising

Some of these were expressed in the comparisons between outdoor and transportation advertising at the beginning of this chapter, but certain others are worth commenting upon.

(*a*) The variety of kinds of site is so great that it is more versatile than ordinary outdoor advertising. For example, a small bill announcing a sale can be placed on the window of a local bus, a holiday resort may advertise on every main-line station in the country, and a secretarial bureau may use cards in the compartments of London Underground trains. This adaptability makes it a medium which in one form or another can be exploited to meet specific markets.

(*b*) The medium attracts **public goodwill** which is enjoyed by the advertisers using it. When people are waiting for a bus or a train to arrive, or when they are actually travelling, the advertising overcomes their sense of time-loss or their boredom. For these reasons the copy can be lengthier than with most forms of street advertising, and it can do a more thorough selling job. Outdoor advertising is mainly reminder, but transportation advertising can be hard selling. These remarks are worth pondering upon: the British travelling public tends to be unsociable, but will be grateful for advertisements that help to pass the time amusingly or informatively. The British tend to be inhibited about selling and advertising, yet in the transportation atmosphere these inhibitions tend to falter.

Two of the organisations principally concerned with transportation advertising in the UK are **London Transport Advertising** and **British Transport Advertising,** and the following accounts, with details of actual advertisers using their media, set out the highlights of their services to advertisers.

23.6   London Transport Advertising

London is an exceptional market. It is the biggest consumer market in Britain and the richest, Britain's biggest touring centre, and the biggest concentration of people who influence buying decisions. Ten million people live in the London Transport area. Like other media, transportation advertising changes and expands as new bus routes and new Underground lines and stations are introduced. The road and rail systems carry millions of passengers a day, and commuters and shoppers generally make at least two journeys a day. The repetition value of transportation advertising is therefore great, while pedestrians and motorists are aware of external transportation advertising.

The following are the different sites available on public transport vehicles, properties and premises:

Double crowns on buses. The fronts are sold only in pairs but the rear positions may be bought singly. Because they are high up on double-decker buses it is important that the message is legible at a distance. The fault is sometimes made of using posters with small print which might be suitable for an Underground station wall.

Targets. These positions on the outside of bus stairways have good impact, are lower down than double crowns, and are used by mass consumer advertisers.

Lower rears. Since they face the drivers of following cars, these are favourite positions for motor trade advertisers promoting motor-cars, accessories and oil.

Double-deck sides. With illuminated spaces on the offside only, these are very impactive too, being high up and very wide so that they lend themselves to full-length figures for advertising, say, holidays, sun-tan oils, jeans or for big name displays for football pools, drinks or airlines.

Monopoly advertisers, to give them a name, cover those who have taken all the outside positions on a bus, and these are very dominant travelling advertisements. Johnnie Walker whisky made very effective use of this medium with numerous Johnnie Walker figures displayed.

Overall Painted Bus. This special form of monopolised bus advertising is popular in many parts of the world. Until their withdrawal in October 1975, Londoners were either astounded or infuriated by the sight of buses painted as a complete advertisement on a yearly contract. Silexine paint, Thomson Yellow Pages, Bertorelli ice-cream, BCM Uniparts, Sharp Electronics, Younger's Tartan Beer, Ladbroke's and Home Pride Flour were among those who used these incredibly gaudy advertising monsters. Unipart even painted the roof of their bus for the benefit of office viewers. For six months during the 1977 Silver Jubilee Year, there were 25 silver buses, each devoted to a single advertiser.

This was an example of how advertising changes, and media come and go. A problem was that in cities where there are buses of familiar colour, e.g. red and green, it could be confusing to waiting passengers if the once-familiar red or green were decorated in a riot of advertising colours. Some passengers objected to sitting on a travelling advertisement.

Now let us turn to the London *Underground*, where the following sites and sizes are available:

Double crowns (508 mm by 762 mm). This popular-size vertical poster space is available on walls throughout Underground stations, e.g. corridors and platforms.

Quad crowns (1016 mm by 762 mm). Twice the size of double crowns and horizontal, these are the spaces on station walls which are used a lot by the entertainment industry.

4-Sheets (1016 mm by 1524 mm). Even more dramatic, these larger spaces are again available throughout stations.

16-Sheets (2032 mm by 3048 mm) (across the tracks). Unlike 16-sheets on roadside hoardings, these posters are seldom limited to the usual slogan, picture and brand name. Enterprising advertisers of drinks, restaurants, building societies and so on have produced elaborate, witty and complex posters to beguile waiting passengers.

Lift and escalator panels (413 mm by 565 mm). Once the favourite sites for ladies' underwear and swimsuit advertisers, these panels are now used by a variety of advertisers from theatres to menswear.

Spectaculars and illuminated panels. Spectaculars span the escalator system and are up to 18 metres wide, permitting dramatic advertisements with, say, more than life-size figures.

Advertisement rates are based on the traffic enjoyed by the different stations, and for advertisement rate purposes they are grouped as Class A, Class B and Class C. Thus, Piccadilly Circus, Euston, Knightsbridge and Holborn are Class A stations; Bayswater, Gants Hill, Kennington and

Uxbridge are Class B; and Brent, Ickenham, Pinner and Hainault are Class C. There are more than a hundred Class A and Class C stations, less than a hundred Class B stations. Sites are rented weekly or monthly, usually in multiples of 50 or 100.

Car cards (476 mm by 165 mm). This is a fairly inexpensive form of advertising, with the opportunity to place a detailed message in a small space but placed high up so that it is easily seen by seated or standing passengers. It is popular with jewellers, secretarial agencies, publishers, stores and tuition centres.

23.7 British Transport Advertising Ltd

This is the largest company of its kind in the world, and is responsible for selling and servicing commercial advertising on the properties and vehicles of the country's nationalised transport undertakings. These comprise the National Bus Company, Scottish Transport Group, British Transport Hotels, British Transport Docks Board, British Waterways Board, Hoverspeed Ltd, National Freight Company Ltd, Scottish Freight Company Ltd and Freightliners Ltd.

(Many civic bus services offer advertising sites too, and the contractors include Kemps Specialist Media Ltd and WHS Advertising Ltd. The latter also handle advertising sites at airports, air terminals, exhibitions, shopping centres and on bus shelters.)

BTA Ltd has been particularly enterprising in creating special forms of transportation advertising such as the 4-sheet poster lightbox, bringing rear illumination to static advertising. This consists of the poster being placed between two sheets of acrylic and illuminated from behind by fluorescent tubes, giving the advertisement a brilliance equal to photographic projection. This system has been adapted to various sites and sizes. Cards can also be displayed in a light box. Light boxes are available on Sealink ships.

Another innovation is the provision of display and exhibition space at main-line stations, such as the concourse at Euston.

The Polybus was introduced in early 1981. This name was given to a new system of bus advertising developed and patented by BTA Ltd. It allows the advertiser to encircle a double-decker bus, in the space normally occupied by busfronts, sides and rears between the lower and upper deck windows, with a continuous message on vinyl. The Polybus has now been replaced by the **Colorbus** and the **Unibus**.

The Colorbus is restricted to one trade category in any one bus depot area, and resembles the former painted bus.

The Unibus has a continuous painted advertisement about 80 ft. in length. This encircles the bus. It appears below the windows on a single-deck bus, and occupies the fronts, sides and rears between the lower and upper deck windows on a double-deck bus.

23.8 Buying Outdoor Advertising

As shown by the examples of London Transport, British Transport, Kemps

Specialist Media and WHS Advertising, their services are very well organised commercially. It is a lively medium, adaptable by advertisers, and continually enlivened by the introduction of new advertising opportunities. For many years outdoor advertising suffered from a multiplicity of local billposting contractors together with a number of amalgamated groups so that site renting was a complicated business. Today there are consortia through which outdoor advertising campaigns can be booked.

One such central supply point is Independent Poster Sales Ltd of London. IPS have 26 contractors in membership, and access to thousands of other sites, with 'on-line' booking facilities. This means that a package can be bought with one order and one invoice. Advertising agencies receive 15 per cent commission, with 5 per cent specialist bureau fee in addition where applicable. The rates charged include poster despatch and Poster Audit Bureau levy.

23.9   Inspection of Posters

One of the industry's biggest problems—poster damage and quickly remedied action—was tackled by the creation in 1977 of the Poster Audit Bureau referred to above in the paragraph on IPS. Periodic inspections are made of poster sites to report damaged posters and to ensure their replacement.

24
Sales Promotion and Point-of-Sale

24.1 Sales Promotion or Merchandising?

There is conflict between various authorities on the meaning and usage of the terms 'sales promotion' and 'merchandising'. The modern tendency, as seen in the definition of the Institute of Sales Promotion and in the sales promotion features in the trade press (e.g. *Marketing*), is to dispense with the expression merchandising altogether and to use sales promotion as the all-embracing term for promotional exercises at the point-of-sale.

Further argument exists as to whether sales promotion is a form of advertising or marketing, but since advertising is part of the marketing mix it would seem logical to classify sales promotion among the below-the-line advertising media.

However, at the 1984 annual conference of the Marketing Education Group held at Moor Hall, Francis Buttle of the University of Surrey defined merchandising as 'any form of behaviour-triggering stimulus or stimuli, other than personal selling, which takes place at retail or other point-of-sale'. This reverts to the interpretation of merchandising used in previous editions of this book, but which the author now replaces with the omnibus term of sales promotion.

24.2 Definition

The ISP definition reads: *Sales promotion is the function of marketing which seeks to achieve given objectives by the adding of extrinsic, tangible value to a product or service*. In plainer English, the ISP definition refers to all the schemes described in this chapter under the heading Sales Promotion. Other items which may or may not be used in sales promotion schemes for retail display will be referred to as point-of-sale (or point-of-purchase) material.

From the retailer's point of view, *merchandising* has another meaning, that is the buying and selling of merchandise or goods, and this can include store layout or the footage allocated to brands on supermarket shelves. In this book we are concerned with sales promotion schemes which in effect bring the customer and the manufacturer closer together. It has developed to the point that sales promotion is seen by some companies such as Nestlé and their product Nescafé as being more effective than media advertising.

In Chapter 11 reference has been made to agencies which specialise in creating sales promotion schemes. According to the ISP, about £4,000 m. is spent on sales promotion in the UK, including printing and production costs.

24.3   Current Trends

Many forms of sales promotion are described in the following pages, but there has been an interesting change in the forms currently used. Because of more competitive High Street trading in the 80s, it has become less attractive for consumers to collect tokens and send them with cash for items such as household goods. With less trouble they can buy these goods just as cheaply in the shops. Consequently, there are today fewer self-liquidating offers, and also mail-ins which involve the consumer in postage costs. The current trend is to organise schemes which require the least effort on the part of the consumer and the following list of schemes has been extended in this edition to include them. At the same time, money-matching schemes (collecting coupon halves of different money values) have become popular again with petrol companies and other firms.

Shelf space in supermarkets is reserved for a limited number of fast-selling lines, and the manufacturer has to adopt fast-acting techniques of moving goods out of the store. Consequently, he has to introduce sales promoting methods at the point-of-sale, maybe using impactive media like television, but jumping ahead of slower-moving media, and deliberately trying to induce what is often called 'impulse buying' by means of packaging, offers and other devices.

24.4   Sales Promotion

The principal forms of sales promotion are:

(*a*) **Gift coupons.** One of the oldest devices to secure regular purchase, gift coupons have been used by cocoa, tea, cigarette and petrol companies, also by magazines and newspapers, and they appeal to the collecting or acquisitive instinct.

(*b*) **Picture cards.** Again, the appeal is to the collecting habit. Cards have been given away with cigarettes, ice lollies, tea, children's magazines and petrol, but none has excelled the pre-war series of Players which are still available from collectors' shops, or the Wills series which could be exchanged for prints of the pictures formed by the complete set. Wills also issued miniature playing cards which could be exchanged for a full-size pack. The modern tendency, with collecting items, is to have shorter sets than the 50 or 52 cigarette cards. Goodwill is maintained by offering to supply cards not yet obtained when the scheme closes, thus avoiding disappointment among collectors who are often children. With most sales promotion schemes it is very necessary to observe the PR aspects.

(*c*) **Cash dividends.** As with the former Brooke Bond's Dividend Tea, and Co-op trading stamps, cash dividends have a combination of gift and saving scheme not unlike the original Co-op 'divi'. It has both a bargain and a collecting appeal and once again has the merit of achieving regular sales and brand loyalty.

(*d*) **Putting halves of coupons or pictures together.** This is another collecting scheme which seems to be a favourite with petrol companies, having been used by Shell and Texaco, the latter being linked with a competition. It can be irritating if one seems to get too many of the wrong halves!

(*e*) **Cash premium coupons or vouchers.** Provided the retailers do not accept them in exchange for any goods, they are very effective in moving the promoted brand. There is some risk of irritating dealers who have to stock the goods demanded and are put to the trouble of claiming redemption even if a handling charge is paid. Some retailers regard cash premiums as a nuisance, but manufacturers are often unsympathetic because, after all, the retailer is getting extra business.

There are several kinds of cash voucher: (i) they may be delivered house-to-house; (ii) published in the press; (iii) published in shopping magazines which contain collections of current offers; (iv) printed on the pack to encourage repeat purchase; (v) printed on the pack of another product (e.g. £1 off an automatic toaster at Currys on a large box of Ship matches).

(*f*) **Free gifts.** This really is a method of inducing impulse purchases as with the free comb attached to the toothpaste package, or an ingenious offer on the label of Cadbury's drinking chocolate of a free bar of dairy milk chocolate to those who entered a £5,000 contest. Few people can resist a free gift, even if they have to buy something else to get it! Free offer **mail-ins** are those where a gift is offered in return for the label or package, or for a number of tokens. It is important to limit such offers one to a family and to have a stated maximum number of gifts or a closing date, otherwise demand may outrun both supplies and the budget. Lyons tea have offered rubber gloves, tights and rose trees, indicating the variety of gifts that can be given in this way. The handling of these offers is simpler since there is no monetary transaction, and it is not necessary to seek self-liquidation of the cost.

(*g*) **Self-liquidating premium offers.** These are the non-profit-making offers of merchandise such as beach balls, coffee tables, fine art prints, towels, cutlery and other items offered for carton tops or labels and a cash payment. A criticism has been made that the quoted normal retail price may not be realistic if the item has been specially produced for the offer and is not otherwise available. Nevertheless, thousands of people have taken advantage of these offers and goodwill has been extended towards the supplier.

However, ill-will is easily provoked if the brand manager responsible for buying the offer does not make sure (i) that the product can be supplied in sufficient quantities to meet the short-term demand, and (ii) that the product is well packed so that it is not damaged in transit. There have been instances where the manufacturer of the premium offer has been so swamped by demand that he has not been able to deliver, causing great resentment among customers; and some items such as gramophone records and picture frames have been sent out with such poor protective packing that the item has arrived damaged, once again causing annoyance to customers.

(*h*) **Free samples.** This is surely one of the very best forms of sales promotion, customers being invited to try the product and decide whether they like it or not. If, in a store sampling booth, they express liking the demonstrator can move on to make a sale. If the sample is delivered to the house, another effort is necessary at the point-of sale to remind people to purchase. Either way, it does invite goodwill for the manufacturer is obviously not afraid to let people try the product first before committing themselves to a purchase. Free trials and demonstrations of motor-cars, washing machines, sewing machines and other consumer durables are other versions of the same thing. Similarly, Butlin's invite visitors to spend a trial day at their holiday camps, although this is not absolutely free.

(*i*) **Trade characters,** either in stores or calling door-to-door and using specially decorated vehicles, are a dramatic form of sales promotion.

(*j*) **Cash awards for use of product.** This is a very old one (e.g. the ten-shilling note to the man who provided the smoker with a light by producing a box of Blue Cross matches). This resulted in many men carrying a box of Blue Cross for years, just in case they were stopped in the street and asked for a light! Similarly, housewives are given cash awards by the caller if they have certain brands of goods in the larder.

(*k*) **Multiple packs.** Sometimes called jumbo packs, these are used to encourage the sale of small items in multiples; bars of chocolate, chocolate biscuits, bars of soap, razor blades, paperback books are packed collectively in a single wrapper (or banded together), and usually offered at an advantageous price. Thus, instead of buying one bar of chocolate one buys a number which makes production and distribution much more economic. A typical example is the Oxo cube and the razor blade where single sales used to be quite normal. It is perhaps a sign of the times that people can afford to buy in larger quantities. But it is also an effective way of achieving repeat usage. Carry packs of canned beer are another example.

(*l*) **Flash packs.** Provided they do not offend the *Trade Descriptions Act*, these are a method of making price-cut offers, and are used especially in the confectionery trade.

(*m*) **Children's contests,** such as painting and colouring competitions, have been used by circuses, soft drink manufacturers, publishers and confectionery firms. The method lends itself to the distribution of many small consolation prizes which make a lot of competitors happy.

(*n*) **Competitions** for adults need big prizes to make them seem worth entering after the extravagant football pool winnings, Premium Bond and Irish Sweep prizes. It is also necessary to avoid prize-winning by doing all the possible permutations, and tie-breaking 'slogan writing' is one of the devices used to reduce the number of prize-winners and so retain a big prize. A competition should be simple to enter, and should not be run over such a long period of time that contestants get bored or forget to enter. Today, competitors are usually protected by the Institute of Sales Promotion ISP Standard Competition Rules, and this will be stated on entry forms.

(*o*) **Charity promotions.** With these schemes the pack usually carries a token with a cash value which the manufacturer promises to redeem as a contribution to a charity or cause named in the promotion.

(*p*) **High Street redemption schemes.** This is another on-pack scheme, and the premium coupon entitles consumers to discounts off goods bought from named retailers. One scheme offered discounts off rail tickets, another off the cost of dry cleaning. These schemes are welcomed by the associated retailers because purchases are usually made in excess of the value of the voucher.

There are also many ways of encouraging dealers to stock up apart from helping them to sell out—some of which are:

(*a*) **Special trade terms.** Like the old 'baker's dozen', 13 for the price of 12, a free quire of copies of a newspaper or magazine, or one free case with so many cases, are typical ways of giving the dealer a bonus to take up stock. This is frequently the method used to secure initial stocks of a new product.

(*b*) **Dealer contests.** A typical dealer contest is a window display competition, using the supplier's point-of-sale material. Manufacturers of cameras and wine shippers have used this device, with prizes of holidays for two, cine cameras or cash.

(*c*) **Special displays.** In return for a certain minimum value order, the dealer is provided with a special display such as a working model or a system of dispensing the product, usually on loan for a specified period.

(*d*) **Publishing of stockists' names.** Either names are given to enquirers, or names are listed in advertisements, thus helping to direct customers to a source of supply. Makers of cars, paint and clothing and organisers of packaged holidays do this.

(*e*) **Training of sales staff.** In some trades it is important that the stockist can explain the product to the customer, and 'schools' are run to train sales assistants, as in the cosmetics industry.

(*f*) **Works visits.** Retail sales assistants are better able to sell a product if they have visited the factory and seen how it is made. This is common in the furnishing, bedding and soft furnishing industry.

(*g*) **After-sales service.** With most consumer durables, a good after-sales service is essential, otherwise the trader will not take stocks or act as an agent or distributor. Guarantee of spare parts or repairs, or the training of the retailer's own service staff are forms of this back-up service.

(*h*) **Instruction and service manuals.** When the product is technical, or complicated in its application, the dealer may have to be supplied with simple-to-follow manuals explaining use, fitting, special applications, maintenance and repair.

The production or handling of these eight selling aids will usually come within the duties of the advertising manager, involving as they do creative and production work. Another item is the **sales portfolio,** usually a ring binder setting out the sales offer, and incorporating pulls of advertisements and photographs of the product.

Finally, there are **co-operative advertising schemes** whereby the stockist is offered a discount on space rates if he advertises the product in the local press, or free blocks or artwork for use in his local advertising, together with various items of display material which may include showcards, pelmets, mobiles, posters, transfers, crowners, price tickets, give-away leaflets, catalogues and other sales promotional material.

24.5 Two Kinds of Sales Promotion Material

Two forms of sales promotion material may be used as regular items or as part of a promotional scheme, these being *point-of-sale* (*POS*) *material* and *sales literature*. They may be analysed as follows:

Point-of-sale Material—for windows, shelves, counters, floors.

(*a*) **Posters.** Sometimes called bills, these are usually of crown or double-crown size (381 by 508 mm and 508 by 762 mm respectively).

Some of the best posters are the scenic ones distributed by airlines, and usable anywhere in the world served by the airline. Among the best are those of KLM, depicting Dutch scenes. News bills are another example of the use of the poster at the point-of-sale, and some of the most attractive are those issued by the holiday and travel industry and used to decorate travel agencies. Less artistic perhaps but very effective are the silk-screened posters seen on department store windows to announce sales and on supermarket windows to advertise bargain buys.

(*b*) **Showcards** made of card or metal, strutted or suspended, are one of the original forms of POS and are being ousted by the increase in self-service stores where display space is limited. They remain major display pieces in the confectionery and tobacco trades where shops tend to be smaller and more traditional. Showcards can be made three-dimensional to carry specimen products—e.g. pipes, ballpoint pens—or as dispensers from which the product may be taken by the customer. The decision to produce showcards depends very much on the typical outlet. While they have the advantage of portability they may have a brief life (and therefore be uneconomic) since only a few can be used at any one time by the shopkeeper.

(*c*) **Mobiles.** Suspended displays, often made up of a number of items, are useful in supermarkets where the ceiling is about the only unoccupied space, and they attract attention by their movement and novelty.

(*d*) **Pelmets** are a fairly permanent means of gaining window display, being pasted to the top edge of the window.

(*e*) **Dumpers and dump bins** are tubs for containing packages, and here is the attempt to thrust the product right under the nose of the customer and urge purchase. The fact that the goods are presented in a tumbled fashion is dramatic and usually implies a special offer. The advantage is that the line is isolated from rival brands.

(*f*) **Wire, metal and plastic stands.** These range from 'beanstalks', comprising a stack of trays or shelves, to smaller dispensers not unlike filing trays. Like the bins, these stands isolate and identify the product but they are liable to abuse as when a mixture of brands is placed in one by the shopkeeper who likes the utility of the stand but does not reserve it for its original user. It pays the supplier to see that the stand itself is identified by the manufacturer or his brand.

(*g*) **Dummy packs.** Packaged products should be for sale, not display, and for window-dressing purposes the manufacturer usually supplies dummy packs. However, dummy packs are again more suitable for products sold by non-self-service shops such as the small grocer, tobacconist, confectioner, ironmonger or chemist.

(*h*) **Display outers.** For small packaged units such as confectionery, razor blades, medicines or soups, the original container can form a useful dispenser, the lid folding back to make a display panel.

(*i*) **Display stands** are useful when the product is not a mass packaged item and can stand to advantage by itself on a tasteful stand. Clocks, watches, jewellery and china models look well on display stands.

(*j*) **Cash mats, open/closed door hangers, drip mats** and **dart match floor mats,** mostly made from plastic or rubber, can be useful reminder advertisements at the point-of-sale.

(*k*) **Plastic shopping bags,** carrier bags and boxes for men's suits and ladies' wear are striking means of conveying publicity from the point-of-sale. Elliott shoe shops, Marks and Spencer and various airport duty-free shopping centres provide extremely attractive bags for carrying purchases.

(*l*) **Crowners** carry price tags or slogans and when slipped over the necks of bottles make ideal POS material where space is limited.

(*m*) **Models, static or working,** provide a means of miniaturising items that would be impossible to display otherwise, the airliner or cruise ship being a typical example, while some products are characterised by a familiar trade figure such as the Michelin rubber man and the Abbey National couple with an umbrella-like roof over their heads. The working or moving model is an attention-getter, often proving an attraction to window-shoppers when the shop is closed.

Sales Literature

Printed material serves to promote the sales of manufacturers, mail-order traders, travelling representatives, wholesalers and retailers. It has the advantage, rather like direct mail advertising (of which it may be a part), of providing detailed information in a permanent and portable form. The following are the chief kinds of sales literature:

(*a*) **Data or specification sheets.** Usually A4 size, and sometimes with a gate-fold, these sheets set out statistical information about components, materials and products of interest to architects, quantity surveyors, electronic engineers, designers and others who have to specify items. Binders are generally supplied by the manufacturers who then keep the recipient up to date with sheets ready punched for filing.

(*b*) **Catalogues, price lists, timetables, tariffs.** As the different names suggest, these booklets, folders or leaflets give tabulated or illustrated information about a large number of items and are usually issued periodically.

(*c*) **Leaflets** are pieces of print consisting of one unfolded sheet printed on one or both sides; **folders** are pieces of print folded in various ways to produce four or more pages; **brochures** are small, bound booklets, mostly wire stitched; and **broadsheets** are very large folders with pages often as large as those of a newspaper, or folding out like a map.

(*d*) **Wall charts** are informative posters and are long-lasting and ideal for educational purposes, or for presenting instructions, charts or maps.

(*e*) **Calendars.** Once the Christmas gift of every family butcher and grocer, the calendar has become a most sophisticated sales promotion medium. A novel idea has been the despatch of calendars at unorthodox dates so that they do not clash with those sent out at Christmas.

A particularly ingenious calendar was issued in 1977 to promote Idem carbonless paper made by Wiggins Teape. It was unusual in both appearance and supply. The subject was a nude blonde, but the calendar was issued in three four-month editions, each calendar showing the model in a different pose. The calendars were also an unusual size and shape, being 965 mm deep by 388 mm wide, with the calendar dates set at the foot. The object was to establish the brand name Idem through printers to the end-user, and the calendar presented an ideal medium for doing this both in end-user offices and in printers' sales departments where staff are as important sometimes as external salesmen. Photographic and printing technique were combined to produce an artistic calendar inoffensive to mixed staffs. It was produced by advertising agents George Hynes & Partners.

A new point-of-sale advertising device, which in larger sizes also has outdoor applications in shopping precincts, is the **Rotasign.** This is the successor to earlier audio-visual advertisements in grocery outlets, the mature modern version being a lightbox that is illuminated to show a continuous reel of up to forty colour transparencies. The box measures 3 ft 4 in by 2 ft 6 in. and is placed 7 ft above the ground at the end of the first aisle of the supermarket. Those for outside locations are four-sheet in size, 60 ins by 40 ins.

Other types of promotional print include blotters, picture postcards, note pads, telephone number hanging cards, pocket and desk diaries, and other pieces which happen to best serve a particular advertiser.

From the variety of items discussed in this chapter it will be appreciated that sales promotion is a complex area of opportunity and expenditure. Those responsible for this sort of advertising need to be extremely selective, and we have scarcely touched upon 'give-aways' such as pens, ash trays, book-matches and keyrings. On the other hand, the range of items makes it possible to choose what is likely to be most economical, original and successful.

24.6 Supermarket Advertising

Supermarkets, hypermarkets and discount stores lend themselves to public address system commercials and advertisements on the trolleys used by customers.

Part 4: Creating Advertising Campaigns

25
Voluntary and Legal Control of Advertising

In this final part of the book we shall consider the actual creation and execution of advertising, and practical demonstrations are given in the case studies. There are, however, three other aspects: the protection of (*a*) the public, (*b*) the good name of advertising, and (*c*) the reputation of the media from harmful, fraudulent, misleading or tasteless advertising. This leads to two other considerations: advertising may be abused by *dishonest or unscrupulously competitive advertisers* so that the user, not the tool, is to blame, or it may be unintentionally misused by overenthusiastic creators. Sometimes an apparent offence may be a matter of opinion and interpretation, bearing in mind that advertising does have to be larger than life if it is to be noticed at all and if it is to compete with other advertisements.

The ethics of advertising have become a major public relations exercise for the advertising industry, notwithstanding the consumer protection aims of politicians and organisations which seek to regulate advertising. The advertising industry recognises that *unless advertising is believed and acted upon it cannot work*. If it does not work it is a wilful waste of money, and it is not cynical therefore to say that ethics are good economics. Consequently, it is essential that the public are encouraged not merely to overcome their inhibitions but to have no grounds for complaint about advertising. It should be a public as well as a commercial service.

Similarly, media owners are not only anxious to attract revenue from advertising but know that their reputations depend on trustworthy advertising. Mail order traders, for example, have to sign an undertaking about their ability to supply goods as advertised and to indemnify publishers who operate a reader protection scheme against loss of money.

The expanded work of the Advertising Standards Authority and the Code of Advertising Practice Committee is explained in Chapter 5. Members of the public are now invited to send written complaints about advertising (other than radio and television) to the ASA. Case Reports are published regularly. The full Code may be purchased, or a short version may be obtained free of charge, from the ASA. From time to time the Code is amended as when Appendices M and N, covering cigarette and alcoholic drink advertising respectively, were added. This is a self-regulating system. The expansion has been made possible by a levy introduced into rate-card prices and administered by the Advertising Standards Board of Finance.

Radio and television advertising is controlled by a similar but more extensive Code which is included in the *Independent Broadcasting Authority*

Act, 1973, so that its strictures have the force of law. Cigarette, political, religious, and certain other classes of advertising are forbidden. Commercials are vetted by the broadcasting trade associations and the Independent Broadcasting Authority. In fact, it is best to discuss commercials with these authorities at the script and storyboard stage, or at least at the double-head stage before the married print is completed.

Legal control falls into two areas, those of common and private law and statute law, and the reader is recommended to obtain a copy of *Advertising Law*, by R. G. Lawson and published by Macdonald and Evans.

Anyone engaged in advertising should be familiar with the law of contract, defamation (libel, slander, slander of goods), copyright, trade descriptions, trade marks, passing off and any special legislation relevant to his industry, company or client.

Legislation is constantly being introduced or revised which affects advertising. The following is a selection from some of the sixty or so statutes and statutory instruments which are listed in Appendix L of the *British Code of Advertising Practice*. Although the Code sets out voluntary controls, 1.1 of the Preamble states '*All advertisements should be legal, decent, honest and truthful.*'

> *Advertisements (Hire Purchase) Act, 1967*
> *Betting, Gaming and Lotteries Act, 1963*
> *Business Advertisements (Disclosure) Order, 1977*
> *Consumer Credit Act, 1974*
> *Copyright Act, 1958*
> *Defamation Act, 1952*
> *Fair Trading Act, 1973*
> *Food & Drugs Act, 1955* (as amended)
> *Independent Broadcasting Authority Act, 1973*
> *Lotteries and Amusements Act, 1976*
> *Medicines Act, 1968*, and regulations
> *Misrepresentation Act, 1967*
> *Prices Act, 1974*
> *Race Relations Acts, 1968, 1976*
> *Resale Prices Act, 1976*
> *Restrictive Trade Practices Act, 1976*
> *Sex Discrimination Act, 1975*
> *Supply of Goods (Implied Terms) Act, 1973*
> *Trade Descriptions Acts, 1968, 1972*
> *Unsolicited Goods & Services Act, 1971*

In other countries, voluntary and legal controls also exist, although they are likely to be different from those operating in the UK. They may be conditioned by religious, social and political considerations. The exporter should familiarise himself with such controls, and may be advised by the Institute of Practitioners in Advertising (see Chapter 5), which publishes booklets on European advertising. Useful legal information is contained in the *Hints To Businessmen* booklets on 140 countries published by the British Overseas Trade Board, Export Services and Promotions Division, Export House, 50 Ludgate Circus, London, EC4M 7HU (01-248 5757).

Trade Descriptions Act and the 28-day Clause

Retailers who advertise price reductions are supposed to obey the '28-day clause' meaning that the goods should have been on sale at the full price for the past 28 days. In practice, as certain well-known advertisers have proved by their advertisements in the popular press, the law is an ass in respect of this seeming restriction. It does *not* stipulate that the goods have to have been on offer for 28 days at any particular store! So, if an advertiser has many stores, it can sell at the higher price in just one and pretend to a special sale price at any or all of the others! This deception has been exploited, and the Office of Fair Trading has been unable to make the 28-day clause effective, or to stop what would seem to be fraudulent sales or shopping events. At least Marks and Spencer display notices stating that goods offered at reduced prices have been on sale at their main London store at the full price.

26

The Creation and Production of Advertisements

When advertising is criticised it is almost always because of its influence and power. The ironical implication of such criticism is that advertising works. Not only that, but like the Double Diamond slogan, *it works wonders*! Not that it is a waste of money, or crude and ugly, or untrue, but that it is liable to encourage people actually to buy things. The materialistic barb is usually added—'which they do not want'.

Well, no one is likely to want to buy a square wheel until someone is able to convince buyers that it works better than a round one. And if people don't want instant tea, or Edsel sports cars, or a multipurpose insecticide, they simply won't buy them no matter how persuasive the advertising. The old adage that you can take a horse to water but you cannot force it to drink is absolutely true of the consumer.

As an example of this, on entering a Tesco supermarket a schoolboy stared at the array of orange banners suspended above the aisles and made the very apt remark that there was so much advertising you couldn't take any of it in. He was so right. He happened to be interested in advertising in connection with his 'A' Level economics.

British advertising owes its influence and power to good planning, including media planning, but as shown by the preference of advertisers for 'creative agencies', much is also owed to the high standards of advertisement creation and production. Some of these standards far exceed those of American advertising whose crude press and TV advertising results from the inevitable economics of more localised advertising. Our compact islands permit national press and networked TV so that creative and production costs can be spread more economically. Consequently, we have TV commercials produced by technicians who also produce full-length films, while Royal Academy and international artists are not ashamed to illustrate advertisements. Many copywriters are published authors, poets and playwrights. Advertising has become a major patron of the arts, and this is substantiated by the case studies which follow this chapter.

26.1 The Creative Task

There are six key stages in the task of a successful advertisement, these being:

(a) **Awareness.** The reader, viewer or listener must be made aware of the existence of the product or service. This awareness may be won by the brand name, picture, logo, special colour scheme, slogan or jingle, or trade characters like the Bisto Kids or Johnnie Walker or an actor like John Cleese or Joan Collins who always appears in the commercials for Sony and for Cinzano respectively.

(*b*) **Knowledge.** It must inform. The advertisement itself may provide the information, or it may offer literature or direct the reader to the showroom, exhibition or demonstration. It may offer a free sample or trial. (In some cases this knowledge may have to be presented by advance or supplementary PR techniques such as product news, feature articles and documentary films.)

(*c*) **Desire.** A liking for the product translated into the wish to possess or enjoy it is the next step. Pleasant shape, attractive colour, mouth-watering flavour and other inducements such as novelty, fashion, or improvement may create the necessary desire.

(*d*) **Conviction.** But desire is not enough. We like lots of things but we do not or cannot afford to buy everything. What makes the subtle difference? It is often the conviction that A or B is better—it performs better, looks better, is a better bargain. This conviction can be gained by use of testimonials, test reports, money back guarantees, and sometimes because there is a corporate image that wins goodwill.

(*e*) **Brand preference.** But we may be attracted by the advertisement, interested in its content, desirous of buying the product and convinced about its qualities and yet we cannot decide between seemingly identical teas, toothpastes, holiday resorts, motor-cars or insurance policies. This is where brand preference has to be distinguished, the reason why so many advertisements use house styles, show packages, repeat the name, and are repeated consistently.

(*f*) **Decision.** Finally, there is the admonition, the action-provoking device which urges the reader, viewer or listener to fill in the coupon, ring up the distributor, go to the store or in some way turn attention, interest, desire and conviction into a reality.

If we now consider press advertising, and printed media in particular, there are seven essentials of a good layout:

(*a*) **It should attract attention,** otherwise no one will notice it. Size, shape, colour, position, headline, picture and typography may all influence attention-getting.

(*b*) **It should be original**—that is, unlike its neighbours. It should avoid following design clichés which tend to make advertisements all look alike. Such clichés have included heavy black borders, triangular coupons, whole sentence headlines, free-style lettering drawn with a crayon, and scraperboard drawings. These fashions seem to occur in advertising, somebody starting a new style and rival firms copying it. (It happens to such an extent on TV that it is sometimes difficult to distinguish between one beer, detergent or dog food ad! Probably the most blatant example of this was Pepsi-Cola's all-singing follow-up to the Coca-Cola 'I'd like to buy the world a Coke' commercial.)

(*c*) **The layout should have a focal point** which rivets the wandering eye.

There should be a point of major interest. The simple cigarette advertisement that illustrates the pack has a very definite focal point, whereas some of the more sophisticated cigarette advertisements are so 'busy' that it is hard to tell what is being advertised, guns, pictures, wine, glassware or pedigree dogs! As an example of this, the author was very much aware of a beautifully photographed full-colour advertisement in the weekend colour magazines which he was convinced was advertising sherry, until a student corrected him and pointed out that the product being advertised was a cigarette! To all intents and purposes the packet of cigarettes had seemed to be the 'prop', not the glasses of sherry.

(d) **The advertisement should be immediately comprehensible**—as the cigarette advertisement mentioned above obviously was not. Readers will not study each advertisement in turn, and the layout can do much to select readers. There was the case a few years ago of the advertisement illustrated by a girl wearing a bikini that had women writing in to know where they could buy the bikini. The address was an advertiser who was inviting financial investments, not selling bikinis! Sometimes an advertisement can be so clever it detracts attention from its real purpose.

(e) **There should be a logical sequence of factors.** The layout should set out its offer and information in a logical style, perhaps making use of sub-heads or illustrations which carry the eye through the advertisement.

(f) **The layout should have movement.** The eye should be helped to travel comfortably through the advertisement, absorbing the message and arriving at the decision-making admonition.

(g) **It should be a unified whole.** The advertisement should be seen as a piece, not as isolated bits. Even a catalogue-type advertisement for a mail-order or retail store should be seen as an entity before the reader becomes selective within this whole.

26.2 Basic Principles of Design

A good design is one that cannot be changed without ruining it. Unnecessary borders, too many different type faces (or only one that becomes boring), unusual type faces, badly distributed colour, 'busy' layouts may be deterrents to the first essential of good design, **unity**. This is the first of the eight basic elements or laws of good design which are:

(a) **Unity.** There should be perfect union of the parts of a layout which may comprise the headline, picture, text, sub-heads, coupon and logo. They need to be held together as a visible whole. Emphasis or contrast is an aid to unity, one feature providing a focal point with which everything else is associated. But all emphasis is no emphasis and the message is lost. Contrast also helps to get the advertisement noticed and at least partially absorbed by the 'glancer' who may subsequently become converted into a 'reader'.

(b) **Variety.** Change and happy harmonious repetition is a combination that permits variety without confusion. One way of doing this is to use the different weights, sizes and variations within the whole family of a particular type face. Severe regularity can be boring (like all those orange banners mentioned at the beginning of this chapter) but alternate patterns like a chess-board can be interesting.

(*c*) **Balance.** Related to the law of gravity, the eye is happiest when it views things north, south, east and west fashion. Shapes should be arranged to form a balanced pattern. There are two kinds of balance: symmetrical which means even balancing with a mathematical centre—this can be very formal, dull and lacking in movement; with occult or dynamic balance, the east-west midway horizontal is raised to the 'optical centre' which resembles the handle of a sword or the French Cross of Lorraine. This is helpful in arranging headlines which are often better read at this position of optical centre rather than at the extreme top or in the precise centre.

(*d*) **Rhythm.** This is the principle that directs the movement of the eye throughout the design. There should be a natural 'flow', the simplest example being movement in the shape of the letter 'S'.

(*e*) **Harmony.** The layout should be pleasing to the eye. There should be no offensive, jarring notes of undue emphasis. In an advertisement much of this harmony will lie in the typesetting. Type sizes and measures must harmonise so that the copy is pleasant to read, small type for a narrow measure, larger type for a wider measure.

(*f*) **Proportion.** Care should be taken in the ratio of length to width, making subtle use of margins. Usually, the margin at the foot is greater than the other three margins.

(*g*) **Scale.** Here we refer to the extent of visibility, optical illusions occurring with densities and certain colours. Black seems to be closer to the eye than grey, either emphasising what is in black or destroying what is in grey if there is too much black. There are also dominant colours like red and orange (on which, incidentally, black stands out best), and receding colours such as light blue and pastel shades which can create the impression of space or distance, peace or solitude.

(*h*) **Emphasis.** Rather similar to scale, emphasis is particularly valuable in black-and-white advertising which constitutes most of press advertising. Too much emphasis is self-defeating while none at all is uninteresting. White space—giving the layout some 'daylight'—is one of the surest ways of achieving emphasis.

Let us reiterate the chief points:

(*a*) Unity means emphasis of just one feature; (*b*) Variety means pleasant change; (*c*) Balance can be either static (symmetrical) or have movement (dynamic) and the optical centre is a third of the way down from the top; (*d*) Rhythm is won by repetition; (*e*) Harmony calls for regularity and continuity; (*f*) Proportions need to be subtle, not violently geometrical; (*g*) Scale is proportion related to the density of masses and the density characteristics of colours; and (*h*) All emphasis is no emphasis.

26.3 Headlines

One of the most effective ways of attracting attention to an advertisement lies in the careful choice of the kind of headline that should be used. A headline should not just be a catchy phrase or slogan that seems all right, but a positive contribution to the style and mood of the advertisement. A few of the many different kinds of headline are these five:

(a) *Declarative*: Brown's Beer is Best
(b) *Identification*: Brown's Best Bitter
(c) *Testimonial*: 'I always drink Brown's Beer,' says Johnnie Smith.
(d) *Interrogative*: Have You Tasted Brown's Bitter?
(e) *Curiosity*: Why Does Brown's Beer Taste Different?

26.4 Text or Body Matter

There are three easy rules for inducing readership of the copy in the body of the advertisement: (a) short paragraphs; (b) short sentences; and (c) short words. Of these number three is most important for if a reader pauses at a long or unknown word his attention is lost. The flow of reading must never be halted.

There are three ways of presenting text matter:

(a) **Make it attractive to look at.** Attractive copy is legible copy, and this is where the expert typographer will use his skill in choice of face and type size, and the setting out of indented paragraphs with spacing between the paragraphs, using a comfortable measure and if necessary running the copy in columns. Leading between the lines—that is, spacing with strips of metal or setting type on a larger body—can help to make a lot of small type more readable.

(b) **Make it interesting.** Devices should be exploited which make a lot of words look attractive to read, these being sub-headings, the setting of alternate paragraphs in italics, or setting the first paragraph in larger or bolder type.

(c) **Style of writing.** The above will be ineffectual if the copy is not worth reading, or is difficult to read. This is where the copywriter may indulge in breaking the pure literary rules if it helps to carry the reader's interest from point to point. For example, the copy may be punctuated by dashes instead of full stops and commas, e.g. 'Wonderful Worthing—so clean—so sunny—so make it your holiday choice this year.'

26.5 Typography

Typography is one of the greatest arts in the hands of the advertisement creator, but, judging by the monotonous frequency with which sans serif types are used in advertisements and in print designed in advertising agency studios, typography is almost a lost art. This is a great pity because the correct or tasteful selection of type faces, and their deployment according to variations within a family, can contribute greatly to the legibility, attractiveness, power and influence of advertisement copy. However, serif faces are returning!

Sans serif types are clean and bold, and have their place as display types, for short paragraphs of text, for gaining clarity in items set in small print such as coupons, and as a means of creating a contrast with serif types. But they are hard to read in the mass, and difficult to . . . . with a shiny surface. Generally speaking, sans serif type face. . . misused and abused, presumably by specifiers who are too lazy ent to learn how and when to use type faces to advantage. A typ. is the use of photo-set sans serif faces for the text in sales . . . . . ure produced by offset-litho where the combination of high gloss ink and a nicely finished paper tends to dazzle the eye and makes a serif type much easier to read.

Typography is important for three reasons: (*a*) it makes the advertisement or print legible if the right type faces are specified; (*b*) similarly, good typography is attractive; and (*c*) apt choice of type gives the work style and character.

However, there are many hundreds of different type faces, and there are also very similar designs produced by rival foundries, IBM, and photo-typesetting systems. Before specifying any type face it is essential to discover first whether the printer or typesetting house has in fact got the types which are being specified.

Type faces fall into two main groups: display or decorative and text or body faces. The blending of the two makes interesting and attractive print. The **face** is the particular design; the **fount** is a complete alphabet of characters; and the **family** is the series of variations of one type design, e.g. light, medium, bold, condensed, italic, expanded, titling and shadow.

The point system is used for the measuring of type, and because it would mean changing all the type in every print shop there will be no metrication of typography. A point is a seventy-second of an inch. A pica em, commonly used in printing as a unit of measurement, is 12 points wide or a sixth of an inch.

There are numerous ways of setting type faces or making use of lettering. It may be set by hand by a compositor, or on a Monotype typesetting machine which sets individual characters, or on a Linotype, Harris Intertype or Ludlow typesetting machine which set slugs or type to determined widths. Nowadays, much typesetting is done by means of a computerised photo-typesetting machine, characters being photographed from a fount on a small disc. The set copy is stored on magnetic tape or floppy disc, while the operator sees his work on a visual display unit like a television screen. A print-out can be made from tape or disc. Corrections are made easily by retrieving the original stored setting. Letraset can be used for display lines.

26.6 Humour in Advertising

Should the creative advertising man or woman use humour in copy, pictures or presentation? With a basically entertainment medium like television or cinema, humour can score, but the following is a check list of advantages and disadvantages:

Problems

(i) It is difficult to appeal to all tastes.

(ii) There is risk of slowing down the sales impact.

(iii) Humour may be accepted for its own sake, and obscure the sales message.

(iv) It has its limitations, and doesn't apply to every product or service.

Advantages

(i) It helps to make advertising pleasant and acceptable—ideal for an entertainment medium.

(ii) Lends itself to slogans, jingles, doggerel, and easily read messages.

(iii) It can be combined with illustrations—situations—characters—cartoonists—comedians.

(iv) It can have topicality, making use of current catch-phrases.

26.7 Slogans and Jingles

Slogans and jingles make possible the association of memorable phrases with the product or service. Ideally, the product, or the name of the advertiser should be stated in the phrase. Here are 12 reasons why slogans and jingles can be successful:

(*a*) They provide a very simple, direct form of message, making small demand on the reader, viewer or listener.

(*b*) Being short, they are easily displayed in big letters on signs or posters.

(*c*) They are easily remembered, and often become sayings that go on working overtime for advertisers. They help to overcome the ephemeral nature of some advertising.

(*d*) They reiterate the brand name.

(*e*) They may well become characteristic of products, so that they are linked with a friendly phrase.

(*f*) Universal application throughout every kind of media makes slogans work hard for advertisers. They can be printed, spoken, sung, illuminated, maybe written on the sky.

(*g*) They can be useful when conducting next-day recall research.

(*h*) They can be funny and therefore entertaining.

(*i*) Idiomatic slogans are long remembered.

(*j*) They can plug selling points.

(*k*) They can be bright, topical and up to date, helping to suggest a wide-awake company.

(*l*) They can be emotional and psychologically right for some advertisers.

But against those 12 advantages it is worth considering at least five possible disadvantages:

(*a*) Slogans and jingles can become dated and therefore a liability.

(*b*) There is a problem when changing agencies. The new agency will obviously want to be inventive and make changes so that a well-established slogan has to be abandoned, perhaps resulting in an inferior one. This is one of the penalties of changing agencies.

(*c*) People may get bored with the same old slogan and not bother to take in the rest of the copy.

(*d*) There is a risk of being copied so that what was an original slogan becomes a cliché such as 'First in its class' or 'The Number one . . .'.

(*e*) Rivals may play havoc with your slogan, the classic example being 'Who made the going great?' (Pan-Am) which was capped by BOAC's 'Who made the Boeing great?'

Here are a few quite old slogans which go on living. Some of them are over 40 years old!

> Don't Be Vague, Ask For Haig
> Ah, Bisto!
> Send it to Vernons
> Listen to Breakfast (Kelloggs Rice Krispies)
> I'm Getting Younger Every Day

And here are a few more recent ones which make excellent use of sloganising especially as punchline 'signature slogans':

> Top breeders recommend it (*Pedigree Chum*)
> Simply years ahead (*Philips*)
> This is the age of the train (British Rail)
> Don't just book it—Thomas Cook it.

Meanwhile, here are some discarded ones which were once very good:

> Top People Take *The Times*
> Tide's In—Dirt's Out
> That Was Shell That Was
> Friday Night Is Amami Night
> For Your Throat's Sake Smoke Craven A

26.8 Creative Sounds for Radio, TV and Cinema Advertising

Finally, in this brief survey of creative advertising, let us consider the use of creative sounds in electronic media. There are four main kinds:

(*a*) Background music, either 'library' or original.
(*b*) Voices on or off.
(*c*) Product sounds.
(*d*) Sound effects.

Background Music

Signature tunes help to extend the memorability of advertising that has the benefit of sound, and the best jingles ring in the mind like favourite tunes. For instance, *'You've never had a better bit of butter on your knife'* and *'That calls for a Holstein'* immediately conjure up their products, even if one is not watching the screen.

Voices On or Off

The use of familiar voices, rather than professional presenters, has been one of the features of commercial TV, well-known voices being acceptable without undue implication of unlikely personal testimony. There is the advantage to the advertiser that the voice is familiar and the personality is liked, and this encourages viewers to accept the message.

Product Sounds

Just as television and cinema advertising provide the reality of vision and colour, so can sound reality be introduced if the product or service can be heard. The snapping of crisp biscuits, the crunching of potato crisps and even pickled onions, the shaking of coffee beans, and the roar of aircraft engines are all advances upon copy or script writing and pictures whether still or moving.

Sound Effects

The washing of waves on the seashore, the hooting of owls, the breaking of icicles, and skidding of car tyres are typical sound effects to be heard in commercials, reminding us of all the tricks of steam radio which for decades had relied upon its manipulators of coconut shells and sheets of zinc. Scriptwriters for commercials have had to exploit many of these old devices, or use 'library' records and tapes of many familiar sounds which may be hired for the purpose.

27
Case Studies

27.1 British Airways Shuttle Service

This is a study of a product change to counter inflation. After 1973, when fuel rationing began, airline costs mounted higher than their prices, and after fifty years of falling real air fares the trend was reversed while market growth was halted. Efforts to economise produced the inevitable responses of customer resistance and industrial unrest.

Cost-push was having a serious effect on British Airways' busiest route between London and Glasgow, on which 12 flights were operated Monday to Friday in the summer, 11 in the winter, until the introduction of Shuttle in 1975. In two years the price of aviation fuel increased fourfold and wages by 38 per cent. In one year, landing fees went up by 54 per cent and navigation fees by 100 per cent. In 1974, fares were increased twice, by 20 per cent and 12 per cent. Passenger reaction showed in a traffic fall-off of 15 per cent.

British Airways did not have a monopoly of the route, being in competition with British Caledonian, the one flying from Heathrow and the other from Gatwick. Both airlines faced the same economic challenge. There was also increasing competition from British Rail, and the disturbing prospect of a third London airport at Maplin.

Marketing is about selling at a profit what customers will buy. The question was what would prospective passengers on the London–Glasgow service buy which would reverse this loss situation? They wanted simple, convenient, flexible air travel—comparable with surface travel but with all the advantages of flying. The answer was a customer decision, and therefore it was good marketing. It was called *Shuttle*.

Shuttle meant a no-reservation, high-frequency, guaranteed seat. All the customer had to do was arrive at the airport, collect a boarding card, join the next flight and buy a ticket on board, almost like travelling by bus. It was ideal for domestic short-haul travel with its demand for punctuality. The new service was summed up in the slogan *Just turn up and take off*.

While British Airways' Shuttle Service is a major innovation in Europe, and was entrepreneurial in its incalculable business risks, the idea was borrowed from Eastern Airlines of the United States. Eastern Airlines had introduced their Air-Shuttle in 1962, operating first between New York and Washington and then between New York and Boston, and carrying one million passengers on these routes in the first 14 months. Air-Shuttle was then extended to the Newark–Washington, Newark–Boston and New York–Montreal routes and by 1970 three million passengers a year were being carried in this fashion. At La Guardia Airport a special Air-Shuttle terminal building has been converted from part of a hangar.

The first British Airways Shuttle service was launched on January 12, 1975. Then the Edinburgh service was added on 1 April 1976, followed by Belfast on 1 April 1977.

In charge of the advertising campaign was Keith Tottem, advertising manager, British Airways travel division. The campaign was produced by Foote, Cone & Belding Ltd, the account director being Peter Dobb, copywriter Stuart Winning, and art director David Lindsay.

The Shuttle concept has four characteristics: (i) flights operate to a regular all-the-year-round daily pattern; (ii) bookings are unnecessary; (iii) a seat is guaranteed to every passenger who checks in at the gate at least ten minutes before departure time; (iv) passengers have the option of purchasing their ticket on board with cash, cheque or credit card.

The word *Shuttle* was short and urgent, and the advertising fully exploited that basic ingredient of good, hard-selling advertising, *repetition*. The word *Shuttle* became a four-decker headline, and this was the copy for the introductory (Phase 1) press ad:

S h u t t l e
S h u t t l e
S h u t t l e
S h u t t l e

Repeat after us.

If I'm going to Glasgow from Jan 12th, I don't need to book.

All I have to do is turn up at Heathrow airport any time up to the hour, any hour from 8 in the morning till noon or from 2 till 9 at night any weekday (every 2 hours 8.00 a.m. to 8.00 p.m. at weekends), and there'll be a jet waiting for me.

I can get my ticket in advance from my British Airways Travel Agent.

Either way I'm guaranteed, repeated guaranteed, a seat.

It's easy coming back, too.

Shuttle. Just turn up and take off.

It's as simple as that.

British
airways

We'll take more care of you.

(The three phases of this first campaign will be detailed further on. In the second phase the words 'or pay on the plane' were added after 'Travel Agent' in subsequent press ads.)

Obviously, there were two areas in Britain for the advertising, London and Scotland, calling for mainly regional media. This was not a national campaign.

In London, the two evening newspapers of that time, the *Evening Standard* and the *Evening News*, each carried two large insertions, and the *Daily Telegraph* was also used twice because in spite of some waste circulation it did have a strong South of England readership. Thirty-second commercials were shown on Thames and Weekend TV, and time was taken on

Capital and LBC independent local radio. Bus side posters were placed on both London Transport and British Airways' own buses, and 4,000 car cards were placed in compartments of London Underground trains. At strategic points, such as on the road to the rival airport of Gatwick, solus supersites or bulletin boards were used.

On the aircraft, a point-of-sale folder was placed on seat backs prior to the Shuttle introduction to advise regular passengers. The folder was also mailed to business customers. On the cover, reversed white on red, were the words:

> Just turn up and
> take off
> Shuttle
> Shuttle
> Shuttle
> London Glasgow

This was an example of the 'triple Shuttle' being used as a logotype. Inside the concertina folder was a coloured picture and caption narrative of the simple Shuttle procedure. The copy was terse and brief, in keeping with the image of the service. Typical captions read:

> No fuss with Shuttle
> It's true! Just pick up your boarding card and
> go straight through to Gate 3 at London
> Heathrow, Gate 26 at Glasgow Airport.
>
> Just fill in the
> boarding card
> It's all so simple. Just your name and
> address on the Card—sign it—and go
> straight to your waiting Trident. No hold-
> ups, no hang-ups. That's Shuttle.
>
> Guaranteed seats
> for good timekeepers
> As long as you're actually at the gate
> precisely on the hour or before, you'll be
> sure of a seat. If the first Trident's full, you'll
> travel on the second, or even the third!

The style was nearly as disarmingly persuasive as the mail-order club advertisements, yet the idea of Tridents queueing up to be filled was irresistible. On the back was a timetable that could be clipped and kept in the wallet.

The initial Scottish advertising was a little more dispersed in that it not only covered the catchment area for Glasgow but also took in Edinburgh (which did not yet have its own Shuttle) and the hinterland where there were feeder air services.

Press advertising in the same style appeared in the *Glasgow Herald, Aberdeen Press and Journal, The Scotsman* and the short-lived *Scottish Daily News*. The STAGS TV group was booked for 30-second commercials, and the newly opened Radio Clyde was included in the campaign.

The red and white motif was adopted for the London–Glasgow Shuttle service, and the same presentation was repeated in the press ads. by reversing *Shuttle* white on black in the four-decker headline which filled more than half the depth of the space.

The copy platform was directed chiefly at the business market, but it was not forgotten that 30 per cent of passengers are travelling on personal visits.

The TV commercial (Phase 3) showed a businessman speaking on the telephone to his boss in Glasgow, finding he has time to catch the next Shuttle, getting out of his taxi at Heathrow, filling out his boarding card, receiving a newspaper from a stewardess on board the plane, and being met by his boss at Glasgow Airport with the words 'What kept you?'

As with the crisp press ads, and the pictorial folder, the TV commercial visualised the service but had the musical backing of the British Airways theme tune—*just turn up and take off*.

The Underground car cards carried the promise *Read This And You Need Never Book Another Seat To Glasgow*.

The subsequent radio commercials, first introduced in April 1975, called for a different technique and perhaps one of the most interesting examples was one put out the following year when the producers borrowed from the popular Mastermind TV programme made famous by Magnus Magnusson. The question-master asked *'What is the fastest means of travelling to Glasgow from 1975 until the present day?'* to which a Cockney contestant replied that it was *'Shuttle'*. Then a voice-over said *'Shuttle to Glasgow—just turn up and take off—it's as easy as that,'* and this was followed by the Shuttle jingle.

However, because of various industrial relations problems, advertising for the Glasgow launch had to be issued in three phases which were:

Phase 1: *January/February 1975*
      Press London and Glasgow and *Daily Telegraph*
      London bus sides
      London Underground car cards
      Supersites—a few at both ends (on-going)
Phase 2: *April 1975*
      Press London and Glasgow
      Radio, London and Glasgow—short bursts
Phase 3: *June/July 1975*
      TV, press and radio at both ends.

Approximately £110,000 was spent on the three phases. This was divided 26 per cent press, 29 per cent TV, 13 per cent radio, 8 per cent Underground car cards, 11 per cent bus sides and 13 per cent supersites (whole year).

To cope with demand, British Airways had not only nine 100-seater all one class Trident 1's (restyled with fewer seats giving more legroom and greater comfort) as the workhorses of the service, but three 130-seater Trident 3's for rush periods, and 330-seater Tri-Stars as specials when there were football and rugby matches. The operation was given its own special management and passenger handling and cabin crew organisation.

Initially, with no experience of what would happen, it looked as if an hourly service would be needed. But experience proved that some flights could be dropped. Shuttle permitted passengers to choose the flight time frequencies which could be matched by an adequate back-up of aircraft to meet demand. The situation has not yet occurred when too many aircraft were at the wrong end of the route.

From the bleak sales situation of the previous year Shuttle in 1975 produced a 16 per cent increase in traffic in spite of disruptions such as a strike at Glasgow Airport lasting five weeks. Summer traffic was 28 per cent up on the previous summer, although there had been an 8 per cent rise in fares since 1973.

When the Shuttle idea was market researched—and got a firm *'yes'* from the majority of customers sampled—the proposed service had been described as two-hourly, with no in-flight meals and beverages since cabin staff would be taking fares. But when Shuttle became operational the busy Monday to Friday services were flown hourly except for 13.10, and complimentary beverages, soft drinks and biscuits were served in the airport gaterooms.

On April 1, 1976 the London–Edinburgh Shuttle was brought in with this press ad in the London *Evening News* and *Evening Standard* using the 'triple Shuttle' logotype at the base:

Now
you can
Shuttle to
Edinburgh
and
Glasgow

On April 1st, our brand new London–Edinburgh Shuttle gets off the ground. And if you've tried our London–Glasgow Shuttle you'll know you've got a lot to look forward to.

All the same principles apply. A *guaranteed* seat on a Trident jet, all the convenience of London's Heathrow Airport, a choice of paying in advance at your Travel Agent or British Airways, or on board the aircraft. Only difference is a two-hourly service—0730 to 2130 every weekday. On Saturdays the last departure is at 1930, on Sundays the first departure is at 0930. So you just turn up any time up to the time you want to fly—and away you go. It's as easy coming back too.

You'd like a self-drive car waiting at the airport?

You've got it—we've arranged a special service with Godfrey Davis called Shuttle-Drive—ask for details.

Add to this a vastly improved Turnhouse Airport at Edinburgh, with a brand new extended runway, and you've got yourself the fastest, most efficient way of getting between the two cities ever.

The British Airways London–Edinburgh Shuttle. Just turn up and take off. It's as simple as that.

British
airways

We'll take more care of you.

Shuttle   Shuttle   Shuttle

For the *Scotsman*, the Edinburgh morning newspaper, the headline read *Now you can Shuttle to London from Edinburgh*, and the copy had special Scottish interest as these opening paragraphs show:

This Spring, Edinburgh has two more things going for it. First, a vastly improved Turnhouse Airport, with a brand new extended runway. Second, a service to London from April 1st to match the streamlining—called Shuttle.

  For a year now Glasgow's enjoyed the benefits of Shuttle—now it's your turn.

The Edinburgh service was given the colour code of blue for its directional signs at airports, though the red and white motif of the original launch was retained as the Shuttle brand image.

For the Edinburgh launch, some £50,000 was spent and the breakdown was 30 per cent press, 40 per cent radio, 4 per cent Edinburgh bus sides, and 26 per cent supersites (whole year). During the summer of 1976 business improved by 19 per cent over the previous summer when there had been no Shuttle service.

Shuttle was further extended to Belfast, Northern Ireland, on April 1, 1977, and for this white was chosen for directional signs. Thus, all three principal domestic routes were transformed to the Shuttle concept.

The budget for the Belfast launch was about £39,000. This was divided 40 per cent press, 50 per cent radio, 10 per cent TV, with some additional expenditure on outdoor sites.

From an advertising point of view this is an interesting exercise in that the selling proposition was the simplicity of Shuttle, and this characteristic was maintained creatively. David Bernstein, in his book *Creative Advertising* (see Bibliography), says the job of the creative advertising man is to convert a proposition into an idea. With Shuttle, Foote, Cone & Belding had to promote an idea, one of the techniques being the reiteration of the word *Shuttle*. It was a form of image advertising: the airline passenger public had to understand clearly and accurately what the British Airways Shuttle service was. Given this understanding, the sales appeal became attractive, superior and successful. It was also basically informative, gaining from and contributing to the overall British Airways image.

On July 17, 1975 *Flight* ran an article headed *London–Glasgow: speed and comfort*. The first and last paragraphs of the article read as follows:

'British Airways' Shuttle, from London Heathrow to Glasgow Abbotsinch, has an immediate advantage over Eastern's in that both airport terminals are new, modern in concept, and (coincidentally) of suitable layout for shuttle operations.

'Comparison between "father and son" services shows that British Airways has learnt well from Eastern. Several of the Eastern Air-Shuttle's shortcomings have been avoided (obscure signposting, low seat-pitch, awkward fare level). As for the passenger, it is hard to imagine how the service could be improved to give even faster door-to-door times. It is now possible to travel from city-centre to city-centre in a little over 2½ hr, which is just about as instant as any transport over 400 miles can get.'

In January 1977 British Airways were able to announce that the Shuttle flights had turned out to be money spinners. In two years, a £3,800,000 loss on the London–Glasgow and London–Edinburgh routes had been converted into a £¼m profit. The first year alone, 1975, saw the annual loss on the London–Glasgow route halved and the traffic increased by more than a fifth. Between April 1976 and January 1977 the loss of

£206,000 on the London–Edinburgh route had been turned into a profit with 21 per cent more passengers. Between them, the two Scottish Shuttle services carried more than 1½ million passengers in 1975 and 1976. With the introduction of the Belfast service in April 1977 it was estimated that 1,700,000 passengers a year would be flying on the three 'walk on and pay on board services', while by 1978 British Airways forecast that these services would be carrying 44 per cent of the airline's domestic revenue.

The Shuttle story does not end there. In February 1977 the Americans carried out test flights at Edwards Air Force Base with a Boeing 747 bearing a space vehicle piggy-back fashion. By the 1980's the space vehicle is expected to fly a cargo shuttle service between the USA and outer space, retrieving satellites and ferrying into orbit a manned space laboratory. Perhaps by that time British Airways will have yet another Shuttle service?

Maybe not to the moon, but within two days of the space shuttle story there was an announcement in the press that British Airways were discussing a London–Dublin shuttle service with Aer Lingus, and continental shuttle services with KLM of Holland, Sabena of Belgium and Air France.

Meanwhile, the third Shuttle service—London to Belfast—was launched with a five weeks' campaign during March and April 1977. Once again there was press advertising at both ends of the route, in the London *Evening News* and *Evening Standard* and in the *Irish News, Belfast Newsletter* and *Belfast Telegraph*. Good use was made of commercial radio. There were two types of commercial, one being a job interview skit in which the applicant got the job because he knew he could attend his employer's Belfast branch by means of Shuttle, and the other being another play on *Mastermind* called Masterbrain. These were broadcast on LBC and Capital Radio, while Irish versions in County Antrim accents were made for the Belfast Downtown station. A TV commercial was also shown on Ulster Television, special leaflets were distributed at Belfast Airport, while in London the supersites were amended to include the third Shuttle route.

This campaign completed the three-year scheme to convert British Airways' three major domestic routes to Shuttle.

Since that time British Airways have continued to use aggressive advertising to promote the Shuttle. The product was extremely successful and fulfilled a real customer need. The prime reason for success was more complicated. Shuttle provided more capacity, whereas a traditional seat reservation system, with a high 'no-show' profile, frustrated the consumer demand.

Selling activity for Shuttle, after the initial launch, was reduced to a drip for a considerable period. In the main this was reminder-type advertising on local radio stations in London and Scotland. But the proof of success was reflected by the airline's introduction of a Shuttle service between Belfast and London and in 1980 between London and Manchester.

A major marketing problem arose when the recession hit the UK in the early part of 1980. The total market shrunk and it became obvious that traffic between Scotland and London by rail, air and road would remain depressed for a considerable time. These factors forced the airline to reappraise its promotional effort. TV was used in London, Scotland, Manchester and Belfast, supported by large outdoor poster sites.

The strategy was simple: hold market share at the expense of rail travel.

The airline did hold its market share, but numbers fell. Not until the Autumn of 1981 did the total market start to increase and then at only single percentage figures.

The campaign material, which made direct comparisons with the time of the train won major awards at the Cannes Film Festival and the UK travel industries' own award ceremonies. Both TV commercials, which were shown in Scotland and London with matching posters, won major advertising awards at every international advertising seminar.

27.2 Shuttle Awards

(a) USA award *'CLIO'* at International Television and Cinema Advertising Awards.
(b) *Gold Lion* at Cannes International Advertising Film Festival.
(c) British Television Advertising Awards *Bronze Arrow*.
(d) Second prize Television Travel Section at Institute of Marketing/ Travel Trade Gazette Awards.

While Shuttle was the first of all BA flights to be affected by the recession, it was also the service which showed signs of coming out of recession ahead of any other route. During 1980 and 1981, a range of promotional fares, from standby to weekend excursions, was introduced to retain market share and to compete with intensive competition from long-distance buses and Inter-City trains.

Super Shuttle Campaign

From a monopoly situation British Airways were faced with competition when British Midland Airways were allowed to introduce a scheduled service on two Shuttle routes, Glasgow and Edinburgh, in 1983. The new BMA service included hot meals, and a lower basic fare. Under the Thatcher government, encouragement was being given to private enterprise and BMA enjoyed the image of a small, profitable and independent regional airline doing battle with a presumed inefficient state corporation. Added to this was the prospect of British Airways being privatised as part of Government policy to sell off nationalised industries.

In nine months BMA succeeded in taking 11 per cent of the BA Shuttle market and gaining a rising 33 per cent of the total market on the Glasgow/Edinburgh routes which were also serviced by BCAL from Gatwick. With the busy August bank holiday approaching it was essential for BA to fight back, regaining its premier position without appearing to 'crush the opposition by sheer weight of advertising spend or clout'.

A two-months' Super Shuttle re-launch campaign in August–September 1983 was planned and created by Saatchi & Saatchi Garland-Compton Ltd at a cost of £1m. plus £100,000 production costs. It covered television, radio, poster and trade press advertising. The objectives were: (i) to convince passengers that the new in-flight service was the best available; and (ii) to establish/re-establish the relevance of the Shuttle concept.

The consumer proposition was that 'Shuttle gives the best in-flight service plus a guaranteed seat'. The reasons why were:

(*a*) Bucks Fizz and superlative hot breakfast
(*b*) Free bar
(*c*) Free newspapers
(*d*) Allocated seats
(*e*) Cabin staff trained by TWFA
(*f*) Guaranteed seat (via back-up aircraft)
(*g*) More flights which equals more convenience

The following is the script of the 50 second, one-up Super Shuttle TV commercial:

Picture	*Sound* (voice-over)
Open on a beautiful sunrise as 757 passes gracefully through the screen. The sun glints through the window.	On this flight from London to Edinburgh are Two pilots Four cabin crew
Cut to ECU man's hand cleaning specs.	And one very important passenger.
Cut back to 757.	He's not a film star He's not a sheikh He's not a politician Yet he's treated like a VIP.
Cut to close up man's hand selecting newspaper from tray.	His favourite papers
Cut back to 757.	
Cut to breakfast tray sliding onto table.	A five star breakfast.
Cut back to 757.	
Cut to close up of bottle of wine and glass on tray.	Free drinks.
Cut back to 757 and zoom in on to silhouette of man in window of plane.	Who is he?
Cut back to view of man establishing that he is the sole passenger.	A passenger on British Airways Super Shuttle.
	Super new service at no extra cost.
	You can't beat the New Super Shuttle.
Cut back to plane as it peels away out of top of frame.	Who else puts on an extra plane for one passenger simply because his flight was full?
Dissolve to end title sequence against the title 'The World's Favourite Airline'.	Only the world's favourite airline.

And this is one of the regional back-up radio commercials on Scottish independent local radio:

Sound effects	*Dialogue*
Cab in heavy traffic throughout.	*American*: (George Segal type) Hey, Cabbie, what's going on here for Heavensake? Didn't we just pass the Cathedral ten minutes ago? I mean how many Cathedrals are there around here, anyway?

You don't realise I have got *one* meeting *in* London *this* lunchtime. At present I find myself an impressive twenty-eight yards from the Holy steps.

Look at the time, the plane leaves at twelve fifteen. Oh shucks I'll never make it.

Cabbie: (Philosophical Glaswegian) Dinna worry. We'll get you there with a guid ten minutes to spare.

American:
What!

Cabbie:
Och, on British Airways it's just turn up and take off on the London flight, sir.

American: (Slightly mollified)
Oh, well yeah assuming there's a seat left.

Cabbie:
Och, no problem, if the plane's full up they'll put on another one for you.

American: (Encouraged)
Oh really!

Cabbie:
Oh yes, standard procedure on British Airways Super Shuttle.

American:
Oh good . . . but, hold the plane Jo! I don't have a reservation.

Cabbie:
Just get a ticket in the departure lounge.

American:
Oh, well that's alright then. Say, isn't this George Square again.

Cabbie:
Yes, well, it has got four sides you know.

American:
Oh, I see.

Voice-over
The new British Airways Super Shuttle service to London. Simply turn up and take off. And if one plane's full we'll put on another one just for you. You can't

Sound effects

Dialogue

beat the new British Airways Shuttle
Service.
     Contact your travel agent for details or
British Airways. The world's favourite
airline.

The posters were bold and brief with a large picture of a shuttlecock.
One version carried the headline 'Breakfast is now being served' and below
the shuttlecock were the words 'Five star breakfast. You can't beat the
new Super Shuttle service'. In the bottom right hand corner was the red
and blue British Airways logo and the slogan *The World's Favourite Airline*.

27.3 Brooke Bond Oxo Ltd

One of the success stories of modern advertising has been the TV campaign
for Brooke Bond PG Tips which, at the time of writing, has consistently
used the same slogan: 'the tea you can really taste'. The company has used
the same advertising agency for this product, Spottiswoode Advertising
Ltd, which following a merger became known as Davidson Pearce, Berry
and Spottiswoode Ltd, and is now Davidson Pearce Ltd. This study spans
nearly 30 years.

It is one measure of this success that in a market information report
published by Pye in May 1972, the following were the viewers' Top Ten
commercials: Coca-Cola; Manikin; Brooke Bond PG Tips; Cadbury's;
Guinness; Kelloggs; Heinz Beans; Esso Blue; Typhoo Tea; and Home
Pride. Brooke Bond PG Tips commercials have been one of the viewers'
favourites consistently ever since, establishing an unprecedented record in
TV advertising.

The tea market is a huge one, twice as big as either the canned dog or
canned cat foods. On average, the British drink nearly five cups of tea a
day. Of all the hot beverages drunk in the UK, 66 per cent is tea, 28 per
cent is coffee and 6 per cent are others. Tea is bought by 97 per cent of the
population who average over 300 g a week (more than two packets a
week).

In 1956 Brooke Bond told their advertising agents that they wanted to
use the new medium of commercial TV which had been launched in Britain
only the previous year. Spottiswoode were also told to produce something
really original. The agency creative director took himself off for a walk in
Regent's Park, visited the Zoological Gardens, and stopped to watch the
famous Chimps' Tea Party. *Tea! PG Tips! Chimps!* They thought he had
gone mad when he returned to the agency with the idea of a TV commercial
using chimpanzees. But gradually the other members of the plans board
began to like the idea, and their enthusiasm rapidly blossomed. But they
were convinced that the client wouldn't buy it.

Until the advent of commercial TV, the end of resale price maintenance,
and the ascendancy of supermarkets, tea firms as a whole were among the
most conservative of advertisers. To present the bare idea to the client was

tantamount to resigning the account, so the agency decided to back its judgement, make a speculative film in spite of the cost, and present it to the Brooke Bond management as a *fait accompli*.

Spottiswoode coined the slogan 'tea you can really taste', hired Peter Sellers for £100 (and there were no repeat fees in those days!), hired a troupe of performing chimpanzees, and then invited the client to see the result. The two films were uproariously funny, if somewhat crude by more recent production standards and achievements, but humour was a strong point with the first TV commercials, to recall only Guinness and Murray-mint at that time. The Brooke Bond directors were not only astounded, they were delighted.

Associated with the campaign have been PR, point-of-sale and sales promotion activities. One of the first PR efforts was a tie-in with Twycross Zoo, and car stickers were supplied which read: 'We have been to Twycross Zoo, Home of the Brooke Bond Chimps'. This was printed in the house colours of PG Tips, green and red. One of the early point-of-sale devices was a window-bill which pictured a chimp policeman.

The next series of commercials had topical or humorous situations. There was a Father Christmas theme with baby chimps bringing presents, and one film showed Madame Zodiac reading not only her crystal ball but tea leaves.

Brooke Bond's famous red delivery van—famous since the old chain-driven Trojans in the 20s and 30s—was also featured. Production problems occurred here because chimps are only child-size, and model vans had to be built for the studio shots, real vans being used on location. The voice-over was Valentine Dyall's. When this film was shown in 1957–8 super-markets had not yet captured 40 per cent of retail trade, and the idea of a small van delivering tea to small shops was legitimate. Another part of the growing-up process in TV commercial production was the introduction of the jingle.

Give-aways were introduced for children. There was a colouring book of stories, games and puzzles, given free with purchases of the tea, and there were also balloons and badges bearing pictures of chimps.

As more films were made the production became more sophisticated, with more costume effects and special studio techniques. To induce the chimps to open and close their mouths to simulate speech they were either given chewing gum to chew or honey was put on their lips. Normally, chimps bare their teeth only when they are nervous! The completed films are a model of editing, and for some of these earlier productions 30,000 feet of film were shot to get the final 30-second commercials.

Topicality has been characteristic of the PG Tips films, and having signed up Peter Sellers for voice-over effects another series took off the very popular *Goon Show* in which Sellers starred on the radio. The next series was even more ambitious, bringing in Bob Monkhouse as voice-over. Using the theme of 'A matter of taste', the chimps performed a cowboys and bar-shooting incident, an artist and model episode, a tie-in with the picture cards given in the packets, and an hilarious card game. In these commericals there was much more human characterisation.

About this time, Typhoo was the market leader, with Brooke Bond Dividend Tea second and Brooke Bond PG Tips third. PG Tips were gaining sales at the rate of £1m. a year. It was a battle of the giants, with PG Tips making consistent use of the new advertising.

In these early 60s the commercials were supported by a 'What the chimp says' contest in the press; a self-liquidating offer of Bendy toy chimps with a total of 100,000 redemptions; and postcards featuring the characters in the commercials were sold to the general public. These efforts pointed to their popular acceptance. The chimps had entered upon an almost Disney-like realm of subsidiary enterprise and exploitation!

The fourth television campaign made excellent use of Bruce Forsyth's very appealing sense of humour in a set of situation comedies, using the theme 'When things go wrong a cup of tea puts them right'. One featured a call by the gas man; another showed a policeman helping to mend a puncture; and a third made a play on a businessman going to the City. The theme was associated with the then current 'Don't ask a man to drink and drive' campaign of the Ministry of Transport. There were also window-bills with the wording 'DRINK AND DRIVE Brooke Bond PG Tips'.

Retailer exclusive contests were another sales promotion scheme, contests being set up in association with a particular large retailer in different localities, Tesco for example. This was a 'Name the Chimps' competition, the public being invited to put apt names to pictures of chimps. The prize was a year's free groceries.

On four occasions Brooke Bond gave the chimps a rest.

In 1968–9 the chimps returned with the 'Tea On Your Mind' theme. A troupe of talented Dutch chimps were engaged for this extremely funny series. Incidentally, some fifty different animals have been used by Brooke Bond during the past twenty years. The 'Tea On Your Mind' series—'can't concentrate until you've had a good cup of PG Tips'—brought in even more characterisation. There was a chimney sweep, a woman doing house-work, a pop group recording session, and a band playing in the street. These were the most sophisticated chimp films made so far, heralding the brilliant commercials of the 70s.

Humans were introduced into the next series. So was colour. One featured a man buying chocolate at a railway kiosk—where the chimp assistant was drinking PG tips. Again, this meant studio filming of the kiosk (because of the small size of the animal) but actual location of the human model at Harold Wood station. This experiment of mixing chimp and human being was not repeated. It was agreed that chimps were best filmed on their own, even when in the golfing sequence one chimp knocked out another with his club! If put together with humans the chimp became an inarticulate animal, whereas their main success was in appearing more human than humans. By itself, the animal could portray a recognizable human character and situation. The chimp, more than any other animal, had this remarkable and amusing facility to caricature man.

More PR and promotions took place at this time. One of the PG chimps was actually entered in the 1969 *Daily Mail* Air Race. Letraset transfer toys and games were given away, and there were also gift handkerchiefs with chimp designs.

By now market shares had changed, with PG Tips in first position, Typhoo in second and Dividend in third. In 1970, tea bags—pioneered some years earlier by Tetley—were catching on, and in 1971 the sixth series of chimp commercials promoted PG Tips in tea bags—the same tea as in the packet. Two episodes showed a garden fête and the launching of a ship. This took Brooke Bond PG Tips into a growing sector of the market. No chewing gum was used to make the animals seem voluble, and they were trained to move their mouths. Irene Handl, Fred Emney and other stars provided the voice-over effects. Accidents were inevitable during filming, one lively chimp thrusting his fist through a ship's side in the model built for the launching scene. Producer Berny Stringle had to be remarkably patient.

Now a marketing decision had to be made. The competition was spending a large amount of money on the promotion of tea bags. Should Brooke Bond put their money behind tea bags or packet tea? It was decided to combine both packs in the same commercials. They did not want people to switch from packets to tea bags. But they had to recognise the coming market for tea bags.

Before producing the 1972 series research was conducted to discover what people thought about the chimp commercials. They did not present such a hard sell as some TV ads, and were interesting and entertaining in themselves. A problem with humour is that it is difficult to repeat a joke, and a problem with brief TV commercials is that the content is so easily absorbed that repetition can provoke irritation and boredom. The research showed that people found it so unusual that the chimps should *appear* to talk like humans. That couldn't be said even about Donald Duck or other animal cartoon characters for they still sounded like non-human creatures speaking words. This incongruity, revealed by the research, was the main attraction, so it was decided to build in as much talking as possible, and to create more surprising and elaborate situations.

Something like a year's work goes into the making of four commercials—reduced to two in 1976—Brooke Bond's marketing manager and the brand manager working closely with their advertising agency account executive and creative team. Eight months' planning and looking at story boards take place before the final situations are accepted. Then the chimps have to be trained for four months before filming can begin, and this includes training them to move their mouths.

The 1972 series won the *TV Mail* award, and was one of the Top Ten in the Pye survey of colour television. This inventive and highly comic series featured army manoeuvres, the Tour-de-France bicycle race, road menders and a pair of piano shifters. Both PG packet and tea bags were shown. For these commercials, 12,000 feet of film was shot, the rushes being viewed at seven o'clock next morning after overnight processing. This was a brilliant series using many animals, a lot of well-practised action and several well-known voices. Moreover, it was a most economic series because these commercials were repeated in succeeding years with successful results.

A prototype series—the PG Tips Show—was pilot pre-tested on Southern Television in early 1972. At the time it was thought to be the ultimate in the succession of chimp commercials, since extraordinary synchronisation was achieved in the mouth-movement/ voice-over combination to present an old-time music hall impression of Marie Lloyd singing a Cockney song. It was pre-tested by transmitting the Marie Lloyd commercial from the Chillerton Down transmitter, while one of the 1972 series was transmitted from the Dover station, and a recall test was conducted among viewers in the two areas next day.

A chimp standing on a stage dressed up like Marie Lloyd and singing an old song was static, unrealistic and lacking in plain earthy humour. Moreover, the idea of a series called the *PG Tips Show* failed because the well-known human artists would not lend their names to such an idea. So the four 1972 commercials were brought back again, although in one test area in 1975 they were replaced by totally different commercials with human actors. Of these perhaps the most memorable was of an old lady in hospital talking the night nurse into making her a cup of tea, a very charming character study which, like the chimp commercials, had the merit of standing up to a lot of repeat showings. However, the test showed no business increase, and so the chimps campaign continued nationally.

In 1972 shop audit reports indicated that Brooke Bond PG Tips possessed more than 26 per cent of the packet tea market. Up to that time £5m. had been spent on the chimp commercials, counting both production and air time. By 1977 they had 26 per cent of the packet and tea bag market.

The chimps returned with two commercials shown in 1976–7 that had a new marketing strategy, promoting the superiority of tea bags by having a chimp reject a cup it had been given in favour of a cup of PG Tips. These commercials moved on to challenge the more competitive market pressures in the growth sector of tea bags.

These hilarious films contained recognisable situations leading up to tea drinking, and were highly topical. One showed the chimps on holiday in Spain. The supplied tea was horrible and the English tourist saved the day by producing the PG Tips tea bags which he had resourcefully brought with him. The other showed a tea break for garage mechanics, making a pun of the MOT test, converting Ministry of Transport into 'made 'orrible tea', and closing with one of the funniest of all chimp scenes. Once again, the chimp commercials cleverly exploited everyday situations and idiomatic expressions, while at the same time being entertaining and therefore ideal for the advertising medium.

The Brooke Bond PG Tips campaign can be summed up as follows:

(*a*) TV made it possible for the chimps to appear as recognisable human beings, in fact as familiar English characters such as the army sergeant, road mender, furniture remover or garage mechanic. Moreover, there were the vocal effects of well-known British comedians. Consequently, viewers responded to them not as lovable little beasts but as people they knew and to whom they could relate. Yet there was the incongruity, novelty and humour of animals acting just like ordinary people.

(*b*) The packs, both packets and tea bags, were at various stages in the campaign well identified in the centre sequence, and often elsewhere in the commercials.

(*c*) The same slogan was used consistently and persistently. The agency and the client stayed with a good idea, something which is often lost in the mania for switching agencies.

(*d*) The same agency was retained, which suggests good agency/ client relations, with the creative team developing ideas from year to year.

One spin-off from training chimpanzees to perform in commercials was the making of a 10-minute film, 'Golfer's Progress', produced by Jim Clark and Augusta Productions. Non-advertising films should avoid commercial references but perhaps it was excusable to mark all the golf balls with the letters 'PGT'! Made for private audiences, the film is often shown at golf clubs, and has indirectly resulted in catering contracts.

The four 1972 commercials cost about £10,000 each to make, but such was the effect of inflation that the latter films were costing £25,000 each. No doubt, budgeting demands resulted in the making of two films in 1976 instead of four in 1972.

Nevertheless, while above-the-line expenditure was £450,000 in 1972, it was raised to more than £1m. in 1977 and in 1981 was increased to over £2m. This was spent entirely on TV. All TV regions except Ulster are used. The money is allocated in proportion to sales in each region, a case of exploiting success. The frequency of the 30-second commercial is determined by a points rating system keyed to audience rating figures. The agency is instructed to seek showings in each area that secure a minimum of 500 rating points a month, the vast proportion of spots being transmitted at peak viewing.

Brooke Bond's annual expenditure has been very consistent, the company believing in persistent advertising, expenditure increasing as sales have risen. This has proved successful judging by the different and less successful policies of rivals, one of which made the serious mistake of dropping advertisements for a whole year, while the erratic expenditure of another is reflected in its erratic sales figures. The benefits of advertising have been very apparent to Brooke Bond, and that includes the special value of the TV medium for a very homely, family product.

The proof of the tea was clearly the drinking! Tea is today a £310m.-a-year market. In 1956, PG Tips was third or fourth brand with 11 per cent of the market: in 1977 as brand leader, its market share of packet tea and tea bags exceeded 26 per cent, and it remains brand leader in the 80s.

27.4   Developments of PG Tips (1980–84)

A new theme was adopted in 1980, moving away from the chimps in normal every-day situations, to them acting in film-style commercials. The story centred around 'Brooke Bond', the top spy of the British Secret Tea Service, and featured his escapades to protect the secret of the PG Tips blend. These were launched by a trailer advertisement advertising that the new commercials were 'coming soon'—the first treatment of this kind.

With innovations in packaging for PG Tips, foil-wrapped packet tea, and new flavour-flow tea bags, the advertising moved away from the chimps to use other means to communicate these developments of the brand.

However, in 1983 the chimps continued as the main advertising theme, and the slogan changed from *Tea you can really taste* to *There's no other tea to beat PG*.

The return to everyday situations was made in the Spring of 1983 with the characters of Ada Lott and Dolly Potts providing a vehicle to allow 'flash back' situations showing some of the favourite chimp commercials since 1971. This assures enough material for this campaign to continue for many years to come.

27.5 Latest Developments in PG Tips Chimp Advertising

In 1984 a new direction was determined for the creative use of the chimps in future PG Tips advertising.

The company felt that while the Brooke Bond advertisement, like all other previous chimp advertising, demonstrated extremely good results relative to competitive advertising in the company's extensive advertising research work, the basic vehicle of the chimps was probably not being used to its greatest potential on this campaign.

The result of this thinking was a new campaign based on two chimp characters called Ada Lott and Dolly Potts, referred to generally simply as Ada and Dolly. Both of these characters had already seen exposure in previous famous chimp commercials. Ada and Dolly represented a move away from the elaborate, fantasised world of Brooke Bond to much more down-to-earth, realistic but still highly amusing slices of life.

The response in the tracking research was immediate and gratifying. Awareness of the Ada and Dolly campaign registered to the highest levels seen in recent years and within a very short space of time, the commercials showed a much slower 'wear-out' trend than other commercials in the tea market. Ada and Dolly were thereby firmly established as two talkative women to communicate the new message of the brand, which was *there is no other tea to beat PG. It's the taste*.

Given this solid foundation, the company felt that the immense back catalogue of chimp advertising offered a further opportunity for the brand. Many consumers still remembered characters like Mr Shifter and Cyril the Cyclist, the former having been shown more than any other TV commercial in British history. The combination of Ada and Dolly and the treasure house of past footage created an ideal opportunity to present a brilliant new campaign on low production cost, and so the 'flash-back' series was born.

In this series each commercial opens with Ada and Dolly talking together and their conversation turns to an event which they remembered. At this point, footage from one of the famous previous commercials appears, giving the consumer a chance (or for some their first chance) to see these memorable scenes. Each commercial closes back on Ada and Dolly and the latest buy-line for the product *there is no tea to beat PG. It's the taste*. The long history of the chimp campaign gave an opportunity for a large number of commercials without new footage being shot, since the 'tops and tails' of Ada and Dolly all come from previously shot footage of these two characters.

The 'flash-back' series was first shown in the Spring of 1984, and continued until the end of the year.

The very latest development of chimp advertising has been to adopt the chimps for use on breakfast time TV-am and on Channel 4 where the position taken by the actors' union Equity on repeat fees was a negative factor in assessing this medium. The solution was to find again existing footage shot of the chimps, which had not been used before and where the chimps were not talking, to accompany a voice-over. In each case a particular breakfast time or domestic situation was referred to, e.g. cooking the breakfast, washing the dishes or reading the newspaper. In each case the commercial was of 10 seconds duration. From the point of view of using TV–am this was ideal since 10 seconds can economically be used to cover the full transmission period from a medium which is known to have an audience which on average actively views for only 10–20 minutes at a time.

All of these different campaigns illustrate the durability of the total campaign and the company's ability to extract maximum advantage not only from the creative vehicle but also from the actual film footage shot. On this basis there is no reason why the chimps should not continue for many years to come.

Tony Toller, creative director of Davidson Pearce, has been responsible for the Brooke Bond account and the filming of the chimps commercials for 20 years. He is also kept busy giving talks and making video presentations to societies and groups.

A measure of the universal success and popularity of the PG Tips commercials is that the Mr Piano Shifter one is featured in the *Guinness Book of Records* as the commercial which has been broadcast more than any other on British television.

Bibliography

Annual Publications

Advertiser's Annual, Thomas Skinner Directories, East Grinstead, West Sussex.
Benn's Press Directory, Benn Business Information Services Ltd, Tunbridge Wells, Kent.
Blue Book of British Broadcasting, The, Tellex Monitors Ltd, London.
Hollis Press and Public Relations Annual, Hollis Directories Ltd, Sunbury-on-Thames, Middlesex.
Marketing Pocket Book, The Advertising Association, London.
Public Relations Year Book, Financial Times Business Publishing Ltd, (for Public Relations Consultants Association), London.

Trade Press

Admap, (monthly), Admap Publications, London.
Advance (Information about forthcoming editorial, advertising features, monthly loose-leaf pages for binder), Themetree Ltd, Aylesbury, Bucks.
British Rate & Data (BRAD), (monthly), Maclean Hunter, London.
Campaign (weekly), Haymarket Publishing Ltd, London.
Direct Mail Magazine, (quarterly), Ferrary Publications, Tenterden, Kent.
Direct Response (monthly), Macro Publishing Ltd, Hoddesdon, Herts.
International Journal of Advertising (quarterly), Holt, Rinehart and Winston Ltd, (for the Advertising Association), Eastbourne, Sussex.
Marketing (weekly), Haymarket Publishing Ltd, London.
Marketing Week (weekly), Centaur Communications, London.
PR Week (weekly), Rangeline Ltd, London.
Public Relations (quarterly), Longman Ltd, (for Institute of Public Relations), Harlow, Essex.

Books

Advertising, Frank Jefkins, Macdonald & Evans, Plymouth.
Advertising Association Handbook, The, Eds. Jeremy Bullmore and Mike Waterson, Holt, Rinehart and Winston, Eastbourne.
Advertising Law, R. G. Lawson, Macdonald & Evans, Plymouth.
Advertising Today, (3rd Edn), Frank Jefkins, International Textbook Company, Glasgow.
Advertising Works, Ed. Simon Broadcast, (IPA Effectiveness Awards case studies, annual editions), Holt, Rinehart and Winston, Eastbourne.
All About PR, Roger Hayward, McGraw-Hill, Maidenhead.
Assessing The Effectiveness of Advertising, Jack Potter and Mark Lovell, Business Books, London.

British Code of Advertising Practice, (6th Edn.) The Advertising Standards Authority, London.

Career in Marketing, Advertising and Public Relations, A, Ed. Norman Hart and Gilbert Lamb, Heinemann, London.

Case Studies in Marketing, Advertising and Public Relations, Ed. Colin McIver, Heinemann, London.

Consumer Choice, Gordon R. Foxall, Macmillan, London.

Corporate Personality, The, Wally Olins, Design Council, London.

Craft of Copywriting, The, Alastair Crompton, Business Books, London.

Creative Advertising, David Bernstein, Longman, London.

Dictionary of Marketing, Advertising and Public Relations (2nd Edn.), Frank Jefkins, International Textbook Company, Glasgow.

Dictionary of Trade Name Origins, Adrian Room, Routledge & Kegan Paul, London.

Effective Publicity Writing, Frank Jefkins, Frank Jefkins School of Public Relations, Croydon.

Effective Use of Advertising Media, Martyn Davies, Business Books.

Forecast of Advertising Expenditure, The Advertising Association, London.

Fundamentals and Practice of Marketing, The, John Wilmshurst, Heinemann, London.

Introduction to Marketing, (2nd Edn.), John Frain, Macdonald & Evans, Plymouth.

Introduction to Marketing, Advertising and Public Relations, Frank Jefkins, Macmillan, London.

Management Guide to Market Research, James Livingstone, Macmillan, London.

Marketing: An Introductory Text, (3rd Edn.), Michael Baker, Macmillan, London.

Marketing, A French Approach, Robert G. I. Maxwell, Pan Breakthrough Books, London.

Marketing: Theory and Practice, (2nd Edn.), Michael Baker, Macmillan, London.

Marketing Communications, Colin J. Coulson-Thomas, Heinemann, London.

Marketing Made Simple, B. Howard Elvy, Heinemann, London.

Marketing Plans, Malcolm H. B. McDonald, Heinemann, London.

Marketing Research For Managers, Sunny Crouch, Heinemann, London.

Modern Marketing, Frank Jefkins, Macdonald & Evans, Plymouth.

Practice of Advertising, The, Ed. Norman Hart and James O'Connor, Heinemann, London.

Practice of Public Relations, The, (2nd Edn.) Ed. Wilfred Howard, Heinemann, London.

Printing Reproduction Pocket Pal, (4th Edn.), Advertising Agency Production Association, London.

Profitable Product Management, John Ward, Heinemann, London.

Public Relations, Frank Jefkins, Macdonald & Evans, Plymouth.

Public Relations For Business Success, Frank Jefkins, Croom Helm, Beckenham.

Public Relations Made Simple, Frank Jefkins, Heinemann, London.

Index

9 2   9